Money, Value, and the State

Decolonization in East Africa was more than a political event: it was a step toward economic self-determination. In this innovative book, historian and anthropologist Kevin P. Donovan analyzes the contradictions of economic sovereignty and citizenship in Tanzania, Kenya, and Uganda, placing money, credit, and smuggling at the center of the region's shifting fortunes. Using detailed archival and ethnographic research undertaken across the region, Donovan reframes twentieth-century statecraft and argues that self-determination was, at most, partially fulfilled, with state monetary infrastructures doing as much to produce divisions and inequality as they did to produce nations. A range of dissident practices, including smuggling and counterfeiting, arose as people produced value on their own terms. Weaving together discussions of currency controls, bank nationalizations, and coffee smuggling with wider conceptual interventions, *Money, Value, and the State* traces the struggles among bankers, bureaucrats, farmers, and smugglers that shaped East Africa's postcolonial political economy.

KEVIN P. DONOVAN is Lecturer at the Centre of African Studies, University of Edinburgh.

African Studies Series

The African Studies series, founded in 1968, is a prestigious series of monographs, general surveys, and textbooks on Africa covering history, political science, anthropology, economics, and ecological and environmental issues. The series seeks to publish work by senior scholars as well as the best new research.

    Editorial Board

David Anderson, *The University of Warwick*
Carolyn Brown, *Rutgers University, New Jersey*
Christopher Clapham, *University of Cambridge*
Richard L. Roberts, *Stanford University, California*
Leonardo A. Villalón, *University of Florida*

Other titles in the series are listed at the back of the book.

Money, Value, and the State

Sovereignty and Citizenship in East Africa

KEVIN P. DONOVAN
University of Edinburgh

Shaftesbury Road, Cambridge CB2 8EA, United Kingdom

One Liberty Plaza, 20th Floor, New York, NY 10006, USA

477 Williamstown Road, Port Melbourne, VIC 3207, Australia

314–321, 3rd Floor, Plot 3, Splendor Forum, Jasola District Centre, New Delhi – 110025, India

103 Penang Road, #05-06/07, Visioncrest Commercial, Singapore 238467

Cambridge University Press is part of Cambridge University Press & Assessment, a department of the University of Cambridge.

We share the University's mission to contribute to society through the pursuit of education, learning and research at the highest international levels of excellence.

www.cambridge.org
Information on this title: www.cambridge.org/9781009501330

DOI: 10.1017/9781009501385

© Kevin P. Donovan 2024

This publication is in copyright. Subject to statutory exception and to the provisions of relevant collective licensing agreements, no reproduction of any part may take place without the written permission of Cambridge University Press & Assessment.

When citing this work, please include a reference to the DOI 10.1017/9781009501385

First published 2024

A catalogue record for this publication is available from the British Library.

Library of Congress Cataloging-in-Publication Data
Names: Donovan, Kevin P., author.
Title: Money, value, and the state : sovereignty and citizenship in East Africa / Kevin Donovan, University of Edinburgh.
Description: Cambridge, United Kingdom ; New York, NY : Cambridge University Press, 2024. | Series: African studies series | Includes bibliographical references and index.
Identifiers: LCCN 2024002339 (print) | LCCN 2024002340 (ebook) | ISBN 9781009501330 (hardback) | ISBN 9781009501347 (paperback) | ISBN 9781009501385 (ebook)
Subjects: LCSH: Africa, East–Economic conditions–20th century. | Africa, East–Economic policy–20th century. | Africa, East–Politics and government–20th century.
Classification: LCC HC860 .D657 2024 (print) | LCC HC860 (ebook) | DDC 330.9676–dc23/eng/20240228
LC record available at https://lccn.loc.gov/2024002339
LC ebook record available at https://lccn.loc.gov/2024002340

ISBN 978-1-009-50133-0 Hardback

Cambridge University Press & Assessment has no responsibility for the persistence or accuracy of URLs for external or third-party internet websites referred to in this publication and does not guarantee that any content on such websites is, or will remain, accurate or appropriate.

To my family, with much love and appreciation.

Contents

List of Figures		*page* viii
Acknowledgments		x
A Note on the Text		xv
	Introduction: The Government of Value	1
1	The Moneychanger State: Money after the End of Empire	51
2	A Monopoly on Valuation: Economic Sovereignty and Citizenship in Uganda	92
3	Restricted Value: Bank Nationalization and the Price of Decolonization in Tanzania	148
4	Crimes against Economy: The Economy of Accusation in 1970s Uganda	211
5	*Magendo*: Arbitrage and Ambiguity on an East African Frontier	263
	Conclusion: A Neoliberal Government of Value	304
Archival Collections Consulted		327
Bibliography		329
Index		356

Figures

1.1 A manager for Barclays Bank in Tanzania counting money in June 1966 — page 58
1.2 Julius Nyerere pictured at the opening ceremony for the Bank of Tanzania — 87
2.1 Uganda Credit & Savings Bank mobile vans — 104
2.2 Vans used for promoting and selling the Premium Development Bonds around the country — 120
3.1 Julius Nyerere announcing the Arusha Declaration — 150
3.2 Citizens from Tanga marching to State House in Dar es Salaam to support the Arusha Declaration — 159
3.3 Government bureaucrats attending a training course at the Tanzania Bank of Commerce where they are shown various foreign currencies in 1966 — 172
3.4 An NBC customer deposits money in his account — 187
3.5 The first meeting of the board of the National Bank of Commerce, shortly after nationalizations in 1967 — 191
3.6 A newly constructed NBC branch in Arusha — 193
3.7 A mobile NBC agency serving customers — 195
3.8 Villagers in Mugandu were awarded an NBC shield in recognition of their high levels of deposits with the bank in 1978 — 196
3.9 Amon Nsekela addresses the opening of a bank branch manager seminar (held in the former Standard Bank branch of Dar es Salaam) — 208
4.1 An unnamed woman photographed before the Economic Crimes Tribunal in 1975 — 212
4.2 Governor of Central Province Nasur Abdullah addresses agents for essential commodities in 1975 — 232

List of Figures

4.3 Domestic goods seized as evidence at an Economic
    Crimes Tribunal in 1975   247
4.4 An unnamed Kenyan pictured with the Kenyan
    currency he is accused of illegally exchanging for
    Ugandan shillings in 1975   250
4.5 Smuggled paraffin seized near the Uganda-Zaire
    border in 1978   252

Acknowledgments

I depended on the kindness, support, and expertise of many along the way to publishing this book. I am deeply grateful to those people in Kenya, Uganda, and Tanzania who spoke with me about the history discussed here, often introducing me to their families and friends. Moreover, this work was only possible due to the labors of archivists who guided me through their collections. I am grateful to them all, but Richard Ambani's dedication is especially remembered and missed.

The circuitous path to this book began when I was a doctoral student in Anthropology & History at the University of Michigan. I could not have asked for a better team of advisors. Gabrielle Hecht is the best combination of creative, demanding, and caring. She has gone beyond the call of duty, opening doors that allowed for somewhat unorthodox routes. I am grateful for her combination of attentiveness and inventiveness as an "undisciplined" scholar. Jatin Dua was a pivotal influence, not only on specific arguments that follow but also on how to weave together anthropology, history, and political economy. He is a valued model for how to make sense of and creatively intervene in disciplinary debates. From our first meeting, Derek Peterson provided concrete suggestions and a more general sensibility that made possible the work I endeavored to do. I can think of few who match his commitment to research and the region; he is an exemplar worth emulating. Paul Edwards shepherded me through my years in Ann Arbor, not least through his commitment to teaching me what does not necessarily appear in a syllabus but is nevertheless necessary. He encouraged me and cultivated a wider intellectual world that made my work all the better. Mike McGovern provided critical interventions, some of which suggested he knew where I would end up far before I did.

Michigan Anthro-History is a gem – one that thrived thanks to the dedication of the faculty involved. More widely, I benefitted from enormous expertise and support in History, Anthropology, African

Acknowledgments

Studies, and Science & Technology Studies. I am grateful to the faculty who taught me and to the staff who made everything work so smoothly. Their insightfulness was matched by their congeniality, and the combination of serious thought and vibrant sociality was an ideal setting in which to conduct doctoral work. The Graduate Employees' Organization makes doctoral education at the University of Michigan feasible.

In Ann Arbor, I was surrounded by exceptional peers who challenged and inspired me. Emma Nolan-Thomas, Jamie Andreson, and Amanda Respess were comrades in Anthro-History. Nana Osei Quarshie, too, and he kept me honest and much more. Simeon Newman made our seminar all the better. R. J. Koscielniak's combination of intellect and commitment pushed me to be a better scholar. Nishita Trisal, Nick Caverly, Sonia Rupcic, Daniel Williford, and Zehra Hashmi are valued fellow travelers. Davide Orsini, Dan Hirschman, Brady G'sell, Tara Dosumu Diener, Kristen Connor, Tara Weinberg, Shana Melnysyn, Ashley Rockenbach, Doreen Kembabazi, Adam Fulton Johnson, Katie Wataha, Katy Holihan, Sara Katz, Lauren Whitmer, Geoffrey Hughes, Richard Reinhardt, Lamin Manneh, Benedito Machava, Ozge Korkmaz, and Adriana Chira taught me much and made Ann Arbor a better place. I was lucky that Emma Thomas and Guy Willoughby could do the same in Berlin, too.

I am so grateful for age-mates who became friends during this project. Emma Park has read every word here – often twice – and usually served as a sounding board before they were written. She is my most important of colleagues and dearest of friends. Given how much Basil Ibrahim taught me about East Africa, it is no small thing to say they taught me as much about the rest of the world. Amiel Bize clarified more than they will know over the course of our friendship – about Kenya, research, and beyond. The opportunity to combine research and parenting with Basil and Amiel has made both all the better. Robyn d'Avignon has been an inspiration and a friend; I am happy to treat her advice as the final word on matters big and small. Edgar Taylor's comments on a draft chapter pulled together missing pieces and gave me confidence that crucial arguments were not completely off the mark; from the early days of my doctorate, his careful arguments made me pause and reconsider in crucial ways. I also thank Zoltán Glück, Manissa Maharawal, Zeb Dingley, Pete Lockwood, Tom

Cunningham, Wangui Kimari, Tyler Zoanni, Joella Bitter, Angela Okune, Lindsay Erishman, and Feri Marko. Robert Mwanyumba has been an important friend throughout, as have Sam Dinger and Rishi Arora. Collaborating with Aaron Martin and Chris Mizes has been a joy and taught me much.

Research also provided an opportunity to meet and learn from academics across the region. I am grateful for the insights and support of Godfrey Asiimwe, Pamela Khanakwa, Oswald Masebo, Peter Wafula Wekesa, Radha Upadhyahya, Wafula Okumu, Evarist Ngabirano, Colman Msoka, Vincent Simiyu, Moses Muhumuza, Adolf Kimbugwe, and Moses Akugizibwe. Mahiri Mwita started me on Kiswahili, introduced me to his family, and provided important early lessons on the meaning of East Africa.

David Anderson welcomed this draft manuscript enthusiastically and provided expert insights along the way; in a different and difficult moment in 2019, he provided kindness and wisdom I will not forget. Rohit De, Emma Hunter, Paul Nugent, and Justin Willis read a version of the entire manuscript, and I am incredibly grateful for the combination of generous critique and detailed feedback they provided. At other moments, I have been helped and guided by Howard Stein, Kelly Askew, Matt Hull, Webb Keane, Liz Roberts, Anne Pitcher, Gerard McCann, Chris Vaughan, Julie MacArthur, Ismay Milford, Joseph Nye, Keith Breckenridge, Parker Shipton, Bill Maurer, Taylor Nelms, George Roberts, Antina von Schnitzler, Hannah Appel, Janet Roitman, Philippe Frowd, Joshua Walker, Xenia Cherkaev, Paul Bjerk, and Alicia Decker. James Brennan, Carol Summers, and Justin Willis have been particularly generous senior colleagues. Comments from Toni Marzal, Marco Goldoni, Rebecca Tapscott, Nida Alahmad, Jake Blanc, Nicholas Tunanukye, and various audiences made the chapters here stronger.

I could not ask for a better post than Edinburgh. The Centre of African Studies (CAS) is filled with colleagues who combine dedication and kindness. The mix of methods, disciplines, and geographies is as important as the shared ethos. My dissertation could not have become this book without CAS. I thank Tom Molony, Hazel Gray, Andrew Bowman, James Smith, Rama Salla Dieng, Akin Iwilade, Kathy Dodworth, Paul Nugent, Maggie Dwyer, J.B. Falisse, George Karekwaivanane, Simeon Koroma, Hugh Lamarque, Rob Macdonald, Jose Muñoz, Amir Anwar, Gerhard Anders, Clayton Boeyink, Barbara Bompani, Thabani Mutambasere, Nelson Oppong, Ian Russell, Sam

Spiegel, Myriam Bousbia, Becky Moody, and the others who make CAS such an ideal place. I also thank Jamie Cross, Alice Street, Sara Dorman, Di Paton, Meha Priyadarshini, Jake Blanc, Izzy Pike, Martin Chick, and others in SPS, HCA, and the UCU who have made the university more than a job and Edinburgh feel like home.

Three anonymous reviewers for Cambridge University Press were important for improvements prior to the final version. I appreciate their diligence and enthusiasm. A version of Chapter 5 previously appeared in *Cultural Anthropology* 36(1), and I am grateful to the editorial guidance it received, especially from Brad Weiss. A version of Chapter 4 was published in the Journal of African History, and I appreciate Michelle Moyd and Sam Severson's editorial labors. Malachi Kabaale at the Uganda Broadcasting Corporation, John Lukuwi at the Tanzania Information Services, and Andrea Stultiens and Canon Rumanzi of History in Progress Uganda assisted with the photographs. Maria Marsh, Natasha Burton, and Biju Singh guided me through the publishing process with care.

The sorts of financial and institutional support on which I depended for this work are worryingly scarce today. Both Michigan and Edinburgh have been supportive in terms of time and money. A Graduate Research Fellowship from the US National Science Foundation provided the type of flexibility and security that should be available to all graduate students. A dissertation fieldwork grant from the Wenner-Gren Foundation provided an opportunity to work across the region. A visiting position at the Max Planck Institute for the History of Science, kindly facilitated by its director Dagmar Schäfer, was formative in more ways than one. A grant from the Royal Society of Edinburgh's Arts & Humanities initiative proved crucial in the final stages. Research permission was granted by the Uganda National Council of Science & Technology, the Tanzania Commission for Science and Technology, and the National Commission for Science, Technology & Innovation in Kenya.

In countless ways, my parents laid the foundation for this work. They have continued to support me, encouraging commitment and learning. My siblings, too, have contributed with love and other gifts (including not a few books that confused their algorithmic recommendations). More recently, my in-laws have asked all the right questions and provided support and much love. In all these relations, I am extraordinarily fortunate.

But the most important outcome of this research was the least expected. I knew work in East Africa would be meaningful; I did not expect it to be as consequential as it became for the rest of my life. A chance encounter in Dodoma led Emily and me to Fort Collins, Berlin, Edinburgh, and many places in between. It also led to Josephine. (Margot, too!) They bring me more joy, insight, and resolve than I could ever imagine. As I write these acknowledgments in Nakuru, we are trying to find a model for simultaneously parenting and researching. So far, it involves more bouncy castles than I expected (or budgeted for).

So far, so good.

A Note on the Text

Between the 1920s and 1965/66, the currency in Kenya, Uganda, Tanganyika, and Zanzibar was the East African shilling. A shilling was divided into 100 cents. Twenty East African shillings were equivalent to one pound.

Until 1971, the British pound was divided into 20 shillings (abbreviated by the letters "Shs."). Each shilling was composed of 12 pence (abbreviated by the letter "d."). As a result, £1 was equivalent to Shs. 20 or 240d. In 1971, the British shilling was eliminated, and the pound decimalized so that each £1 was worth 100 pence (abbreviated by the letter "p").

Beginning in 1965/66, the countries of Kenya, Uganda, and Tanzania issued their own currencies. Each currency was called the shilling. The respective national shillings were abbreviated as KSh., USh., and TSh., though in non-comparative contexts, one national currency might simply be abbreviated Shs.

Introduction
The Government of Value, 1945–1980

I.1 The Moneychanger State

In early October of 1977, John Wesonga returned to the Office of the Governor for Southern Province in Uganda. Wesonga was "a desperate man," exasperated by his repeated entreaties. He recently lost his wife and anxiously wished to return to Kenya, his home country. Yet, without the approval of the Governor of the Bank of Uganda, he was stuck, unable to exchange his Ugandan shillings for their Kenyan equivalent.[1] Like others at the time, he was required to apply to the country's central government for foreign currency. Before he could be issued money that would be accepted across the border, he was forced to await a response from the Bank of Uganda, located nearly three hundred kilometers away.

The restricted access to foreign currency was not limited to would-be emigrants; it extended to all categories of residents and citizens who wished to travel or make purchases abroad. In the years after independence, Uganda expanded a system of currency controls that stipulated for what purposes and in what amounts foreign currency was legally acquired. The government assessed the worthiness of applicants according to a patchwork of laws and regulations. These frequently changing rules sought to calibrate the expenditure of precious US dollars, British sterling, and other foreign currencies earned through Uganda's exports. In doing so, they differentiated between types of applicants: individuals studying in the UK, buyers of commodities only available in Nairobi, or immigrant laborers seeking to return home: each qualified for different amounts of foreign currency in exchange for their Ugandan shillings. All were, however, subject to the state's monetary authority. The government sought to manage a severe shortage of foreign exchange by tying individuals to their infrastructure of

---

[1] Bank of Uganda (BoU) GOV.104.16: Governor, Southern Province to Governor, Bank of Uganda, October 12, 1977.

value: the Ugandan shilling. Yet, given the limits of this currency – namely, its virtual absence of purchasing power outside the borders of the country – the effect for men like Wesonga was immobilizing. Without access to the means of external exchange, he and others found themselves constricted to the territorial boundaries of a country which, in his case, was not even his own.

For many postcolonies, a national currency – like a constitution, flag, or passport – was a necessary accompaniment to independence. Money was a potent symbol of decolonization, and it was a means of settling debt and saving wealth. But money was also an instrument of governing people and commanding commodities. More than a matter of markets alone, money constituted a new political order.[2] Mandated as the only legal tender within a country, national currency was a means of making postcolonial nation-states and ruling their territory and citizens. It helped define what was valuable and influenced how that value would be distributed. In doing so, national currencies were designed to further the goal of economic sovereignty, through which postcolonial states might meaningfully determine their own fortunes. Yet, as an infrastructure for governing value, money was contradictory and limited. A core contradiction was that the value of *national* currency depended on the accumulation of a reserve of *foreign* money. States were obliged to hold dollars and sterling in order to pay for imports and repay loans. In a regional political culture where claims to autochthony mattered a great deal, and in a political order where domestic authority was greatly valued, the national currency was fundamentally dependent upon alien money. This severely limited the capacity to use national monies to secure postcolonial sovereignty, and it occasioned struggles between citizens, states, and companies that are the subject of this book.

Money, Value, and the State examines the contradictions and tribulations of economic sovereignty and citizenship. It analyzes how the

---

[2] For the colonial period, see Wambui Mwangi, "The Order of Money: Colonialism and the East African Currency Board," PhD dissertation, University of Pennsylvania, 2003. For arguments in this vein from the North Atlantic, see Christine Desan, *Making Money: Coin, Currency, and the Coming of Capitalism* (Oxford University Press, 2014); Brian Gettler, *Colonialism's Currency: Money, State, and First Nations in Canada 1820–1950* (McGill-Queen's University Press, 2020). Generally, see also the work of Michel Aglietta, including *Money: 5000 Years of Debt and Power* (Verso, 2018).

I.1 The Moneychanger State

governments of Kenya, Tanzania, and Uganda sought to control the production and distribution of wealth, through monetary and other means, in the two decades after independence. Decolonization was more than a political event; for colonized people, political independence was a step toward economic sovereignty. The end of European empires set the stage for broader ambitions of self-determination, including transforming the racial capitalism inherited from the colonial era. Yet, the ensuing decades were marked by paradoxes and limits, not only ambition and opportunity. The experiences of men like John Wesonga are exemplary of these dilemmas of postcolonial statecraft and citizenship, where governing money for some purposes entailed subjugation and constraints. Whether self-determination – in its political, economic, or cultural valences – could be achieved without such incongruities, and where the limits to independence would be drawn, mattered deeply to East Africans. Throughout the work, I trace how different people – from bankers and bureaucrats, to farmers-cum-smugglers – differed over what counted as valuable and how it should be controlled. This book explores how such predicaments and disputes were worked out and how the project of economic sovereignty was transformed from the late colonial period through the end of the 1970s.

East African states sought a *monopoly on valuation* through which economic and social worth was legitimately defined and apportioned.[3] In determining who qualified for foreign exchange, postcolonial bureaucrats intervened in family life and trade networks, deeming some activities permissible and others proscribed. States claimed the sole right to govern a range of economic instruments and exchanges. Foreign money was the resource monopolized in Wesonga's case, but just as important to East African states was their monopoly on the valuation of key export crops. Due to their need to acquire foreign currencies, states obliged citizens to earn export value, most centrally

---

[3] This idea was developed over the course of many conversations with Emma Park. She first used the term in an of how European colonists in nineteenth-century eastern Africa struggled to assert sovereignty via taxation. Their novel "revenue regime" struggled against competing visions of legitimate authority and "metrics of value" among Africans, and the imposition of colonial money was a key mediator for the establishment of work. Emma Park, "The Right to Sovereign Seizure? Taxation, Valuation, and the Imperial British East Africa Company," in Gurminder K. Bhambra and Julia McClure (eds.), *Imperial Inequalities: The Politics of Economic Governance across European Empires* (Manchester University Press, 2022), pp. 79–97.

by cultivating crops that could be sold abroad. At the time of independence, coffee and cotton were preeminent in Uganda. In Kenya, coffee and tea predominated. Tanganyika was especially reliant on sisal exports, and Zanzibar earned almost its entire export value from cloves. The history of export crop regulations in "East Africa is a history of a movement towards centralization and monopoly sales of crops," and independent states built upon the colonial inheritance.[4] The institutionalized control of exports was most manifest in farmers' obligation to accept for key crops the prices determined by the state. Oftentimes, this price setting was done at the cabinet level, or even by the president himself – such was the political importance of this monopoly on valuation.[5]

When states assigned price, they were intervening in more than the cost of buying coffee or cotton. They were enforcing a social order that had implications for political constituencies and familial relations. For instance, the price of coffee was issued with an eye toward maintaining support among cultivators who were also voters; the price was also set with an assumption that wives and children would do unpaid farm and domestic labor, allowing the state to pay less than otherwise. In other words, the material price carried with it ethical ideas about where effort should be expended, how allegiances should be formed, and who had authority to command others. Valuation is the ability to assign worth, and through explorations of export agriculture, currency controls, and commodity regulations I show that states endeavored to control how value was established to sediment their own sovereignty.[6] I demonstrate how the techniques of valuation – its pricing protocols, standards of measurement, and legal enforcement – were central to statecraft, and how the results had implications for a wider field, from the position of women to the power of executive office. Valuation often coheres into a price, but the calculations through which prices emerge

---

[4] R. M. A. van Zwanenberg with Anne King, *An Economic History of Kenya and Uganda, 1800–1970* (Macmillan Press, 1975), pp. 202–210.

[5] In the idiom of economists, this is a monopsony from the perspective of the farmers and a monopoly from the perspective of international buyers.

[6] On valuation, see Fabian Muniesa, "A Flank Movement in the Understanding of Valuation," *The Sociological Review* 59 (2011): 24–38; Marion Fourcade, "Cents and Sensibility: Economic Valuation and the Nature of 'Nature'," *American Journal of Sociology* 116(6) (2011): 1721–1777.

I.1 The Moneychanger State

are rarely self-evident.[7] Economic value implicated ethics and politics, making a history of valuation techniques and justifications a history of struggle to establish worth.

These crop marketing regimes worked hand in glove with postcolonial monetary controls, though the latter have received little historical study. Marketing boards earned foreign exchange while central banks preserved and allocated it. The intermediation of exports, as many have noted, allowed states to impose a margin between the international price received and domestic price paid, and it was through that surplus that states funded their expenditure. In Uganda, for instance, domestic coffee prices were set by subtracting the cost of state marketing and revenue needs from the expected international price; the remainder was divided among farmers, sometimes amounting to less than a third of the world price. Less well appreciated is that postcolonial economic statecraft depended not merely on the difference between international and domestic prices for cotton, coffee, or sisal. Perhaps more important was the *controlled conversion* between different monies. When East African farmers sold their produce to their governments, they were paid in domestic currency. When East African states sold these exports to international buyers, they were paid in US dollars, British sterling, or other foreign money. There was not only a quantitative difference that financed independent states (i.e., the price differential) but also a qualitative difference (i.e., the different instruments of payment). In other words, the state strategy was not only to mediate exports so as to pay farmers less than was received from multinational buyers. The fiscal model of postcolonial states depended on monopolizing currencies and controlling the conversion between them. This was *the moneychanger state*.

The different qualities of different monies had political effects and set in motion various dramas and struggles.[8] There are three

---

[7] Andrea Ballestero, "The Ethics of a Formula: Calculating a Financial-Humanitarian Price for Water," *American Ethnologist* 42(2) (2015): 262–278.

[8] In pointing to the different types and qualities of money, I am following an anthropological tradition that sees "moneyness" as a contextual result and not a universal status. When, where, and for whom something is valid money – and when that money reflects wider values – were the stakes of struggles in East Africa. See Allison Truitt, "Money," in Felix Stein (ed.), *Open Encyclopedia of Anthropology* (Open Knowledge Press, 2020); Jane Guyer and Karin Pallaver, "Money and Currency in African History," in Thomas Spear (ed.), *Oxford Research Encyclopedia of African History* (Oxford University Press, 2018).

implications of note. Most evidently, different monies had different geographic qualities. Payment in Ugandan shillings meant farmers were territorially restricted while the state commanded money with value beyond its territory. Historians of East Africa have pointed to a variety of ways independent states tried to enforce territorial identities, from the violent suppression of separatist projects to the promulgation of cultural nationalism.[9] For men like John Wesonga and many others, it was monetary infrastructure that produced the national territory as a consequential container of economic, political, and social life.[10] In addition to geography, money governed time. On the one hand, financial instruments – in the form of agricultural credit, or simply bank savings accounts – could remake time.[11] Farmers lacking liquidity would draw upon loans to buy inputs, repaying after harvest. The ability to access different money also shaped what futures one could reasonably envision and pursue. The national currencies of Kenya, Tanzania, and Uganda were potentially volatile and prone to erosion of their purchasing power, especially as economic slowdown and crises became commonplace in the 1970s. In this context, dollars or sterling – so-called hard currencies – better maintained their value, allowing those who held them to save or invest them on longer horizons than would be available to holders of "soft" money.[12] It was this differential

---

[9] On Kenya's suppression of separatism, see Derek Peterson, "Colonial Rule and African Politics (1930–1963)," in Nic Cheeseman, Karuti Kanyinga, and Gabrielle Lynch (eds.), *The Oxford Handbook of Kenyan Politics* (Oxford University Press, 2020), pp. 29–42; Julie MacArthur, "Decolonizing Sovereignty: States of Exception along the Kenya-Somali Frontier," *The American Historical Review* 124(1) (2019): 108–143; Hannah Whittaker, "Frontier Security in Northeast Africa: Conflict and Colonial Development on the Margins," *The Journal of African History* 58(3) (2017): 381–402. For Uganda, see the discussion in Richard Reid, *A History of Modern Uganda* (Cambridge University Press, 2017). For Tanzania's cultural nationalism, see Kelly Askew, *Performing the Nation: Swahili Music and Cultural Politics in Tanzania* (University of Chicago Press, 2002). For its suppression of dissent, see James Brennan, "Julius Rex: Nyerere through the Eyes of His Critics, 1953–2013," *Journal of Eastern African Studies* 8(3) (2014): 459–477.

[10] For the start of a national currency in Sudan, see Alden Young, "A Currency for Sudan," in Stephen Macekura and Erez Manela (eds.), *The Development Century: A Global History* (Cambridge University Press, 2018), pp. 130–149. For the case of Ghana, see Harcourt Fuller, *Building the Ghanaian Nation-State: Kwame Nkrumah's Symbolic Nationalism* (Palgrave Macmillan, 2014).

[11] Cf. Thomas McDow, *Buying Time: Debt and Mobility in the Western Indian Ocean* (Ohio University Press, 2018), pp. 8–9.

[12] Jane Guyer, "Soft Currencies, Cash Economies, New Monies," *Proceedings of the National Academy of Sciences* 109(7) (2012): 2214–2221.

durability that obliged central banks to hoard foreign monies in the service of domestic currency. Finally, monetary regimes were hierarchical, with control over more valuable types of money raising one's rank and power. Access to less liquid or stable monies relegated others to more subordinate roles. This worked internationally, as postcolonial states struggled under the inequalities of the sterling and dollar regimes, and domestically, as only some citizens could access better money than others. Forming their own central banks and national currencies was an effort by East African states to carve out a measure of monetary independence from the international system, but in doing so they positioned themselves as the proper authority governing citizens.[13] The management of currency – and the wider government of value it implied – were therefore emblematic of the double-binds, constraints, and contradictions of the nation-states which came to predominate after empire.

The moneychanger state was not, in other words, unique to Uganda. A shared set of predicaments animated states: from Stalin's "quest for gold" to the *Banque de France* carefully calibrating credit to manage international payments, and across the decolonizing world where foreign reserves were an object of constant anxiety.[14] The very aspiration to self-determination – even autarky – depended on the reality of an international economic order that obliged states to mediate the relation between currencies.[15] And nor did the moneychanger state work merely through currency conversion; rather, it depended on a linked set of institutions, instruments, and ideologies. If, for Africans, currency controls were emblematic of a long history of extraverted statecraft, it is also a reminder that the politics of gatekeeping could extend far beyond territorial borders, to rural hamlets and even the structure

---

[13] Cf. Maha Ben Gadha et al., eds., *Economic and Monetary Sovereignty in 21st Century Africa* (Pluto Press, 2022); Ilias Alami et al., "International Financial Subordination: A Critical Research Agenda," *Review of International Political Economy* 30(4) (2022): 1360–1386.

[14] Elena A. Osokina, *Stalin's Quest for Gold: The Torgsin Hard-Currency Shops and Soviet Industrialization* (Cornell University Press, 2021); Éric Monnet, "Une coopération à la française. La France, le dollar et le système de Bretton Woods, 1960–1965," *Histoire@Politique* 19(1) (2013): 83–100.

[15] The Bretton Woods monetary regime arrayed all currencies against the US dollar, which in theory was convertible to gold. Capital controls were widespread in the postwar decades, only eroding significantly after 1974. Eric Helleiner, *States and the Reemergence of Global Finance: From Bretton Woods to the 1990s* (Cornell University Press, 1996).

of family relations, for it was the productive labor of cultivating kin on which the moneychanger state ultimately depended.[16]

This necessary rapprochement between the domestic populace and moneychanger state did not always occur. Many citizens disputed the priorities of the postcolonial states, challenging the legitimacy of their putative monopoly and rejecting the idea that monetary sovereignty suited popular interests. In times of economic trouble, the consolidation of foreign money by central banks was even more significant, encouraging a desperate and sometimes coercive state effort to maintain a monopoly on the controlled conversion between national and international monies. While Wesonga expressed desperation at his confinement within Uganda's monetary territory, many others took matters into their own hands, smuggling and defrauding the state's government of value. East Africans often refer to such practices as *magendo*, a Kiswahili term that points to illegal but not always illicit acts. In the 1970s, magendo reached new heights as smugglers and counterfeiters rejected the terms of their unequal inclusion in the postcolony and demonstrated their own ideas about what was valuable and how it should circulate. They tried to escape the confines of the postcolonial monetary hierarchy, convinced their interests were best served by illegal trade and transactions.

In other words, any single monopoly on valuation was very much a matter of struggle. Over time, citizens' diverse ideas about how to govern value – what should be produced, how it should be distributed – fundamentally challenged state sovereignty. I demonstrate that the state's assertion of a right to govern value was one of many competing valuation practices, including those proffered by East Africans of various persuasions and the multinational corporations that operated across the region. No state attempted to determine all valuation, but even in the domains that were central, like export crops and currency conversion, the state could only do so much to convince, cajole, and compel adherents. Indeed, often the state's own regulatory efforts created new opportunities for what I gloss as "arbitrage," meaning

---

[16] On gatekeeping, see Frederick Cooper, *Africa in the World: Capitalism, Empire, Nation-State* (Harvard University Press, 2014), pp. 30–31; on extraversion, see Jean-François Bayart, "Africa in the World: A History of Extraversion," *African Affairs* 99(395) (2000): 217–267.

I.1 The Moneychanger State

the opportunistic, strategic, and pluralistic movement between regimes of valuation.[17]

Citizens had their own ideas about what was worthwhile, who should labor for it, and who deserved a cut. When Idi Amin upbraided a gathering of Buganda's elders in 1971 for only buying land, not investing in trade, he was joining a long tradition of insisting East Africans imbue some goods with value and not others.[18] Whether it was women using coins as jewelry or pastoralists refusing to bring their herds to market, officials have long struggled to channel worth in ways they deem productive and useful. Equally ethical and material, these ideas and practices competed and only sometimes aligned with states. This book builds on anthropological theories to explore the entanglement of economic value and ethical values. While the English language and some theories separate *value* and *values*, I am more interested in how these putatively divergent domains are the result of historical processes and the space of ongoing tensions. Put simply, the accumulation of economic worth implicates ethical ideas; likewise, ethical values reflect (albeit not mimetically) the prevailing economic systems. What people have reason to desire is something that is made in relation to each other – sometimes in relatively consensual ways, sometimes in more antagonistic dramas.[19] Value(s) – whether that be the accumulation of commodities, the spread of one's fame, or the maintenance of family honor – are the result of practical and imaginative activity, as well as sometimes more forceful impositions. This means that they are not uniform across a culture or society, nor are they settled once and for all.[20] They are, in other words, historical products of valuation. The chapters that follow examine the relationships between different sorts of production – including the production of subsistence goods, of human relationships, of ethical consciousness, of forms of wealth – and

---

[17] See also Jane Guyer, *Marginal Gains: Monetary Transactions in Atlantic Africa* (University of Chicago Press, 2004).

[18] Opening Conference of Buganda Elders, August 5, 1971, in *Speeches* (Kampala 1973).

[19] David Graeber, "It Is Value that Brings Universes into Being," *Hau* 3(2) (2013): 219–243.

[20] Brad Weiss, *The Making and Unmaking of the Haya Lived World: Consumption, Commoditization, and Everyday Practice* (Duke University Press, 2012).

of the forces that institutionalize and subvert this social order.[21] It shows how they aligned or conflicted as states and firms tried to install their own ethos on workers and cultivators.

States may have claimed unique legitimacy in the governing of value, but this was hardly a universal perspective. To pick one example, Chapter 5 discusses how people living around Mount Elgon did not think what was valuable could be reduced to money, but nor did they think their values were somehow purified of commercial concern. Rather, I demonstrate how value was understood as the careful arrangement among social relations and between people and commodities. The social hierarchies and material interdependencies were mediated by labor undertaken, property accumulated, and respect earned on extended timelines. If this was a locally hegemonic notion of value – that is, of the proper relationship between moral virtues and material resources – it was hardly immune from outside influence, let alone challenge. Interventions by the colonial and postcolonial states and the imaginative responses of residents were longstanding trends. It was also internally contested by those excluded from its rewards, or anxious to reap more quickly than they sowed. I analyze how external changes – not least of which the prevailing price for coffee beans – led to a situation where ethical challenges, economic rewards, and existential risks were all dramatically implicated.

Scaling History

Money, Value, and the State is not a study of macroeconomics or monetary policy. It has little to say about how interest rates changed foreign exchange flows, or how the economic models of development plans were calculated. There is no quantitative analysis. It is, rather, a historical ethnography of economic action and its inevitable entanglement with political struggle, social life, and ethical ideas. Like Alden Young's attention to the economic "styles of reasoning" in Sudan or Ritu Birla's focus on "market governance" in India, I analyze how state infrastructures and imaginaries worked to transform economic and social life.[22] I position topics such as money and smuggling within

---

[21] Terence Turner, "Marxian Value Theory: An Anthropological Perspective," *Anthropological Theory* 8(1) (2008): 43–56.

[22] Alden Young, *Transforming Sudan: Decolonization, Economic Development, and State Formation* (Cambridge University Press, 2018); Ritu Birla, *Stages of*

1.1 The Moneychanger State

a long horizon of decolonization, where competing ideas about self-determination and interdependence were worked out through arenas that were equally economic, cultural, and political.

In ranging across Kenya, Uganda, and Tanzania, this book departs from the typical scales of analysis in East Africa – the ethnic community or the nation-state. There are important reasons to narrate history along these axes, yet as Toby Green writes in his history of Atlantic Africa, the localism of African historiography has militated against more expansive geographies of scholarly analysis.[23] Likewise, Derek Peterson has argued that "East Africa's historians have been seduced by the logic of the archivist, the administrator, and the census taker. The administrative grid structures the way we write history."[24] The result is an inattention to the fact that even parochial projects were motivated by supranational concerns. Diverse communities faced shared predicaments, not least of which was how to secure well-being and self-determination. My approach joins an emerging "regional turn" in African studies, working at the various scales East Africans produced and subverted in the course of the twentieth century.[25]

Ugandans receive the most attention in what follows, while Tanzania is the focus of Chapter 3 and Kenyans appear with most sustained discussion in Chapter 5. In part, this unevenness reflects the contingent nature of all research projects; in part it reflects the purposeful foregrounding of key elements of economic sovereignty and citizenship. Uganda was a fertile research site because I benefitted from the considerable expansion of archival access in Uganda over the past two decades.[26] In addition to central and district government records, I was provided access to the collection of the Bank of Uganda, which to

Capital: Law, Culture, and Market Governance in Late Colonial India (Duke University Press, 2009). See also Timothy Mitchell, *Rule of Experts: Egypt, Techno-Politics, Modernity* (University of California Press, 2002); Manu Goswami, *Producing India: From Colonial Economy to National Space* (University of Chicago Press, 2004).

[23] Toby Green, *A Fistful of Shells: West Africa from the Rise of the Slave Trade to the Age of Revolution* (Penguin Books, 2020), pp. 6–7.
[24] Derek Peterson, *Ethnic Patriotism and the East African Revival: A History of Dissent, c.1935–1972* (Cambridge University Press, 2014), p. 26.
[25] Ismay Milford, Gerard McCann, Emma Hunter, and Daniel Branch, "Another World? East Africa, Decolonisation, and the Global History of the Mid-Twentieth Century," *Journal of African History* 62(3) (2021): 394–410.
[26] Derek Peterson, "The Politics of Archives in Uganda," in *Oxford Research Encyclopedia of African History* (Oxford University Press, 2021).

my knowledge has only been studied by the institution's official historian.[27] These archival sources provided surprising insights that encouraged me to foreground the findings. Not least among these were the continuities between the Obote and Amin eras when approached through the perspectives adopted in this book. I was likewise pleased at the detail available in the archive of Barclays Bank, much of which provided insights into Tanzanian policymaking that is otherwise quite difficult to grasp given the status of archives in that country. Other chapters reflect more local concerns, the sort of findings best approached through fieldwork and oral histories. Chapter 5, for instance, was the result of interviews on both sides of the Kenya–Uganda border, as well as participant observation on more contemporary dynamics. Subsequent archival research in the two countries provided additional evidence, but my understanding of the relationship between gender, generation, money, and smuggling was only evident through the conversations I had with residents around Mount Elgon, which straddles the border.

The Horizon of Decolonization

The effervescent historiography of decolonization has focused on the political and cultural work that produced an indeterminate and multivalent experience. Rather than a straightforward transition, as Luise White writes, decolonization "took place in fits and starts, with overtures exploited and procedures scaled back."[28] The nation-state was not a self-evident scale for independent polities, nor was it a very agreeable one in the eyes of many Africans. Some loyalties and aspirations were smaller than the colony, as ethnic patriots promulgated a vision at odds with the nation.[29] Other visions were larger than the nation, linking people across the borders drawn by European powers.[30] There was considerable inventiveness, as histories were written and futures projected in order to build new constituencies

---

[27] Phares Mutibwa, *The Bank of Uganda (1966–2006): A Historical Perspective* (Bank of Uganda, 2006).
[28] Luise White, *Unpopular Sovereignty: Rhodesian Independence and African Decolonization* (University of Chicago Press, 2015).
[29] Peterson, *Ethnic Patriotism*.
[30] Frederick Cooper, *Citizenship between Empire and Nation: Remaking France and French Africa, 1945–1960* (Princeton University Press, 2014).

and cartographies.[31] A major strand of scholarship focuses on the remaking of identities during the 1950–1960s, as cultural pioneers promoted new sorts of subjectivities, behaviors, and solidarities. Some of these were expansive, as previously distinct peoples were called forth as fellow believers, nationals, or Africans. For instance, the adept politicians within the Tanganyika National African Union enrolled local concerns into a territorial movement.[32] Others came to identify as "East Africans," layering a regional sensibility onto more local identities.[33] In contrast, some cultural politics were more exclusive. Jockeying for political power hardened divisions.[34] In Uganda, the question of who would rule the so-called Lost Counties not only cast Bunyoro and Buganda as antagonists; it made it impossible for the central government to be seen as anything but friend or foe.[35] In Kenya, *majimboism* arrayed smaller groups against the fear of Luo and Kikuyu dominance.[36] Elsewhere, demands for unanimity minoritized some people.[37] Throughout East Africa, Asians were cast as an internal other, insufficiently loyal and native to the

---

[31] Kate Skinner, *The Fruits of Freedom in British Togoland: Literacy, Politics and Nationalism, 1914–2014* (Cambridge University Press, 2015); Paul Nugent, *Smugglers, Secessionists & Loyal Citizens on the Ghana-Togo Frontier* (James Currey, 2002).

[32] Susan Geiger, *TANU Women: Gender and Culture in the Making of Tanganyikan Nationalism, 1955–1965* (Heinemann, 1997); Paul Bjerk, *Building a Peaceful Nation* (University of Rochester Press, 2015).

[33] Chris Vaughan, "The Politics of Regionalism and Federation in East Africa, 1958–1964," *The Historical Journal* 62(2) (2018): 519–540.

[34] In Kenya, see Justin Willis and George Gona, "Pwani C Kenya? Memory, Documents and Secessionist Politics in Coastal Kenya," *African Affairs* 112 (446) (2013): 48–71; Jeremy Prestholdt, "Politics of the Soil: Separatism, Autochthony, and Decolonization at the Kenyan Coast," *Journal of African History* 55(2) (2014): 249–270; James Brennan, "Lowering the Sultan's Flag: Sovereignty and Decolonization in Coastal Kenya," *Comparative Studies in Society and History* 50(4) (2008): 831–861.

[35] Derek Peterson, "Violence and Political Advocacy in the Lost Counties, Western Uganda, 1930–64," *The International Journal of African Historical Studies* 48 (1) (2015): 51–72; Shane Doyle, "Immigrants and Indigenes: The Lost Counties Dispute and the Evolution of Ethnic Identity in Colonial Buganda," *Journal of Eastern African Studies* 3(2) (2009): 284–302.

[36] David Anderson, "'Yours in Struggle for Majimbo': Nationalism and the Party Politics of Decolonization in Kenya, 1955–64," *Journal of Contemporary History* 40(3) (2005): 547–564.

[37] Jonathon Glassman, *War of Words, War of Stones: Racial Thought and Violence in Colonial Zanzibar* (Indiana University Press, 2011).

postcolonies.[38] Over all, this new historiography links the opportunities and alternatives of decolonization to the cultural work of making identities, detailing the rhetorical, cultural, and sartorial politics of the era.

This book shifts focus to the economic aspirations and experience of decolonization, tracing how self-determination was understood by citizens and states to require remaking money and markets. In doing so, it also challenges the timeline of decolonization, concurring with Young's argument about "the distinctiveness of the late colonial and early postcolonial state."[39] Decolonization was neither an "event" nor a "moment." It was not coterminous with a changing of the political guard, nor was it only an interlude of foreclosed opportunity. Rather, decolonization was – and in some corners is – an expansive horizon marked by the gap between experience and aspiration.[40] It was debated in a variety of idioms, including "independence," "self-determination," and "neocolonialism" in English, *madaraka* and *uhuru* in Kiswahili, and *eddembe* in Luganda.[41] Across the 1950–1970s, the meaning of decolonization and the means to achieve it shifted between political, legal, cultural, and economic registers. Nowhere were these domains clearly delineated.

My focus is economic sovereignty and economic citizenship. By elaborating these notions, I account for what could make

---

[38] Sana Aiyar, *Indians in Kenya: The Politics of Diaspora* (Harvard University Press, 2015); James Brennan, *Taifa: Making Nation and Race in Urban Tanzania* (Ohio University Press, 2012); Edgar Taylor, "Claiming Kabale: Racial Thought and Urban Governance in Uganda," *Journal of Eastern African Studies* 7(1) (2013): 143–163; Anneeth Kaur Hundle, "Insecurities of Expulsion: Emergent Citizenship Formations and Political Practices in Postcolonial Uganda," *Comparative Studies of South Asia, Africa and the Middle East* 39(1) (2019): 8–23.

[39] Young, *Transforming Sudan*, p. 6.

[40] Compare to the gap between the space of experience and the horizon of expectation: Reinhart Koselleck, *Futures Past: On the Semantics of Historical Time* (Columbia University Press, 2004).

[41] On Tanzanian debates about uhuru, see Emma Hunter, *Political Thought and the Public Sphere in Tanzania: Freedom, Democracy and Citizenship in the Era of Decolonization* (Cambridge University Press, 2015). On eddembe, see Edgar Taylor, "Eddembe," in Dilip Menon (ed.), *Changing Theory: Concepts from the Global South* (Routledge, 2022), pp. 111–126. For wider Ugandan debates about politics, see Jonathan Earle, *Colonial Buganda and the End of Empire: Political Thought and Historical Imagination in Africa* (Cambridge University Press, 2017).

decolonization meaningful – a practical and substantive ambition rather than a formal status.[42] Matters of income, finance, and trade were necessarily correlates of self-determination. They were subject to popular struggle in which cultural values framed the debate. But they were often contradictory promises that could undermine liberation and belonging. I am especially interested in how economic aspirations and constraints unfolded after political independence. While the ferment of political imagination may have waned with the assumption of territorial power by national politicians, the imperatives of economic sovereignty remained alive. The idea that production, exchange, and consumption needed to be transformed in order to meet the needs and aspirations of East Africans motivated political and social life for at least the two decades after political independence.[43] Economic matters were not divorced from debates about political authority, social belonging, or ethical life. Historians of the region have perhaps been less attentive to this in recent decades, but a new wave of diplomatic and intellectual historians have emphasized the continuities.[44] Most prominent is Adom Getachew's important reconstruction of African and diasporic political thought in which questions of self-determination are equally political and economic. Tanzania's Julius Nyerere features prominently.[45] His vision of *ujamaa* (literally, familyhood; more commonly, African socialism) and *kujitegemea* (self-reliance), as well as his championing a New International Economic Order (NIEO) – in which African economies would escape their continued subordination to metropolitan interests – were visions for a future without arbitrary domination. Only by remaking monetary orders, trade regimes, and international law would self-determination be achieved. Yet, for Getachew and others, these are ultimately tragic narratives, as the inspiring alternatives run ashore

---

[42] On how Africans have pursued "meaningful freedom" and "meaningful citizenship," see Phyllis Taoua, *African Freedom: How Africa Responded to Independence* (Cambridge University Press, 2018); Lahra Smith, *Making Citizens in Africa: Ethnicity, Gender, and National Identity in Ethiopia* (Cambridge University Press, 2013).

[43] Dharam Ghai, ed., *Economic Independence in Africa* (Kenya Literature Bureau, 1973).

[44] Christopher Dietrich, *Oil Revolution: Anticolonial Elites, Sovereign Rights, and the Economic Culture of Decolonization* (Cambridge University Press, 2017). See also Christopher Lee, *Making a World after Empire: The Bandung Moment and Its Political Afterlives* (Ohio University Press, 2010).

[45] Adom Getachew, *Worldmaking after Empire: The Rise and Fall of Self-Determination* (Princeton University Press, 2019).

and succumb to more restrictive models that reproduce Africa's marginalized position.[46]

This book shares the view that political changes need to be seen in a longer horizon of economic struggles, but its focus is less on diplomatic or intellectual maneuvering. Rather, it starts from productive activity and the everyday struggles to govern it. In order to understand self-determination, it is necessary to see something like Nyerere's speeches in the context of domestic circumstances, not only international argumentation. Likewise, ideas about the international regulation of commodities must be understood from the perspective of African cultivators, the practical struggles to convince soil and seed to bear fruit, and ideas about what use such labor should be put toward. The most prominent imaginaries for economic sovereignty – in the writings of Nkrumah or Nyerere that anchor recent scholarship – were often rejected or refused by the African citizens for whom the leaders claimed to speak. My approach is more attentive to these uncaptured, dissident practices and their implications for state-centric accounts of self-determination.[47] For while the dynamics of international capitalism and neocolonialism did much to circumscribe sovereignty in East Africa, ultimately, the divergent trajectories and values of East Africans cannot be discounted.

I.2 Colonial Subjects and Economic Claims

Economic self-determination was so salient in the mid-twentieth century because East Africans did not only experience colonialism as a denial of political rights. They also clamored for long-denied commercial liberties, including the right to open shops, export their crops, and receive loans. Oftentimes, the political and economic were so entwined as to be indistinguishable, and economic uplift was seen as formative of political advance. This section briefly explores how Africans made claims to economic rights in the late colonial period before returning in the next section to the postcolonial era on which this book largely focuses.

---

[46] Samuel Moyn, *Not Enough: Human Rights in an Unequal World* (Belknap Press, 2018).

[47] "Uncaptured" is Goran Hyden's term for popular refusal of Nyerere's economic regime in *Beyond Ujamaa in Tanzania: Underdevelopment and an Uncaptured Peasantry* (University of California Press, 1980).

I.2 Colonial Subjects and Economic Claims

Although colonialism did encourage some cases of African commercial production, the more common experience was one of official impediment and popular frustration. The push into export production was often thwarted, not least by "experts in colonial economy [who] were too steeped in images of African backwardness" to effectively support their commercial advance.[48] European planters – wary of competition – claimed Africans' unkempt coffee would provide a breeding ground for disease and sully the quality of their exports.[49] When African production was facilitated, it often produced contradiction and crisis. Communities willing to further colonial export agriculture might receive support, especially after the Second World War, but most East Africans were denied economic opportunities or relegated to subordinate roles.[50] Land alienation and conservative regulations inhibited agricultural production in some locations. A combination of burdensome taxation, neglectful policy, and austere underinvestment constrained other areas. African employees received paltry wages with few benefits and only the lowest rungs of employment were open to Africans. Likewise, entrepreneurial ventures such as shopkeeping, trade, or transportation were long reserved for non-Africans, especially the Asian diaspora that colonial policy positioned as an intermediary commercial minority in East Africa.[51]

Colonial subjects responded with a variety of tactics. Frustration about pay and conditions animated a series of protests, strikes, and riots beginning in the 1930s.[52] In Kenya, Mombasa and Nairobi were hotbeds of industrial action, often sparking agitation far along the railways they served.[53] Farmers, too, disputed the terms of their economic incorporation into the empire. All across the region, illegal trade

---

[48] Cooper, *Africa in the World*, p. 25.
[49] C. C. Wrigley, *Crops and Wealth in Uganda: A Short Agrarian History* (East African Institute of Social Research, 1959), p. 40.
[50] D.A. Low and John Lonsdale. "Introduction: Toward the New Order 1945–1963," in D. A. Low and Alison Smith (eds.), _The History of East Africa, vol. 3_ (Clarendon Press, 1976): 1–63.
[51] In a large literature, see van Zwanenberg with King, *An Economic History*; Bruce Berman, *Control & Crisis in Colonial Kenya the Dialectic of Domination* (James Currey, 1990).
[52] Frederick Cooper, *Decolonization and African Society: The Labor Question in French and British Africa* (Cambridge University Press, 1996).
[53] Frederick Cooper, *On the African Waterfront: Urban Disorder and the Transformation of Work in Colonial Mombasa* (Yale University Press, 1987); R. D. Grillo, *African Railwaymen: Solidarity and Opposition in an East African Labour Force* (Cambridge University Press, 1973).

challenged colonial economic rule.[54] The early Kikuyu political organizations led by Harry Thuku protested, among other things, the restrictions on African coffee cultivation.[55] The Luo Thrift and Trading Corporation established by Oginga Odinga in 1945 combined ethnic patriotism and entrepreneurial retail.[56] Both of Tanganyika's successful coffee-growing communities, the Chagga and Haya, rioted in 1937 over the limits imposed on their cultivation, and leading politicians like Paul Bomani got their start organizing African traders and growers.[57] In Buganda, a series of widespread protests in the 1940s were galvanized by frustration over the price paid for cotton, the role of Asian intermediaries, and the regulation of farmer cooperatives.[58] Baganda organized mass boycotts of Asian traders and foreign imports to challenge the structure of colonial racial capitalism.[59] To the east, Gisu coffee farmers insisted on better prices and protocols for selling their crops.[60] To the west, the Bwamba Rwenzori Growers Association carried on an extended campaign for their own coffee processing plant and less exploitative middlemen.[61] In both cases, they carried their produce to neighboring countries to protest the colonial monopoly on valuation. And, of course, at the core of the Mau Mau crisis was a struggle for self-mastery and freedom understood in terms equally material and moral.[62]

[54] David Anderson and David Throup, "Africans and Agricultural Production in Colonial Kenya: The Myth of the War as a Watershed," *Journal of African History* 26(4) (1985): 337.
[55] Phoebe Musandu, *Pressing Interests: The Agenda and Influence of a Colonial East African Newspaper Sector* (McGill-Queen's University Press, 2018), pp. 189–200.
[56] E. S. Atieno-Odhiambo, "'Seek Ye First the Economic Kingdom': A History of the Luo Thrift and Trading Corporation 1945–1956," in B. A. Ogot (ed.), *Hadith 5* (East African Publishing House, 1975).
[57] John Iliffe, *A Modern History of Tanganyika* (Cambridge University Press, 1979), pp. 274–286.
[58] David Apter, *The Political Kingdom in Uganda: A Study of Bureaucratic Nationalism*, 3rd ed. (Routledge, 1997 [1961]), pp. 181–194.
[59] Edgar Taylor, "1959 and 1972: Boycott, Expulsion, and Memory," *AwaaZ*, www.awaazmagazine.com/volume-19/issue-2-volume-19/cover-story-issue-2-volume-19/1959-and-1972-boycott-expulsion-and-memory.
[60] Stephen Bunker, *Peasants against the State: The Politics of Market Control in Bugisu, Uganda, 1900–1983* (University of Chicago Press, 1991).
[61] Kabarole District Archives 628/1: Economic Crops, 1950–1970.
[62] John Lonsdale, "The Moral Economy of Mau Mau," in Bruce Berman and John Lonsdale, *Unhappy Valley Book 2: Violence & Ethnicity* (James Currey, 1992), pp. 265–468.

I.2 Colonial Subjects and Economic Claims

East Africans were often vocal and lucid in petitioning for the transformation of commercial regulations. They appeared at government inquiries, wrote letters, and made submissions to official commissions. For instance, when the East African Royal Commission was established in 1953 to investigate "economic development" and the "social problems" arising from urbanization, population growth, and industrialization, many wrote to and appeared before the commission to present their troubles and propose solutions.[63] They saw the official inquiry as an appropriate stage for positioning themselves as worthy economic actors. Commodity markets, property rights, and concerns about inequality were not novel concerns for East Africans, as the Commission posited, but rather the subject of extensive reflection and debate. As Emma Hunter argues, the extensive meetings and tours by the Commission provided a platform for Africans to work through the proper place of "a distinctive form of capitalism" within African social life, and the submissions provide a trove of insights into their concerns.[64]

Some reflected personal concerns and interests, but there was also a shared discourse into which Africans placed their concerns, united in the promise of agricultural productivity and commercial advance. The Catholic Mission Elders of the Nyeri Diocese, for instance, called for adult farming courses and critiqued existing agricultural instruction for being coercive rather than persuasive.[65] Restrictions against African traders should be lifted, they contended, and the color bar in jobs be removed. Hezekiah Asamba of Maragoli in western Kenya agreed with these concerns. In his submission, he detailed the extent of African exclusion, not only from government and religious roles, but also from employment and trading. Asamba asserted that whatever activities the Europeans or Asians were undertaking in Kenya, "the African is ready to do." Unfortunately, these interlopers "help themselves with the best

---

[63] Scholarly assessments of the Commission have largely dismissed it as misguided, obsessed with private land ownership and "detribalization," but see Andrew James Hood, "Developing the East African: The East Africa Royal Commission, 1953–1955, and Its Critics," PhD dissertation, Rice University, 1997.

[64] Emma Hunter, "'Economic Man in East Africa': Ethnicity, Nationalism, and the Moral Economy in Tanzania," in Bruce Berman, André Laliberte, and Stephen J. Larin (eds.), *The Moral Economies of Ethnic and Nationalist Claims* (UBC Press, 2016), pp. 101–122.

[65] UKNA CO 892/5/1: Submission by the Catholic Mission Elders of the Diocese of Nyeri, Kenya, May 29, 1953.

jobs." To justify their lucrative positions, "all the foreigners including the Government join together and say that the African is lazy and untrustworthy." Against this slander, Asamba appealed to the Commissioners as upright arbiters of industriousness, asking,

> Since you came here, have you visited a place and found people at work? What did you see? Did you confirm the saying that Africans work for five hours a day?

Answering in the negative, Asamba explained that the trouble was not so much African sloth but foreigners' deceit. The government, he explained, defines the workday as eight hours during the week, with work stopping at 1:00 p.m. on Saturday "so that he may get time to wash clothes and to prepare for the Sunday as God commanded that that day shall be the day of rest." However, "The Indians are robbing the Africans of their time. Instead of working for 8 hours, they work for 9 hours or ten hours a day."[66]

Asamba thought Africans were deprived of economic liberties by a combination of official controls, moral impugnment, and foreign subterfuge. Stephen Gichina of Naivasha similarly condemned "being debarred from wealth."[67] Such a condition threatened his own masculine standing in the world and simultaneously contributed to the political problems in Kenya:

> Being given freedom to advance ... will make an African feel that he is a man like the men of other races here and show him that they are not envious of him, and it will free him from fear of them, because he will realize although these other races continue to dwell here, he will be happy here in his own country and not be afraid of being deprived of his right.

Asamba's and Gichina's concerns about economic subordination were echoed across the region. The Nyamwezi chief Abdullah Fundikira believed that native agriculture needed "nothing short of a revolution in methods and systems."[68] This would require mechanization which, in turn, would require more financial resources for African farming,

---

[66] UKNA CO 892/5/4: Submission by Hezekiah Asamba, Maragoli, December 26, 1953.
[67] UKNA CO 892/5/4: "Memorandum on Things to Be Done in Future" by Stephen Gichina, Naivasha, December 15, 1953.
[68] UKNA CO 892/10/3: Memorandum presented by Abdullah Fundikira, n.d., but 1953.

"preferably for a start by Government funds." Others called on the government to expand its financial role, approving of the Royal Commission's suggestion that more loans be provided to Africans. The Kenya African Union branch in Nyanza noted that only non-Africans receive bank loans, despite the needs of African traders and farmers. C. N. W. Siganga, president of the Abaluyia People's Association concurred, saying credit must be matched by improved commercial training and facilities for obtaining commodities from abroad.[69] Even submissions that disagreed on the virtues of registering and commodifying land – widely seen as a prerequisite for expanded lending – were united in the belief that Africans deserved more loans.[70] The Uganda Growers Co-operative Union, an organization with more than 10,000 Ganda members, rued that African interest in commerce was "submerged and chilled by poverty and lack of capital."[71] Others emphasized the restrictive role of government regulations: the Bagishu Khuheentsa Co-operative Union in eastern Uganda complained about the official price and the "oppressive" rules around selling cotton.[72] A letter from Bataka of Busoga pointed to the same rules, saying as a result agriculture was suffering because it is "only the Indians who earn enormous profits from it." The effort, cost, and risk taken by African farmers were not reflected in the "fixed" prices paid to them; meanwhile, "the Indian simply sits in his chair" and reaps the higher profit of a racially discriminatory pricing formula.[73]

I.3 Money, Borders, and the Remaking of Transactional Territories

The result of these frustrations was a widespread sense that political independence would entail a remaking of the economic order. Citizens demanded the ability to trade, open shops, and receive fair payment for their crops and work. They wanted respectable jobs with good wages

---

[69] UKNA CO 892/6/1: Submission by C.N.W. Siganga, President, Abaluyia People's Association.
[70] Hunter, "Economic Man."
[71] UKNA CO 892/15/1: Submission from the Uganda Growers, Co-operative Union, 1953.
[72] UKNA CO 892/15/1: Memorandum from Bagishu Khuheentsa, Co-operative Union, Mbale, April 1953.
[73] UKNA CO 893/15/1: Memorandum from Bataka of Busoga, May 10, 1953.

and the training to carry out those duties. When opportunities arose, they were frequently embraced: by 1966, for example, there were reportedly 300,000 sewing machines sold in Uganda on the basis of hire-purchase contracts.[74] Independence leaders surrounded themselves with an array of expatriate advisors and a new generation of African technocrats who filed into ministries and parastatal companies. Some changes were a matter of policy decisions, such as raising the minimum wage. Other changes required new economic institutions and infrastructures. I argue that this economic statecraft was preeminently shaped by the imperatives of sovereignty, rather than "development." While development was a potent discourse – all the more so given its protean, shifting qualities – it was especially important as a means to secure and advance the self-determination of East African countries. Economic progress was necessary to maintain legitimacy in the eyes of citizens and to meet the monetary imperatives of statehood. Postcolonial nation-states required a substantial reserve of foreign money; therefore, expanding exports, calibrating imports, and growing the commercial domain were the bases on which the new countries would both survive and thrive. In other words, behind the aspirations of development often lay the imperative to expand and sustain a reserve of foreign money. Such an imperative existed across the region, despite rhetorical and policy divergences.

Economic sovereignty needed both to change how money was governed and to secure more of it. In the 1960s, considerable effort went into a series of financial initiatives that tried to change how value was produced and governed. Some of these were short-lived experiments: Chapter 2, for instance, analyzes the difficulties of selling "development bonds" to Ugandan citizens in 1964–1965. Doing so was intended to provide additional financing to meet the state's ambitious spending goals, but ultimately not enough Ugandans were willing to invest in the novel debt instruments to provide a lasting fiscal model. Other projects were of lasting consequence. Fundamental to the analysis that follows is the creation of central banks and national currencies in 1965–1966. The colonial economy was based around the East African shilling, a currency common to the region and administered by the East African Currency Board. As Wambui Mwangi showed, the Board was a political force used to discipline and dominate the

---

[74] Walter Tessier Newlyn, *Money in an African Context* (Oxford University Press, 1967), p. 60. The population in 1959 was 6.5 million.

region.[75] Chapter 1 discusses African dissatisfaction with this monetary regime, not least for how it facilitated the export of wealth to Britain and constrained long-term investment in East Africa. By allowing for the free conversion between shilling and sterling, the Currency Board facilitated the easy international movement of capital.[76] In its place, the three independent states created national currencies, independently administering Kenyan, Tanzanian, and Ugandan shillings under the direction of central banks. The central banks were important and novel institutions, designed to not only administer a national money but also influence commercial banks and credit. They worked to consolidate wealth in usable forms (e.g., foreign reserves) and influence its distribution among deserving citizens. As the national leadership put it at their respective opening ceremonies, the central banks and the currencies they controlled were the next step to secure independence. As I discuss in Chapter 1, doing so provided a measure of autonomy compared to colonial money, but it also compelled citizens to fall in line with the centralization of monetary authority within nation-states.

This reformulation of money and power in East Africa was not the only path out of empire. In Francophone West Africa, the monetary regime continued to be controlled by the former metropole, despite political independence. The CFA franc maintained the currency at a fixed exchange rate with the French franc and enshrined free convertibility between the African and French monies. Sixty-five percent of foreign exchange reserves were to be deposited with the French Treasury. Those who resisted were undermined, starting with Guinea whose vote to leave France in 1958 resulted in, among other subterfuge, France printing fake currency to undermine Sékou Touré's rule.[77] In the eyes of its critics, the CFA franc remains a "colonial currency," denuding African countries of monetary sovereignty, subsidizing European livelihoods, and giving French firms preferential access to West African markets.[78] The currency is an element of wider political

---

[75] Mwangi, "The Order of Money."
[76] John Loxley, "The Development of the Monetary and Financial System of the East African Currency Area, 1950 to 1964," PhD dissertation, University of Leeds, 1966.
[77] Elizabeth Schmidt, *Cold War and Decolonization in Guinea* (Ohio University Press, 2007), p. 172.
[78] Fanny Pigeaud and Ndongo Samba Sylla, *The Last Colonial Currency: The CFA Franc Story* (Pluto Press, 2021).

and military subordination, so-called *Françafrique*.[79] Others acknowledge the desirability of greater exchange rate stability, lower inflation which may result from being yoked to France, and fewer impediments to cross-border movement.[80] In this case, the situation is at best "voluntary servitude."[81] Whichever the case may be, the commitment in East Africa to managing money locally marked a departure from British colonialism and postcolonial Francophone countries.

In East Africa, the creation of national currencies allowed for the centralized consolidation and controlled conversion between different types of money, thereby expanding the economic power of the postcolonial state in ways that were impossible in the colonial monetary system.[82] In this way, central banks and national currencies exemplify a monopoly on valuation. By promulgating a singular standard for valuation, the national currency jostled with alternative measures of worth; by doing so across the entire territory, the state tried to eliminate the types of arbitrage and niches in which citizens made their own value. In other words, currency was less a reflection of national identity or imagined community than an instrument for the national government of value. To be sure, this was spatially uneven – areas producing export value, more heavily commodified cities, and transportation corridors were different from less monetized areas – yet national currency worked as an infrastructure to rescale exchange away from imperial circuits toward territories governed by nation-states.[83]

Nationalisms had limited power in East Africa, but nationalized money worked to bind people to the nation-state and its territory.[84]

---

[79] Ian Taylor, "France à Fric: The CFA Zone in Africa and Neocolonialism," *Third World Quarterly* 40(6) (2019): 1064–1088.

[80] Rahmane Idrissa, "Countries without Currency," *London Review of Books*, December 2, 2021.

[81] Kako Nubukpo, "Politique monétaire et servitude volontaire," *Politique africaine* 105(1) (2007): 70–84.

[82] For a comparison, see Tinashe Nyamunda, "Money, Banking and Rhodesia's Unilateral Declaration of Independence," *Journal of Imperial and Commonwealth History* 45(5) (2017): 746–776.

[83] As Dodd correctly insists, "state currencies have intermingled with other monetary forms for as long as they have been in circulation." Nigel Dodd, *The Social Life of Money* (Princeton University Press, 2014), p. 212; Eric Helleiner, *The Making of National Money: Territorial Currencies in Historical Perspective* (Cornell University Press, 2002).

[84] Jeffrey Herbst appreciated the territorial power of currency, but his analysis was mired in the questions of urban bias and "overvaluation," *States and Power in*

I.3 Money, Borders, & Remaking of Transactional Territories 25

They were akin to what Etienne Balibar calls the "networks of apparatuses" necessary to maintain the nation-state in popular life.[85] For holders of national currency, the territory and the nation-state assumed new significance.[86] Bearing *Tanzanian* shillings in one's pocket – rather than Kenyan ones, or US dollars, or gold jewelry – subordinates one to the Tanzanian government of value. It translates other forms of value into an infrastructure designed and managed by the state. It fastens users of Tanzanian shillings to the perturbations in its value and obliges them to consider its future prospects. It also confines their purchasing power to the jurisdiction of that money. In other words, national currency is an important bordering technique, as Gustav Peebles has argued.[87] When combined with other controls – including controls on the conversion into foreign money – currency worked to enclose people within a territorial jurisdiction.

National currency was part of a wider project of delineating territory and categorizing people.[88] This book approaches money and statecraft from the territorial margins, for residents of the border regions were never far from the concerns of East African central banks.[89] The imperative of maintaining sufficient foreign reserves encouraged states to view some populations with suspicion. In particular, borderland residents and Asian communities were seen as improperly extraterritorial in their management of goods and money. An iconic example is the stepwise expansion of Asian diasporic family businesses across East Africa. Facilitated by colonial regulation and the common East African currency, marriage and merchant trade created a regional formation. As the

---

Africa: Comparative Lessons in Authority and Control (Princeton University Press, 2000).
[85] Etienne Balibar, "The Nation Form: History & Ideology," *Review* 13(3) (1990): 329–361.
[86] For the geography of African states, see Catherine Boone, *Political Topographies of the African State: Territorial Authority and Institutional Choice* (Cambridge University Press, 2003).
[87] Gustav Peebles, "Inverting the Panopticon: Money and the Nationalization of the Future," *Public Culture* 20(2) (2008): 233–265.
[88] Nandita Sharma, *Home Rule: National Sovereignty and the Separation of Natives and Migrants* (Duke University Press, 2020).
[89] Veena Das and Deborah Poole, *Anthropology in the Margins of the State* (SAR Press, 2009); Aidan Russell, *Politics and Violence in Burundi: The Language of Truth in an Emerging State* (Cambridge University Press, 2019); Paul Nugent, *Boundaries, Communities and State-Making in West Africa* (Cambridge University Press, 2019).

government of value became increasingly territorialized, these regional networks became an object of popular opprobrium and official sanction. "We have records of Asians," wrote Bank of Uganda officials in 1972, "who claim to be based in Zaire and Rwanda" but are operating in Uganda. Their lack of clear residence allowed Asians to transfer funds out of Uganda, draining the already limited foreign reserves.[90] And the ambiguity of their location confounded attempts to confine them within the territorial limits of monetary sovereignty.

It was not only Asians who crossed the borders of money.[91] Tanzanian, Rwandese, and Burundian migrant workers returning home from Uganda's fields brought nearly half a million shillings with them in only six weeks in 1970.[92] In the frontier between Uganda and Kenya, cross-border lives and livelihoods were historically maintained by kinship ties, as well as ritual and commercial exchange. Chapter 5 details how Bagisu and Babukusu people along the border drew on shared cultural resources and language to facilitate a spectacular coffee smuggling trade in the second half of the 1970s. This was an especially notable perforation of a monopoly on valuation, but all along East Africa's borders were transactional territories that could present a threat to territorial money and a resource for "fiscal disobedience."[93]

These frontier livelihoods and kinship reflected popular ideas about what sorts of production and exchange should take place, as well as the uses to which wealth should be put. Cattle, for instance, frequently eluded state control as it was passed back and forth in cross-border dowries.[94] Bureaucrats saw in these international families and exchanges an affront to the monopoly on valuation. In response, currency and border controls tried to remake *transactional territories*,

---

[90] Bank of Uganda (BoU), "Director of Exchange Control to Governor, 20 July 1972. Reciprocal Banking/Currency Exchange Arrangements Between Uganda and Rwanda."
[91] On "hybrid identities" across the Congo–Uganda border, see Timothy Raeymaekers, *Violent Capitalism and Hybrid Identity in the Eastern Congo* (Cambridge University Press, 2014).
[92] BoU GOV.120.9: General Manager to Governor. "Border Posts," 1970.
[93] Janet Roitman, *Fiscal Disobedience: An Anthropology of Economic Regulation in Central Africa* (Princeton University Press, 2004); Dereje Feyissa and Markus Hoehne, *Borders & Borderlands as Resources in the Horn of Africa* (James Currey, 2015).
[94] Mbale District Archives MBL/6/25: Cattle Imports into Uganda, including Dowry, 1974.

those geographies of economic exchange and social conviviality.[95] Given the histories of colonial cartography, labor migrancy, and extended family networks, many transactional territories crossed state borders.[96] Sometimes, postcolonial states could countenance these frontier practices; in cases where it contributed to their own revenue or trade interests, cross-border networks were even actively supported.[97] Yet, when they subverted the monopoly on valuation – drawing off foreign exchange or export commodities – the states often worked to interrupt and reorient transactional geographies to be more territorial. Their success was hardly guaranteed, and I show that central bankers and police worked to stop illegal trade in export crops or currency only to find their controls to falter in the face of such deep-seated networks.

I.4 State and Corporation as Competing Monetary Authorities

It was not only workers and farmers whose cross-border ties became a target of official rebuke. The British companies who dominated the capitalized economy were, to varying extents, also a source of state consternation. Colonial economic policy supported a relatively narrow set of dominant firms, often with regulations that created near-monopoly conditions.[98] Banking, for instance, was dominated by three firms: Barclays, Standard, and National & Grindlays.[99] Because of their role in financing other sectors, the banks were especially important for the wider economy, yet they routinely frustrated African

---

[95] My thinking on this is inspired by Lana Swartz's idea of "transactional communities" in *New Money: How Payment Became Social Media* (Yale University Press, 2020) and by Francis Nyamnjoh, "Incompleteness: Frontier Africa and the Currency of Conviviality," *Journal of Asian and African Studies* 52(3) (2017): 253–270.

[96] Achille Mbembe, "At the Edge of the World: Boundaries, Territoriality, and Sovereignty in Africa," *Public Culture* 12(1) (2000): 259–284.

[97] On shifting regimes of territoriality, see Brenda Chalfin, *Neoliberal Frontiers: An Ethnography of Sovereignty in West Africa* (University of Chicago Press, 2010). On divergent interests, Gregor Dobler, "The Green, the Grey and the Blue: A Typology of Cross-Border Trade in Africa," *Journal of Modern African Studies* 54(1) (2016): 145–169.

[98] Colin Leys, *Underdevelopment in Kenya: The Political Economy of Neo-Colonialism, 1964–1971* (University of California Press, 1975).

[99] Compare to the role of expatriate banks in colonizing the Caribbean. Peter James Hudson, *Bankers and Empire: How Wall Street Colonized the Caribbean* (University of Chicago Press, 2018).

entrepreneurs and policymakers. The expatriate banks overwhelmingly issued short-term loans to export-oriented firms, especially agricultural brokers who borrowed in order to pay cultivators and then repaid the banks when the crops were sold internationally. This was lucrative and largely risk-free work, and the banks stubbornly refused to expand their lending into other sectors that required taking more risk and issuing loans for longer terms. Moreover, they maintained the vast majority of their financial reserves and profits in Britain, where it was invested in London's capital markets, to East Africa's detriment. As decolonization advanced and Africans envisioned an economy responsive to their demands, the foreign banks became a frequent target of opprobrium. Oginga Odinga, for instance, told a cheering crowd in Embu in May 1965 that their independence was not yet complete. Recalling the violent struggle for independence, the vice president said it was necessary "that Africans became masters of the wealth in Kenya as soon as possible." Controlling the banks that exported money to London and New York was essential, he explained. Drawing on an East African idiom that linked exploitation to selfish consumption, Odinga insisted that it was necessary to cut the straw through which "imperialists sucked the pot and grew fat."[100]

Foreign banks were of the most concern in Tanganyika.[101] The territory had long been the poorest and least diversified economy, and the leadership of the Tanganyika African National Union (TANU) had an especially strong territorial sensibility.[102] As a result, the refusal of British banks to finance new industries or invest their surplus at home was all the more frustrating. Leading policy intellectuals like Amon Nsekela distinguished between banking in the service of people's needs versus banking in the pursuit of profit. It was clear to TANU that the latter predominated, even after independence. They took various steps to redirect capital toward citizens' needs, including establishing entities to compete with British firms. Ultimately, these proved insufficient, spurring the complete nationalization of all foreign

---

[100] *East African Standard*, May 10, 1965. See James Brennan, "Blood Enemies: Exploitation and Urban Citizenship in the Nationalist Political Thought of Tanzania, 1958–75," *Journal of African History* 47(3) (2006): 389–413.
[101] Tanganyika and Zanzibar became Tanzania in 1964.
[102] As argued in Iliffe, *A Modern History*. The class composition of TANU – largely civil servants – likely contributed to the direction of its economic policy. Issa Shivji, *Class Struggles in Tanzania* (Tanzania Publishing House, 1976).

I.4 State and Corporation as Competing Monetary Authorities

banks in 1967. "Our independence is not yet complete," announced Julius Nyerere when taking the action, and only by repurposing banking could political sovereignty be secured through economic independence.[103] Nationalization would stop the easy export of capital, allowing a more purposeful control of foreign exchange. Chapter 3 provides a detailed reconstruction of the ensuing struggles between the Tanzanian government and Barclays. Tanzania was obliged to pay for the expropriated business, but how exactly the banking operation would be valued was another matter. The state and corporation had competing perspectives on banking. Where Barclays claimed its global reach was productive of Tanzanian development, TANU thought financial value had to be governed by the state and cooperatives on behalf of workers and peasants. I analyze how both the state and corporations tried to impose their own ideas about valuation. Technical accounting standards fused with political considerations, and the resulting price for decolonizing banking reflected less the state's ability to monopolize how value was affixed than a compromise between competing ways of organizing the economy – a socialist state or a multinational corporation.

Nationalization tried to tame the international circuits of capital inherited from the empire by using banking as an instrument of state planning. It was indicative of how international capital constrained politically independent states. Nyerere was a vocal advocate for what a 1974 UN declaration called a New International Economic Order. The NIEO tried to reorganize global property and trade regimes in the interest of postcolonial states, but it was often at the scale of the nation-state that such ideas could actually be implemented. Chapter 3 provides insights into the practical work of implementing new economic orders, attending both to notable events like nationalization and the mundane drudgery that followed. In this regard, institutions like the National Bank of Commerce (NBC), which amalgamated the expropriated banks, were on the frontline of remaking finance to meet people's needs. The NBC became a lynchpin in Tanzania's muscular implementation of African socialism and self-reliance, the philosophy elaborating Julius Nyerere's vision for economic sovereignty. The NBC was the key parastatal in Tanzania, serving to finance an elaborate range of state

---

[103] "Tanzania Nationalises Banks," *East African Standard*, February 7, 1967; Paul Bjerk, "Sovereignty and Socialism in Tanzania: The Historiography of an African State," *History in Africa* 37 (2010): 275–319.

enterprises after the 1967 Arusha Declaration. These aimed to more closely monopolize a range of production and exchange, including an expanding price control regime. The NBC also became a workshop for pioneering new economic morality. Under the leadership of Amon Nsekela, discriminatory credit policies would be equalized, commercial profitability balanced with social costs and benefits, workers organized into management councils, and financial "superstition and ignorance" in the public overcome through public cinema and radio.[104]

I.5 Savings, Loans, and Citizens

Just as important as government takeovers was the creation of new financial institutions, directed by government to pursue official policy goals. Postcolonial governments created a range of new banks that would serve agricultural cooperatives, traders, and farmers. Some of these initiatives aimed at remaking the racial structure of colonial capitalism. British banks were historically reticent to lend to Africans, and what credit was available from Asian merchants to purchase vehicles, hoes, or other manufactured goods was costly and embroiled in wider resentments at the middlemen.[105] Decolonization offered to change this status quo.[106] In Kenya, for instance, state lending was combined with the revocation of trade licenses to displace Asian merchants who lent to Africans.[107] The Kenyan government worked with external donors to establish the Agricultural Finance Corporation in 1963, and three years later the Cooperative Bank of Kenya was created to lend to farmers and other cooperative groups.[108]

---

[104] Amon Nsekela, "The Public Corporation as an Instrument of Economic Development in Africa," *Mbioni* 7(3) (1972): 5–37.

[105] The small but lucrative loans that Asians provided to African growers in northwest Tanganyika earned the merchants the appellation *wachuluzi*, from the Swahili "to trickle" – a reference to the relative pittance received by indebted farmers. Brad Weiss, *Sacred Trees, Bitter Harvests: Globalizing Coffee in Northwest Tanzania* (Heinemann, 2003), p. 94.

[106] Though it hardly eliminated it: In 1972 Kenya, one leading Asian businessman estimated £10 million outstanding in loans to Africans. Robert Gregory, *Asians in East Africa* (Westview Press, 1993), pp. 104–112.

[107] David Parkin, *Palms, Wine, and Witnesses* (Intertext Books, 1972), p. 51.

[108] Parker Shipton, *Credit between Cultures: Farmers, Financiers, and Misunderstanding in Africa* (Yale University Press, 2011). In addition to establishing its own bank, the Kenyan government also negotiated equity stakes in previously private corporate banks. Alice Amsden, "A Review of Kenya's

I.5 Savings, Loans, and Citizens

Just as important as lending was unearthing the "considerable currency which is sterilized by hoarding on the part of the African population." Postcolonial states worked to overcome the "psychological attitude" that militated against depositing savings with banks.[109] In the 1970s, the Cooperative Savings Scheme grew to include 150,000 depositors and more than KSh. 60 million within just a few years. This was an explicit part of producing citizens.[110] In Tanzania, despite a wariness about the monied economy, it was an ambition of African socialism to expand banking in order to "extend the monetary sector to people at the subsistence level."[111]

Chapter 2 draws on internal records to explore the Uganda Commercial Bank (UCB), a government-owned entity established in 1965. The UCB was intended to cultivate the "banking habit." As Joseph Mubiru, the Governor of the Bank of Uganda, put it in 1967, "mobilizing savings" would help the country "deal with the problem of encouraging the small man to save his current earnings for his future but also for the overall well-being of the economy."[112] This was a political and economic project, but it was also cultural: it would convert wasteful subjects into economizing citizens. Citizens were encouraged to adopt new technologies for ensuring credibility, including cooperative farming and bookkeeping. These would reform citizens to align with the demands of economic sovereignty, turning individual wealth into a collective resource without depriving individuals of their earnings.[113] Even more importantly, UCB would expand the amount of money available for development financing. Expanded banking would serve a critical role in wider economic systems, whereby increased export productivity would be achieved through

---

Political Economy since Independence," *Journal of African Studies* 1(4) (1974): 418. See also Peter Marris and Anthony Somerset, *African Businessmen* (Routledge, 1971).

[109] Kenya National Archives (KNA) MAC/KEN/56/2: Scope for a 'Commercial Bank of Kenya,' n.d. [but 1965?].

[110] Government pamphlets to "Teach Yourself Citizenship for Self-Government" included one on money. KNA MAC/KEN/86/2: "Jifunze – Uraia No. 11 Pesa," 1962.

[111] "Banks Take-Over Legalised," *East African Standard*, February 15, 1967.

[112] BoU G.56.70, GOV.806.4: Oral Evidence of Mubiru, July 18, 1967.

[113] The key was that people could keep their wealth (in a savings account) while simultaneously permitting others to use that wealth (as a bank loan). Gustav Peebles, "Rehabilitating the Hoard: The Social Dynamics of Unbanking in Africa and Beyond," *Africa* 84(4) (2014): 595–613.

mechanization and other inputs purchased on credit. While historians of development have focused on the role of foreign aid, international financing was often too little in the eyes of East African policymakers. "We need more money than ever before," said Uganda's Minister of Finance in late 1964, yet it was not forthcoming from abroad. When it was available to meet their spending goals, it would arrive late, with conditions and other drawbacks. At worst, "gifts and loans" would turn independent countries into subservient states.[114] By collecting citizen savings domestically and converting them into loans, UCB could provide capital to priority sectors, at a cost and time frame that would further export earnings.

Ugandans vocally demanded an expansion of banking, seeing it as the proper role for the state. While urban centers were sufficiently served by the 1950s, citizens demanded in the coming decades an expansion of branches to smaller towns and the use of mobile banking vans for more rural areas. In 1977, for instance, UCB sent J. M. Kasobya to Kagadi, a town in western Uganda. The trip was meant to be an exploratory visit, seeing whether the area could support a bank branch, yet it turned into a spectacle. Residents appeared in droves to insist Kasobya open accounts for them. More than USh. 50,000 was deposited that day "to show the support they had for the Bank," he reported to superiors. The offerings worked: a convinced Kasobya reported that Kagadi was populated by "outstanding progressive farmers" who can grow almost anything. A UCB branch in Kagadi would be an "undoubted" success, he decided. Elsewhere, too, citizens decried the absence of resources to further their productive activities, and they drew upon a variety of registers to position themselves as both worthy investments and deserving of assistance – including calling on the state's finances as youthful clients of a senior patron. Citizenship moved across the scholarly ideal types of dependent subordination or egalitarian individuals.[115]

[114] This was Nyerere's position in the Arusha Declaration, but such a sensibility was also evident elsewhere, including in Kenyatta's insistence on *harambee*, wherein self-help would drive development.

[115] Code-switching between rights and patronage, and the importance of productive inequalities, are central to Kristin Phillips's sensitive ethnography and idea of "subsistence citizenship." *An Ethnography of Hunger: Politics, Subsistence, and the Unpredictable Grace of the Sun* (Indiana University Press, 2018). See also James Ferguson, *Give a Man a Fish: Reflections on the New Politics of Distribution* (Duke University Press, 2015), pp. 160–162.

I.5 Savings, Loans, and Citizens

Access to credit could also provide the material trappings of modernity, yet in practice there were always those left behind. Its political and moral significance also made credit the subject of fractious dispute. In Kenya, agricultural credit was part of the independence settlement for land-deprived citizens, but troubles with repayment brought into focus the competing loyalties of borrowers and obligations of the state.[116] A narrow idea about what constituted legitimate value – namely, economic output – led to continual conflicts with citizens whose more expansive values led them to spend loan money on funerals, weddings, education, or a new bicycle or radio.[117] Farm credit flowed most readily to large landholders, and only 15 percent of smallholders received loans by 1973. It was also ethnically stratified.[118] In Tanzania, as the government came to control the levers of finance, bank loans entered a fraught contest over the distribution of wealth and prestige. For instance, an NBC subsidiary that provided loans to civil servants to purchase cars became the target of leftist students at the University of Dar es Salaam. Private cars were insufficiently socialist and a drain on the national reserve of foreign currency. They critiqued the vehicle loans as the exclusive preserve of 'Nizers – a derogatory term for those few beneficiaries of Africanization. 'Nizers were condemned as "slothful and decadent," and populist periodicals sensationalized young women being picked up in glamorous private cars. Even poetry was used to complain that the 'Nizer "does not pay his debt."[119] Such accusations of improper privilege were salient enough to eventually find a home in parliamentary debate in June 1966, and in 1970 the loans for private vehicles were banned.[120] By objecting to preferential access to credit and conspicuous consumption, these citizens mobilized the state's own rhetoric against its

---

[116] Shipton, *Credit between Cultures*; Kara Moskowitz, *Seeing Like a Citizen: Decolonization, Development, and the Making of Kenya* (Ohio University Press, 2019), pp. 135–142; Ambreena Manji, *The Struggle for Land & Justice in Kenya* (James Currey, 2020).
[117] Parker Shipton, *The Nature of Entrustment: Intimacy, Exchange, and the Sacred in Africa* (Yale University Press, 2007); Parker Shipton, *Mortgaging the Ancestors: Ideologies of Attachment in Africa* (Yale University Press, 2009).
[118] Amsden, "Kenya's Political Economy," pp. 425–431.
[119] Joshua Grace, *African Motors: Technology, Gender, and the History of Development* (Duke University Press, 2021), p. 148.
[120] Andrew Ivaska, *Cultured States: Youth, Gender, and Modern Style in 1960s Dar es Salaam* (Duke University Press, 2011), p. 203.

policies; they demanded state banks live up to the goals of conserving foreign reserves and reducing social stratification.

I.6 Cultivating Credible Citizenship

As is clear in the case of banking, the government of value was not merely a state imposition. Certainly, bureaucrats could be unwelcome arbiters of worth – mandating prices, intervening in farming, and extracting taxes. Many of the disputes I examine in the pages to follow are the result of conflicting ideas about these very topics. Chapters 4 and 5, for instance, depict the widespread smuggling economies of the 1970s as subversive offenses against the state's control of commodities. Fraudulent cheques or the contravention of currency controls were not simply criminal malfeasance; they were an insistence that wealth circulate at odds with state dictates. When farmers loaded cotton on canoes to cross Lake Victoria, they did so because they thought the product of their labor was worth more than their own state would pay and because they had enduring commitments to cross-border transactional territories. When Kenyan farmers around Bungoma were in arrears to a "staggering" KSh. 14 million to the Agricultural Finance Corporation, as they were in 1975–1976, they likewise revealed that certain obligations were more important to them than financial debts owed to banks.[121]

In other cases, though, citizens assented to the state direction of resources, its setting of prices, and its limits on international trade. Indeed, popular economic ethics could be important drivers of state monopoly. In the 1970s, the Idi Amin state oversaw an elaborate crackdown on "economic crimes" such as hoarding, smuggling, and overpricing goods. In Chapter 4 I discuss how many citizens demanded the government intervene when the Ugandan economy buckled. They petitioned and protested against economic criminality deemed to cause inflation and shortages. Indeed, even the Asian expulsion – so often reduced to the whims of one man – reflected a wider demand to remake the racialized economic order in ways befitting popular ideas about the ethical distribution of wealth.[122] These ideas had various influences – from the inequalities of income and taxation, to histories of personal

---

[121] Kakamega Records Centre KRC AGB/1/127: Bungoma District Annual Report, 1976.
[122] Edgar Taylor, "Asians and Africans in Ugandan Urban Life, 1959–1972," PhD dissertation, University of Michigan, 2016.

I.6 Cultivating Credible Citizenship

indignity and mistreatment, to expectations of personal and collective benefit.[123] Yet, common to the history was an expectation that the state could and should remake economic relations, property, and regulations. In the face of widespread shortages, Ugandans denounced bureaucrats as corrupt, neighbors as smugglers, and shopkeepers as hoarders. And they demanded official intervention. Nor was this unique to Uganda: Tanzanians and Kenyans likewise called for the state to more closely intervene in a variety of domains, from providing credit to redistributing trade licenses and policing economic crimes.[124]

Petitioning the state, calling upon it to act, and offering one's voluntary assistance were modalities of economic citizenship. The chapters that follow trace the emergence and contradictions of what I call *credible citizenship*. Citizens of Kenya, Uganda, and Tanzania positioned themselves as reliable producers. Elements of this formation were already evident in the 1950s. As the submissions to the East Africa Royal Commission convey, Africans insisted that they were trustworthy recipients of loaned capital, viable managers of shops, and essential producers of cash crops. For many, access to land – including the land expropriated by colonial forces – was foundational to such project. With independence, the colonial discrimination and political interests that made it possible to deny economic liberties to Africans faded, and citizens were better able to demand their entrance into further market domains. In each case, the commercial rights of credible citizenship were yoked to responsibilities. Shopkeepers were expected to contribute taxes; income was to be saved in bank accounts where it might be converted into loans for others. Above all, the responsibility of credible citizenship was to contribute to the expansion of export value. Credible citizenship was therefore formative of a productivist ethos, in which the virtues of output were extolled and those who were unable to yield fruitful work were consequentially

---

[123] On inequality, see Vali Jamal, "Asians in Uganda, 1880–1972: Inequality and Expulsion," *The Economic History Review* 29(4) (1976): 602–616; on interpersonal experience, see Taylor, "Claiming Kabale"; on expectations of benefit, see Chapter 4.

[124] On credit, see Brennan, *Taifa*, pp. 185–186; on trade licensing, see Aiyar, *Indians in Kenya*, chapter 6; for economic crimes in Tanzania, see Ronald Aminzade, *Race, Nation, and Citizenship in Postcolonial Africa* (Cambridge University Press, 2013), pp. 230–234.

denigrated. Merit was revealed through industrious contributions to the collective. Deviations from this responsibility incurred discipline, sometimes to the point of state violence.[125]

Engaging in productive market activity was a way to earn both money and esteem. As I discuss in Chapter 4, commercial contribution was also a key means of justifying access to consumer commodities, especially as shortages prevailed in the 1970s. Credible citizenship provided a means to achieve a range of culturally salient aspirations, from affording the material trappings of married life to educating one's children. It was also a way of legitimating one's position within a regime of economic self-determination. In one register, it was through productive activity that belonging in the polity was justified; in this way, its effect was generally felt throughout the populace. More often, though, it was a means of justifying access to limited resources by fashioning oneself as more deserving than others; in this way, it was a practice of distinction. Credible citizenship was always an unequal and exclusionary formation, as the standards of citizenship were routed through economic modalities characterized by risk, competition, and profit. The areas conducive to export crops produced a class of cultivators who could advocate on their own behalf. States had a material incentive to privilege these enclaves, directing more resources to boosting output (and sometimes income). What resulted from this productivism were masculine regimes of control, as export crops were sold and money governed in ways that diminished the role of many women – even as they labored in the fields. Over time, more women found a form of freedom in the markets of East Africa's cities and towns, trading the obligations and inequities of rural patriarchy for a mixture of economic opportunity and precarity.[126] Yet, just as frequently their burden was doubled as the compulsion to produce and earn was coupled with the work of caring and raising children.[127] And there was no guarantee their commercial contributions would be

---

[125] On productivism, cf. Ferguson, *Give a Man a Fish*, pp. 51–60.
[126] Bessie House-Midamba and Felix Ekechi, eds., *African Market Women and Economic Power: The Role of Women in African Economic Development* (Greenwood Press, 1995).
[127] Esther Boserup, *Woman's Role in Economic Development* (George Allen & Unwin, 1970).

I.6 Cultivating Credible Citizenship 37

recognized as such. The result, as Kara Moskowitz argues in her study of Kenya, was uneven, multivalent, and pluralistic citizenship.[128]

Such an approach departs from those who see African citizenship principally through the lens of legal identity.[129] Legalism risks extracting dichotomies of political belonging from the imperatives of accumulation and the struggles to define and control wealth. Rather than distinct domains, the borders of *political* inclusion were *economic* matters. The lens of credible citizenship also brings into focus the insufficiency of Euro-American theories, especially the genealogy of "social citizenship."[130] In contrast to the situation prevailing in 1940s Britain – where welfare institutions promised to soften capitalist volatility and immiseration – colonial officials were "very reluctant about implementing international standards of social security."[131] Social citizenship was fundamentally tied to a waged industrial working class that never prevailed in the colonies; as a result, the idea of using state institutions to redistribute economic surplus to those temporarily unable to work – due to being young, old, or unwell – never had much purchase in East Africa. Far more important was the state fostering economic opportunity for the unwaged producers who predominated. Issuing trade licenses or agricultural loans may have changed who could truck, barter, and trade, but credible citizenship made little claim to egalitarian redistribution. Few thought that the resources existed for meaningful redistribution, and in many cases hierarchical ideas about dependence and worth militated against it. Stratification was the result. Insofar as inequality was a concern, the promise of "development" – that there would be more tomorrow than today – justified deferring redistribution. Yet, the fluctuations of the market, the deepening of under-development, and the ghostly presence of indebtedness as the flip side of credit ultimately stymied many of the aspirations of credible citizenship.

---

[128] Moskowitz, *Seeing Like a Citizen*, p. 9.
[129] The most important of which is Mahmood Mamdani, *Citizen & Subject: Contemporary Africa and the Legacy of Late Colonialism* (Princeton University Press, 1996).
[130] T. H. Marshall, *Citizenship & Social Class* (Cambridge University Press, 1950). Cf. Niraja Gopal Jayal, *Citizenship and Its Discontents: An Indian History* (Harvard University Press, 2013).
[131] Andreas Eckert, "Regulating the Social: Social Security, Social Welfare and the State in Late Colonial Tanzania," *Journal of African History* 45(3) (2004): 467–489.

I.7 Inclusion, Exclusion, and Enforced Belonging

Like all forms of citizenship, credible citizenship was double-edged.[132] It had both assimilating and exclusionary aspects. As the rights and responsibilities of citizenship were extended to some, they were necessarily refused to others. Nationality could define the boundaries of inclusion, but it intersected with class, gender, race, and ethnicity. The poor faced uphill battles. Despite often doing much of the farm labor and provisioning for children, women had less access to credit and the proceeds of their work. Sometimes entire ethnic groups were cast as backward, draining the economic vitality of the nation. The Maasai, for instance, were depicted as stubbornly traditional Others who needed reform in order to enter postcolonial modernity.[133] It is perhaps not an accident that they frequently subverted the state's monopoly on valuation by moving their valuable livestock across the Kenya–Tanzania border.[134] The racial divisions of East Africa were among the most evident zone of conflict in regard to economic citizenship. It was not that the Asian residents of Kenya, Uganda, and Tanzania were unproductive *per se*, but many believed that their productivity came at the expense of others. Because Asian earnings were posited to come at the expense of the nation, their position of economic and legal belonging was suspect. This antinomy between citizenship as inclusion and exclusion is well recognized by African studies. In moments of economic and political stress – including the divisions of decolonization or the xenophobia of the neoliberal era – cultures of assimilation give way to more exclusive, competitive positioning. Expulsion and violence may result.[135] As I have suggested, national currency was an instrument of such bordering dynamics, used

---

[132] Emma Hunter, ed., *Citizenship, Belonging, and Political Community in Africa: Dialogues between Past and Present* (Ohio University Press, 2016); Frederick Cooper, *Citizenship, Inequality, and Difference* (Princeton University Press, 2018).
[133] Leander Schneider, "The Maasai's New Clothes: A Developmentalist Modernity and Its Exclusions," *Africa Today* 53(1) (2006): 101–131.
[134] Perhaps as many as 100,000 heads of cattle from Tanzania were annually sold illegally in Kenya during the 1970s. Dorothy Hodgson, *Once Intrepid Warriors: Gender, Ethnicity, and the Cultural Politics of Maasai Development* (Indiana University Press, 2001), pp. 202–222.
[135] Peter Geschiere, *The Perils of Belonging: Autochthony, Citizenship, and Exclusion in Africa and Europe* (University of Chicago Press, 2009).

I.7 Inclusion, Exclusion, and Enforced Belonging

to socially sort insiders and outsiders in the pursuit of material resources.

A focus on monetary infrastructure and governance also suggests a different dynamic, not well captured by the dualism of inclusion and exclusion. Rather than seesawing between assimilation and expulsion, money has been used to *enforce* membership, enclosing people within political and economic jurisdiction. Here, the trouble is not rejection or removal but rather the imposition of belonging. Confining citizens within a particular way of governing money and wealth served to raise the barriers to exiting, often with troubling effects for East Africans whose attachments were not limited to one state, nation, or territory.[136] "Inclusion," in this approach, is not an unalloyed good. Instead, it can subject communities to extraction and predation.

Enforced belonging was not only a problem for extraverted residents with cross-border ties. The inclusion in monetary infrastructures could further inequality within these circuits. This began before political independence: anticolonial activists argued that the financial regime inherited from Britain drained wealth from across East Africa to, first, Nairobi and, then, London. What is less appreciated is that the system built after independence had similarly unequal effects. In 1972, a Bank of Uganda study found that "the banking system operates to pump money from poorer counties into the most developed parts of Uganda, adding to the processes of concentration."[137] In other words, credible citizenship offered no guarantee of collective benefit. The dynamics of capitalist production and economic inequality within and between nation-states continued to deprive some areas to the benefit of others. Here the trouble was more akin to what scholars working elsewhere have called "adverse incorporation" or "predatory inclusion."[138]

Many East Africans recognized it was wise to equivocate about one's inclusion in a given monopoly on valuation. In the chapters that follow, I show how the enforcement of inclusion led to various forms

---

[136] MacArthur, "Decolonizing Sovereignty," p. 113; Keren Weitzberg, *We Do Not Have Borders* (Ohio University Press, 2017).

[137] Bank of England Archives BoE OV75/9: The Banking System and Regulation of Liquidity in Uganda, by G. Durin, 1972.

[138] For the former, see Rama Salla Dieng, "Adversely Incorporated Yet Moving Up the Social Ladder?" *Africa Development* 47(3) (2022): 133–166; for the latter, see Keeanga-Yamahtta Taylor, *Race for Profit: How Banks and the Real Estate Industry Undermined Black Homeownership* (University of North Carolina Press, 2019).

of subterfuge, not least of which was smuggling, as citizens resisted limits to their transactional territories and captured arbitrage opportunities. For many, states remained coercive and capricious at the same time they were ineffective. Asian East Africans are perhaps exemplary, though hardly alone, in this regard: wary of their standing and obligated to relatives in multiple territories, those who could afford to do so "salted money away" and invested in ties across the borders.[139] Borderland residents were also purposefully pluralistic, holding a bit of savings in both currencies, making claims to land and kin in both territories, and perhaps acquiring identity cards from both states. Rarely was this formally dual citizenship; it was rather an ethic of spreading one's resources across territories in order to provide alternative pathways when others closed down.[140] Extraterritorial ties were especially effective, but similar hedging strategies were available within countries, too. For instance, urban Kenyans have long maintained what access to rural land they can, not least to support themselves in times of economic slowdown.[141] The ability to rely on subsistence production proved a valuable backstop against the risks of market and state. What this suggests is that although citizenship was routed through economic circuits, and although the state was called upon to have an active role in that effort, East Africans did not reduce their attachments to the state alone. Credible and legal citizenship remained one tactic, arrayed with others, for securing a decent life and belonging. As I discuss in Section I.8, the practice of state sovereignty had to unfold in ways that reflected this popular dispensation.

I.8 Between Domination and Hegemony

The pluralism of many citizens – their ability to flee, to turn to subsistence, or to smuggle in the face of government coercion – obliged sovereign power to work through more than coercion. Historians of Africa have long recognized this for earlier eras, where the relative

---

[139] BoE OV75/11: Uganda Asians, August 21, 1972.
[140] Scholars of pastoralism have perhaps been best attuned to these pluralistic practices, including Peter Little et al., "Avoiding Disaster: Diversification and Risk Management among East African Herders," *Development and Change* 32 (3) (2001): 401–433.
[141] Lyn Ossome, "Can the Law Secure Women's Rights to Land in Africa?" *Feminist Economics* 20(1) (2014): 155–177.

I.8 Between Domination and Hegemony

abundance of land made it difficult to corral followers and laborers without a degree of persuasion. Scholarship has been particularly attentive to how reciprocal obligations attached people to certain polities. Leaders proved their worth through hospitality, healing, and other ways of winning assent; followers earned their membership through decorous behavior, industrious contributions, and ritual incorporation.[142] In the colonial era, too, large-scale migrations were referenda on European presence, and Africans' ability to materially provide for themselves often served as a bulwark against colonial demands.[143] Such insights are less explored in postcolonial settings, and an attention to economic statecraft gives new insights into the exercise of sovereign power.

Economic sovereignty required persuading citizens that a state monopoly on valuation was in their interests. A national currency would be rejected or unused if it seemed otherwise. This was very clear in the case of Uganda: at the time the Bank of Uganda began issuing its own currency in August 1966, the central government and Kingdom of Buganda were in the midst of a violent struggle over political supremacy. A few months before, Uganda's Prime Minister Milton Obote abrogated the constitution and drove the Kabaka into exile after a bloody confrontation.[144] Longstanding antagonisms by Ganda patriots toward the central state were never more vehement. The technocrats and politicians planning to introduce the new Ugandan shilling were worried that Baganda would refuse to use the money. Not only was it a symbol of the central state's power, some people complained that the security features on the notes depicted the emblem of Obote's political party, now even more loathed in Buganda.[145]

---

[142] Steven Feierman, "Reciprocity and Assistance in Precolonial Africa," in Warren Ilchman et al. (eds.), *Philanthropy in the World's Traditions* (Indian University Press, 1998), pp. 3–24.

[143] A. I. Asiwaju, "Migrations as Revolt: The Example of the Ivory Coast and the Upper Volta before 1945," *Journal of African History* 17(4) (1976): 577–594.

[144] I. R. Hancock, "The Uganda Crisis, 1966," *Australian Outlook* 20(3) (1966): 263–277.

[145] Mutibwa, *Bank of Uganda*, p. 108. On East African monetary symbolism, see Wambui Mwangi, "The Lion, the Native and the Coffee Plant: Political Imagery and the Ambiguous Art of Currency Design in Colonial Kenya," *Geopolitics* 7(1) (2002): 31–62; Catherine Eagleton, "Designing Change," in Ruth Craggs and Claire Wintle (eds.), *Cultures of Decolonisation: Transnational Productions & Practices, 1945–70* (Manchester, 2016), pp. 222–244.

Economic boycott and activism were nothing new to Buganda, and the refusal in the country's richest area to take up the national currency would thwart the massive, consequential undertaking. Fortunately, from the perspective of central government planners, the introduction of the new currency coincided with the payment to coffee growers in Buganda. As long as marketing boards, banks, and brokers paid farmers in the new currency, Buganda's patriotic cultivators would have little option but to accept the new money. They were, technically, able to refuse payment, but in practice they were confined by circumstance and interest to use the Ugandan shilling.[146]

This situation is akin to what Max Weber called "domination by virtue of a constellation of interests." This form of power "has its source in a formally free interplay of interested parties," who are not under any obligation to submit but do so because they find it suits their purposes. Weber suggested domination through a constellation of interests is especially apt in situations of monopoly power, including "any large central bank or credit institution." They may dominate an economy, but they do not do so through explicit coercion. Rather,

> they simply pursue their own interests and realize them best when the dominated persons, acting with formal freedom, rationally pursue their own interests as they are forced upon them by objective circumstances.[147]

A monopoly on valuation through a central bank and national currency is exemplary of this type of domination. States promulgated and maintained their own monetary infrastructures because they had a perceived interest in doing so: it provided better control over credit, it allowed them to monopolize foreign money, and it put their symbolic presence in pockets across the country. Citizens used the national currency because it was the sole legal tender, required to pay taxes and purchase goods, thus allowing them to pursue their own ends.[148] When Ugandans adopted the Ugandan shilling in 1966 – and Kenyans and Tanzanians did similarly with their national monies – they did so because it was in their perceived interest to do so. In the settling of debts and the buying of commodities, they were "formally free" to use

---

[146] BoE OV75/3: Commonwealth Office to British High Commission, Kampala, August 6, 1966.
[147] Max Weber, *Economy and Society* (University of California Press, 1978), pp. 942–945.
[148] Paul Nugent has discussed similar dynamics in terms of social contracts in "States and Social Contracts in Africa," *New Left Review* II(63) (2010): 35–68.

I.8 Between Domination and Hegemony

other instruments, but they adopted the money "simply [to] pursue their own interests and realize them best."[149]

That a monopoly on valuation unfolded best through a constellation of interests provides a new lens on sovereignty, citizenship, and the state in East Africa. It emphasizes the ambiguity of domination, where opportunity and complicity – not merely deprivation – characterize subjects of sovereign power.[150] States are heterogeneous ensembles, with competing components and pressures.[151] In contrast to a literature that winnows the state to spectacle and violence, *Money, Value, and the State* demonstrates how overlooked entities such as central and parastatal banks mediated conflicting demands through their government of value.[152] Weber is, of course, better known for defining states as "a human community that (successfully) claims the monopoly on the legitimate use of physical force within a given territory."[153] Pointing to a monopoly on valuation – and disputes over its legitimacy – is intended to clarify how African states rule through mundane matters of money and pricing, not merely coercion.[154] Violence is not always absent in this form of domination, and such histories did undergird currency and crop regulation in East Africa.[155] But in contrast to those who think coercion is the "prevalent mode of political rule" in postcolonial Africa, I argue that state force is insufficiently compelling without exercising domination through a constellation of interests.[156] The violence of East Africa was evidence of the weakness of rule, and sovereignty worked in more layered ways.[157] To see the

---

[149] Weber, *Economy and Society*.
[150] Srirupa Roy, *Beyond Belief: India and the Politics of Postcolonial Nationalism* (Duke University Press, 2007).
[151] Bruce Berman and John Lonsdale, *Unhappy Valley*, Book One (James Currey, 1992).
[152] Achille Mbembe, "Necropolitics," *Public Culture* 15(1) (2003): 11–40.
[153] Max Weber, "Politics as a Vocation," in H. H. Gerth and C. Wright Mills (eds.), *From Max Weber: Essays in Sociology* (Routledge, 1948), pp. 77–129.
[154] For an assessment of the imprecision of coercion and consent, and the role of credit instruments, see Béatrice Hibou, _The Force of Obedience: The Political Economy of Repression in Tunisia_ (Polity Press, 2011).
[155] As Weber notes in his own discussion, large credit institutions can shift into more overt relations of command and obedience, as in the case of a debtor who is required to give a creditor a seat on a management board to receive a loan.
[156] Issa Shivji, "The Rule of Law and Ujamaa in the Ideological Formation of Tanzania," *Social & Legal Studies* 4 (1995): 147–174.
[157] David Graeber, "Dead Zones of the Imagination: On Violence, Bureaucracy, and Interpretive Labor," *HAU: Journal of Ethnographic Theory* 2(2) (2012): 105–128.

state as brutish Leviathan is to ignore the plurality of people's values and how they articulate with sovereign power.

In this way, the history discussed in *Money, Value, and the State* reflects a view of sovereignty as necessarily a limited achievement. A monopoly on valuation was in practice never totalizing, even if it did serve as a regulatory ideal shaping state and popular action. From the perspective of state regulators, this incompleteness drove ambitions to further their economic sovereignty. From my perspective, it is a reminder that sovereignty is never a characteristic of an autonomous actor working through autocratic decree or generalized consent.[158] Rather, it is characterized by a series of interdependencies, pluralized and fragmented.[159] In working to attain economic sovereignty, East African states were interdependent on maintaining shared interests with their citizens, as well as negotiating their connections overseas. The result was a political formation less characterized by the pronouncements of a singular sovereign than the indeterminant composition of a sovereignty distributed across currency notes, coffee fields, and smuggling routes.[160]

Considering aligned interests also reframes theories of the relationship between citizens and states. Many have noted that patriotism can encourage a contribution to wider, often abstract, virtues – including through self-sacrifice. At times, belonging and allegiance in East Africa have indeed been matters of life and death. More prosaically, they have frequently inspired restraint and renunciation as loyal members contribute to projects in support of larger publics. In her study of Buganda, Holly Hanson emphasized that submission and giving to monarchical authority were virtuous acts through which individuals upheld collective well-being. Tribute, gift-giving, and labor given freely were the basis on which reciprocity would sustain the proper order of Ganda society.[161] Such loyal sacrifices for a higher good similarly motivated

---

[158] Thomas Blom Hansen, "Sovereignty in a Minor Key," *Public Culture* 33(1) (2021): 41–61.

[159] As Jessica Cattelino writes in her study of Florida Seminole sovereignty, "both money and sovereignty are more usefully understood as constituted by relations of interdependency than imagined to be based on autonomy." *High Stakes: Florida Seminole Gaming and Sovereignty* (Duke University Press, 2008), pp. 199–200.

[160] Achille Mbembe, *On the Postcolony* (University of California Press, 2001), p. 25; p. 128.

[161] Holly Hanson, *Landed Obligation: The Practice of Power in Buganda* (Heinemann, 2003).

I.8 Between Domination and Hegemony

Ugandans to contribute at personal cost to Britain's struggle in the Second World War.[162] After independence, the politics of self-reliance (*kujitegemea*) in Tanzania and self-help (*harambee*) in Kenya were calls of personal forbearance for collective advance.[163]

In contrast, credible citizenship worked less through self-sacrifice than self-interest.[164] The enterprise and labor of citizens were called upon equally in the service of the nation and as a means of advancing one's own ambitions. Rather than forbearance and restraint, credible citizenship was premised on a merger of individual and collective interest. As discussed above, this was most evident among the commercially oriented denizens of East Africa's productive export enclaves and towns. Yet, whether enunciated by citizens demanding loans or by politicians distributing trade licenses, there was a perception that the pursuit of commercial advance would serve the collective and the individual. For instance, when citizens were called upon to save their wealth in bank accounts, they were not being asked to sacrifice their earnings; they were promised their money back – plus interest – while simultaneously furthering national development. Their interests were not purely financial, even if they were routed through monetary infrastructures: a wider range of motivations – from honor and prestige, to ethical obligations and a sense of daring – are evident in why various people aligned, or did not, with the state architecture.[165] There was nothing inevitable about such a lamination of personal and collective purpose, and, indeed, the rights of economic citizenship were matched by corresponding duties: in

---

[162] Carol Summers, "Ugandan Politics and World War II," in Ahmad Alawad Sikainga et al. (eds.), *Africa and World War II* (Cambridge University Press, 2015), pp. 480–498.

[163] Peter Ngau, "Tensions in Empowerment: The Experience of the 'Harambee' (Self-Help) Movement in Kenya," *Economic Development and Cultural Change* 35(3) (1987): 523–538.

[164] See a related discussion in Holly Hanson, *To Speak and Be Heard: Seeking Good Government in Uganda, c.1500–2015* (Ohio University Press, 2022), chapter 4.

[165] As Bayart put it when describing an ethic of accumulation that characterized postcolonial politics, the power to "amass and redistribute wealth" can be productive of socially sanctioned honor, too. Yet, while his view is grounded in the 1980s – and therefore emphasizes "the highly personalized regulation of the State rhizome" – a perspective based on archival evidence from earlier decades shows patrimonialism is only one form of action and legitimation. Jean-François Bayart, *The State in Africa: The Politics of the Belly*, 2nd ed. (Polity Press, 2009).

return for loans, agricultural inputs, or trade licenses, citizens were obliged to produce the sorts of goods and revenue on which the state depended. Yet, the economic and political model of the postcolonial period worked best insofar as a constellation of interests held together, and divergent values among citizens could make that hard to do. East Africans positioned their financial architecture to overcome such antagonisms. Where conflicts between the individual and collective were perceived, the idea of "development" promised to ameliorate them; that is, by depicting a more prosperous future through industrious action, the shortcomings of the present were justified as temporary experiences, not permanent conditions.

I.9 Unmaking Economic Sovereignty from Within and Without

By the second half of the 1970s, it became ever more difficult to maintain this careful choreography. After years of exporting capital around the world, the United States' departure from the gold standard in 1971 encouraged wealth to flow back to New York and increased the cost of borrowing in Africa.[166] The spike in oil prices beginning in 1973 wreaked further havoc on the foreign exchange positions of East African states, as they had to spend considerably more for declining amounts of petrol, fertilizers, and industrial inputs.[167] A series of bad rains and harvests also set in. In some cases, crisis was averted by the especially good price received for coffee beginning in 1976, but in other cases long-term declines in export revenue prevailed. In Uganda, Idi Amin's government proved especially ill-equipped to maintain a constellation of interests, and the Asian expulsion in 1972 deprived the country of considerable expertise and capital.

The second half of this book explores how farmers, workers, and others pursued their own interests in the face of shortages, slowdowns, and inflation. The states did not concede the government of value, but more and more citizens insisted on their own authority to determine

---

[166] Giovanni Arrighi, "The African Crisis," *New Left Review* II(15) (2002): 21–22.

[167] Emily Brownell, *Gone to Ground: A History of Environment and Infrastructure in Dar Es Salaam* (University of Pittsburgh Press, 2020). Subsequently, Aili Tripp, *Changing the Rules: The Politics of Liberalization and the Urban Informal Economy in Tanzania* (University of California Press, 1997).

I.9 Unmaking Economic Sovereignty from Within and Without 47

what was valuable and how to achieve it. For instance, many refused to sell crops to the cooperative organizations that states used to monopolize export value. In response, exhortations and regulations in each of the countries tried to boost production and regulations attempted to conserve foreign exchange. On the front lines were men like Chief Amini Keresi who moved about Uganda's Kibaale county and turned to radio broadcasts to convince citizens to "put much effort on digging ... [for] that is where most of our wealth comes from."[168] Yet, Keresi often met disinterest and resistance as citizens believed their interests were served otherwise. In practice, Ugandans were displaying alternative ideas about what was valuable, coming to see subsistence and other activities as worthy of their time and labor rather than the export-oriented production on which the state depended.

Instead of relying on government jobs or financial regimes, more and more East Africans turned to alternative networks. They still called upon the state to rectify the situation and provide effective economic stewardship, yet few reduced their aspirations to the state – struggling as it did to coordinate between popular and official interests. Instead of monopoly, the practice of citizenship pluralized, with belonging best achieved through multiple attachments to various relations beyond the state. This pluralism was a hedge against the failure or volatility of any one livelihood or identity. As a repertoire of belonging and survival, it often existed at odds with state efforts to secure a monopoly on valuation, but as conditions worsened in the 1970s, pluralism became a generalized condition.[169] Emily Brownell has depicted how Dar es Salaam residents balanced between multiple tactics in the 1970s, as inflation ate away at wages. They moved between what employment they could secure and other livelihoods that were relatively insulated from what she calls the "foreign exchange economy."[170] In place of a finished cement home, they relied on piecemeal brickmaking; in place of purchased foods, they cultivated a garden on the edges of the city. In Kenya, too, more and more citizens found themselves making ends

---

[168] KDA 270: Amini Keresi to Information Officer, Toro, January 26, 1978.
[169] The pluralization of "regulatory authority" is a focus of Roitman, *Fiscal Disobedience* and Raeymaekers, *Violent Capitalism*.
[170] Emily Brownell, "Re-territorializing the Future: Writing Environmental Histories of the Oil Crisis from Tanzania," *Environmental History* 27(4) (2022): 747–771.

meet through *jua kali* – earning an income under the "hot sun" in labor ranging from carpentry to street vending.

Uganda's citizens likewise turned to alternative tactics for making a living. After 1972, many factories came to a standstill and shortages of spare parts became the order of the day. Uprooting coffee to plant vegetables and absconding from urban employment for rural homes, they used subsistence farming to avoid the increasingly ungovernable world of commodities. Many others relied on trade that was criminalized by the state, not least for depriving it of essential revenue. By 1974, illegal access to foreign currency was "very common."[171] Chapter 5 shows how coffee farmers marshalled relations between Uganda and Kenya to facilitate access to wealth and security. Drawing on extended families, mutually understandable languages, and histories of ritual exchange, frontier residents smuggled coffee and other commodities in the magendo circuits.[172] In Kenya, this trade allowed previously marginalized populations to enjoy a new range of commercial goods, while in Uganda – where the situation was more dire – smuggling provided the basic goods through which a decent life might be secured.

States tried to clamp down on these subversive practices. Kenyans came to think too many of their consumer goods were being smuggled into Uganda, driving up prices. The Price Control Office for Western Province "had to work around the clock" in 1978, but it was only able to bring a few smugglers to magistrates in Bungoma and Busia. They scoured the entire province to find shopkeepers "over-charging, failing to issue cash sale receipts, ticketing of goods, price lists, hoarding, refusing to sell, obstructing authorities, and failing to stop." In all, they charged 168 with offenses against the state pricing regime and raised KSh. 150,000 in fines in 1978.[173] In both Tanzania and Uganda, "economic crimes" became a public panic, as merchants refused to sell goods at the price or timing demanded by the state. Tanzania's Preventive Detention Act was used to arrest 500 people for foreign exchange violations in 1975–1976 alone.[174] In Joshua Grace's

---

[171] BoU GOV.305.1: Minutes of EA Exchange Controllers Meeting, January 18, 1974.
[172] Peter Wafula Wekesa, "The History of Community Relations across the Kenya-Uganda Boarder," PhD dissertation, Kenyatta University, 2011.
[173] KRC AUS/1/5: Provincial Price Control Office, Annual Report, 1978.
[174] Aminzade, *Race, Nation, and Citizenship*, p. 233.

I.9 Unmaking Economic Sovereignty from Within and Without 49

discussion, what the Tanzanian state called "economic sabotage" was in fact a threat to its own power to spread socialist development "across national space ... through set government prices."[175] In other words, the transactional territories of smugglers were an affront to the state's own territorial government of value. In Chapter 4, I discuss the work of Uganda's Economic Crimes Tribunal, which was established in 1975 and arraigned thousands of citizens for hoarding or smuggling goods. It was in part a response to the desperate cry by Ugandans for "essential commodities" such as salt and sugar that were no longer readily available, upsetting their ideas about economic ethics. Such juridical interventions, though, were of limited utility. Already by 1974, the situation was so dire the directors of the Bank of Uganda thought the country faced an existential threat due to the "problem of foreign exchange." If "the country is not to perish," the Bank's management argued, they needed to "break the vicious circle" that drained the national reserves through limited exports and currency smuggling.[176] Pulling their various levers – credit restrictions, border controls, and public pronouncements – was only getting them so far. The result threatened not merely pocketbooks and bottom lines, but the very survival of the nation. As commodities slipped out of controlled channels and money lost its value, it was an ever more desperate effort to govern value.

Kenya, Uganda, and Tanzania mobilized money and finance to help constitute independent nation-states, but the infrastructural power of currency and finance was ultimately limited. It proved incapable of consistently controlling citizens and commanding commodities. In this way, by the late 1970s, the project of economic sovereignty was being undone from within, as farmers and workers refused the state's authority to govern value. The ethical values and economic interests of citizens diverged from the state's putative monopoly on valuation. Living a decent life, fulfilling moral obligations, and achieving one's ambitions were less compatible with the legal circuits of value. Central banks, national currencies, and economic crimes tribunals tried to govern popular value and values, but they increasingly stumbled. Just as importantly, they could not govern *capital*. This may seem

---

[175] Grace, *African Motors*, p. 238. See also T. L. Maliyamkono and Mboya Bagachwa, *The Second Economy in Tanzania* (Ohio University Press, 1990).
[176] BoU Minutes of the Board of Directors, December 6, 1974.

counterintuitive; after all, money and credit are often equated with capital. But undergirding my analysis is a distinction between capital as an abstract form of value and money as the temporary instantiation of capital. Capital is a social relation of unceasing "value in motion," sometimes manifest in commodities, sometimes in labor power, sometimes in money. It is what David Harvey calls "an immaterial but objective force" – immaterial because it is not reducible to its physical manifestation in commodities or money, but objective in its real-world consequences.[177] It works through impersonal and abstract force which is, nevertheless, a coercive sort of power.[178] In other words, while a state currency (or a cheque or another monetary token) might represent and embody capitalist value, capitalist value supersedes money in its material forms. At times, East Africans could harness capital; at other times, they could suppress it. In many cases, they actively facilitated it. But ultimately, the contradictions of capitalism relegated many East Africans to further immiseration and crises. In such a situation, economic self-determination slipped out of reach. As their exports were replaced by less expensive substitutes and their money could purchase less and less, East Africans faced a receding horizon of sovereignty. What came in the 1980s under the sign of "structural adjustment" was an effort to install a new government of value – one that traded national economic sovereignty for the sovereignty of capitalist markets – and it is where this book will conclude.

[177] David Harvey, *The Limits to Capital* (Verso, 2006 [1982]), p. xx.
[178] Søren Mau, *Mute Compulsion* (Verso, 2023).

1 *The Moneychanger State*
Money after the End of Empire

1.1 Introduction: The Critique of Colonial Currency

In August 1964, the manager of the Ottoman Bank in Nairobi wrote to John Loynes at the Bank of England in London. "I suppose one should not rumour monger," opened the banker, Colin Kerr, "but straws in the wind are sometimes helpful."[1] Kerr was not merely passing rumors with friends or colleagues. He was writing to the most influential monetary authority of East Africa: John Loynes almost singlehandedly ran the East African Currency Board (EACB), the institution responsible since 1921 for issuing the East African shilling. From the end of the 1950s and continuing in the years after political independence, Loynes governed a currency regime under considerable strain. The colonial economic formation had long been the subject of African critique. In the 1940–1950s alone, a series of strikes, protests, and riots focused on working conditions, agricultural marketing rules, and land management.[2]

With the advance of political independence in the 1960s, the conditions were present for a more extensive reformation of the infrastructures and institutions through which value was governed. Currency was no exception, and African politicians began to agitate for changes to the EACB. In their view, it was an unnecessarily conservative institution that deprived Africans of the monetary authority they needed for full independence and economic development. Changing the rules governing money would help provide the resources necessary for the ambitious spending priorities of the new states. It would also offer, some argued, the means to undo the uneven development of East Africa and its subordination to metropolitan economic demands.

The critique of the EACB was most pronounced in what became Tanzania, where leadership of the Tanganyika African National Union

---

[1] BoE OV76/3: Kerr to Loynes, August 12, 1964.
[2] Frederick Cooper, *Decolonization and African Society: The Labor Question in French and British Africa* (Cambridge University Press, 1996).

(TANU) advocated for change. As the Minister of Finance, Paul Bomani was central to overseeing a series of technocratic financial inquiries into the matter after 1961. Bomani and his colleagues tried to balance competing desires: to better control their state finances and to maintain the infrastructures of regional cooperation of which the East African shilling was perhaps most important. As a result, nearly three years into political independence, the future of the Currency Board remained uncertain. While Nyerere, Bomani, and others continued to profess a commitment to a regional monetary order, they were clear that the status quo could not continue indefinitely. Doing so would subordinate their economic self-determination to a conservative and outdated Currency Board. Despite political independence, the East African shilling maintained a racialized monetary hierarchy that starved the region of investment and facilitated the export of already limited capital. What they wanted instead was an East African central bank – capable of adept financial regulation and expansive development financing – but were it to not arrive, they would be forced to go it alone, creating a national currency and central bank.[3]

It was in this uncertain interregnum that Colin Kerr sent his speculative letter. Continuing from his modest apology for speculating, the banker informed Loynes that while Kerr was on leave the last week, a representative of the De La Rue corporation, Mr. Wethered, stayed in the Kerr home. Two days later, Paul Bomani's secretary rang Kerr's house because the Minister wanted to urgently speak to De La Rue's Wethered. The Tanzanian bureaucrat did not know Wethered had already departed, but was keen to track him down. When Kerr received this mistaken call, he knew it portended potentially significant news. Kerr did not need to tell Loynes that De La Rue was one of a few companies hired by governments around the world to securely print currency. Nor did he have to be explicit about what this phone call may augur: "What horrible conclusions one is supposed to draw from this, I leave to you to decide," he finished his missive.[4] Nor did Loynes – who responded to Kerr with his appreciation – need encouragement to keep tabs on the African ministers who were his ostensible

---

[3] Paul Bjerk, "A Preliminary History of the Bank of Tanzania," in Salvatory Nyanto (ed.), _A History of Post-Colonial Tanzania: Essays in Honor of Prof. Isaria N. Kimambo_ (James Currey, forthcoming).

[4] BoE OV76/3: Kerr to Loynes, August 12, 1964. On the ties between De La Rue and the Bank of England, see Sarah Stockwell, *The British End of the British Empire* (Cambridge University Press, 2018), p. 216.

colleagues. Weeks before, Loynes learned that Bomani was on official business in London at the same time a West German monetary advisor to Tanzania was holidaying in England, raising the possibility that a "private conspiracy [was] being hatched."[5] Keen to hold together his regional monetary regime, Loynes viewed the actions of independent African states with suspicion. Hints that they may be printing their own currency or designing new institutions without Bank of England guidance were worrying. They were warning signs that the fate of the colonial monetary system would soon match that of the colonial political system. From Loynes's perspective, such an end to the Currency Board threatened not only East African monetary stability; it would also undo the economic power exerted by Britain in the region.

This chapter examines the end of colonial money and the establishment of national currencies and central banks in 1965–1966. Monetary matters have largely been neglected in the study of East African decolonization, yet these were the infrastructural firmament for postcolonial economies and identities. The East African Currency Board was a contradictory institution: despite African politicians' criticisms, many aspired to maintain the regional monetary regime but transfer control to independent states. The question of independence was at what *scale* identity, polities, and economies would cohere. In part, these were worked out through questions about monetary authority and financial arrangements. I show how the transition from the EACB to a planned East African central bank was tied up with wider aspirations for an East African Federation. Currency became a topic of intense debate among African elites and their expatriate economics advisors, and I use rarely discussed archival sources to detail the high-stakes politics of money in the era of decolonization.

Ultimately, though, an East African central bank and currency proved irreconcilable with other political and economic imperatives. This led to the establishment of national institutions and infrastructures to govern value. Coming a few years after political independence, the central banks and currencies of Kenya, Tanzania, and Uganda were framed as necessary steps toward economic sovereignty. Politicians and citizens hailed them as a way to foster development; credit creation and financial regulation were instruments to author national futures. But as I indicate below, these were at best means toward "arrested

---

[5] BoE OV76/3: Kessels' Memo, July 29, 1964.

autonomy" in which international money and foreign influences continued to have a determining position – not least of which was the requirement to accumulate and maintain a significant reserve of foreign assets under the stewardship of central banks.[6] The result was an ongoing imperative to earn export value – a burden especially placed on farmers cultivating the countries' major export crops. Citizenship was to be economically productive, and as I argue in the subsequent chapters, this inaugurated a range of political struggles over inequality, belonging, and worth.

1.2 Colonial Money after the End of Empire

By the postwar era, the East African shilling and the Currency Board that administered it were the predominant state money across the region; however, it was a monetary regime that emerged through a series of historical struggles over value. Europeans in East Africa at the end of the nineteenth century faced, in the words of Emma Park, a "proliferation of value forms."[7] Their administrative and commercial ambitions – not least of all taxation – depended on the existence of a dominant currency, yet they were confronted by a dizzying mix of competing ideas and instruments. Preferences for livestock, brass wires, cowrie shells, and other objects impeded the colonial ideal of uniformity. As Karin Pallaver writes, the colonial monetary order was characterized by the "coexistence sometimes for decades, of multiple currencies, circulating in different currency circuits and often performing different functions."[8] As a result, the path to standardization was at best a crooked line.

It was also a process marked by crises, including what Wambui Mwangi calls the "social and political delirium" known as the "East

---

[6] "Arrested autonomy" is Juno Parreñas's term for the constraints on self-determination. *Decolonizing Extinction: The Work of Care in Orangutan Rehabilitation* (Duke University Press, 2018).

[7] Emma Park, "The Right to Sovereign Seizure? Taxation, Valuation, and the Imperial British East Africa Company," in Gurminder K. Bhambra and Julia McClure (eds.), *Imperial Inequalities: The Politics of Economic Governance across European Empires* (Manchester University Press, 2022), pp. 79–97.

[8] Karin Pallaver, "The African Native Has No Pocket," *International Journal of African Historical Studies* 48(3) (2015): 474.

1.2 Colonial Money after the End of Empire

African rupee crisis."[9] This complicated fracas unfolded between 1919 and 1921, pitting Asian merchants against white settlers in a conflict not merely over the proper value of East African money but also over what structure racial capitalism would take in the region. In brief, while the Indian rupee had until that point been the prevailing government currency in East Africa, its revaluation after the First World War led to considerable losses to white wealth in Kenya. In contrast, the diasporic Asian population benefitted financially and resisted actions by the colonial state to their detriment. African employees and producers, for their part, were caught in the middle, at risk of losing what coined savings they had accumulated. The government muddled through, with four official monies in two years to try to tame the severe currency fluctuations and political passions.[10]

The eventual result was the EACB and its East African shilling.[11] A number of institutional arrangements are worth mentioning. The first is that every East African shilling issued was required to have a corresponding amount of pounds sterling deposited with the EACB. For instance, by 1955 the £60.4 million in East African shillings that the EACB had issued was backed by £61.8 million in sterling reserves.[12] These sterling deposits came from two predominant sources: foreigners settling in East Africa and East Africans selling their goods to foreigners.[13] And while these sterling deposits were exchanged for East African money, they were not invested in East

---

[9] Wambui Mwangi, "Of Coins and Conquest: The East African Currency Board, the Rupee Crisis, and the Problem of Colonialism in the East African Protectorate," *Comparative Studies in Society and History* 43(4) (2001): 763–765.

[10] Robert Maxon, "The Kenya Currency Crisis, 1919–21 and the Imperial Dilemma," *The Journal of Imperial and Commonwealth History* 17(3) (1989): 323–348; Karin Pallaver, "A Currency Muddle: Resistance, Materialities and the Local Use of Money during the East African Rupee Crisis," *Journal of Eastern African Studies* 13(3) (2019): 546–564.

[11] This is not to say the EACB was an immediate success. Financial missteps in 1919 meant that it took until 1950 to accumulate the mandatory 100 percent sterling reserves.

[12] The fact the EACB was more than 100 percent covered reflects the conservatism of its administration. Joachim Kratz, "The East African Currency Board," *Staff Papers (International Monetary Fund)* 13(2) (1966): 233.

[13] In the first case, a British farmer might convert their British currency to East African shillings when settling in Kenya; they would then hold the corresponding amount of East African currency to use for their expenses. In the second case, East Africans sold their produce to merchants who had, themselves,

African concerns; rather, the sterling reserves were put into London's financial markets.[14] The result was a huge sum that was not available in the region – "sterilized" in the view of some critics.

Closely related to this one-to-one backing was another element: the unimpeded convertibility between colonial and metropolitan money. Holders of East African currency could always acquire British sterling – at the time one of the world's most reliable and acceptable monies. In the language of the Currency Board and its proponents, the full sterling backing and convertibility instilled "confidence" in the East African economy. Businesses were willing to trade in East Africa because they knew they could always return to the more international currency, sterling. In practice, only wealthy individuals and major commercial entities did so because few Africans accumulated enough or had reason to leave the region.

Mediating the financial system were the expatriate banks who transferred money between London's sterling markets and East Africa's shilling sphere. The largest of these – National & Grindlays, Standard Bank, and Barclays Bank D.C.O. – were all established by the First World War, working as government bankers and lending to export agriculture. The EACB regime boosted their fortunes.[15] They were vocal proponents of currency convertibility because it allowed them to move customer deposits to London, and as a result they advocated against what they called the "monster of exchange control."[16] Thanks to the Board's regional scope, the private banks could operate across Tanganyika, Kenya, Uganda, and Zanzibar as one market, with Nairobi serving as headquarters. As colonial development became the order of the day, the banks opened "development corporations" that provided modestly enlarged financing to East

---

converted sterling into East African money to pay for the cotton, coffee, or sisal they wished to buy.

[14] John Loxley, "The Development of the Monetary and Financial System of the East African Currency Area, 1950 to 1964," PhD dissertation, University of Leeds, 1966; John Letiche, "Dependent Monetary Systems and Economic Development: The Case of Sterling East Africa," in Willy Sellekaerts (ed.), *Economic Development and Planning: Essays in Honour of Jan Tinbergen* (Palgrave Macmillan, 1974), pp. 186–236.

[15] Irving Gershenberg, "Banking in Uganda since Independence," *Economic Development and Cultural Change* 20(3) (1972): 510.

[16] Julian Crossley and John Blandford, *The DCO Story: A History of Banking in Many Countries 1925–1971* (Barclays Bank, 1975), p. 101.

1.2 Colonial Money after the End of Empire 57

African businesses.[17] The banks also benefitted from the EACB's lack of regulation and its comfort with commercial collusion. By the 1940s, a formally organized cartel agreement fixed prices and services with what an observer called "strictness and wideness in scope [that were] unparalleled." "The practical effect," he wrote of the oligopoly, was to "completely eliminate any competition between the [British] banks on the matters laid down by the agreement."[18] The savings deposits of their customers were largely invested in London and their cushioned profits were distributed to metropolitan shareholders.[19] The result was that "these banks were actually involved in a process of exporting capital from the underdeveloped countries of East Africa for use in a developed country."[20]

The imperial architecture of money in East Africa suited metropolitan interests (see Figure 1.1). Capital produced in East Africa and invested in Britain was a form of what one scholar calls "unrequited exports."[21] Monetary authorities at the Bank of England and Treasury worked diligently to rebuff claims to exported wealth from the colonies. This was all the more important in the context of postwar Britain's parlous finances. Convertibility into sterling facilitated inexpensive production in the colonies, and barriers to transfers beyond the sterling area tried to blunt the rising power of the US dollar.[22] Warding

---

[17] Frances Bostock, "The British Overseas Banks and Development Finance in Africa after 1945," *Business History* 33(3) (1991): 167.

[18] This included collusion on prices for interest, commissions, and fees, as well as prohibitions on offering services not covered by the agreement. Ernest-Josef Pauw, "Banking in East Africa," in Peter Marlin (ed.), *Financial Aspects of Development in East Africa* (Weltforum Verlag, 1970), p. 233.

[19] One of the few public institutions of the colonial era to serve Africans financially was similarly extractive. The Post Office Savings Bank began in Kenya in 1926 before expanding to three-quarters of a million accounts across the region in 1966. For decades, it invested Africans' accumulated savings into assets in Britain that paid "ultra-low rates of interest," amounting to a "large-scale export of capital at extremely low prices." Pauw, "Banking," p. 226.

[20] Walter Tessier Newlyn, *Money in an African Context* (Oxford University Press, 1967), p. 43.

[21] Paul Robert Gilbert, "The Crown Agents and the CDC Group: Imperial Extraction and Development's 'Private Sector Turn'," in Gurminder K. Bhambra and Julia McClure (eds.), *Imperial Inequalities: The Politics of Economic Governance Across European Empires* (Manchester University Press, 2022), p. 102.

[22] The rise of the US dollar and the troubles of the sterling area weighed heavily on the British state, and even when some quarters of officialdom were prepared to reduce the amount of colonial earnings held in London, the Colonial Office

Figure 1.1 A manager for Barclays Bank in Tanzania counting money in June 1966.
Source: Tanzania Information Services.

off the decline of sterling was a "central preoccupation" of government officials, and the easy movement of capital from the colonies to London was a critical ingredient to muting austerity in Britain.[23]

The double drain of easily exported wealth and the metropolitan investment of capital was more glaring as political independence neared. Colonists' anxiety about decolonization heightened the flight of money from East Africa. For instance, after the Lancaster House Conference secured constitutional advances for Kenyan Africans in March 1960, £900,000 was transferred from the colony in one week

---

"took the view that colonial austerity was worth the sacrifice it entailed: what was good for the sterling area was, in the long term, good for colonial development." Gerold Krozewski, "Finance and Empire: The Dilemma Facing Great Britain in the 1950s," *International History Review* 18(1) (1996): 55.

[23] P. J. Cain and A. G. Hopkins, *British Imperialism: Crisis and Deconstruction 1914–1990* (Longman, 1993); Wadan Narsey, *British Imperialism and the Making of Colonial Currency Systems* (Palgrave Macmillan, 2016); Yusuf Bangura, *Britain and Commonwealth Africa* (Manchester University Press, 1983).

alone. This figure grew to nearly £5 million by early July. "So ravaged were Kenya's finances," writes Robert Tignor, that the British cabinet – which rarely deigned to discuss individual colonies – met to discuss how to "inspire investor confidence" in Kenya.[24] Yet, without substantive changes, including the end to convertibility and full sterling reserves, there was little to be done.

This was because the colonial regime institutionalized a monetary hierarchy, with East African shillings subordinated to British sterling. In effect, shilling notes and coins were tokens, referring back to sterling deposits. While they had a quantitative equivalence, the shilling was geographically circumscribed to the territory of the EACB.[25] The greater acceptability of sterling – it could be used in London *and* Nairobi – made it a more valuable money from the perspective of colonial capitalists. It also meant that East African shillings were dependent upon availability of sterling. Closely related to this hierarchy of acceptability were the inequalities of time that the Currency Board maintained.[26] Money is always a temporal instrument, whether advancing resources in the form of loans or storing wealth in more enduring ways than other assets. But not all money has the same ability to rework time or project a viable future. The greater international acceptability of sterling and the consolidation of financial investments in London meant sterling assets were far more effective as long-term instruments. Shilling was largely confined to the present, unable to be used for purposes beyond immediate purchases or short-term loans to agricultural brokers. This suited the colonial economy well enough, but African development aspirations required longer-term money to be invested in roads, hospitals, and other infrastructure that would not provide short-term returns.

---

[24] Robert Tignor, *Capitalism and Nationalism at the End of Empire: State and Business in Decolonizing Egypt, Nigeria, and Kenya, 1945–1963* (Princeton University Press, 1997), p. 357.

[25] This included Kenya, Uganda, Tanganyika, and Zanzibar, but also Aden and Somaliland – a geography that reflected the shifting frameworks of colonial control.

[26] On monetary hierarchies, see Stephanie Bell, "The Hierarchy of Money," *Levy Institute* Working Paper no. 231 (1998). On money and temporality, see Jane Guyer, "Prophecy and the near Future: Thoughts on Macroeconomic, Evangelical, and Punctuated Time," *American Ethnologist* 34(3) (2007): 409–421; Stefan Eich, *The Currency of Politics: The Political Theory of Money from Aristotle to Keynes* (Princeton University Press, 2022).

From the perspective of African activists, the system's bias toward expatriate economies had detrimental effects and politicians demanded increased monetary authority.[27] They were appalled by the capital flight and refusal to invest in the region, seeing every shilling converted to sterling as a resource Africans could no longer marshal for national purpose. They wanted the ability to contain wealth within the region and to invest it according to African needs. Neither of these goals was possible with an institution purposefully designed to do little more than exchange between shilling and sterling. Instead of a currency board, what was needed was a central bank. Such institutions were not only *de rigueur* in Europe and America, they were fast becoming part of a standard suite of postcolonial statecraft. By 1961, central banks were established in Ghana, Nigeria, Ceylon, and other former colonies.[28] Central banks had a variety of functions beyond a currency board's role in issuing money. They could provide banking services to government, regulate commercial banks, influence commercial credit, and control foreign exchange flows. Through their policy levers, they could end the British banks' practice of responding to London's market perturbations and interest rates even when they mattered little to East Africa. They would also be the stewards of the reserves of foreign currency held by government, opening the possibility of investments that furthered African goals rather than subsidizing London's money market.[29]

Importantly, the goal in the years before 1965 was not the establishment of *national* central banks for each East African territory. Rather, they would trade the EACB for an East African central bank, operating across Kenya, Tanganyika, Uganda, and Zanzibar.[30] Such a scale for imagining African monetary governance was not unusual given the

---

[27] They were not alone, as one economist memorably summarized, "Conservative ministers and Communist spokesmen, practical bankers and impractical spenders, *The Economist* and *The Daily Worker* have all agreed that the sterling balances represent exploitation of the colonies and that they ought to be repaid." Ida Greaves, "The Colonial Sterling Balances," *Essays in International Finance* no. 20 (September 1954).

[28] BoE OV7/81: Loynes address to Kenya Economic Society, January 10, 1961.

[29] S. K. Basu, *Central Banking in the Emerging Countries: A Study of African Experiments* (Asia Publishing House, 1967); A. Mensah, "The Process of Monetary Decolonization in Africa," *Utafiti* 4(1) (1979): 45–63.

[30] P. G. Clark, "The Role of an East African Central Bank in Accelerating Development," Makerere Institute of Social Research, EDRP 46.

importance of the common market and currency at that time. Most of the people involved never had reason to question the acceptability of their money across the region, and enterprises had likewise structured their business on a regional scale. Bank branches in Tanganyika and Uganda answered to Nairobi, and factories in Kenya sold their wares across British East Africa in exchange for the same currency. Yet, the chronology of decolonization decoupled political independence from economic matters: when Tanganyika became independent at the end of 1961, the date for Kenyan independence was still unknown, with some influential voices expecting it to not come for some years more.[31] Much the same held the next year when Ugandans took control of their state. Divergent independence timelines invited divergent fiscal policies, as Tanganyika and then Uganda urgently went about developing their national planning apparatus. Yet, political and economic authority could not proceed without reference to each other.

As I discuss more fully below, it was in this context of maintaining and furthering their shared economic status that ideas about an East African Federation reached new salience. The idea was familiar to most of the political class, even if views differed as to its desirability or proper composition.[32] Its prominence only grew in June 1960 when Julius Nyerere addressed the Second Conference of Independent African States in Addis Ababa, capturing headlines with his proposal to delay Tanganyikan independence in order to decolonize with Kenya and Uganda within a federation. Few African leaders were outright opponents of federation, moving its plausibility into the domain of reasonable expectation, at least until 1964. As a result, hopes for the East African central bank were pinned on the formation of a regional political authority that would ground the shared monetary institution.

Securing Colonial Capitalism at the End of Empire

Nevertheless, the task of reforming monetary authority could not wait for federation. Already in the 1950s, the expanding economy and African protest obliged the Currency Board's management to begin

---

[31] Kevin P. Donovan, "*Uhuru Sasa*! Federal Futures and Liminal Sovereignty in Decolonizing East Africa," *Comparative Studies in Society & History* 65(2) (2023): 372–398.

[32] Chris Vaughan, "The Politics of Regionalism and Federation in East Africa, 1958–1964," *Historical Journal* 62(2) (2018): 519–540.

expanding its historically narrow function of exchanging between monies. The evolution of the EACB was directed by John Loynes, the longtime Bank of England associate who exerted unparalleled control on the East African money in those years.[33] Loynes acknowledged the eventual need for a central bank, but he insisted it proceed on a firm political basis. If an East African central bank was responsible to three or four different governments, it would face the unwieldy – even impossible – task of executing a uniform monetary regime across divergent fiscal policies. Unlike a currency board that exerted an automatic ability to "control" government finances, a central bank would be more likely to succumb to what he saw as the temptation of irresponsible government spending.[34] In his view, an East African political settlement was a necessary precondition for an East African central bank; until that was available, he worked to insulate the Currency Board from African influence.

Loynes worked against what he saw as the undue haste of African politicians. He repeatedly insisted the time was not right for ending the Currency Board. "We must accept that no central bank," he said at the end of 1960, "however elaborately endowed, can make bricks without the straw of the right financial surroundings." He cast scorn on those who rushed toward central banking, saying they were naively taken by the "mystique and prestige" of such institutions. Instead of a muscular instrument for governing value, Loynes told his audiences that a central bank was of limited utility to African aspirations. While a central bank could create money, it "cannot automatically create wealth and resources." In fact, "in the wrong hands" a central bank was "the finest instrument not only for inflation but also for giving inflation a spurious air of respectability."[35] Economic independence – a term he put in scare quotes – was something that could only occur slowly and with sufficient appreciation for what he saw as the hard facts. "We are dealing with real life, not fairy tales," he insisted when confronted by alternative views.[36]

---

[33] As Sarah Stockwell writes, "More than any other, one man was instrumental in the Bank's efforts to exercise influence" across late colonial Africa. Stockwell, *The British End of the British Empire*, p. 151. In 1965, he changed his surname to an old family name of "de Loynes." For simplicity, I have only used the older name.

[34] BoE OV7/82: Loynes to Kenneth Bolton, September 13, 1962.

[35] BoE OV7/81: Loynes address to Kenya Economic Society, January 10, 1961.

[36] BoE OV7/86: Loynes to Editor, Tanganyika Standard, December 10, 1964.

1.2 Colonial Money after the End of Empire

Instead of rushing to a central bank, Loynes proffered an evolved Currency Board as the solution to East Africa's demands. As he proudly insisted to his many contacts in the region and beyond, there was much the Currency Board could do to take on the functions of a central bank. He thought this evolution of functions would buy time against the demands of East Africans. Evolving the EACB into an "embryo" central bank would "reduce pressure for the premature creation of a central bank endowed with all the normal powers and duties."[37] He carefully stage-managed this transition, brandishing widely the "central banking look" (without its full functions) in order to avoid appearing "in any way to drag my feet."[38] He was keen to manage appearances, with public statements often purposefully crafted to maintain the authority of the Currency Board over which he had nearly single-handed power.[39]

While the EACB did, indeed, undergo a transformation in those years, it remained a fundamentally conservative financial institution, shaped by metropolitan anxieties to maintain sterling's international standing.[40] Critics condemned it as a paragon of "Gladstonian" liberalism, where the free circulation of capital within imperial circuits was commonsense and grounded in necessity.[41] "A currency authority," Loynes wrote in East Africa's newspapers, "has the prime task of safeguarding the value of its currency."[42] What Loynes deemed "sound finance" was premised on limits to African monetary sovereignty; indeed, in his judgment, Africans were unlikely stewards

---

[37] BoE OV7/79: Loynes to Julian Crossley, May 13, 1964; BoE OV7/78: Loynes to Rendell, September 14, 1962.

[38] BoE OV76/3: East African Currency Board, September 6, 1963; BoE OV7/78: Loynes to the Governors, September 11, 1962. Aware of the "colonialist" connotation of the Board's name, EACB officials were also in favor of rebranding as a "Monetary Institute or Currency Authority" BoE OV7/85: Loynes to Minister Gichuru, May 28, 1964; BoE OV7/79: H.R. Hirst, "Office Note (154)," October 19, 1962.

[39] An unpublished Bank of England history notes with curiosity how the institution "lent its name and prestige" to Loynes's work conducted "on a highly personal basis." BoE OV18/4: E.P. Haslam, *Central Banks in the Making*, p. 949.

[40] For the colonial policy debates in this context, see David J. Morgan, *Official History of Colonial Development: A Reassessment of British Aid Policy, 1951–1965* (Macmillan Press, 1980).

[41] BoE OV7/83: B.W. Meynell to F.A. Reynolds, Commonwealth Relations Office, February 5, 1963.

[42] BoE OV7/77: Draft Newspaper Article Enclosed in Loynes to A.N. Galsworthy, October 6, 1960.

of monetary affairs. His correspondence drips with condescension and his policy advice insisted on expatriate management wherever possible.[43] Loynes saw his African interlocutors as, at best, well-meaning and naïve; more often, their divergent views on how money should be governed made them incapable and untrustworthy.[44] He reduced Kenyan opposition to continued British monetary oversight as evidence of "political allergies of the black men" in that former settler colony.[45] In practice, he worked to shore up the racial hierarchy of money, akin to what Allan Lumba has traced in the Philippine colony where monetary authorities intervened to maintain "racial order and capitalist security."[46]

Extending the EACB's mandate past political independence was done in order to "maintain one stable and convertible currency for the whole East African area."[47] While currency volatility was certainly a risk, guarding the value of the East African shilling had the effect of starving the region of investment capital. In choosing to emphasize the former over the latter, Loynes and the EACB erred on the side of maintaining the racial capitalism of British colonialism. The continued value of the East African shilling was nowhere more important than in the settler and expatriate-dominated economy of Kenya. The property owners in these "islands of white" stood to lose from the devaluation of their assets.[48] They also faced the considerable risk of being unable to easily convert their shillings into sterling should they want – as many did – to remove their wealth from the jurisdiction of independent African governments. As Loynes told the heads of British banks in February 1962, a currency board "seems likely to remain the only type of issuing authority which can preserve the measure of discipline

---

[43] This is most evident in his personal letters to other British officials, such as BoE OV76/4: Loynes to H.J. Hinchey, December 31, 1964.
[44] He also rebuffed those he could less readily condemn as lacking expertise: As the International Monetary Fund (IMF) began consulting on the design of Tanganyika's central bank, Loynes moved to "have an Englishman on the team" to represent the interests of sterling. BoE OV78/4: Loynes to Rootham, September 28, 1964.
[45] BoE OV78/4: Loynes to Jasper Rootham, September 28, 1964.
[46] Allan E. S. Lumba, *Monetary Authorities: Capitalism and Decolonization in the American Colonial Philippines* (Duke University Press, 2022), p. 4.
[47] BoE OV7/81: Loynes to Michael Curtis, December 20, 1960.
[48] Dane Kennedy, *Islands of White: Settler Society and Culture in Kenya and Southern Rhodesia, 1890–1939* (Duke University Press, 1987).

necessary in present circumstances to keep the one currency in being."[49]

The model that developed in the years after 1955, then, was a cautious expansion of the Currency Board's work in order to curtail more radical demands and maintain the fundamental monetary hierarchies. Perhaps the most prominent example of the EACB transitioning to an "embryo" central bank was the ostensible departure from one-to-one sterling backing and the start of lending by the EACB within East Africa. As discussed above, to African observers these were two of the most frustrating aspects of the currency board model, not least because they meant that the EACB offered little in the way of expansionary monetary policy. The EACB, in effect, hoarded its reserves in London where they were "sterilized" rather than putting them to use in East Africa.[50] Loynes's commitment to this cautious model is all the more striking because it was only in 1950 that the Board managed to accumulate a full backing of sterling reserves for the outstanding East African shillings; missteps at the EACB's start in 1919 meant that actual reserves were far short of the full mandate.[51]

In response to such critiques, the EACB began a "fiduciary issue" in 1955. This permitted the Currency Board to buy East African local securities up to £20 million without corresponding sterling deposits. In the coming years, the limit was expanded so that by 1964–1965, up to £35 million could be issued in this way. For East Africans, this was not merely a valuable financial instrument; it also presented little risk to the Currency Board. After all, it was exceedingly unlikely every East African shilling would be presented for redemption at the same moment, exhausting the EACB's reserve of sterling.[52]

Relaxing the requirement for sterling would in theory free up capital for investment in economic development, including the sort of infrastructural spending that struggled to find other support.[53] Yet, even in

---

[49] BoE OV78/4: Loynes to J.K. Michie, February 9, 1962.
[50] Basu, *Central Banking*, p. 63.
[51] Newlyn notes that the EACB "survived" the Great Depression "with an initial reserve of less than 50 per cent of currency outstanding," belying the idea that the reserves alone maintain confidence in the money. Newlyn, *Money in an African Context*, p. 31.
[52] BoE OV7/81: Loynes to Galsworthy, October 12, 1961.
[53] In July 1963, one economist calculated that about £40 million from the EACB reserve might be redirected to economic development. BoE OV78/4: British Trade Commission, Kenya, July 17, 1963.

this expanded role, the EACB was mired in financial conservativism in at least three ways.[54] Loynes used his position to curtail aspirations for longer-term investments, hewing close to the ideology of sound finance wherever possible. What credit the EACB supported was required to be profitable in short order. The possibility of "mobilizing currency reserves for development purposes" was depicted by British administrators as a danger because "money spent on roads and bridges does not turn over." Economic infrastructures were disparaged as "prestige projects" unworthy of investment.[55] Instead, the fiduciary issue was to be spent on "short-term and self-liquidating" loans, mostly to finance the export of crops.[56] As a result, what novel monetary powers the states gained were used to reproduce the inherited structure of export agriculture.[57] Moreover, the amount of fiduciary issue also remained insufficient to the financial aspirations of the new states as the Currency Board continued to prioritize the demand of international capitalists for money easily converted into sterling. Finally, it was not merely that the fiduciary issue was directed toward a very narrow set of purposes and in small amounts. It was also that the Currency Board continued to adopt an overly cautious view of what monetary reserves were necessary to maintain confidence in the currency. In May 1962 it did not merely have one-to-one backing of its issued currency; in fact, it was 118 percent covered.[58] For its British overseers, such a status was a point of pride: in a period of "gloom about the economy" and political upheaval, the excessive reserves meant the "reputation and standing of the East African shilling remains untouched."[59] Yet in a region lacking usable capital, it compounded the financial constraints.[60]

---

[54] For a summary of debates, see John Loxley, "Sterling Reserves and the Fiduciary Issue in East Africa," *Economic Affairs* 11(5) (1966): 217–226; Basu, *Central Banking*, pp. 59–61.
[55] BoE OV7/88: Milner-Barry to Galsworthy, Colonial Office, August 3, 1965.
[56] BoE OV76/3: Personal and Confidential, April 8, 1963.
[57] In some cases, its remit was actually narrow in terms of crop finance, intended for the financing of crop transport and not storage. BoE OV7/79: Loynes to Gordon, September 16, 1964.
[58] BoE OV78/4: Draft: East African Currency Board, May 11, 1962.
[59] BoE OV7/82: East African Currency Is Strong, *Uganda Argus*, October 22, 1962.
[60] It was not only Africans who found the British overly restrictive. American experts also thought the financial models were "conservative and [provided] inadequate contribution to development, particularly in medium-term lending to

1.3 Halting Steps toward Monetary Nationalism

Tanganyikan independence at the end of 1961 cast the Currency Board into an even starker light. Leadership in the region's first sovereign country was frustrated that the "country's money is still under colonial control."[61] In an effort to calm the dissent, the EACB was moved to Nairobi and representatives of the member governments were appointed to the board. Yet, the Currency Board was not to be a "department of government ... [and the] prime aim is and will be to preserve a stable and convertible currency."[62] The monetary regime remained stacked against prevailing African views of how money should be governed, and it was designed to resist popular redirection of its resources.[63]

The half-measures frustrated TANU leadership, which was especially vocal on these matters. Before independence, Governor Turnbull reported with frustration that the African government-to-be was "sticking firm" to their decision to have their own currency. The chief proponent was Nsilo Swai, whose views on the topic made him an "extremist" in the eyes of Britain. "There seems," Turnbull wrote,

> to be more than national pride in this, and it is being argued that one's own Central Bank with its currency issue is necessary for planned economic development ... [and] that the Currency Board system diverted Tanganyika's persistent favourable balance of trade to support Kenya's persistent adverse balance.[64]

Turnbull was puzzled by the TANU's desire for monetary authority. Yet, his bewilderment reflects less the oddity of Tanganyikan aspiration that the imperial commonsense that stable and convertible currencies were the bedrock of economic well-being. The colonial

---

agriculture." BoE OV7/85: H.L. Engberg on "Banking in East Africa," May 11, 1964.

[61] BoE OV7/82: Loynes to A.L. Adu, July 12, 1962.
[62] Convertible to sterling, that is, BoE OV7/77: Draft Newspaper Article Enclosed in Loynes to Galsworthy, October 6, 1960.
[63] On the genealogy of insulating money from democratic forces, see Eich, *The Currency of Politics*. For more recent attempts to "encase" property from political interference, see Quinn Slobodian, *Globalists: The End of Empire and the Birth of Neoliberalism* (Harvard University Press, 2018).
[64] BoE OV76/3: Roger Turnbull to Secretary of State for the Colonies, March 30, 1961.

monetary regime, after all, was designed to facilitate the movement of people and commodities within – but not beyond – Britain's imperial geographies. That money might be managed differently was startling, thought officialdom, and likely a passing error of judgment that would be corrected when confronted with implacable economic realities. As a result, the best thing to do, the Governor thought, was to "alert the Bank of England quickly" so they might provide "expert advice" to Tanganyika on the matter, steering them toward British interests.

Independent Tanganyika did not insist upon an immediate change to the monetary regime. Rather, they continued to call for its reform in the context of wider East African decolonization. Nyerere and colleagues worried that scuppering the existing monetary ties would ruin their aspirations for an East African Federation, so they resolved to remain within the Currency Board until that eventuality came to pass.[65] This was not without costs, however. When Minister of Finance Paul Bomani rose to speak at the annual meeting of the IMF in September 1962, he told the assembled technocrats that "Tanganyika became of age last December when it achieved its independence." Yet, their initiation into the world of states was only partial, limited not only by resources and low standards of living. It was also curtailed by the "established rules of the game" that are not designed to suit citizens' "real needs." Despite being "an independent state, we have only a partial and minority say in the control of our currency." Such a "handicap" was a price they were willing to accept to maintain the common market – but only for so long.[66]

The year before, the Government of Tanganyika sponsored an inquiry by an official from the Deutsche Bundesbank, Erwin Blumenthal. Blumenthal was the most prominent of a new crop of expatriate economics advisors who arrived in East Africa after 1960. John Loynes worked diligently to maintain his hegemony on currency expertise, but political independence allowed Tanganyika and then Uganda to hire outside advisors and promote citizens to positions of authority.[67] These monetary experts could marshal evidence and argument against the EACB's preference for the status quo. They could also use their professional standing to challenge the status quo on behalf of

---

[65] See the discussion in TNA Acc.469 CIC 9/84/01 Part C EAHC / EACSO 1961.
[66] BoE OV7/82: Statement by Paul Bomani, September 19, 1962.
[67] In addition to trying to contain Blumenthal's inquiry to Tanganyika alone, he hoped to delay its findings – perhaps for six or nine months – to buy him time for his own plans. BoE OV76/3: Loynes to Maurice, November 9, 1962.

1.3 Halting Steps toward Monetary Nationalism 69

the African officials who hired them. For instance, Blumenthal insisted his work could only be done by investigating the entire region, despite Britain's insistence that his inquiry be contained to Tanganyika's currency and banking. As a result, Blumenthal visited Uganda and Kenya, consulting widely with officials, politicians, and businessmen. Across the region he found "readiness" among the leading personalities to move toward a more expansive monetary regime, departing from the Currency Board model.

His ultimate report – printed and circulated in March 1963, much to the Currency Board's dismay – was critical of the existing system. He faulted the EACB for its restricted investment policy and fiduciary issue, its inability to be a lender of last resort, not providing banking services to the governments, not administering exchange controls, and not properly regulating commercial banks (including their credit policies).[68] Going further, Blumenthal's report emphasized how the EACB facilitated a banking industry at odds with East African aspirations. These banks were known for their conservative approach.[69] Blumenthal went further, denouncing the cartel agreement between British banks (the secretive price fixing "Summary of Banking Arrangements") as artificially limiting competition and raising the cost of borrowing and transferring money.[70] Yet, despite all the problems with the current system, Blumenthal did not recommend Tanganyika create its own central bank and currency. Such a move would damage the common market, which Blumenthal agreed was important for generating more economic activity. Instead, he proposed a two-tier system, with one East African central bank and four subsidiary central banks (in each of the constituent territories). The regional entity would issue currency, determine monetary policy, and administer key international regulations (such as exchange control and the foreign reserves). The state banks would provide national payment services and banking to the government, as well as supervise commercial

---

[68] Erwin Blumenthal, *The Present Monetary System and Its Future: Report to the Government of Tanganyika* (Government Printer, 1963). See discussion in BoE OV76/3: Loynes to Roothman, December 21, 1962.

[69] Barclays, for instance, was more conservative in its lending in Africa than it was in the UK. Margaret Ackrill and Leslie Hannah, *Barclays: The Business of Banking 1690–1996* (Cambridge University Press, 2001), pp. 281–282.

[70] For the banks' defense against these charges, BoE OV76/3: The Summary of Banking Arrangements, East Africa & the Blumenthal Report, February 27, 1963.

banks. Such an idea clearly had its roots in West Germany, where the Bundesbank historically worked through subsidiaries in German states, yet Loynes thought it "naïve" and "preposterous," unsuited to what he called "African conditions."[71] At the very least, it was likely to be expensive; more likely, it would prove unable to control the inevitable divergences in national policymaking and expenditure.[72]

The actual merits of the proposal – as well as a similar one by an economics advisor to Uganda – were never known because it was shelved before being tested. Loynes carried out an extensive lobbying exercise with Blumenthal's supervisors in Frankfurt, the newly influential IMF, as well as British and African officials in London, Entebbe, and Nairobi.[73] The interference in 1963–1964 meant the currency question continued to hang in abeyance – an object of considerable importance whose time, it was said, had not come. "The main need is really to buy time," Loynes said while strategizing against the momentum of Blumenthal's report.[74] Instead, the Currency Board was still up to the job: "Our machine creaks a bit but does quite a lot and can do much more."[75]

The Currency of East African Federation

For their part, the ministers of finance for the four territories met in Zanzibar on July 5, 1963, to discuss the various reports and inquiries. Paul Bomani, James Gichuru, A. K. Sempa, and Juma Aley were mired in long technical discussions and competing ideas about what model would suit their citizens' preferences and national needs. A month before, Jomo Kenyatta, Julius Nyerere, and Milton Obote had joined their voices to call for the formation of an East African Federation before the end of the year. They created a working group to hash out a constitution and various federal policies. As a result, there seemed considerable promise that Tanganyika's patience with the Currency Board was justified, so the delegates commissioned additional studies

---

[71] BoE 76/3: Loynes to the Governors, February 12, 1963; BoE OV76/3: Loynes to Roothman, December 21, 1962.
[72] BoE OV76/3: Loynes to Roothman, December 21, 1962.
[73] The Bank of England's "reaction [to Blumenthal] was one of horror." BoE OV18/4: Haslam, *Central Banks*, p. 954.
[74] BoE OV76/3: Loynes to the Governors, March 21, 1963.
[75] BoE OV76/3: Loynes to A.L. Adu, April 8, 1963.

1.3 Halting Steps toward Monetary Nationalism

and resolved to continue their discussions in tandem with the Federation working parties.[76]

Both this suspended animation and Blumenthal's two-tier central bank proposal reflect the awkward liminality of decolonization.[77] Rather than an abrupt change, East Africans experienced decolonization as a drawn-out affair. As Blumenthal's inquiry proceeded in 1962, it still seemed that Kenya would go through a "lengthy period of 'internal self-government' before full independence is granted."[78] During that time, they would be unable to federate and progress on currency reform would likewise stall. Different pacing in the territories resulted in discordant temporalities: while Tanganyika was already creating a national economic development plan in early 1963, Kenya remained under British control. Nevertheless, the countries were sutured together by shared infrastructure, not least of which was the common currency. The two-tier proposal reflected the desire to maintain the benefits of economic coordination while navigating distinct political statuses. It also reflected the imperfectly nested scales of political solidarity and allegiance. It was not evident in 1961 what scale of political community would come to predominate in East Africa. The nation-state was, after all, a historical novelty, and in large parts of the region it was viewed with apathy; in places like Buganda, it was often greeted with outright hostility. Yet, people of the time did not identify merely with kingdoms or ethnic patria. Many understood themselves as members of a nation. Still others included "East African" as another scale of collective belonging. Sometimes this was an overarching category that subsumed national and ethnic appellation; in other cases, the multiple scales of identity existed in more tension.[79]

These different scales of identity were not presumed to be incompatible. Monikers that today may seem to hold together contradictory

---

[76] BoE OV76/3: Note of Meeting of Finance Ministers and Their Advisers at Zanzibar, July 5, 1963.
[77] Donovan, "*Uhuru Sasa!*"
[78] BoE OV76/3: Loynes to M.H. Parsons, November 4, 1962.
[79] For a recent interpretation, see Chris Vaughan, Julie MacArthur, Emma Hunter, and Gerard McCann, "Thinking East African: Debating Federation and Regionalism, 1960–1977," in Matteo Grilli and Frank Gerits (eds.), *Visions of African Unity: New Perspectives on the History of Pan-Africanism and African Unification Projects* (Springer International Publishing, 2020), pp. 49–75; for an earlier assessment, see Joseph S. Nye, *Pan-Africanism and East African Integration* (Harvard University Press, 1965).

positions, such as "pan-African nationalist," were commonsensical positions for political activists who understood themselves to be representatives of multiple identities. These multiscalar identities, however, needed institutional firmament to endure. Much has been written about the formation of identities in the 1950–1960s, whether those are national, ethnic, religious, gendered, or otherwise. Less has been written about the delicate dance of holding together or remaking institutions throughout this period of change. Yet, the decolonization of East Africa proceeded through these more technocratic exercises, as well, and this cumbersome coordination spurred a variety of ideas about how the region might become independent. The East African Federation and an East African central bank were two such ideas.[80]

Nyerere and colleagues were willing to remain in the existing currency union as long as the possibility of federation remained viable.[81] In a federation, an East African central bank could govern money in the interest of the entire region, including making up for inherited inequalities. Yet, as the feasibility of federation faded in 1964, Tanganyika was increasingly "restive" on the matter of currency. When they met in March 1964, Nyerere told Loynes that Tanganyika "must now control our credit and our economy," and he blamed Kenya and Uganda for obstructing Federation.[82] His rhetoric was part of an increasingly exclusive nationalist idiom. While Nyerere still spoke in favor of larger regional and pan-African groupings, holding the levers of statecraft and bearing formal responsibility to Tanganyika's new citizens encouraged higher priority for the interests of the nation. Insofar as those interests were perceived to be at odds with neighbors, it became harder to hold together the position of pan-African nationalist. Instead, those two labels fractured into competition with one another.

Tanganyikan officials had at least three reasons to fear the *laissez-faire* economic regime. First, the concentration of industry around Nairobi continued with frustrating endurance. More than two years into independent statehood, Tanganyika continued to struggle to

---

[80] Arusha Records Centre [ARC] 148/10: EACSO Economic Advisory Unit: Federal Problems, 1964.
[81] Paul Bjerk, "Postcolonial Realism: Tanganyika's Foreign Policy under Nyerere, 1960–1963," *International Journal of African Historical Studies* 44(2) (2011): 215–247.
[82] BoE OV7/85: East Africa, March 12, 1964.

1.3 Halting Steps toward Monetary Nationalism

attract factories and other investments away from the Mombasa–Kampala railway corridor.[83] Second, the long-standing tendency for surplus capital to be exported from Tanganyika reached worrying heights in the first half of 1964. European owners of sisal estates, white farmers in the southern highlands, and Asians were sending money to Nairobi and London. The common currency offered no means to limit this drain. Tanganyikan officials pressed hard for capital controls against, at a minimum, the rest of the sterling area, yet they received little assistance stemming the tide.[84] Finally, Tanganyika was trying to find the resources to implement its first five-year development plan. Every shilling converted to sterling was wealth they could not direct to their own purposes. A lack of effective monetary authority only contributed to their deficit of economic sovereignty.

TANU leadership, including Nsilo Swai and Paul Bomani, began floating the possibility of installing tariffs or quotas on trade with Kenya and Uganda. At a meeting in Kampala on March 17, 1964, Tanganyikan ministers forthrightly declared they were prepared to do so.[85] They knew the risks were high, but felt the costs of doing nothing were even greater. If their actions ended the common market, so be it – they were prepared to create their own national currency and central bank to foster and regulate a national economy.[86]

The next month, the political leadership of Kenya, Tanganyika, Uganda, and Zanzibar held a meeting in Nairobi to try to salvage the increasingly fractured regional sensibility.[87] The verbatim transcript of the private meeting reveals a remarkable record of Obote, Nyerere, Kenyatta, and their senior ministers debating the path toward federation in the face of uneven and combined development. Nyerere's concerns were preeminent, telling the audience that the common market was not

---

[83] In a large literature, see Arthur Hazlewood, *Economic Integration: The East African Experience* (St. Martin's Press, 1975).
[84] BoE OV76/3: Note for Record, April 22, 1964.
[85] BoE OV76/3: J.H. Butter to Loynes, March 18, 1964.
[86] These topics attracted considerable scholarly attention in the 1960–1970s, though the currency aspects were often neglected. Jesse H. Proctor, "The Effort to Federate East Africa: A Post-Mortem," *Political Quarterly* 37(1) (1966): 46–69; Colin Leys and Peter Robson, eds., *Federation in East Africa: Opportunities and Problems* (Oxford University Press, 1966); Ali A. Mazrui, "Tanzania versus East Africa: A Case of Unwitting Federal Sabotage," *Journal of Commonwealth Political Studies* 3(3) (1965): 209–225.
[87] AR/MISR/155/3: East African Common Market; AR/MISR/155/1: East African Federation.

serving everyone equally well.[88] He made his point in various idioms, drawing on Biblical quotes and trade statistics alike. "What is good for the whole should be good for the part, [but] this is not true in economics." Instead, it was possible for some areas to prosper while others deteriorated. While Federation was still important, he no longer thought that it could be done quickly, and the economic matters needed urgent attention. Tariffs, quotas, and a currency "controlled by the governments and not left to the East African Currency Board" were among his suggestions.[89]

When he took the floor, Uganda's prime minister went even further. While Obote condemned what he saw as Nyerere's changing tune on federation and trade policy, his government also worried about the flow of capital and jobs to Kenya.[90] It was difficult to calculate how much money flowed out of his country to Kenya and beyond, but it was certainly substantial. One estimate put it at £30 million between 1959 and 1963.[91] Moreover, Ugandans lost jobs as a result of the common market: all the best jobs and associated benefits (such as housing and entertainment) were concentrated in Kenya.[92] "What is it that the common man in Tanganyika, in Uganda, will gain if all the industries are going to be centered around the facilities available in Nairobi?" Very little, he explained, yet there seemed little the states could do to unmake the uneven geography of capital. Obote continued, asking the ministers to think about it from the perspective of those "masters of their money" – the investors, the capitalists, the industrialists. Before they get to Uganda, they travel through Mombasa, Nairobi, Naivasha, and Nakuru, he explained, tracing the

---

[88] This was not his view alone. It had been established since at least the Raisman Commission. *East Africa: Report of the Economic & Fiscal Commission* (Colonial Office, 1961).

[89] BoE OV76/3: Conference of East African Heads of Government, April 10, 1964.

[90] BoE OV76/4: The East African Common Market and All That, November 10, 1964.

[91] BoE OV7/79: D.G. Badger to East African Currency Board, November 13, 1964.

[92] For Adoko Nekyon, the trouble was compounded by the fact that what jobs existed in Uganda often went to Kenyans or Tanganyikans. "I do not know how much we are paying to Kenya labourers in Uganda or how much we are paying to Tanganyikan labourers in Uganda, but we cannot send them back to their home [in the current arrangement so] that must be balanced against the balance of trade." BoE OV76/3: Conference of East African Heads of Government, April 10, 1964.

1.3 Halting Steps toward Monetary Nationalism

route of the railway through Kenya. Of course they will put up their factories before they get to Uganda.

These complaints pointed to the uneven and combined development of East Africa.[93] East Africa's leaders recognized that the territories under their jurisdiction had divergent fortunes as a result of their interconnections, not least of which was the common market and currency.[94] In other words, it was in part because the East African shilling was formative of a shared commercial market that some areas (such as Nairobi or Jinja) were prosperous while others floundered (such as Bunyoro or southeastern Tanzania). This raised the question of how to govern value across such spaces without entrenching the inequalities born of capitalist integration. Moreover, for Obote, it was not only that inequality was a problem between countries; it was also a problem within countries. He cautioned, this is a problem that will "arise inside Kenya itself by a man in the village saying, 'What do I get out of all these industries I see in Kenya? What is my part in it?'" This was all the more true in Kenya, he intimated, because the economy of Kenya was actually beholden to a more narrow faction. It was not "Kariuki and Onyango," Obote said – invoking names common to the ethnicized ruling party in Kenya – but rather white minorities who ran the factories. When Tanganyika or Uganda purchases from Kenya, they are not buying "Kenyan goods." Rather, "some of the monies that we pay for these goods go to Verwoerd in South Africa. Some of them go to Winston Field in Southern Rhodesia." Government needed to act, he insisted, and it needed to do so in the interest of "the common man." Central planning, Obote suggested, was one of the few means to rectify the unequal effects of market activity.[95]

---

[93] By "uneven and combined development" I mean the simultaneous and interrelated production of development and underdevelopment, wealth and deprivation. For the purposes of East African historiography, the critical insight of this framework is to trouble the ethnic or national scales at which historians work, which have the effect of subdividing the coproduction of these locales and the linked processes by which economic and social transformations occurred in seemingly disparate areas. For a discussion, see the articles in *Cambridge Review of International Affairs* 22(1) (2009).

[94] D. P. Ghai, "Territorial Distribution of the Benefits and Costs of the East African Common Market," in Colin Leys and Peter Robson (eds.), *Federation in East Africa* (Oxford University Press, 1965).

[95] BoE OV76/3: Conference of East African Heads of Government, April 10, 1964.

In response, Kenyatta pleaded innocence: "what we have inherited, good or bad, is not our fault."[96] He claimed ignorance in economic matters and said he only wanted "to find a solution," to the troubles raised by his peers. Yet, the matter was complicated, and the men in the room found it difficult to isolate the issues and focus their response. The debate tumbled over multiple domains, from federation and common currency to industrial planning and inequality. "We are getting mixed up terribly," thought Uganda's Adoko Nekyon.[97] The irresolvable crux was not merely divergent interests but also discordant temporalities. The immediacy with which the East African Federation was once presented had devolved into a languid horizon of lesser possibility. Organizing federation would take time and political will that would only distract from and delay the pressing needs of regional economic coordination. Yet, without greater political control, some of the most promising economic transformations – a regional central bank among them – were themselves incapable of advancing. Instead, the meeting adjourned with instructions to the assembled ministers to return to their working groups to sort out the details of regional economics and federation. Such marching orders, however, were worryingly vague.[98]

The End of East African Money

What was lacking, in the meeting and more generally at this moment, was an authority who could issue decisions and determine the course of action. Sovereignty was suspended between multiple poles, and the erosion of a common colonial antagonist weakened the East African solidarities. In the absence of clear and efficacious authority, the initial response to the disputes of March and April 1964 took the form of a technocratic exercise. The Kampala Agreement, as the resulting deal was known, purposefully allocated major industries to different countries.[99] Uganda would receive bicycle factories, Tanzania would be home to vehicle tires and tubes, and Kenya would manufacture

---

[96] BoE OV76/3: Conference of East African Heads of Government, April 10, 1964.
[97] BoE OV76/3: Conference of East African Heads of Government, April 10, 1964.
[98] A point made by Tom Mboya and Oscar Kambona in BoE OV76/3: Conference of East African Heads of Government held in Nairobi, April 10, 1964.
[99] BoE OV7/87: Explanatory Notes on the Kampala Agreement, 1965.

1.3 Halting Steps toward Monetary Nationalism

electrical lamps. Ongoing trade would be governed by a quota system intended to minimize the existing imbalances. These trade regulations were most obviously a concession by Kenya to the persistent view that they had "the lion's share of investment and industrialisation."[100] The goal was to meet Tanzania's demands for a more equitable distribution of industry and employment, permitting the two smaller economies to "catch up" to Kenya and therefore save the common market and currency.[101] Yet, in effect it did much to further nationalist calculations: the logic of negotiating was routed through national balance of payments, thereby representing the nation-state as the container of economic production.[102] It proved limited in ambition, slow to realize, and ultimately ineffectual.[103]

For Kenya, such agreements may have been something of a bitter pill, but the state elite were willing to swallow them in order to maintain the common market and currency. The economic benefits to Kenya made the common market and currency a prize they would only reluctantly relinquish as Kenyatta's circle began reproducing the colonial economic structure in the independence era. Conservative Treasury officials remained influential in Nairobi after they had been replaced in Dar es Salaam and Entebbe. Loynes impressed upon them that Tanganyika's emerging plans to create a separate currency and central bank was "something that only makes sense if Tanganyika is determined to inflate, impose exchange controls, and generally run its currency into the ground for the sake of 'development'." He continued:

I should not be at all surprised if the planners in Tanganyika, who are not central bankers and who do not understand the money side of the develop-

---

[100] BoE OV76/3: East African Currency Board, memo by Loynes to The Governor of Bank of England, July 14, 1964.
[101] BoE OV7/85: Measures to Strengthen the East African Common Market by Robert Hall, March 5, 1964.
[102] For discussions of similar phenomena in Sudan, Egypt, and India, see Alden Young, *Transforming Sudan: Decolonization, Economic Development, and State Formation* (Cambridge University Press, 2018); Timothy Mitchell, *Rule of Experts: Egypt, Techno-Politics, Modernity* (University of California Press, 2002); Manu Goswami, *Producing India: From Colonial Economy to National Space* (University of Chicago Press, 2004).
[103] For economic assessments, see Hazlewood, *Economic Integration*; Philip Ndegwa, *The Common Market and Development in East Africa* (East African Publishing House, 1968).

ment problem, have assumed that such a move would give them greater resources. This is an illusion.[104]

Loynes also counseled the Minister of Finance, James Gichuru, that Kenya's position gave it a special "interest in preserving one good money for the whole of East Africa." He disparaged Tanganyika's plans as "printing their own bits of paper," an idea surely to lead to ruin.[105]

By August 1964, the prospects of an East African central bank were increasingly grim, despite the EACB's efforts to get a "tighter grip on monetary affairs."[106] The prior month, Paul Bomani told his British counterparts that "it was impossible for three sovereign governments to properly control monetary policy while the control of the currency remained with a single Currency Board."[107] They regretted any knock-on effects a national currency would have on regional federation, but could not countenance the current regime. At the Currency Board, John Loynes tried to maintain support for the status quo, working tirelessly against what he called "separatism."[108] From his perch in London and intermittent trips to East Africa, he tried to keep abreast of developments but was frustrated by how tightlipped Tanzanians were. This encouraged his suspicious stance toward Paul Bomani's travels and phone calls to De La Rue's currency printers (discussed above).

In addition to his private lobbying, Loynes wrote in newspapers and spoke publicly. When Tanzanian newspapers started carrying in 1964 negative coverage of the Currency Board, he sent lengthy rebuttals. A pseudonymous letter writer, *Maendeleo* (Kiswahili for "Development"), especially sparked Loynes's ire for suggesting technical failings of the Currency Board.[109] That same year, Loynes told the Dar es Salaam Chamber of Commerce how much trouble merchants would face from three separate currencies, possibly with varying rates of exchange. "Beyond Arusha, Tanganyikan money would have to be changed into Kenyan money, and beyond Kisumu, it would have to be changed again, with the bankers taking their profits each time." Such impediments would limit their business, removing the

---

[104] BoE OV76/3: Loynes to J.H. Butter, Kenya, March 24, 1964.
[105] BoE OV76/3: Loynes to Gichuru, March 24, 1964.
[106] BoE OV76/3: Loynes to Mladek, IMF, August 19, 1964.
[107] BoE OV76/3: Note for the Record by M.P.J. Lynch, July 28, 1964.
[108] BoE OV76/3: Memo for the Deputy Governor, July 29, 1964.
[109] BoE OV76/4: Loynes to Bolton, East African Standard, December 31, 1964.

1.3 Halting Steps toward Monetary Nationalism

"most important single financial factor in bringing about the rapid development of the whole area."[110] Merchants may have feared additional friction at the borders, but as the years passed, the development of East Africa as a whole had less and less of a constituency. While the British government continued to see its interest in the maintenance of a common market for its multinational firms, African politicians found it harder to see the projects of economic integration and national development as coterminous.[111] Instead, the long-recognized fault lines of combined and uneven development animated a newly assertive economic nationalism.

A visit by the IMF in February 1965 was intended to provide further technocratic guidance on how central banking might work in East Africa. Rather than inaugurating an East African central bank, though, it served as a silent vigil for the East African shilling.[112] Three days before the IMF officials arrived in Kampala, the Uganda Minister of Finance publicly announced their plans for two new institutions, the Uganda State Bank and the Bank of Uganda. The first would serve as a government-owned commercial bank to boost savings and loans. The second, their press release said, would "perform such central banking functions as will be reserved to it under the East African Reserve Bank Constitution."[113] The Bank of Uganda was not, they insisted, intended to detract from East African monetary cooperation, but would rather form a part of what seemed to be a two-tier central banking institution. No agreement had been made along those lines, and no East African Reserve Bank Constitution existed. These were certain to be topics of discussion with the IMF, but the two preemptive working papers from Uganda were mostly greeted by confusion or hesitation.

Whether Uganda's proposal was an evolution of East African monetary governance, a departure from it, or its death knell – as various observers thought – mattered little by the time the IMF reached Dar es Salaam a few days later.[114] There, in a secret speech to the visitors and

---

[110] BoE OV7/85: Address to the Dar es Salaam Chamber of Commerce by Loynes, n.d. [but mid-1964].
[111] BoE OV7/87: Draft Note for Meeting with Gichuru, 1965.
[112] IMF ref: 75873 East Africa Currency Board: East Africa Currency and Economic Union, June 1965.
[113] BoE OV76/4: Uganda to Have Two New Banks, press release from Minister of Finance, February 1, 1965.
[114] For the confusion caused by Uganda's announcement, see "State Banking Systems," *East African Standard*, February 4, 1965.

neighboring dignitaries, Minister of State and Acting Finance Minister Swai announced Tanzania's intention to go its own way. As you will appreciate, he said, "it is customary for a sovereign government to control its monetary and banking system and to regulate the general level of activity in the economy through its own central bank."[115] While they had been willing to work in a regional fashion, that now seemed untenable due to the divergences in economic structures, trade relationships, overseas borrowing, and development objectives of the three states. The path forward, he said, would be to coordinate through independent central banks rather than pining for an eventuality that always receded beyond the horizon.[116]

As monetary nationalism gained the upper hand over East African integration, the Currency Board moved to protect what Loynes called the "key territory" financially – Kenya.[117] His effort to maintain an East African monetary union reflected, in part, his belief that a regional currency was nowhere more important than in Kenya.[118] Indeed, as Tanzania moved unilaterally, Loynes made a last-ditch effort to persuade Uganda to remain in a common currency – a project aimed at maintaining the economic benefits to Kenya.[119] His preference for Kenya was not, however, a preference for all Kenyans. His work to "safeguard Kenya's interests," he wrote to a Bank of England colleague, was "worth doing, above all for the sake of helping the whites."[120]

Decolonization was a considerable threat to the relationships between property, inequality, and race in Kenya.[121] A vocal and

---

[115] BoE OV76/4: Statement by A.Z.N. Swai, Minister of State, February 12, 1965. See also IMF ref: 75873 East Africa Currency Board: Memorandum by Tanzania, February 1965.
[116] For the IMF's role establishing the Bank of Tanzania, see IMF ref: 76110 Tanzania Central Banking Legislation, 1965–1969. For their critique of Uganda's initial legislation, see IMF ref: 76137 Central Bank of Uganda, 1965–1969.
[117] BoE OV7/87: Loynes to L.B. Walsh-Atkins, Commonwealth Relations Office, March 22, 1965.
[118] BoE OV7/85: Loynes to Minister Joseph Murumbi, March 13, 1964.
[119] BoE OV7/87: Loynes to H. Kessels, Deutsche Bundesbank, June 19, 1965.
[120] BoE OV78/4: Loynes to Jasper Rootham, September 28, 1964.
[121] See the context in Paul Mosley, *The Settler Economies: Studies in the Economic History of Kenya and Southern Rhodesia, 1900–1963* (Cambridge University Press, 1983); Colin Leys, *Underdevelopment in Kenya: The Political Economy of Neo-Colonialism, 1964–1971* (University of California Press, 1975).

1.3 Halting Steps toward Monetary Nationalism

organized movement of landless and marginalized Kenyans made radical calls for redistribution.[122] Yet, the potential for more significant economic transformation was interrupted by the Kenyatta state and his British partners.[123] By mid-1964, Kenyatta and his allies were neutralizing their opposition, including more radical economic visions that would call into question the distribution of property and the ownership of capital.[124] The sanctity of property was protected, the assets of white settlers were secured or purchased at taxpayer expense, and a narrow network of largely loyalist Kikuyu assumed preeminent roles in the economy.[125]

Historians have emphasized how the threat to this economic dispensation was overcome through state violence, Kenyatta's charismatic influence, and British aid. Less appreciated is the role of the EACB, but during this time it had an important role in securing and reproducing racial capitalism in Kenya. Ready currency convertibility into sterling facilitated the significant export of capital from Kenya while the maintenance of the shilling's value protected the worth of those assets.[126] Capital flight sparked the condemnation of some like the Kenya Freedom Party and Oginga Odinga, but such voices did not prove decisive.[127] Laissez-faire continued to rule. As early as 1963, Loynes expressed surprise that the territory previously racked by the Mau

---

[122] Daniel Branch, *Kenya: Between Hope and Despair, 1963–2011* (Yale University Press, 2011).

[123] One of the key figures was John Butter, a British official in the Kenyan Treasury (and Loynes interlocutor) who remained until 1969 in order to, as the Acting Governor put it in 1961, keep the African Minister of Finance "on the right lines." Quoted in Poppy Cullen, *Kenya and Britain after Independence: Beyond Neo-Colonialism* (Palgrave Macmillan, 2017), p. 128.

[124] Daniel Branch, *Defeating Mau Mau, Creating Kenya: Counterinsurgency, Civil War, and Decolonization* (Cambridge University Press, 2009), especially pp. 174–177; Anais Angelo, *Power and the Presidency in Kenya: The Jomo Kenyatta Years* (Cambridge University Press, 2020); Tignor, *Capitalism and Nationalism*, pp. 358–385.

[125] Tignor, *Capitalism and Nationalism*, p. 379 notes that British officials "embraced a [land purchasing and resettlement] scheme being touted by the right-wing settler community."

[126] On capital flight from Kenya, see Vanessa Ogle, "'Funk Money': The End of Empires, The Expansion of Tax Havens, and Decolonization as an Economic and Financial Event," *Past & Present* 249(1) (2020): 213–249.

[127] On the KFP, see Donald Rothchild, *Racial Bargaining in Independent Kenya: A Study of Minorities and Decolonization* (Oxford University Press, 1973), p. 151fl18.

Mau counterinsurgency had come to distinguish itself as "the most reasonable and moderate" of the region. In contrast, he thought "African socialism" in Tanganyika and Uganda was a "disturbing trend [of] state interference with existing business and investment."[128] What Loynes saw as reason and moderation in East Africa's largest economy was, in fact, the capture and redirection of African political energies by Britain and its loyalist elite. He lamented where African involvement advanced, telling the Colonial Office that the Africanization of East Africa's bureaucracies by men with "few qualifications and still less experience" meant that "formerly useful and competent bodies ... now have an air of disintegration."[129] "These are sad days" for the settlers, Loynes thought, and "the process of dismantling the European economy of the country will cost a lot more yet."[130]

1.4 The Start of National Central Banks

Remarkably, Minister Swai's announcement in February 1965 about Tanzania's plan to leave the Currency Board remained little known outside the small network of technocratic ministers and financial officials. The Currency Board kept expecting the information to leak, sparking a financial panic, but even rumors of the shift remained at a low level. In reality, there was little cause for panic among the region's propertied class. Those who wanted to escape with their capital had been able to do so without much difficulty for more than half a decade. Most of them would have been in Kenya, and by 1965 they had less cause for concern about their wealth: the Kenyatta government had by then distinguished itself ably from Mau Mau era fears among wealthy minorities.

The relative quiet allowed the governments and the EACB to plan the next steps, including urgently training African staff and drafting the legal statutes. The Bank of England seconded two men to Nairobi to prepare to impose foreign exchange controls between East Africa and

---

[128] BoE OV7/84 Loynes to Parsons, September 6, 1963.

[129] "This is not surprising among people whose past history is tribal and who now, if they look ahead at all, are concerned with opportunities to grab land or to get jobs from which Europeans and Asians are now barred." BoE OV7/84: Loynes to the Governors and Parsons, September 6, 1963.

[130] BoE OV7/83: East Africa by Loynes, May 24, 1963. On the structure of European economic dominance, see Rothchild, *Racial Bargaining in Independent Kenya*, pp. 80–94.

1.4 The Start of National Central Banks

the rest of the world. This was highly secretive work, given Loynes's belief that others shared his distrust of African monetary authority and would panic if word got out. Fearful it would leak, he obliquely referred to "you know what" – rather than sending telegrams mentioning "exchange controls" – and he instructed the Bank of England clerks to keep a low profile and only identify themselves as "balance of payment" experts. Tanzanians in particular had long demanded exchange controls to limit capital flight, but the Bank of England was eager to assist in their formulation so they might be managed liberally, lest the "confidence of your public as well as investors overseas" be diminished.[131] In other words, this was not a muscular constraint on capital mobility.

The quiet was eventually broken in June 1965, when the three governments announced the creation of the central banks and national currencies. In place of a single East African shilling there would be three national shillings. The end of the common currency was not intended to end economic cooperation and trade.[132] The new central banks voiced their commitment to equivalent exchange between the three national currencies. Yet, the most immediate response was a hardening of nationalisms in a flurry of recriminations across the region's airwaves and newspapers. Given the prevailing view that regionalism was a virtue – on pan-African, economic, and other grounds – no side wanted to take the blame for undermining such a high-profile example of integration. Kenya's Minister of Finance James Gichuru placed the blame on his southern neighbor. His Tanzanian counterpart, Amir Jamal, forcefully rebutted the claims, saying it was Kenyan and Ugandan refusal to federate that thwarted the plans for an East African central bank. "How long," he wrote in defense of his government, "is a country expected to remain in 'no man's land', helping to maintain a *status quo* which is increasingly coming into conflict with its own development planning?" Moreover, Kenya had been unduly benefitting from a status quo it refused to improve: "It is Tanzanian and Ugandan money, as much as Kenya's, which is circulating in Kenya through the wages and salaries paid" to employees of East African Common Services (which were inordinately concentrated around Nairobi and Mombasa).[133]

---

[131] BoE OV7/87: Loynes to Swai, March 30, 1965.
[132] BoE OV7/87: Preserving Economic Unity, *East African Standard*, June 25, 1965.
[133] BoE OV7/87: Letter from Amir Jamal to *East African Standard*, June 21, 1965.

Others in Tanzania shed no tears for the death of the EACB. A member of parliament, Mr. Mbogo, lamented that "Our country has been turned by Kenya into a mere market for their manufactured goods." Pointing to the concentration of "all important industrial and commercial establishments" in Nairobi, he said his countrymen were tired of being the "underdog," subject to "exploitation."[134] The new institution would be a means to undo that.[135] Tanzanian citizens wrote into *The Nationalist* to celebrate the move as "one of the most bold, courageous, and important decisions ever taken." It would allow the country to create its own policy and, hopefully, move away from ongoing dependence on sterling.[136] Another told the *East African Standard* that it was shameful that an independent country still used the currency with the head of another country's ruler.[137] Even Kenyans expressed that they were "tired of using foreign currency" and welcomed their own money.[138]

These were important moments of statecraft, allowing national leaders to perform their own centrality to the government of value as well as advertise the newfound powers of sovereign statehood. In a recent assessment, Robert Blunt makes a suggestive argument that focuses on Kenyatta's speech opening the Central Bank as a "spectacular baptismal moment" that "attempted to performatively resolve" the problem of sovereign authority through a speech act that placed the president at the center of monetary and moral value. In this interpretation, Kenyatta emblazons his image on the currency in order to secure a gerontocratic power – especially his own elderhood – at risk of debasement by insolent, undisciplined youth. For Blunt, this is a novel response to a particularly Kikuyu problematic of power and value – one through which "Kenyatta implicitly claimed to have power over the creation of money."[139] Yet, if this was true for Kenyatta, it does

---

[134] BoE OV7/87: Untitled Clipping from *The Standard (Tanzania)*, June 16, 1965.
[135] Bjerk, "A Preliminary History."
[136] R.C. Mzeru Letter to the Editor, *The Nationalist*, June 22, 1965.
[137] BoE OV7/87: E. African Money Troubles, *East African Standard*, n.d. [but June 1965]. At the time, the old notes with Queen Elizabeth's image were being swapped for different iconography. Wambui Mwangi, "The Lion, the Native and the Coffee Plant: Political Imagery and the Ambiguous Art of Currency Design in Colonial Kenya," *Geopolitics* 7(1) (2002): 31–62.
[138] BoE OV76/4: New Kenya Money Pledge, *The Standard*, March 3, 1966.
[139] Robert Blunt, *For Money and Elders: Ritual, Sovereignty, and the Sacred in Kenya* (University of Chicago Press, 2019), 91–117. In an earlier version of the argument, Blunt writes that Kenyatta presented the money as "ultimately

1.4 The Start of National Central Banks

little to explain why similar assertions were made in very different ethnic and national dispensations. In Kampala and Dar es Salaam, it was likewise the presidents who used the nationalization of money as an opportunity to burnish their own image and secure the value of new currency.

More important than inaugural speeches were the regulatory regimes and productive imperatives implied by the central banks and national currencies. Emphasizing the spectacular "promissory acts" of *Mzee* Kenyatta rather than the more humdrum protocols of monetary controls distracts from the particular potency of state assertions of economic sovereignty, including its depoliticization within technocratic institutions. It also downplays the importance of accumulating and maintaining a sufficient reserve of foreign currencies, particularly through the obligation to labor on the land. The politically independent states were subordinated to international capital, and the shift to central banks was self-consciously depicted to placate fleet-footed finance.[140] While the currency board model meant there could be no collapse in the value of shilling relative to sterling, central banking brought with it the risk that the domestic currency would prove unable to maintain its worth. Yet as officials in each country were keen to emphasize to domestic and international audiences, there should be no cause for diminished confidence in the new currencies because they were backed by sufficient foreign reserves.[141] This is the paradoxical status of national monetary value – founded on the accumulation and maintenance of foreign money, not on promissory statements. Just as importantly, this was not personalized power but rather an institutionalized guarantee, embodied not least in the sturdy, imposing central

---

backed by the guarantee" of "the father of the nation." "Old Age and Money: The General Numismatics of Kenya," *Suomen Antropologi* 41(1) (2016): 43.

[140] For the constraints on central banks, see Catherine Schenk, "Monetary Institutions in Newly Independent Countries: The Experience of Malaya, Ghana and Nigeria in the 1950s," *Financial History Review* 4(2) (1997): 181–198. For the intended scope of monetary policy in East African central banks, see Walter Tessier Newlyn, "Comparative Analysis of Central Bank Acts," East African Institute of Social Research, EDRP 101, 1966.

[141] Rather than one-to-one backing, the legal requirements for reserves were expressed as a proportion of the cost of imports (in Kenya and Tanzania) or demand liabilities (in Uganda). For Kenya and Tanzania, this worked out to a reserve requirement of four months of imports and in Uganda the equivalent of two months of imports. See Newlyn, "Comparative Analysis," pp. 15–16.

banks opened in prominent downtown locations of Nairobi, Dar es Salaam, and Kampala.[142]

If these new institutions marked critical junctures for the moneychanger state, it was not in the bureaucrats alone that citizens must place their trust; rather, the value of the currency was to be a burden citizens would carry. As subsequent chapters discuss at length, in each of the countries the establishment of national currencies entailed some combination of promising mutual advance and exhorting productivity. In Nyerere's words, the Bank of Tanzania started on a firm foundation of proportionally more "foreign assets" than "many countries whose currency is acceptable throughout the world." But, he continued:

Our people know that it is their responsibility to increase the wealth of our country, and that this can only be done by producing more goods. We shall not make a mistake of imagining that our problems can be solved by a printing press; we know that real wealth is goods, not money. And the Bank, the Government, and the people will work together on this basis.

In these public remarks, Nyerere addressed those who may worry about a departure from monetary prudence (see Figure 1.2). The talisman of "printing" money was explicitly invoked and the temptation denied. This was an international audience, to be sure, but it was crucially one composed of citizens – "the people" that he claimed as partners in this work of governing value. The people of Tanzania were told to dedicate themselves to this work, for in Paul Bomani's words, "It was through self-sacrifice that the country would achieve self-reliance."[143] The prevailing slogans were "*Uhuru na kazi. Uhuru na kilimo.*"[144] Likewise, Amir Jamal told newspaper readers across the

---

[142] These bureaucracies, of course, were staffed by bureaucrats, thus running the risk of personalizing the institutions through the ethnic partisanship of their staff. This was a risk noted at the time. The first Governor of the Bank of Uganda was a Muganda, a status that sometimes raised concerns he was at odds with Obote's government, but also demonstrated a degree of independence from Obote's northern allies. BoE OV7/89: Untitled Memo, April 4, 1966. In Kenya, parliamentarians alert to Kikuyu and Luo dominance called for the Central Bank of Kenya's (CBK) board to be constituted of members from all ethnicities. BoE OV76/4: Central Bank Will Not Harm New Currency, *East African Standard*, March 2, 1966. The Bank of Tanzania's directors included a union leader, an academic, a large Asian plantation operator, and a representative of the cooperative movement.

[143] BoE OV7/87: Untitled Clipping from *The Standard (Tanzania)*, June 16, 1965.

[144] Kiswahili for "Freedom through work. Freedom through farming." TNA Acc.593 CB/1/2: Safaris, Public Engagements and Affairs of R. Kawawa, 1962–63.

1.4 The Start of National Central Banks

Figure 1.2 Julius Nyerere pictured at the opening ceremony for the Bank of Tanzania.
Source: Tanzania Information Services.

region that the strength of the currency will "be based on hard work and increasing rates of production of exportable goods and commodities."[145] This call for economic citizenship was a call for productivity, but also a submission to the nation-state. Bring out your old money, Nyerere told Tanzanians, because in swapping it for the new notes and coins, we will receive the sterling assets "essential" to the Bank of Tanzania's operations. And once you receive your new Tanzanian Shillings, do not "re-bury" it, for it is "much better to open a savings account, either in a bank or in the Post Office." Doing so will not only earn you interest and reduce the risk of theft or fire. "However small the amount" you can deposit will have "enormous benefits" by allowing the banking system to lend "to those who need it."[146] Economic citizenship, in other words, required discipline at the Bank of Tanzania but also among citizens whose wealth was not theirs alone, but rather a collective resource for the nation.

Similar statements accompanied the opening of the Bank of Uganda and the Central Bank of Kenya. Ugandan Minister of Finance

---

[145] BoE OV7/87: Tanzania's Case in Break-up of Currency Union, from Amir Jamal, *East African Standard*, June 17, 1965.
[146] BoE OV7/89: Speech by Julius Nyerere, June 14, 1966.

Lawrence Kalule-Settala introduced the Bank of Uganda Bill in May 1966 to Parliament, promising a stable currency with "sufficient capital reserves to enable policies in the public interest to be pursued."[147] Government had "no intention of indulging in unlimited borrowing from the Bank" and the laws under consideration would preclude such wantonness. Such "evils" as inflation and the loss of currency value would be avoided by the collective pursuit of a "rapid and sustained rate of growth of Uganda's economy."[148] A few months later, when Milton Obote spoke at the opening of the Bank of Uganda building – a massive, expensive monument to its own futurity – he said it marked the start of Uganda's "monetary independence." He assured listeners it would not be a "charity institution" but rather follow sound policies.[149] Jomo Kenyatta founded the CBK emphasizing that it was "ultimately the productive work done by the people" on which the economy and money depended.[150] His words alone could not attract foreign money, so the management of the new CBK spent the first year anxiously searching for sufficient foreign reserves to protect the Kenyan shilling. Only by drawing on the resources of the Post Office Savings Bank – itself capitalized by small citizen savers – could they protect the value of the national money.[151]

The speeches articulated such similar visions because the countries faced such similar imperatives: their national currencies required substantial backing by foreign currencies in order to maintain their purchasing power. These states were not divorcing from international capitalist circuits so much as reworking the terms of their subordinate incorporation. To do so, they established regimes that would consolidate value within their territory and mediate its exchange beyond their borders. While they would no longer require one-to-one backing for domestic currency, the independent central banks did commit to earning and controlling a substantial holding of foreign reserves (lest they lose the confidence of investors). So, while the institutions did

[147] BoE OV75/3: Speech by the Minister of Finance at the Introduction of the Second Reading of the Bank of Uganda Bill, May 16, 1966.
[148] BoE OV75/3: J.B. Houldsworth to J. Brasnett, May 20, 1966.
[149] BoE OV75/14: "Bank of Uganda" Memo, August 25, 1966.
[150] Jomo Kenyatta speech, September 14, 1966, in *Report for the Year Ended 30th June 1966* (East African Currency Board, 1966), p. 118.
[151] Mahesh Gheewala, "The Early Days of the Central Bank of Kenya," in Patrick Njoroge and Victor Murinde (eds.), *50 years of Central Banking in Kenya* (Oxford University Press, 2021), pp. 225–228.

1.4 The Start of National Central Banks

mark a change from the colonial regime, and while the old Bank of England advisors had some disagreements with the new IMF ones, this hardly marked a complete rupture. Foreign reserves would be under the stewardship of a central bank, but they could still only be earned by the laborious initiative of citizens producing commodities for export.

To maintain the worth of their national currency would require ongoing work in the retail shop, the factory floor, and, above all, the soil. Jomo Kenyatta told Kenyans that "in land lies our salvation and survival," yet popular compliance was hardly guaranteed.[152] Duncan Ndegwa, who ran the Central Bank of Kenya for its first decade and a half, recalls the numerous times he needed to remind citizens that monetary wealth came not from the vaults of his institution or its printing press. Instead, it required enterprising production of export value. Jomo Kenyatta concurred, always supporting a balanced budget and promising to fire Permanent Secretaries who overspent. Rather than pulling the levers of money creation, Kenyatta's rule worked often enough by withholding public finances. As Ndegwa relates, Kenyatta understood that "money was a representation of things. After money was land. And after money were the cows he loved." In other words, money was to be created and managed with an eye toward the proper, enduring sources of value: land and cattle. As a guard against "monetary indiscipline," Ndegwa pursued a conservative stance to "safeguard the value of money" and urge citizens toward productive labor.[153]

As I discuss more extensively in the chapters that follow, this government of value would require the ongoing policing and regulation of money, its movement, and its conversion. The end of the Currency Board and the start of national currencies and central banks reflected a more overt reliance on enterprising citizens. How, exactly, they were hailed and compelled would differ in the coming years and in the different countries. For instance, in Kenya a large population of landless would be neglected as surplus to the needs of economic accumulation, while in Tanzania a more uniform idea of productive contribution was demanded of all. Yet, in each of the countries there was a material imperative – not merely a symbolic opportunity – to guarantee wealth through labor productive of export earnings. And in each country

---

[152] Quoted in Muey Saeteurn, *Cultivating Their Own: Agriculture in Western Kenya during the "Development" Era* (University of Rochester Press, 2020), p. 1.

[153] Duncan Ndegwa, *Walking in Kenyatta Struggles* (Kenya Leadership Institute, 2006), chapter 35.

there was also the difficult reality that national monetary value was only as good as the reserve of foreign monetary wealth. Such a reality formed a significant impediment to the pursuit of effective sovereignty and complicated all aspirations to national administration and development by subjecting the postcolonial states to the volatility of international capitalist trade. And this, in turn, obliged the sorts of coercive controls elaborated by the moneychanger state.

1.5 Conclusion: The Infrastructure of Postcolonial Statecraft

To be sure, East Africa's monetary technicians operated within significant constraints, not least of which was the persistence of globally hegemonic money over which they had little control. Yet, national currency was an important infrastructure of postcolonial statecraft. It set the stage for more substantial departures from the model sustained by the EACB. For one, it permitted the installation of foreign exchange controls – first against international sterling operations in 1965 and, beginning a few years later, between the three East African states.[154] It also permitted a greater degree of monetary policy autonomy as the states took differing approaches to issuing sovereign debt, prevailing interest rates, and banking regulations. The inauguration of central banks and national currencies also provided a new repertoire for consolidating wealth within territorial borders. The expatriate banks like Barclays and Standard had previously operated across the region, with management decisions taken in Nairobi or London for all of East Africa. If funds were kept in the region, they were in Nairobi, only transmitted to Ugandan or Tanzanian branches as needed. The end of the regional money meant Ugandan or Tanzanian deposits held abroad were more likely to be kept in their original territory.[155] Insurance firms, too, could be pressured to invest their large holdings within national assets, rather than moving them abroad.[156] This was not an automatic result of the new regime; it required careful and

---

[154] John Loxley, "Financial Planning and Control in Tanzania," in John Loxley et al. (eds.) *Towards Socialist Planning* (Tanzania Publishing House, 1972), pp. 54–55.
[155] BoE OV75/3: Lewis to Loynes, January 20, 1966.
[156] BoE OV75/3: Note for the Record, East African Currency Board, July 14, 1966.

1.5 Conclusion

difficult economic engineering in the years to come, but it was at least now a possibility afforded to the independent states.

The imposition of a national money was always partial. For one, the value of the national currency rested on the accumulation of a sufficiently large reserve of foreign currency, as discussed above. This placed them at some risk of monetary developments abroad. For another, residents frequently used other forms of money, sometimes hedging their bets, sometimes reflecting a more expansive transactional geography. Wealthier, more extraverted residents with commercial ties abroad – notably Asians, but also settlers, politicians, and others – translated their national currency into gold, sterling, dollars, and other financial instruments not authorized by East Africa's states. Borderlands were especially pluralistic monetary zones, with citizens often keeping value in and accepting money from both sides of the border. Finally, money existed in relation to other forms of value, and East Africans have commonly preferred to move their wealth out of state money to the extent possible. Cash earnings were often translated into more culturally salient and politically insulated goods, such as land or cattle. And once embodied as such, they were loath to convert the value back into currency, despite various efforts to commodify cattle and land.

Partial as it may be, national currency was desirable to East African states for its infrastructural power.[157] As an instrument of state power, national currencies worked through the consolidation of wealth within an infrastructure over which the states exerted considerable power. In contrast to the East African shilling – merely a token for sterling, eluding government directives – a national currency gave states a means to influence market activity, raise revenue, and meet many of their own costs. The subsequent chapters discuss some of the ways that tenuous project animated political, economic, and social life in the region.

---

[157] Michael Mann, "The Autonomous Power of the State: Its Origins, Mechanisms and Results," *European Journal of Sociology* 25(2) (1984): 185–213.

2 A Monopoly on Valuation
Economic Sovereignty and Citizenship in Uganda

2.1 Introduction

In late August of 1975, Zerubaberi Were of Mbale wrote to the Uganda Advisory Board of Trade, with copies sent to four other senior provincial and national administrators. "I am a progressive farmer," he opened his petition, "who earns a living by sweating on the land." He was writing to "apply to be allocated foreign exchange for the purchase of a Massey Ferguson 165 Tractor together with a 3-Furrow Disc Plough." In justifying his request, Were detailed his qualifications, both technical and patriotic. He desired to move his 150 acres of arable land from subsistence to commercial agriculture, "an immediate and timely response to His Excellency Alhaji Field Marshal Idi Amin's incentives about double production of the land." He was well positioned to heed this call, noting his training from the Department of Agriculture and financial capability verifiable with his bankers, the Uganda Commercial Bank. "Sir, it is now a common song that the Back-Bone [sic] of Uganda is Agriculture," and it was only appropriate to mechanize farming by exchanging savings in Ugandan currency for their foreign equivalent.[1] For Were and others, personal ambition merged with economic nationalism through productive compliance with the state's exhortations.[2] Yet even as qualified an individual as Were – capable in farming, bureaucratic procedure, and patriotic self-fashioning – could not count on receiving the necessary foreign currency.

Postcolonial states managed a complicated system for controlling and allocating resources, carefully converting between different sorts

---

[1] Bank of Uganda (BoU) 2121, GOV.104.16: Letter from Mr. Zerubaberi Were of Mbale to Chairman of Uganda Advisory Board of Trade, August 26, 1975.
[2] On exhortations, Derek Peterson and Edgar Taylor, "Rethinking the State in Idi Amin's Uganda: The Politics of Exhortation," *Journal of Eastern African Studies* 7(1) (2013): 58–82.

2.1 Introduction

of resources and money in order to govern value. Asserting a monopoly on the allocation of foreign currency and calibrating the exchange between export crops and imported currencies was at the heart of postcolonial statecraft. More than merely commercial, this was a political project that subordinated residents to the monetary protocols of the state and its economic territory. Without the approval of the Bank of Uganda's monetary authority, Ugandans like Were lacked access to the sort of money required to purchase imported goods. Even when they had Ugandan shillings, they needed foreign currencies to buy tractors, ploughs, and the other inputs. As a result, the relationship between states and citizens was routed through currency movement and controls. Citizens like Were needed to properly position themselves within the resulting hierarchy through a combination of solicitous entreaty and the promises of fruitful harvest.

This chapter analyzes the making of economic sovereignty and citizenship in Uganda. In the decades before independence, the Uganda Protectorate was convulsed by strikes, boycotts, and protests that foregrounded the deprivation of economic opportunity and the racialized inequality of market activity. Colonial subjects advocated for a greater share of commerce, the ability to market their crops cooperatively, and access to credit.[3] The politicization of economic activity in the late colonial era marked a watershed in which the production, processing, and pricing of crops became key areas of debate about proper authority and inequality. As a result, few thought of citizenship as merely political. Instead, Africans recognized that a reorganization of economic rules, infrastructures, and practices was necessary to fully realize the possibilities of decolonization – not least of which was the advance of African commercial activities. As Protectorate subjects transitioned – haltingly, imperfectly – into Ugandan citizens, their rights and responsibilities as producers were at the forefront of their concerns. In turn, this put monetary matters at the core of statecraft, as national authority over money was deemed a necessary correlate to political independence and a prerequisite to economic development. To this end, the postcolonial state undertook a variety of new initiatives, from establishing a central bank and

---

[3] B. D. Bowles, "Economic Anti-Colonialism and British Reaction in Uganda, 1936–1955," *Canadian Journal of African Studies* 9(1) (1975): 51–60.

national currency to deploying banking infrastructure and multiplying loans to the public.[4]

Ugandans cast themselves as credible citizens – people who were worthy of resources and status due to their role as productive contributors to national progress. Most significantly, credible citizens emphasized their role in earning export value. In doing so, they responded to the state's own imperative to acquire the economic resources on which its finances and aspirations rested. The claims of credible citizenship were, in part, a call for the unmaking of certain hierarchies, not least of which was the racial ordering of colonial capitalism. Yet it also furthered inequalities among Ugandan citizens, for not everyone could position themselves as credible producers.[5] In some cases, this solidified existing hierarchies; in others, new distinctions emerged. In this chapter, I suggest that money and banking were important means for new hierarchies and their ethics to be worked out. As discussed earlier, an important basis was the hierarchy between foreign money and domestic currency: while the state maintained monopoly control on the former, it distributed the latter among citizens. Maintaining or subverting authority over distinct monies – with their differing durability, acceptability, and geography – was at the core of the struggles discussed in this chapter. Such a hierarchical relationship obliged citizens like Were to cast themselves as "progressive farmers," dutifully contributing to the call of productive labor. Their relationship to imports and foreign currency was not one of rights-bearing individuals, but rather of loyal contributors to a greater whole. If this was often understood to be in one's own interest, it simultaneously required individual aspirations to be joined to the demands of the nation-state.

---

[4] See also Justin Willis, "Thrift, Citizenship, and Self-Improvement: Savings and Borrowings in Uganda from c.1940 to 1970" (unpublished MS).

[5] Hierarchical relations of regard and distribution are a major theme of Ugandan historiography, especially on Buganda. For Carol Summers, such social and material inequalities were formative of vernacular practices of citizenship, in contrast to more horizontal, fraternal notions of nationalism. Ganda belonging was premised on "a vertical, networked, constantly growing hierarchy of reciprocal patronage and protection," she writes in "Local Critiques of Global Development: Patriotism in Late Colonial Buganda," *International Journal of African Historical Studies* 47(1) (2014): 29. Elsewhere, she emphasizes that not all hierarchies are the same: "Grandfathers, Grandsons, Morality, and Radical Politics in Late Colonial Buganda," *International Journal of African Historical Studies* 38(3) (2005): 428. For an earlier era, see Holly Hanson, *Landed Obligation: The Practice of Power in Buganda* (Heinemann, 2003).

2.1 Introduction

The relationship between creditor and debtor was another important formation of economic citizenship. During the 1950s, banking became an interface between Ugandans and the government. I show here how the colonial Uganda Credit & Savings Bank (UCSB) became a model for a wider array of initiatives in the postcolonial era. Colonial officials understood the UCSB as a novel response to African demands for commercial expansion; in an era of buoyant export prices, it also promised to expand state revenue from coffee and cotton.[6] Yet, its design was biased toward wealthy farmers, especially those in the already privileged Buganda. Ugandans without land titles, migrant workers who tilled the fields, and others in penury could not access these new resources. In this way, the UCSB was a harbinger for postcolonial monetary initiatives that may have promised wider access but often shored up or produced new inequalities of wealth and power.[7]

For the independent state, money and finance were valuable instruments of statecraft, used to pursue a monopoly on valuation. A new generation of technocrats and politicians marketed sovereign bonds, savings accounts, and other financial tools as a means of merging individual and collective interests. Opening a bank account, for instance, was a means of contributing to the national good (because your money could be aggregated and lent to someone else's productive enterprise), as well as a method to protect and grow your own wealth. Domestic financial instruments were attractive because foreign loans were expensive and denominated in foreign currency, meaning repayment threatened to drain the national reserve. The order of the day was to "mobilize savings" from individuals and families, turning domestic wealth into a national resource.

The Ugandan state, the national bourgeoisie, and some peasants and workers experimented with novel forms of finance. This chapter tracks two ways in which Uganda did this: the expansion of bank savings and loans and the so-called Premium Development Bonds. In terms of the

---

[6] For similar efforts in Ghana and Algeria, see Catherine Boone, "State Building in the African Countryside: Structure and Politics at the Grassroots," *Journal of Development Studies* 34(4) (1998): 12; Nick Bernards, "States, Money and the Persistence of Colonial Financial Hierarchies in British West Africa," *Development and Change* 54(1) (2023): 64–86; Muriam Haleh Davis, *Markets of Civilization: Islam and Racial Capitalism in Algeria* (Duke University Press, 2022).

[7] *Origins and Growth of Uganda Commercial Bank, 1950–75* (Uganda Commercial Bank, 1975).

former, the Bank of Uganda oversaw an energetic effort to "mop up savings for development purposes."[8] New parastatal banks, branches, and circulating vans were meant to not only turn inert money into investment capital; they were also to produce upstanding citizens, publicly minded and thrifty. Likewise, the Premium Development Bonds tried to convert citizens' cash into a fund that the state would use to invest in social services and economic development. While bank deposits would be mobilized as commercial lending to African traders, development bonds would be under the stewardship of the country's technocratic elite, invested in the pressing priorities of the nation. In both cases, the state tried to align personal and collective interests, drawing on the conjoined promises of patriotism and profitability.

Many studies of nationalism emphasize how citizens are convinced to contribute to a wider good, even to the point of self-sacrifice; cultural attachments and patriotic sentiments subordinate individual direction to a collective purpose. Yet, independent Uganda never marshalled a significant cultural nationalism, divided as it was between subnational loyalties and violence.[9] Economic citizenship, however, tried to sidestep the deficit of affective solidarities by weaving together monetary ties and financial interdependencies. A national currency is perhaps the most evident example of this. Promulgating a national currency created shared interests and demarcated the boundaries of the nation.[10] Deployed across the country, the currency incorporated Baganda landholders, Banyarwanda migrant workers, Karamajong pastoralists, Bakonjo separatists, and all others who wished to legally transact in the country.

But if a national currency had assimilating effects, it also produced its own exclusions. As this chapter details, the inauguration of the Ugandan shilling in 1965–1966 excluded putative foreigners by limiting the convertibility between infrastructures of value.

---

[8] BoU G.56.70, GOV.806.4: Post Office Savings Bank 1967–70. Oral Evidence of Mubiru, July 18, 1967.

[9] A. B. K. Kasozi, *The Social Origins of Violence in Uganda, 1964–1985* (McGill-Queen's University Press, 1994); Nelson Kasfir, *The Shrinking Political Arena: Participation & Ethnicity in African Politics* (University of California Press, 1976).

[10] Gustav Peebles, "Inverting the Panopticon: Money and the Nationalization of the Future," *Public Culture* 20(2) (2008): 233–265; Gustav Peebles, "Rehabilitating the Hoard: The Social Dynamics of Unbanking in Africa and Beyond," *Africa* 84(4) (2014): 595–613.

2.1 Introduction

Governing these frontiers, in turn, cast some as suspicious subverters of the nation's economy – not least of which were Asians, migrants, and residents of the border regions. Their cross-border mobility and kinship were threats to the territoriality of monetary statecraft and the imperatives of maintaining foreign currency. They reflected competing ways of producing and governing value, with practical ethics often at odds with those of the central state. The cross-border circulation of Asian wealth, for instance, was driven by familial obligations as well as a cautious attitude toward nativist policies. As a result, their wealth and monetary dealings were policed and, in some cases, the state's economic sovereignty was used to expel and expropriate.

This antinomy between inclusion and exclusion is central to studies of citizenship in Africa and elsewhere. As many have pointed out, citizenship involves a balance between rights and responsibilities; it also has inevitable tensions between those who fall within its remit and those who are defined as outsiders.[11] This chapter emphasizes that the question of political belonging was hardly the only consequential aspect of citizenship in Uganda; in important ways, the boundaries between inclusion and exclusion were drawn with an eye toward profitable production and resource distribution. Furthermore, experiences like those of Zerubaberi Were also illustrate a less appreciated dynamic: enclosure within a country's regime of governance. National currency presented an impediment for those wishing to leave the sovereign authority of the Bank of Uganda. Here, a long-standing characteristic of African politics – the accumulation of productive followers – took on a new guise, as currency holders were financially fenced in.[12]

***

Central banking, consumer savings, and national currency were political projects of stewardship and authority, animated not by commercial interests and logics alone, but rather as political encounters about the boundaries of belonging, the securing of collective futures, and the making of respectable lives. An attention to these histories not only

---

[11] Emma Hunter, ed., *Citizenship, Belonging, and Political Community in Africa: Dialogues between Past and Present* (Ohio University Press, 2016).
[12] Jane Guyer, "Wealth in People, Wealth in Things," *Journal of African History* 36(1) (1995): 83–90.

crosses the domains of political, economic, and cultural history; it also suggests continuities across Ugandan historiography's assumed ruptures of independence in 1962 and Amin's coup in 1971. Finally, it suggests a more active negotiation between citizens and states than is often assumed in scholarship on postcolonial Africa. Neither the mute recipients of state largesse nor distant fugitives from its impositions, Ugandans actively called upon the colonial and independent states for new sorts of financial infrastructure that would remake the economy. In doing so, they were part of a transformation in the contours of sovereignty and citizenship.

Section 2.2 discusses the late colonial protests and the resulting provision of credit to Africans before turning in Section 2.3 to a discussion of how finance was reformed and expanded after independence. I focus, first, on the Premium Development Bonds that recruited citizens as investors and, second, the expansion of bank savings accounts. The latter especially reveals the continuities in economic sovereignty and citizenship across the Obote–Amin political rupture. If the first half focuses more on demands to incorporate Ugandans into financial infrastructures, the second half of the chapter turns more to the attendant exclusions. In Section 2.4, I show how the expulsion of Asians relied, in part, on the sovereign control of money and banking, but I emphasize how African Ugandans were also subject to the enclosures wrought by the postcolonial monetary order, not least as money worked as a technique of territorial bordering.

2.2 Late Colonial Credit and Capital

Beginning with cotton in 1904 and expanding to coffee by the 1920s, Uganda was the site of an agrarian economic "revolution."[13] Colonial revenue and resource imperatives combined with African ambitions and efforts to build an export-oriented agricultural economy.[14]

---

[13] Michiel de Haas and Kostadis Papaioannou, "Resource Endowments and Agricultural Commercialization in Colonial Africa: Did Labour Seasonality and Food Security Drive Uganda's Cotton Revolution?" EHES Working Papers in Economic History, no. 111 (2017).

[14] C. Wrigley, *Crops and Wealth in Uganda: A Short Agrarian History* (East African Institute of Social Research, 1959); R. M. A. van Zwanenberg and Anne King, *An Economic History of Kenya and Uganda, 1800–1970* (Palgrave Macmillan, 1975).

2.2 Late Colonial Credit and Capital

In Buganda especially, a combination of preferential politics, ecology, and infrastructure aligned to create a class of wealthy elites who spent their proceeds on housing, schooling, and new commodities. Over time, other regions (such as Busoga and Bugisu) also witnessed considerable production for export. Yet, the income growth was not universal; it was geographically uneven and formative of new class divisions. In Buganda, wealthy landholders hired large numbers of migrant workers and, over time, turned away from their historical obligations to coethnic followers. As Holly Hanson and Carol Summers have detailed, these transformations caused a series of turbulent disputes. Ganda ideas about ethical relations between patrons and clients were undermined by new taxes, compulsory labor, and private property.[15] By the postwar years – as export prices boomed and political reforms loomed – the organization of productive activity reached a newly urgent status. Governor Andrew Cohen, who arrived in 1952, was a "development governor par excellence," but Ugandans often disagreed about the specifics of political reform and economic change.[16] The disputes were multiple, ranging from the merits of new commodities to the proper scale of political authority. The cost of living, the conditions of employment, and property reforms animated disputes, but central to many commercially minded cultivators were the rules governing the growing, processing, and selling of cotton and coffee. The disputes fueled new political struggles and organizations, and a series of official inquiries tried to sort out the way forward. In the second half of the 1940s, those claiming the mantle of Bataka (historically, heads of Ganda clans) demanded more accountable government and the right to gin their own cotton and sell their crops abroad.[17] Ignatius Musazi consolidated an important strand of activism by leading a huge number of farmers from Buganda and beyond.[18] They

---

[15] Hanson, *Landed Obligation*; Carol Summers, "Radical Rudeness: Ugandan Social Critiques in the 1940s," *Journal of Social History* 39(3) (2006): 741–770. On calls for "economic autonomy" routed through demands that "government work better than it did," see Holly Hanson, *To Speak and Be Heard* (Ohio University Press, 2022), pp. 104–110.

[16] Summers, "Local Critiques," p. 21.

[17] Uganda Protectorate, *Report of the Commission of Inquiry into the Disturbances in Uganda during April, 1949* (Government Printer, 1950).

[18] Jonathon Earle, *Colonial Buganda and the End of Empire: Political Thought and Historical Imagination in Africa* (Cambridge University Press, 2017), chapter 1.

pioneered their own cooperative organizations to seek collective authority over how the products of their labor were marketed. Farmers complained about the prices set by government, the complicity of chiefs, and the treatment they received from the Asian brokers who bought Africans' crops. African growers asked why they should be paid less than Europeans and Indians for their crops. "Ours is the same coffee as theirs," one gentleman shouted to roars of approval at a meeting organized by Musazi.[19] At the core of this was a demand for "a postcolonial state and economy under African control."[20] In the 1940s, the protests grew as Baganda withheld crops from government-approved channels and petitioned authorities to change the rules over who could sell crops and for what price. In 1945, this took the form of a "general strike" motivated, in part, by the spiraling cost of food and other consumer goods.[21] In 1948, continued popular dissatisfaction sparked government repression, which resulted in an extended state of emergency and violent reprisals.

While Buganda was the most prominent in the Protectorate, people from other regions also refused to accept the racialized structure of the export market, where Africans were confined to farming and not the processing or export of their crops. In Bugisu, for instance, farmers worked collectively to receive better prices and more control over their labor by forcing the state to allow them to organize the Bugisu Cooperative Union.[22] These Gisu advocates were especially effective because they could credibly threaten the state's revenue by withdrawing from coffee production or smuggling its proceeds to Kenya. On the other side of the country, the Bwamba Rwenzori Growers Association likewise carried out a sustained campaign to improve the price they received and to better control the sale of the coffee they grew.[23]

Africans cast their dissent in various forms, but it was often the economic and racial idioms that were most intelligible to British officials. By the 1940s, government officials and farmer activists shared an

---

[19] George Shepherd, Jr., *They Wait in Darkness* (John Day Company, 1955), p. 35.
[20] Aaron Windel, *Cooperative Rule: Community Development in Britain's Late Empire* (University of California Press, 2022), p. 113.
[21] Hanson, *To Speak and Be Heard*, chapter 3.
[22] Stephen G. Bunker, *Peasants against the State: The Politics of Market Control in Bugisu, Uganda, 1900–1983* (University of Chicago Press, 1991).
[23] Kabarole District Archives (KDA) 601/1: Coffee; KDA 628: Economy; KDA 600/5: Bwamba Coffee.

intellectual space shaped by colonial economic and racial thought. Uganda's newly wealthy farmers worked hard to position themselves as capable producers of export value and to remind Britain of their tutelary obligations because these were arguments to which Britain was likely to respond. Just as importantly, they shared a material interest in commercial agriculture.[24] The Protectorate government wanted increased exports and the tax revenue that accompanied it; many Ugandans were only too happy to expand the land and labor dedicated to their own cash crops. As early as the 1940s, bankers at Barclays D.C.O. were surprised that Ganda cultivators readily took to keeping their earnings in bank accounts, even switching providers if they could get a better interest rate.[25] As a result, even if it did not always agree, the colonial state could countenance African economic demands. Success in this regard – such as the decision to provide cotton ginneries to Africans, or cede control of their coffee cooperative to the Bagisu – was always partial, limited by political hesitancy, derogatory views, and the assumed zero-sum relations between races. Yet, in important ways, African insistence did compel the colonial state to reorganize economic institutions to give Africans more autonomy and resources.

One of the more notable initiatives was the provision of credit to Africans. In May 1948, Musazi put this issue at the center of his demands, suggesting that cotton proceeds be used to establish an agricultural bank. The official commission on the protests the next year acknowledged the demand for credit as one of the few legitimate African grievances. "It was clear" that a land bank and building society "was an object of interest to many" Ugandans, it reported, recommending a new financial institution for Africans be established "with all dispatch."[26] Such a commitment to issuing Africans' loans was largely a novelty in East Africa. Instead, the history had been dominated by the conservative paternalism of the colonial state, which historically deemed Africans unfit for credit. Banks, for their part, demanded forms of collateral (such as land) that few could muster.

[24] Mahmood Mamdani, *Politics & Class Formation in Uganda* (Monthly Review, 1976), pp. 177–183.
[25] Billy Frank, "The 'Private' Face of African Development Planning during the Second World War," in J. M. Hodge et al. (eds.), *Developing Africa* (Manchester University Press, 2014), p. 122.
[26] Uganda Protectorate, *Disturbances in Uganda*, pp. 48, 106, 121.

While Asian merchants would issue loans to some Africans, these came with what Eryeza Bwele decried as a "very big rate of interest" in his testimony to the 1949 Commission.[27] As a result, African producers were starved of capital, finding limited doors open to them. Even the most successful African commercial movements, such as the Federation of Uganda African Farmers, found it impossible to acquire the loans that would facilitate their work and growth. George Shepherd, Jr., who worked in the 1950s with the Federation, recalled that bankers could "close all the doors of credit and capital" to the African cooperative marketing movement, "subtly and indirectly strangling us to death."[28]

"Save to Lend"

The Uganda Credit & Savings Bank and the African Loans Fund that it administered were therefore important departures from existing financial policy.[29] Under the motto "Save to Lend," they expanded the financial credit available to Africans.[30] The UCSB was founded in 1950 with the goal of offering banking services to Africans, while the ALF was established in 1954 in order to expand operations, especially to those who could not provide reliable collateral. Both were the result of African activism in prior years, not least by productive farmers and a new class of African traders.[31] They also reflected administrative

---

[27] Uganda Protectorate, *Disturbances in Uganda*, p. 74.
[28] Shepherd, *They Wait in Darkness*, p. 284.
[29] George Bosa, *The Financing of Small-Scale Enterprises in Uganda* (Oxford University Press, 1969), pp. 20–35; Diana Hunt, *Credit for Agricultural Development: A Case Study of Uganda* (East African Publishers House, 1975).
[30] Summers documents the recognition by colonial officials in the 1940s that considerable savings were being accumulated by Africans but not deposited in banks. "Lending to the Empire: Savings Campaigns in Uganda during World War II," paper presented at European Conference on African Studies, 2016.
[31] Windel frames UCSB as a technique to "lure farmers away" from Musazi's co-operative movement and suggests the involvement of the Cooperatives Registrar "seems to have made the bank even more controversial for Ganda farmers" (pp. 132–134). However, the state's response to Musazi was only one element in the expansion of banking to Africans, and the evidence suggests considerable demand for the new financing. Rather than a narrow technique of governing Africans through "cooperative rule," loans fed into a variety of late colonial and African aspirations. Indeed, in the first year of operation, 166 loan applications were approved yet none were to Co-operative Societies (which Windel argues were the target). Instead, loans went to develop land, open brickmaking

2.2 Late Colonial Credit and Capital

Table 2.1 *Savings accounts and balances at the UCSB*[32]

Year	Number of accounts	Amount (£)	Average amount per account (£)
1951	181	7,724	42.7
1952	343	12,101	36.3
1953	520	22,983	44.2
1954	711	44,238	62.2
1955	1,027	88,242	85.9
1956	1,752	214,883	122.7
1957	8,197	565,261	69
1958	19,558	707,641	36.2
1959	30,422	1,110,077	36.5
1960	41,815	1,362,225	32.6
1961	50,420	1,483,746	29.4
1962	56,156	1,463,959	26.1
1963	63,506	1,701,937	26.8
1964	71,689	1,707,843	23.8
1965	82,479	2,058,444	25

concern about the threat that Asian moneylending – including from a raft of small banks that eluded regulation – posed to African borrowers.[33] The UCSB's initial capitalization of £500,000 came from the Price Stabilization Funds, but it sought to expand its assets by recruiting savings accounts, as well. After initial forays in 1956, the UCSB would prove "ingenious in encouraging and collecting small savings," with more than Shs. 29 million held in more than 50,000 accounts by 1961 (see Table 2.1).[34]

Government employees could have part of their salaries automatically diverted to their savings account, and the UCSB even started a school

---

facilities, erect buildings, and start retail shops. Uganda Credit and Savings Bank, *Report of the Board of Management* (Government Printer, 1950), pp. 1–2. On the petty bourgeois advocates, see Mamdani, *Politics & Class*, pp. 201–202.

[32] Adapted from Bosa, *Financing*, p. 38.
[33] UKNA CO 852/1079/12: Banking: Uganda. I appreciate Carol Summers demonstrating the importance of this.
[34] Bank of England (BoE) OV75/2: Extract of "Uganda Survey Mission" in Wilson to H.M. Treasury, April 27, 1961; Uganda Credit & Savings Bank, *Annual Report* (Government Printer, 1961).

Figure 2.1 Uganda Credit & Savings Bank mobile vans.
History in Progress Uganda.

savings scheme to introduce children "to the money economy and the banking habit."[35] Mobile banks drummed up deposits beyond main towns, drawing "small African savings from traditional hiding places, such as holes in the ground or places under the roof."[36] Despite their expense and frequent breakdowns, Ugandans flocked to mobile banks and demanded the UCSB expand their circulation (see Figure 2.1).[37]

The most important UCSB role, however, was the issuance of loans to Africans. Demand was considerable: on the day the UCSB opened its doors in 1950, there was "an immediate rush for application forms,"

[35] BoE OV75/2: Extract of World Bank "Uganda Survey Mission" in Wilson to H.M. Treasury, April 27, 1961.
[36] Uganda Credit and Savings Bank, *Report & Accounts for the period 1st July 1956 to 30th June 1957* (Government Printer, 1957), p. 2. Over time, while these proved expensive and hard to justify as profitable, they were seen as important advertisers of wider services.
[37] Despite the bank's hesitance about profitability, residents of Ankole and Kigezi prevailed upon UCSB to introduce mobile banking in 1961. *Report of the Uganda Credit and Savings Bank, 1961* (Government Printer, 1961), p. 2. Later calculations also suggested they were not profitable. Loxley, "Development of the Monetary and Financial System," p. 78.

2.2 Late Colonial Credit and Capital

and within three months, 830 applications were issued. Of these, 166 were approved, with £829,300 lent to build bricks, erect buildings, open shops, and improve land. All but three were secured against freehold or *mailo* land. In the coming years, the demand would continue, with the number of staff, offices, and loans increasing. These overwhelmingly went to agricultural purposes, but the loans also financed new buildings, shopkeeping, brickmaking, and other businesses. By the end of the decade, the "flood of applications for loans" continued unabated, and more streamlined services were being offered to "progressive farmers" who adopted "farm planning and budgeting" under the supervision of Agricultural Officers.[38]

By 1957, the UCSB had distributed 14,000 loans through the African Loans Fund – 12,000 of which were in Buganda.[39] The unequal distribution of credit reflected a number of influences. Buganda was the most prosperous and politically favored area of the Protectorate. There was a wealthy, propertied aristocracy connected to the Kabaka's court. Baganda also benefitted from connections to the central state, proximity to export infrastructure, and familiarity with cash crop procedures.[40] They also had better ways for convincing the UCSB they were an appropriate credit risk. One method to do so was by having the Buganda government guarantee 50 percent of the loan in case of default. All African Local Governments could do so, but the Buganda Kingdom was comparatively wealthy and well-integrated with its wealthy farmers. When it began backstopping their borrowing in 1956, it unlocked considerable lending: in the first year, more than 10,000 application forms were requested in Buganda, with over 200 completed applications arriving at the UCSB office each week.[41]

The expansion of credit in Buganda also depended on the exceptional legal status of land in the kingdom. The 1900 Uganda Agreement between the Kingdom of Buganda and Britain inaugurated the *mailo*

---

[38] *African Loans Fund Report, 1960* (Government Printer, 1960), p. 12; *Report of the Uganda Credit and Savings Bank, 1961*, p. 4.
[39] JDA 20/3: African Loans Fund, Report and Accounts, 1956–1957.
[40] By the mid-1960s, Buganda produced over 90 percent of robusta coffee exports and around 30 percent of cotton exports, despite having 21 percent of the country's land and 28 percent of the population. W. Senteza Kajubi, "Coffee and Prosperity in Buganda: Some Aspects of Economic & Social Change," *Uganda Journal* 29(2) (1965): 136.
[41] Uganda Credit and Savings Bank, *Report & Accounts for the Period 1st July 1956 to 30th June 1957*, pp. 1–4.

land tenure system in which land was provided to the Kabaka's chosen chiefs, while others became tenants. Reforms in the 1920s provided tenants with protection against eviction and the right to pass their tenancy onto their children.[42] This created a measure of security that facilitated significant agricultural production for export by peasants working small plots of land. It did not, however, lead to considerable bank lending – not least because tenants were unable to mortgage the land they worked. A 1950 survey of Buganda found very little mortgaging on *mailo* land, despite its quasi-freehold characteristic. Its author, A. B. Mukwaya, thought "banks are either not sufficiently understood or not trusted by the Africans."[43] However, the booming economy of the 1950s and more expansive government initiative shifted the financial agenda. The result was the explosive growth of loans. By 1965, a large study of Buganda found widespread borrowing from government schemes and private banks: about half of the coffee farmers sampled received loans from the Uganda Credit & Savings Bank, and almost all who had diversified into commercial farming drew on bank credit.[44]

The inequality of credit did not go unnoticed. In neighboring Busoga, residents were frustrated by the limited lending from the UCSB. Would it not be more useful for all peoples to receive loans – "for it enlarges our trading if somebody is allowed to be given such money and shows an improvement" – wrote one shopkeeper in May 1953, disappointed by the progress of his loan application for Shs. 10,000.[45] By mid-1955, only six of fifty loan applications had been approved in Busoga; in Kigezi, only three of fifty were approved.[46] Even within Buganda, credit was unavailable to many who wanted loans. The Uganda Growers Co-operative Union complained in 1953 that while the UCSB was initially welcomed,

---

[42] Hanson, *Landed Obligation*, especially chapters 5 and 6.
[43] A. B. Mukwaya, *Land Tenure in Buganda: Present Day Tendencies* (East African Institute of Social Research, 1953), pp. 36–40.
[44] Audrey Richards, ed. *Economic Development and Tribal Change: A Study of Immigrant Labour in Buganda* (East African Institute of Social Research, 1954), pp. 261, 301–302. See also the class analysis of this lending in D. Wadada Nabudere, *Imperialism and Revolution in Uganda* (Tanzania Publishing House, 1980), pp. 185–200.
[45] JDA Finance 42/12: Busesa Shops, Bugweri to Secretary UCSB, Application for Shs. 10k on Loan, September 16, 1953.
[46] *African Loans Fund, Report and Accounts, January–June 1955* (Uganda Protectorate, 1955).

our joy was only short-lived when it was brought home to us that the Credit Bank would only give credit to the landed class – the fairly well-to-do class of people who, in the nature of things, are usually unwilling to do "dirty" work i.e. work demanding physical exertion, or a lot of trouble before giving returns.[47]

The Uganda National Congress (UNC) likewise complained that what initially seemed to be a "godsend answer to an acute need" was proving to be a disappointment because 95 percent of Africans could not provide the land or other immovable property demanded as security.[48] For these critics, the trouble was not only inequality of access but also how that furthered existing inequalities within Ugandan society; those without existing resources, who could not marshal sufficient property, or who were located far from transport infrastructure fell even further behind. As the UNC pointed out, even proposals to find means of lending to non-propertied borrowers were set to help the already better off. For instance, to the suggestion that those without land could access credit through the guarantee of 50 percent of the loan by their African Local Government, the political party remarked pointedly that "It can be seen at once what sort of people will manage to take advantage of this amendment." Instead, their demand was to lend to Africans despite the absence of private property. Otherwise, the "average small grower ... some of the most enlightened" in the country will be left behind.

Despite the evident demand, British financial administrators remained anxious about lending without landed collateral.[49] They tried some initiatives, including relaxing security requirements in 1956 and the guarantees from African Local Government mentioned earlier.[50] They also hoped to use cooperative societies: as intermediaries, they might be more easily governed by the state, avoiding loan misuse and ensuring productive output through collective pressure on members.[51] Lending to a group was also an opportunity to spread liability across a wider population than an individual borrower. Mostly though, colonial administrators in the 1950s tried to expand lending by redoubling their efforts to delineate African property regimes. The promise of consolidated and individualized land tenure

---

[47] UKNA CO 892/15/1: Submission of the Uganda Growers Co-operative Union, 1953.
[48] UKNA CO 892/15/1: Submission of the Uganda National Congress, 1953.
[49] UCSB, *Reports and Accounts, 1952* (Government Printer, 1953), p. 2.
[50] UCSB, *Reports and Accounts, 30th June 1956* (Government Printer, 1956), p. 1.
[51] Windel, *Cooperative Rule*.

was central to the East African Royal Commission (1953–1955), and it found expression in Uganda's Land Tenure Proposals published at the start of 1956.

Race was at the heart of this fixation on landed collateral – at least that was the view of the World Bank team preparing its 1961 study of Uganda. Banks, the visitors observed in their draft report, could "do more in the way of extending credit on the basis of character." Creditworthy character was, they thought, a result of "the growth of the money-mentality and respect for debt obligations." However, there was little way for bankers to "know and judge the character of potential African borrowers" due to how "the various communities in Uganda tend to keep to themselves in their social life." Overcoming racial division through greater "social inter-relationships" was a necessary component of learning to lend in the furtherance of "African enterprise."[52] Walter Newlyn agreed, noting that lending decisions in Uganda were made based on "close personal contact between the banker and his customer." Because the British bankers did not socialize with "the African population, the gulf was too wide" to accurately assess creditworthiness.[53]

Nevertheless, the 1950s saw a begrudging escape from some of the strictures of finance. Ugandan subjects continued to demand credit be deployed in ways that challenged British parsimony. The result was lending that sutured together various purposes – not all of which fit neatly together. Bankers and agricultural extension officers who served as the frontline of government lending were at pains to direct capital to what they viewed as productive investments. Revenue and resource imperatives favored lending for agricultural purposes and, to a lesser extent, transportation and shopkeeping. Repayment troubles dogged the UCSB's early days, reaching as high as a third of outstanding loans five years into the initiative.[54] This was a source of consternation for pecuniary-minded administrators who tightened protocols in response.[55] By 1955, UCSB management reported that potential

[52] BoE OV75/2: Extract of World Bank "Uganda Survey Mission," April 27, 1961.
[53] Walter Tessier Newlyn, *Money in an African Context* (Oxford University Press, 1967), p. 44.
[54] Bosa, *Financing*, p. 27.
[55] Almost as soon as they began issuing loans, borrowers began missing repayments. Seeing the early warning signs in 1952, they decided to budget for 5 percent bad and doubtful debts. UCSB, *Report & Accounts, December 1952* (Government Printer, 1953), p. 3. The next year this was raised to 40 percent of the outstanding loans and the need "drastic action" was suggested. UCSB,

2.2 Late Colonial Credit and Capital

borrowers were "beginning to appreciate that the Bank does not exist for the making of free gifts," and ensuing years saw a lower cost from unpaid loans at the UCSB.[56]

But while borrowers acknowledged an obligation to repay, many Africans disagreed about the purpose of credit. They wanted loans to facilitate access to a wider array of goods, most of which the state denigrated as frivolous consumption. The result was many denied applications. The cross-purposes of borrowers and lenders also encouraged elaborate surveillance where local government officials and agricultural extension officers tried to ensure loans were spent on their stated purpose of fertilizer, farm workers, or other commercial ends. Yet, audits consistently proved difficult.[57] As a result of these quandaries, in one case, the government bankers decided an exception would be made: Africans could spend their borrowed money on radios. Such loans, management admitted, were "not an economic proposition" but would help spread the radio – with its promise of inexpensive governance and pedagogy – to rural areas for the first time.[58]

In practice, the point of lending to Africans was not reducible to profit and loss. It moved across commercial propositions and governmental imperatives. The African Loans Fund, for instance, was intended to "educate" Africans on "the proper use of capital and in the necessity to honour obligations."[59] The reform of character and the creation of a "savings minded" public was seen as an appropriate subject for spending, even if repayment was not guaranteed. In the back-and-forth between bureaucrats and subjects, various idioms cast lending to Africans as sometimes humanitarian gifts and other times commercial capital. Officials spoke of "granting" loans to "assist the public," but likewise worried about default and profitability. As a result, would-be borrowers carefully positioned themselves somewhere between deserving subjects of colonial welfare and promising customers with market motivation. Farms and premises were inspected by

---

Report & Accounts, December 1953 (Government Printer, 1954), p. 3. Hunt, *Credit for Agricultural Development*, p. 35 reports that when UCSB did seize landed collateral, it had trouble selling it for a satisfactory price.

[56] UCSB, *Reports and Accounts, December 1954* (Government Printer, 1955), p. 1.

[57] BoE OV7/84: Loynes to Ssentongo, January 1, 1964; Richards, *Economic Development*, pp. 88–89; 143–144.

[58] JDA 20/3: African Loans Fund, Report and Accounts for 1956–1957.

[59] *African Loans Fund Report, June 1959* (Government Printer, 1959), p. 11.

government officials who sought to "weed out applications which are unlikely to prove economic," but they also incorporated a wider set of cultural cues and biases. Africans, reported one official, required close supervision to use loans economically. In their view, this labor could be worth it because the loan was an "extremely effective tool in extension work among progressive farmers. A 'carrot' is far more effective than a 'big stick.' Farmers co-operate readily because they want the loan."[60] Here, a "progressive farmer" was one who not only furthered export and tax revenue but also proved responsive to government demands – equal parts disciplined and enterprising.

Not all who might want financial services met the standards demanded. After 1958, worries about repayment led to focusing less on "the masses where the risk was too large" and more on borrowers deemed safer bets.[61] This was part of a Protectorate focus on "providing guidance to the minority of farmers who were both willing and able to profit from it."[62] As the African advocates of broader access knew, narrowing the UCSB's scope would further wealth inequalities, as those with access to inexpensive migrant labor, a source of nonfarm income, and security of tenure received advances from the state. Partly this was about class formation, but by 1957 Audrey Richards thought, it was coupled with a cultural shift: "the poor were now despised."[63]

Available evidence suggests the UCSB largely served men, though not exclusively because women were not completely excluded from the monied economy. In Buganda, women could own land; one 1950 sample of 687 *mailo* plots identified 70 female landowners, most of whom had inherited or been given the land.[64] The Luganda word *nakyeyombekedde* described divorced or separated women who owned land and a house, sometimes establishing "their own independence through cotton growing."[65] Throughout the protectorate, women and children were essential to agricultural production, and the wives of

---

[60] JDA 57/13: Payment of Loans, January 15, 1959. [61] Bosa, *Financing*, p. 28.
[62] Wrigley, *Crops and Wealth*, pp. 77–78.
[63] Hanson, *To Speak and Be Heard*, p. 139.
[64] The author notes the figure is likely statistically over-represented because one of the survey sample locations was the historic locus of women in the Kabaka's court. Mukwaya, *Land Tenure*, pp. 31–32.
[65] Christine Obbo, "Women's Careers in Low Income Areas as Indicators of Country and Town Dynamics," in David Parkin (ed.), *International African Institute Seminar on Town and Country* (Lusaka, 1972), pp. 7–8.

2.2 Late Colonial Credit and Capital

large farmers in Buganda had an important role in supervising hired labor on their land.[66] Yet, the sale of export crops was largely a masculine domain, with most women in the 1950s excluded from the resulting cash and commodities.[67] Over time, exceptions did arise: by 1965, a relatively isolated bank agency in Bugerere County had a "surprisingly large number of wives [who] held separate saving accounts" from their husbands.[68] While banks would be happy to accept deposits from women, it is less likely they could harness the property and connections necessary to unlock loans.[69] And the well-to-do men advocating for increased financial resources were rarely doing so on behalf of their wives and daughters (let alone their tenants and the immigrants working the fields).[70]

Inequalities were also shaped by the uneven economic geography and administrative prejudices in Uganda. In 1959, the Chief Secretary of the Protectorate denied would-be African traders in Toro Kingdom any financial assistance. In his view, additional commercial facilities were "beyond the evident needs of the local economy at the time."[71] A similar disregard confronted S. Kasenke, a trader in Busoga Province, when he applied for a loan to purchase pumps and chemicals for spraying cotton the same year. The Agricultural Officer had little doubt the bank would "get its money back" and was optimistic that sales of these goods would further the government's "all out lygus

---

[66] Audrey Richards, Ford Sturrock, and Jean M. Fortt, *Subsistence to Commercial Farming in Present-Day Buganda: An Economic and Anthropological Survey* (Cambridge University Press, 1973), pp. 187–188; Ashley Rockenbach, "Contingent Homes, Contingent Nation: Rwandan Settlers in Uganda, 1911–64," PhD dissertation, University of Michigan, 2018.

[67] Female control over land and its produce had grown quite notably after the 1900 Agreement, but a patriarchal reaction to independent women limited the trend. Grace Bantebya-Kyomuhendo and Marjorie McIntosh, *Women, Work & Domestic Virtue in Uganda, 1900–2003* (James Currey, 2006), p. 73.

[68] "Mobile capital," speculated the observer, "is obviously a great advantage where marital relations are so notoriously unstable." A. F. Robertson, "Bugerere: A County Case History," in Richards et al., *Subsistence to Commercial*, p. 261.

[69] I am indebted to Carol Summers for making this point.

[70] In Buganda, it was not uncommon for farm laborers to agree to postponed wages for many months, in effect making them creditors to their employers. Diana Hunt, "Some Aspects of Agricultural Credit in Uganda," EDRP no.106 (East African Institute for Social Research, 1966), p. 6.

[71] KDA 611: Chief Secretary to Toro Native Government, June 8, 1959.

spraying campaign."[72] However, Kasenke's "shop is badly stocked [and] he does not keep books." Not meeting these aesthetic and arithmetic standards meant Kasenke was not recommended for the loan. Perhaps, replied the bank manager, it would be better to work through African Local Government to sell pumps across all Busoga – not merely in Kasenke's shop. In this case, individual entrepreneurship was sidelined in favor of the continued preeminence of indirect rule's institutional structure.

Kasenke was hardly alone in seeking credit. Nor was he alone in the troubles he faced. Dominiko Kiswahili was approved in May 1957 for a three-year loan of Shs. 5,000 to buy a lorry, "provided the applicant purchases a NEW vehicle and puts up the balance of the purchase price himself."[73] Others were denied for lacking sufficient collateral: officials considered Mr. Sebowa was suitable for a large loan, yet his "good permanent house in Katwe built out of the local stone" sat on land for which he had no title.[74] In 1959, a fisherman in Kasenyi submitted a handwritten letter applying for 5,000 shillings to expand his business. He was a man of success, he explained. "I managed to get shs. 4,000/= which I used in building a brick-made shop, from fish." He also had a fishing canoe and gear worth Shs. 6,000. All of this, he pledged "as my mortgage in case I fail to pay this debt within a given period."[75] Failing that, he provided three references to establish his reputability.

Borrowers like Kasenke and Kiswahili worked to position themselves as credible recipients of limited funds. To do so, they hitched their own enterprises to the developmental futures of the Protectorate. Credit offered a temporal redistribution of money – capital today on the promise of future earnings. Lending would provide them immediate access to new resources to construct a future, if only they could draw on that future in the present. Yet, the basis for accessing this value was not only a commercial one: "getting its money back" was not the only concern facing UCSB technocrats. Instead, late colonial loans stood at the intersection of public policy, economic citizenship, and charitable assistance. That sometimes awkward combination of

---

[72] Lygus is an insect that harms cotton production. JDA 57/13: Uganda Credit & Savings Bank, 1953–1959, Agricultural Officer, Busoga to Manager, UCSB, February 6, 1959. S. Kasenke Loan Applicant No. 10776.
[73] KDA 946: Manager UCSB to Dominiko Kiswahili, May 16, 1957.
[74] KDA 946: R.T. Hull Lewis to Manager, UCSB, July 4, 1956.
[75] KDA 946: [Illegible] to D.C. Toro, November 1, 1959.

purposes and ethics would expand in the coming years, and the following section looks at how finance was remade after independence.

2.3 Remaking Money after Empire

Postcolonial Finance

In due course, these late colonial experiments would be adopted, expanded, and reformed by the independent state. The broader array of postcolonial financial instruments would enfold Ugandans as citizens, offering them resources for pursuits insofar as they contributed to the nation's development. While the Protectorate government was often able to disregard or delay their response to subjects' demands, the language of citizenship provided additional legitimacy for Ugandans seeking commercial facilities. But the rights of credible citizens were always linked to duties and responsibilities. A trading license, for instance, came with tax obligations, as well as more mundane requirements to manage your stock and accounts reliably. Politicians extolled these duties in their speeches, while bureaucrats carried out training, supervision, and audits. The singer Fred Masagazi even put the merits of tax in a catchy rumba song, *Atanawa Musolo* (He Who Doesn't Pay Taxes), whose lyrics said "The advice I am giving you, pay tax; it is not good to dodge tax."[76]

If credible citizenship was disciplinary, it was also exclusionary, with some people and areas finding little purchase and others actively expelled from the ranks of the worthy. The independent state prioritized certain demographics and regions above others. This section examines how money, banking, and other financial instruments structured the uneven nature of economic citizenship. It first looks at the construction of the new institutional architecture anchored by the Bank of Uganda and the Uganda Commercial Bank. It then turns to discuss a novel sovereign bond sold to Ugandans and, secondly, the call to "mobilize savings" by converting other forms of money into bank deposits.

---

[76] Michiel van Oosterhout, *The Soul of Uganda Through Song* (Bruttopreis, 2021), p. 6.

The postcolonial financial regime was worked out by a small group of Ugandan officials and expatriates.[77] Chief among them was A. J. P. M. "Jack" Ssentongo (Secretary to the Treasury), Joseph Mubiru (the UCSB boss who would later lead the Bank of Uganda), and Lawrence Kalule-Settala (Minister of Finance). Walter Newlyn, a monetary economist from Leeds University, and George Hoskins, Obote's personal economics advisor, were important in designing the suite of postcolonial institutions, and they received considerable input from the World Bank, the International Monetary Fund, and the East African Currency Board. Ssentongo and colleagues thought the credit and finance system of the country was inadequately arrayed to either control the monetary system or create necessary credit. They took the novelties of the 1950s as a starting point for a new regime under African direction.

At the heart of their reformed system were two entities, a central bank and a commercial bank.[78] They were designed with a belief that "the lack of organization of credit and finance" was stalling national development.[79] As discussed in the prior chapter, the central bank would issue currency and regulate its conversion into foreign money, among other things. Until its demise in 1965–1966, the East African Currency Board worked diligently to insulate money from political events. In contrast, the nationalization of central banking and currency meant the myth of depoliticized money was harder to maintain. Indeed, the Bank of Uganda was subject to political debate from the start as it became an important infrastructure of postcolonial statecraft.[80] Yet, as the Minister of Finance was keen to emphasize, there were limits to its role: it would be "in the hands of technicians responsible to ... experienced men of business, financial and banking affairs" who would "advise Government without fear or favour."[81] When it

---

[77] BoE OV7/84: Uganda Credit & Savings Bank-Development, Memorandum by the Treasury, 1963; BoE OV7/87: Establishment of the Uganda State Bank and Associated Institutions, 1965.
[78] Plans also called for an agricultural credit corporation and industrial finance corporation to provide medium and long-term credit. BoE OV7/87: Untitled memo No. 281/65, February 1, 1965.
[79] BoE OV76/4: "Credit and Finance," Planning Commission Memorandum, 1964.
[80] Phares Mutibwa, *The Bank of Uganda (1966–2006): A Historical Perspective* (Bank of Uganda, 2006).
[81] BoE OV75/3: Speech by the Minister of Finance, May 16, 1966.

2.3 Remaking Money after Empire

began issuing currency in August 1966, Uganda was in the throes of economic stress and political crisis. Early development projects had failed to get off the ground, and Uganda was struggling to find external aid from anywhere beyond Britain.[82] Government costs were too high, but it was difficult to cut back in the most evident category – payments to farmers – because the Obote government thought it would prove politically disastrous.[83] Because the state was spending more than its leaders thought it could afford, the Bank of Uganda was directed to consolidate wealth in usable forms.

Yet, this was troubled by political turmoil. Long-standing political tensions between the central and Buganda governments reached a violent crescendo in the first half of 1966, with Obote suspending the Kabaka from his role as President, sending the Army into a bloody confrontation at the royal palace, and promulgating a new constitution.[84] An important part of the subordination of Buganda involved ending the kingdom's "relative financial autonomy" by centralizing what Apolo Nsibambi called its "financial sinews." Exceptional tax revenue and discretionary spending by the Kabaka's government were ended, and some steps were taken to redirect Buganda's wealth to poorer districts.[85] As a result, the position of financial technocrats like Joseph Mubiru, a Muganda who was expected to take the reins of the Bank of Uganda, was uncertain.[86] Because the new constitution was introduced in a way that contravened the procedures of its predecessor, observers were not even sure if the Bank of Uganda Act was even legal.[87] More importantly, it was unclear if ordinary Baganda would

---

[82] BoE OV75/3: Memorandum to I.D. Lewis, Deputy Governor Designate, Bank of Uganda, July 11, 1966.

[83] BoE OV75/3: Commonwealth Office to British High Commission, Kampala, August 6, 1966.

[84] I. R. Hancock, "The Uganda Crisis, 1966," *Australian Outlook* 20(3) (1966): 263–277; Akiiki Mujaju, "The Gold Allegations Motion and Political Development in Uganda," *African Affairs* 86(345) (1987): 479–504.

[85] Apolo Nsibambi, "Increased Government Control of Buganda's Financial Sinews since the Revolution of 1966," *Public Administration and Development* 10(2) (1971): 100–112.

[86] BoE OV75/3: "Uganda" extract, 1966. Mubiru's biography is in Mutibwa, *Bank of Uganda*, pp. 67–69.

[87] In the view of the UK Commonwealth Relations Office, the situation was "equivalent to a coup," but they decided that Obote had command over most of the country and population so decided to continue recognition of his government. BoE OV75/3: Note for the Record, Mr. Owen, May 17, 1966.

accept the new Ugandan currency, or whether the concentration of symbolic and financial power within the central government would lead to a boycott. Fortunately for the Bank of Uganda, the new currency was due to be issued at the same time as payments to Robusta coffee farmers (who were overwhelmingly Baganda), meaning ethnic patriotism would be confronted by the threat of not receiving any payment for coffee.[88]

For its part, the Uganda Commercial Bank (UCB) was designed to provide savings and loans, especially to the public and ideally on longer time frames than existing models. When it began in 1965, the UCB took over many of the functions and assets of the colonial Uganda Credit & Savings Bank. Indeed, its official emblem was a minor adoption of the UCSB's own coat of arms, with the national bird – a crested crane – flanking a shield bordered by cowrie shells, with major crops – including bananas, maize, and cotton – arrayed generously.[89] Underneath was its motto: Save and Serve. The Obote government gave the UCB pride of place, overseeing its considerable expansion starting in 1966. The new institution reflected a long-standing frustration that expatriate banks mainly provided short-term import–export loans, while "the Ugandan farmers and businessmen lack adequate facilities."[90] Surveying the economy in 1965, both Ugandan and British observers found evident scope for expanding loans to Africans. Globally, former colonies were turning more to domestic resources as they partially delinked from London's finances.[91] In Uganda and the wider region, the hope was to "cut into the business of the British banks who are ... virtually all powerful."[92] Yet, as they observed the UCSB's prior troubles with repayment, the Planning Commission expected borrowers to require careful shepherding and discipline. The trouble, as they put it, was a lack of "expertise viz. the ability of borrowers to carry out profitable development schemes." Technical assistance would, they hoped, ensure loans were put to profitable use, but if repayment continued to be low, it might require additional intervention: "the Prime Minister has been asked to

---

[88] BoE OV75/3: Commonwealth Office to British High Commission, Kampala, August 6, 1966.
[89] The coin at the top of the emblem remained – even in 1971 publications – the East African shilling.
[90] BoE OV75/2: "Uganda Commercial Bank Bill," June 25, 1965.
[91] BoE OV75/2: Loynes to I.D. Lewis, January 13, 1966.
[92] BoE OV7/79: Loynes to Mr. Rootham, October 9, 1964.

2.3 Remaking Money after Empire   117

indicate Government's approval of firm handling and foreclosure, if necessary."[93] The invocation of Obote's approval reflects the political stakes of loans in this moment, as citizens clamored for long-denied commercial rights and states sought to guard against financial losses.

If managed properly, government banking offered additional policy latitude for the state. While the country had limited scope for changing the lending decisions of private banks, they would be able to prioritize sectors within the UCB's operations.[94] The African Trade Development Fund, for instance, had already expanded loans to Ugandans, wishing to compete with the Asian-dominated sector.[95] A range of other initiatives emerged in the first years of independence – many of which were financed by foreign aid.[96] By the 1960s, the US government and World Bank were financing the expansion of the UCSB and African Loans Fund, including £100,000 to relaunch the latter as the Progressive Farmers Loan Initiative.[97] Evidence suggests, however, that off-farm income, and the wealth that provided, remained important to accessing larger loans.[98] Between 1960 and 1966, loans to traders grew most significantly, but policy swung between the industrial, agricultural, and commercial sectors.[99] By 1971, the government planned to issue small loans to more than 150,000 export-oriented farmers to buy equipment and inputs, as well as hire tractors and temporary labor.[100]

As before, credit was not only a financial instrument. Loans were political promises before they were promissory notes. It was not citizenship alone that justified access to credit; rather, the postcolonial

---

[93] BoE OV7/84: "Uganda Credit & Savings Bank – Development," Planning Commission, 1963.
[94] This is not to say UCB was too radical a departure; for one thing, it signed up to the industry's cartel agreement that limited competition. Irving Gershenberg, "Banking in Uganda since Independence," *Economic Development and Cultural Change* 20(3) (1972): 507. See also Holger Engberg, "Commercial Banking in East Africa, 1950–1963," *The Journal of Modern African Studies* 3(2) (1965): 175–200; Holger Engberg and William Hance. "Growth and Dispersion of Branch Banking in Tropical Africa, 1950–1964," *Economic Geography* 45(3) (1969): 195–208.
[95] KDA 611: Trade Development Committees, February 16, 1962.
[96] Hunt, *Credit for Agricultural Development*.
[97] *The Economic Development of Uganda* (The World Bank Group, 1961), p. 99.
[98] Hunt, "Some Aspects," p. 11.
[99] Irving Gershenberg, "The Impact of Independence on the Role of Commercial Banking in Uganda's Economic Development," Makerere Institute of Social Research, 1969, p. 13.
[100] Government of Uganda, *Work for Progress: Uganda's Second Five Year Plan* (Kampala, 1966).

state offered its capacity to redistribute money across time to those it deemed worthy. Troubles with repayment obliged the state to target citizens they deemed credible, to the detriment of smaller, less-legible borrowers. Often, this reproduced the colonial language. "Government is going to assist only those progressive traders who can prove themselves," declared Minister W. W. Kalema at a public rally in Kasese a few years after the UCB opened its doors.[101] But what exactly constituted "progressive" was not always clear. Kalema, for his part, emphasized bookkeeping, forming cooperative associations, and banking "all the money you do business with." Trader training courses offered another means to distinguish oneself as a credible citizen. Yet, the promise of these rites – that is, their capacity to remake the individual – were rarely satisfactory. And like in the case of India, where "progressive farmers" were envisioned as a vehicle for increased agricultural productivity but often a codeword for wealthy peasants and landowners, the vision was profoundly limited and exclusions multiplied.[102]

As a result, some Ugandans turned to supplication and petition, adopting the posture of clientelism. "We are crying with sorrowful voices because we are always too behind in everything," wrote one group of self-identified boys and girls in 1970. "We wish to build a shop which can be called as Toro Boys Trading Company," yet "because we are young people," we failed to collect the necessary capital. "Please sir," they wrote, will the government help us?[103] For these youth, credit was a means to move forward in social time, an instrument not merely of economic well-being but a tool for achieving respectable adulthood. Popular demand for loans involved citizens calling on the state as a source of redistribution – not so much between classes as across generations. They cast the state in the figure of a senior authority who could rework wealth across the years, making it available after decades of foreclosure.

Aligning the Nation via Development Bonds, 1964–1965

The work of the new state required its own resources. In order to deploy loans – let alone pay salaries or build schools – the government

---

[101] KDA 612/2: Hon. W.W. Kalema's Tour of the Western Region, Meeting held at Kasese, January 21, 1970.
[102] Benjamin Siegel, "Modernizing Peasants and 'Master Farmers': Progressive Agriculture in Early Independent India," *Comparative Studies of South Asia, Africa and the Middle East* 37(1) (2017): 64–85.
[103] KDA 612/2: Letter to District Commissioner, Toro, March 13, 1970.

2.3 Remaking Money after Empire

of Uganda needed sources of financing far exceeding the colonial era. It not only turned to taxes and external aid. It also experimented with a variety of novel financial instruments, many of which hailed Ugandans as credible citizens whose claims to legitimate belonging arose through productive contributions. Faced with the limits and cost to foreign aid and borrowing, the government of Uganda turned inward for new sources of liquidity – fungible and exchangeable resources with which to meet its spending aspirations. In the process, citizens were incorporated through new fiduciary infrastructures and the state was able to access wealth that was sometimes unavailable internationally. I focus here on two initiatives: the Premium Development Bonds and savings accounts.[104] The first tried to recruit citizens as investors in sovereign debt, selling them low-cost securities that could be redeemed in five years. The second exhorted Ugandans to store their wealth in banks where it could be loaned out to others. Both were ways to govern wealth, consolidating value under the auspices of the state so that it could be used for new purposes. But unlike taxes, they were voluntary and overtly marketed as a means of merging personal and public interest.[105] As either savings or investment, citizens could contribute to a national collective while improving their own lot in life. These financial experiments aimed to remake temporal rhythms, moving away from both inert private savings and consumptive circulation of cash.[106] Neither long-term savings nor immediate spending, they pioneered a middle path wherein private wealth was committed to a "near future" of public investment.[107] The wealth of citizens was to be aligned with public purpose, drawing innumerable individual transactions into a collective fiscal cadence – taken in from many and spent according to the government's development plans.

---

[104] Discussed also in Willis, "Thrift, Citizenship, and Self-Improvement."

[105] The obligatory nature and ruthless enforcement of tax in colonial Uganda cast a shadow over postcolonial revenue imperatives. See Mahmood Mamdani, *Citizen & Subject: Contemporary Africa and the Legacy of Late Colonialism* (Princeton University Press, 1996), pp. 56–57. More generally, Leigh Gardner, *Taxing Colonial Africa* (Oxford University Press, 2012).

[106] The curtailing of consumption was a major theme of wartime bond sales, but from my investigation it seems less prevalent in the 1960s. Summers, "Lending to the Empire."

[107] Jane Guyer, "Prophecy and the near Future: Thoughts on Macroeconomic, Evangelical, and Punctuated Time," *American Ethnologist* 34(3) (2007): 409–421.

Figure 2.2 Vans used for promoting and selling the Premium Development Bonds around the country.
Courtesy of the Uganda Broadcasting Corporation.

Throughout the mid-1960s, government officials toured the country speaking to audiences about the importance of aggregating "the small money saved by people within the country," thus turning private income into public revenue (see Figure 2.2).[108] In their speeches and radio addresses, they told the citizenry of a new means to do so – the Premium Development Bond. First issued in August 1964 and then with a second phase starting in August 1965, this scheme invited Ugandans to buy financial instruments whose proceeds would be used for public services. As the Minister of Finance put it in a December 1964 interview, Uganda had no shortage of needs. "We need more money than ever before," he explained:

in the field of education more schools are needed, in the field of health more dispensaries and hospitals will have to be provided, and in the field of

[108] JDA Finance 20/11: Speech on the Promotion of the Sale of Uganda Premium Development Bonds, n.d. [but 1965].

2.3 Remaking Money after Empire

agriculture improved agricultural methods through mechanization and better crop husbandry. In the field of commerce and industry, the creation of more employment and in the field of housing the erection of more dwelling housing.[109]

The development bonds responded to a considerable government deficit in 1964–1965, which Jack Ssentongo thought required additional short-term borrowing and taxation were they to avoid "running down" the country's foreign reserves.[110]

Sold at relatively affordable denominations – as little as five shillings each – the Bonds were aimed at a mass public who would benefit from turning their cash into bonds. In some cases, they were explicitly framed as a means to boost savings, yet their promotion also involved other registers. For one thing, the Bonds were also lottery tickets. Purchasers were not only promised the return of their principal in five years; they would also qualify for cash awards between one hundred and fifty thousand shillings at drawings held a few months later.[111] "The more Bonds you buy, the more chances of winning a prize you stand," crowed the District Commissioner for Toro.[112] In the first year of sales, flyers trumpeted 10 percent interest received by bondholders as "profit" – "DO NOT WAIT. BUY YOUR BONDS NOW." In doing so, the government tried to form a constellation of interests: "Whoever buys a Bond assists development of his country."

Assembling such a collectivity required a range of efforts, from novel infrastructures to accounting standards and even public dances. The central government established district-level quotas for sales – 45,000 for Toro, 110,000 for more prosperous Busoga, and a mere 10,000 for marginalized Karamoja – and local committees of government and merchants formed to manage the process.[113] Numerous citizens

---

[109] KDA 788: Premium Development Bond interview on Uganda Television with the Minister of Finance, December 9, 1964.
[110] BoE OV7/86: "A Case," by A. J. P. M. Ssentongo, September 18, 1964.
[111] While the first bond issue paid an interest rate over the course of its maturity, the second repaid only the principal. It sought to make up for this shortfall through "much larger prizes." KDA 743/1: Premium Development Bonds, March 29, 1966.
[112] KDA 743/1: Premium Development Bonds, March 29, 1966.
[113] KDA 788/1: Minutes of the Toro Kingdom Ad Hoc Co-ordinating Committee for Promotion of Premium Development Bonds Sales, January 7, 1965; KDA 788: Premium Development Bonds Second Issue, Administrative and Accounting Arrangements.

volunteered to become salespeople, recruited by the promise of a 5 percent commission and contribution to the nation. For their part, salespeople were proud of "campaign[ing] very hard using good language to convince the buyers."[114] Even unlikely participants tried to become involved, such as a hotel on Lake Katwe that admitted "Trade is very erratic here, and we do not anticipate selling very many Bonds, but we feel 'every little [bit] helps!'"[115]

Vans toured the country with loudspeakers, promotional films, and local and national dignitaries to align the personal and the national. Newspapers and radio heralded the bonds, and after successful events in Arua and Toro, evening socials were held across the country. In Fort Portal, the band from Kilembe copper mines volunteered their performances for a dance that was free to all who purchased a five-shilling Premium Development Bond. "Dance! Dance! Dance!," extolled promotional posters. It "may win you a fortune of Shs. 50,000 and help the development of our country." Counties were encouraged to compete, with an ornamental shield promised to the best performer.[116]

The economic patriotism of buying into the Bond – stressing "the need of unity to nation-building" – was always nestled next to the potential profit for purchasers.[117] Sometimes the collective good was given priority to individual reward, as when schoolteachers were told that the "great privilege" of helping "the development of your country" should be the primary aim – getting a prize the second. But in much of the promotion and design of the initiative, little was asked of citizens. As the Minister of Finance declared, "the money you and I invest in buying Bonds is not lost" since it will eventually be returned. Indeed, what distinguished this sort of economic nationalism was the promise of personal benefit.

Although some Ugandans had experience with wartime bonds, it was largely an unfamiliar form of value.[118] To ameliorate any confusion, the state undertook an education campaign that depicted bonds as money-like. Because they were "bearer bonds" – meaning whoever held the bond could redeem it – and because the physical certificate needed to be presented to claim a prize or receive repayment in five

---

[114] KDA 788: A.O. Owana to District Commissioner, Toro, July 30, 1965.
[115] KDA 743/1: [illegible] to Premium Development Bond Officer, June 5, 1966.
[116] KDA 788/1: Premium Development Bonds, September 30, 1965.
[117] KDA 743/1: Minutes of the 1st Meeting of the Sebei District Ad Hoc Committee, March 25, 1966.
[118] Summers found similar themes of patriotism in "Lending to the Empire."

2.3 Remaking Money after Empire

years, "holders should look after their Bonds just as carefully as they do their money." Banks were the best place for storing such tokens of value, but for those in rural areas, "a tin in a place safe from fire or theft" – next to their birth certificates, tax tickets and other important papers – was suitable. Yet in other ways, bonds were *not* akin to currency. They were not, for instance, to be used to purchase goods because bonds were "money saved," not "ordinary cash."[119] In other words, bonds lacked the immediacy of currency, yet they shared its physical vulnerability. Loss of bonds did occur, as when four were accidentally washed in a shirt pocket, necessitating their replacement. In many more cases, it is likely bonds went unredeemed – subtly turning a citizen's investment into a gift to the state.

From media coverage of lottery winners to dances and door-to-door appeals, the atmospherics of the development bonds were enthusiastic and meant to build a sense of momentum. One survey of nearly 2,000 Ugandans in 1966–1967 found one-quarter of respondents held a PDB, but from the perspective of government, willing buyers could be hard to find.[120] Seven months into the first sales period, Busoga sold only a quarter of its target. Three-quarters of the sales had gone to two large commercial concerns (the Madhvani Group and the Busoga Growers Co-operative Union), meaning they had only "managed to collect" Shs. 17,000 from individuals. "It is obviously nothing compared to the target," the District Commissioner lamented, before telling county chiefs to visit their local marketplaces "where, I am assuredly informed, there are good prospects for the Bonds."[121] When bond promotion committee members missed a meeting in Toro, they were upbraided for their "lack of interest in the responsibility which has been put to you to shoulder."[122] If the public failed to purchase all of an area's quota, the fault lay with the committee members. "From experience," wrote A. O. Owana, the lead organizer

---

[119] KDA 788: Questions Raised with the Minister of Finance, November/December 1964.

[120] Gunther Huber, "Private Savings in Uganda," in Peter Marlin (ed.), *Financial Aspects of Development in East Africa* (Weltforum Verlag, 1970), pp. 94–111.

[121] "Remember," he continued, "this is a national scheme, intended for tapping and pulling together the local resources to be utilized for economic and social development – i.e., for the benefits of the people of Uganda." JDA Finance 20/11: DC Busoga to Chiefs and Bond Sellers, March 5, 1965.

[122] KDA 788: Toro Kingdom Committee for Promotion of Premium Development Bonds Sales, February 8, 1965.

in Toro, "I know that many people would buy the bonds but they are ignorant of what they would expect to get when they have bought them, therefore very wide publicity is very necessary."[123]

The publicity and outreach also dramatized the differentiation among Uganda's citizens. Some populations were more likely contributors to the national good, such as civil servants or agricultural laborers who earned a wage.[124] Asian industrialists may have been inclined to buy them to demonstrate their worth to the nation.[125] Headmasters and school staff in Toro were asked to put aside ten shillings of their monthly salary to buy bonds until the district reached its target.[126] Residents of the country's rural areas were not ignored; indeed, there was considerable expectation that their domestic wealth could be transformed into national resources. The District Commissioner for Toro proudly spoke of the contributions rural areas made to enabling his jurisdiction to exceed its phase one target by Shs. 24,000. To do so, they worked through the administrative structures of indirect rule – with chiefs rousing purchases – and frequent circuits from "Bond Vans on safaris" that attracted a crowd and spread the word through recorded speeches in English, Luganda, and other languages.[127] Yet, reaching rural areas profitably was difficult; petrol and manpower were spent touring the countryside, sometimes without any sales to show for it. In November 1965, the Office of the Prime Minister expressed alarm that many government tours made mileage and expense "claims [that] are far in excess of any profits that will accrue from the sale of Bonds in that area."[128] Over time, the lagging sales reflected an inability or unwillingness of Ugandans to purchase bonds – ultimately a sign of their divergent priorities and values.

"Mobilizing Savings" from Obote to Amin

Bringing diverse forms of value under the control of the state, I have suggested, was a pressing concern for postcolonial Uganda. Whether

---

[123] KDA 788: Sale of Uganda Premium Development Bonds, January 22, 1965.
[124] KDA 743/1: Special Premium Development Bond Drive, March 12, 1966.
[125] I'm grateful to Justin Willis for this point.
[126] KDA 788: Uganda Premium Development Bonds, October 28, 1965.
[127] JDA Finance 20/11: DC Busoga to Premium Development Bonds Officer, February 23, 1965.
[128] KDA 788: F.J.E. Rodrigues, Premium Development Bonds, November 17, 1965.

10 percent of a teacher's salary, proceeds from a smallholder's coffee crop, or myriad other forms of productivity, the state aimed to translate forms of value into ones that could be directed and governed to its own ends. Central to the efforts of "mobilizing savings" in post-independence Uganda were institutions like the Post Office Savings Bank (inherited from the colonial administration) and the Uganda Commercial Bank (founded in 1965).[129] These institutions were part of an ambitious effort to turn the wealth of Ugandans into the financing of national development. The 1966 five-year plan called for £140–150 million to be invested from increased domestic savings. While the IMF deemed this unlikely, there was cause for optimism as the Bank of Uganda reported "a steady increase in saving deposits which, apart from being most encouraging, could suggest a growing spread among the public of the banking habit."[130] Within four years of opening, UCB deposits had increased by more than 50 percent, lending followed suit, and in 1970, it made a net profit of USh. 3.2 million.[131] The red account book where deposits and withdrawals were recorded became for many banking customers a prestige object.[132]

The effort to cultivate this "banking habit" was financial, technical, institutional, and cultural. It required enrolling the public in a new system of distributing and evaluating worth. By moving the private hoards of personal savings into a banking system and then leveraging them to make loans, proponents aimed to gather and shift wealth into activities they deemed more desirable. Moreover, they understood this task as reforming citizens, turning them into contributors to a collective good through the transformation of their habits and ideas. District officers were to spread word about the safety of bank accounts and the benefits of earning interest to "people who keep their money in boxes, etc. in their houses and *shambas*" [i.e., farms].[133] For businesspeople,

---

[129] BoU G.56.70, GOV.806.4 Post Office Savings Bank, 1967–1970. Oral Evidence of Joseph Mubiru, July 18, 1967.

[130] BoU CON.IMF, EAC.601.4: IMF: Uganda Part 1: Staff Report and Recommendations: 1965 Article XIV Consultations, July 6, 1965; BOU GOV.305.1: Second Annual Report, 1967/68, draft.

[131] *Background to the Budget, 1970–71* (Ministry of Planning and Economic Development, 1970).

[132] Though displaying it too proudly could attract unwelcome financial requests from family. Huber, "Private Savings," p. 151.

[133] JDA Finance 43/4: Currency, 1966–1979. Joseph Mubiru, Conversion of East African Currency Board Coins, November 22, 1968.

banking was said to serve as a window into one's success and virtue. As one official enthused,

> Every single penny used for business, you must bank it. Even if you want it that very day, you bank it first, and then draw it out. Because when you go into the Bank, the Manager can look at your sheet, and sees that you bank so much every day, and he must therefore think that you are doing good business, and that he does not use this money for drinking purposes, not connected with business purposes.[134]

Indeed, safely away from temptation, banking could produce moral rectitude, not merely reveal it.

The paradox of financial intermediation – where savings are personally owned while simultaneously distributed to others – could generate confusion. The Governor of the Bank of Uganda, Joseph Mubiru, worried that the public thought the purpose of the Post Office Savings Bank was merely to provide safe custody of their money. In contrast, he saw it as an instrument for encouraging "thrift" and turning savings into investment. If the task was merely safeguarding from theft or damage, citizen-savers would be unlikely to appreciate the full importance of banking. As he put it, they must understand that banks help the country "deal with the problem of encouraging the small man to save his current earnings for his future but also for the overall well-being of the economy."[135] As a technology of the self, banking promised to reform colonialism's subjects into a horizontally affiliated and vertically governed collective – citizens of Uganda.

Mobilizing savings, in other words, was a scalar technique for producing both a future and a collective. The Post Office Savings Bank (POSB) was considered particularly well suited for the effort because, in contrast to full-service banks, it could inexpensively extend into rural areas, where most of the population lived, and "mop up savings for development purposes." Drawing on an existing network of post offices (rather than new bank branches with qualified professionals), the POSB was staffed by village postmasters who used a simplified accounting technique.[136] They also relied on prior

---

[134] KDA 612/2 Hon. W.W. Kalema's Tour of the Western Region, January 22, 1970.
[135] BoU G.56.70, GOV.806.4: Oral Evidence of Mubiru, July 18, 1967.
[136] By the end of 1967, it had 175,000 accounts managed at 700 branches, though banks were out-competing the POSB in some ways. Huber, "Private Savings."

2.3 Remaking Money after Empire

familiarity with customers to lower the risk of fraud. Building on local social relations allowed this capillary network an opportunity for far greater "accumulation of savings in the country."[137] But to do so, it limited the liquidity of savers, forbidding more than one withdrawal a week and requiring notice for any withdrawal of more than 200 shillings.[138] Such a temporal regime ensured the state's ability to project its fiscus across time at the expense of individuals' financial flexibility. It also meant that cash in hand was a materially different sort of money than bank deposits.

For its part, the Uganda Commercial Bank (UCB) pursued an ambitious expansion in the years after its founding. In 1960, there were 15 towns with banking services, and by the end of the decade, there were 123 banking offices in 66 locations plus mobile vans periodically visiting more remote locales. Political independence – and the regulatory latitude it offered – was crucial for convincing expatriate banks that if they "did not make it clear that they have something to offer of benefit to the local population," they would find themselves unwelcome in Uganda.[139] The competition from the UCB also spurred them to action, including driving a 178 percent increase of all banking facilities over the course of the 1960s.[140] In the financial year ending September 1969, the UCB's deposits grew by 40 percent, and the expected takeover of parastatal government accounts (from National & Grindlays) bank would further buoy the UCB.[141]

As the economy stumbled in the 1970s, the importance of centralizing value only increased. After Idi Amin's coup in 1971, banking continued to be an important infrastructure of statecraft. No longer would government neglect the "masses of the people" in favor of "a few progressive farmers." Instead, of "growing paper in the offices," government would help "the people to grow crops in the field," he

---

[137] BoU G.56.70, GOV.806.4: Oral Evidence of Mubiru, July 18, 1967.
[138] JDA Agriculture 17/8: Post Office Savings Bank Account, 1964–1968: Ministry of Works, Communication & Housing to D.C. Busoga, June 7, 1967.
[139] BoE OV75/9: "The Banking System and Regulation of Liquidity in Uganda," by G. Durin, 1972.
[140] Gershenberg, "Banking in Uganda," p. 509.
[141] BoE OV75/7: "Visit to Mauritius, Tanzania, and Uganda," February 1969. In the view of Barclays, Uganda was "heavily banked." DCO 29/443: "Uganda Section Branch," March 31, 1968.

promised.[142] Keen to position himself as a reliable steward of the nation and its African population, Amin spoke of judging each application for a loan "strictly on its merits." He contrasted this with prior days when Asians could access finance that should properly have gone to indigenous Africans. It is "repugnant," he said, in a December 1972 radio broadcast, that less than 1 percent of the population borrows "over 90 percent of the savings of our people."[143] His government would lend not only to the "well known or successful."[144] It would also avail credit to "marginal borrowers," which it defined as businessmen "with neither sufficient security nor previously ascertainable business experience" including those who would "make some rapid expansion of business."[145] The premise was a sort of financial populism, where credit linked the masses to the state and its charismatic boss in return for their loyal production.[146]

For the government, bank branches were a prominent display of their much-touted effort to "take services to the people."[147] At the UCB, the 1970s witnessed a flurry of new banking outreach as the map of Uganda was dotted with more parastatal banking entities. A 1974 plan to open twenty-eight sub-branches was aimed at both facilitating banking for government offices and "the people at large."[148] To do so, the UCB relied on a nested hierarchy of banking infrastructure, with full branches in major centers, sub-branches and agencies in smaller towns, and circulating vans providing intermittent service to more remote locales. Such a variegation reflected and reproduced the uneven development of the territory, with the infrastructurally dense and

---

[142] "Opening of the Uganda Farmers' Forum, 1 July 1971," in *Speeches by His Excellency the President, General Idi Amin Dada* (The Republic of Uganda).

[143] *Uganda's Economic War* (Ministry of Information and Broadcasting, 1975, p. 26.

[144] BoE OV75/11: British High Commission, Kampala, November 13, 1972.

[145] BoE OV75/11: Uganda Development Bank, November 15, 1972.

[146] My thinking on financial populism is informed by James C. Mizes, "Investing in Independence: Popular Shareholding on the West African Stock Exchange," *Africa* 92(4) (2022): 644–662.

[147] BoU GOV.122.6.H: A.C.K. Oboth-Ofumbi to Governor Bank of Uganda, August 28, 1975.

[148] Between 1973–1978, UCB was led by Henry Kajura, an early position in his long career. BoU GOV.122.6.H: Kajura to Minister of Finance, September 20, 1974.

2.3 Remaking Money after Empire

export-oriented South predominating over the arid labor reserves of the North.[149]

For those involved, the virtues of expansion were multiple. Often, the idea was to follow signs of untapped or increasing economic activity. Places like Mpondwe, a rich agricultural area in Bukonjo sub-district, were quickly approved for mobile banking service; situated near the Uganda–Zaire border, northwest of Katwe township, the area's 3,000 taxpayers, agricultural cooperatives, and repair shops for bicycles and radios marked it as an area in which value could be captured and redeployed by the banking system.[150] In fact, noted the Bank of Uganda report on the subject, the area was bigger and richer than many areas where the UCB already had services.[151] Other areas were considered well suited for expanded banking due to their agricultural activities, government offices, or educational institutions (where teachers drew regular salaries).

Yet banking was likewise a political affair. Idi Amin – whose charisma was projected by an elaborate media performance – used branch openings in Mbarara and elsewhere as opportunities to stage his munificence and technocratic credentials.[152] In 1975, Bank of Uganda officials studied the feasibility of opening a UCB branch in Bombo, a town north of Kampala. On "purely economic considerations," they reasoned, neither a branch nor sub-branch was viable. Economic activities in the town had remained the same since 1970, with only around eighty shops and three petrol stations (mostly catering to travelers on the country's main north-south road). Before it closed, the former Barclays agency in the area lost Shs. 61,000 in 1969. Given the "financial and administrative problems" at the UCB, it was inadvisable to open a loss-making branch, particularly when a sub-branch had just been opened ten miles north, in Wobulenzi. Instead, the regulators thought Libyan Arab Uganda Bank, a joint operation between the two governments that had no loss-making

---

[149] BoU 0, GOV.305.3: Bank of Uganda: Currency Issues and Operations During the First 10 Years by B.M. Kume.
[150] BoU GOV.122.6.H: Minister Oboth-Ofumbi to Governor, May 17, 1976.
[151] BoU GOV.122.6.H: Kigangari to Director of Bank Supervision, April 26, 1976.
[152] JDA Finance 20/9: Uganda Commercial Bank Annual Report, 1970–1971. On Amin's use of media, Richard Vokes, Derek R. Peterson, and Edgar C. Taylor, "Photography, Evidence and Concealed Histories from Idi Amin's Uganda, 1971–79," *History of Photography* 44(2–3) (2020): 151–171.

branches, should be encouraged to open there.[153] Nevertheless, Minister Oboth-Ofumbi thought not having the UCB serve the location "might be politically unwise" because the Libyan Arab Uganda Bank was "foreign."[154] Idi Amin, too, weighed in on the Bombo banking situation in a visit to an Army barracks there, stating "every Provincial headquarters should have full-time banking facilities," yet Bombo was the only one without such facilities."[155]

There was vocal demand for banking, with citizens speaking on behalf of the nation. Keesi K. Kyaligonza Adyeeri, for instance, petitioned for a new bank in Fort Portal, where he served as manager of the Uganda Bookshop. It was for "the toiling peasants and developing farmers" that he wished for an extension of the Cooperative Bank.[156] The demand for banking was all the more concerted when fuel and spare part shortages immobilized the vans used to visit rural towns. Traders in Jinja lacked working capital; they wrote to Amin asking that the limit on UCB overdrafts be raised "in light of the present prices of commodities which have gone up more than ten times."[157] Citizen complaints were often funneled through official channels, where government officers justified their locality's importance. Semuliki – a region whose mountainous terrain provides some of Uganda's best coffee – found its geography all the more isolating as banking vans failed to make their way there by the late 1970s.[158]

Throughout the 1970s, officials in Kakumiro maintained a steady stream of complaints, petitions, and inquiries to the Uganda Commercial Bank. The nearest bank branches were 60 miles away, necessitating the movement of "unbelievable sums of money" without proper security. Local government reported "anxiety both in the business world and in the official circles," leading to "the notorious

---

[153] BoU GOV.122.6.H: Director of Bank Supervision to Governor. Bombo Banking Facilities, July 9, 1975.
[154] BoU GOV.122.6.H: Minister Oboth-Ofumbi to Governor. Uganda Commercial Bank Agency at Bombo, May 25, 1976.
[155] BoU GOV.122.6.H: Kajura to Governor. Opening of Sub-Branch at Bombo, May 13, 1975.
[156] KDA 743/2: Suggestion for Opening of a New Bank Branch in Fort Portal, October 23, 1978.
[157] JDA Trade & Industry 23/3: Traders' Memorandum submitted to His Excellency Amin on Commercial and Related Economic Activities in Uganda, n.d. [but 1976–1977].
[158] KDA 864/1: Banking Services for Semuliki District, November 14, 1977.

2.3 Remaking Money after Empire 131

question that I face almost daily: 'when is the bank coming?'"[159] Appeals took on a variety of tones. George Enach-Ongom explained that their "very rich agricultural land" was home to some of the biggest coffee works and cotton ginneries in the whole country, with plenty of commercial – rather than merely subsistence – productivity. "All these farmers are your potential customers," he wrote, appealing to the bank's bottom line. Without banking, they were forced to "hoard money in pots in their houses, at risk of being burnt or eaten by rats and ants." Moreover, such an immobilization of savings contravened government policy which relied on banks to aggregate and redistribute savings. The UCB, he reminded the management, is a "public corporation," with obligation beyond profit. Kakumiro's local government was exposed to "great risks" from robbery and embezzlement, as taxes, school fees, and agricultural payments were left without a bank. If this were not profitable, so be it: "humanitarian considerations may prevail over profit motives."[160]

Two years later, when Kakumiro's pleas were met by the opening of a new UCB branch, it prompted a visit by the Minister of Finance and a public ceremony of dancers and revelry. Even the *prospect* of a permanent UCB branch in nearby Kagadi could occasion popular performances of economic nationalism. At an exploratory visit in 1977 by the UCB's J. M. Kasobya, "people started opening up accounts to show the support they had for the Bank and contributed more than 50,000 in spite of the fact that it had not been known that collections could be accepted" at the meeting. Evidently impressed, the banker noted that "almost anything can grow here" before listing "outstanding progressive farmers" and other entities that would be likely customers. On its present merits, Kagadi branch would be an "undoubted" success, but he reported to superiors its promise was even greater "projecting into the future" when Kagadi would likely become a district headquarters.[161]

For citizens and bureaucrats, banking was an infrastructure to enable personal and collective advance. In many instances, this rehearsed a productivism where agricultural and commercial output

---

[159] KDA 864: Uganda Commercial Bank Branch at Kakumiro, September 1, 1977.
[160] KDA 864: Opening of Uganda Commercial Bank Branch in Kakumiro, September 6, 1976.
[161] KDA 864: Report on Kagadi Uganda Commercial Bank Proposed Branch, July 19, 1977.

was the shared virtue. In such a political culture, it was those who could claim to earn export value who had the most purchase on public prestige. Others – including Ugandans lacking in fertile land or producing less valuable goods – were decidedly marginalized. Women usually had accessory roles, not least because export crops were routed through masculine regimes of control: cotton gins or coffee curing works were populated by men, and cash income was susceptible to male control. In some ways, the era did provide new opportunities for women. The Asian expulsion and economic decline provided some women an opportunity to "step out of the domestic sphere and into the informal labor market."[162] Yet, as Alicia Decker argues, this was at most a partial incorporation into the circuits of value governance, and the women who populated urban economies – renting homes, brewing beer, selling vegetables – received little in the way of state regard, let alone assistance. Women's footholds remained thin and dependent upon economic activity of tenuous viability. Those who could not maintain it suffered even further iniquity.

The productivism at the heart of credible citizenship limited the universalism of notions like "the social" or "the public." Even "citizenship" was stratified as it was subjugated to economic concerns. Despite its considerable expansion from colonial days, the banking system reflected this inequality, remaining concentrated in a small geography. A 1972 Bank of Uganda study found 72 percent of bank deposits and 80 percent of loans and advances were in the four districts of East Mengo, West Mengo, Mubende, and Busoga. Other districts served as sources of funds for the more-privileged geographies: Kigezi was perhaps the most stark, with eight times as many deposits collected as loans made, but it was also a problem for Toro, Ankole, Acholi, West Nile, and Bunyoro.[163] It seemed, in other words, "that the banking system operates to pump money from poorer countries into the most developed parts of Uganda adding to the processes of concentration."[164] While men like George Enach-Ongom, as mentioned earlier, might insist that a

---

[162] Alicia Decker, "An Accidental Liberation: Ugandan Women on the Front Lines in Idi Amin's Economic War," *Women's History Review* 22(65) (2013): 954–970.

[163] In part because they were better served by mobile banks that accepted deposits but did not issue loans.

[164] BoE OV75/9: "The Banking System and Regulation of Liquidity in Uganda," by G. Durin, 1972.

"public corporation" and "humanitarian considerations" must countervail against the imperative of profitable production, these were ultimately less-effective registers of political appeal in postcolonial Uganda, offering a muted egalitarianism at best.[165]

2.4 Governing the Frontiers of Value

It was not only the imperative to produce and earn that shaped sovereignty and citizenship in the postcolony. They were also implicated by the protocols and policing of the moneychanger state. Governor Joseph Mubiru spoke of using "every conceivable device – persuading, cajoling, inciting people, edging the economy a little in this direction, now a shade in that."[166] But sometimes monetary sovereignty required a firmer hand, and when the Bank of Uganda began issuing a national currency, it was obliged to also police the proper use of that money. It did so because the consolidation of value within the state's infrastructures was only possible and meaningful if it did not slip out the country.

Beginning in 1966, the Bank of Uganda became an important means of increasing the amount of foreign exchange the country earned (largely through agricultural output). If the currency earned through cotton, coffee, and other exports was spent beyond its borders, Uganda would be unable to maintain its economic sovereignty. At the moment the Bank of Uganda was established, the country was facing particularly severe pressure on its foreign reserves. Some of this was purchasing imports, but much of it was money moved to Kenya in expectation that the Kenya shilling would prove a more durable store of value. Defensive measures to undo the drain of money were necessary, leading the government to install import licenses, credit controls, and eventually currency controls.[167] Marketing boards were the principal instrument for earning foreign exchange, while a suite of other techniques from the Bank of Uganda – including exchange controls, import licensing, and credit restrictions – were the core repertoire for

---

[165] KDA 864: Opening of Uganda Commercial Bank Branch in Kakumiro, September 6, 1976.
[166] BoU GOV.807.1: Joseph Mubiru, "Central banking with special reference to developing countries," n.d. [but late-1960s].
[167] BoE OV75/3: Commonwealth Office to British High Commission, August 11, 1966.

preserving it within the country. These could be introduced as permanent or temporary measures, but over the course of the decade and a half after the Bank of Uganda's start, they expanded considerably. For instance, while the three countries initially maintained free convertibility between the new currencies, in 1970, restrictions were placed on the conversion between Kenyan, Ugandan, and Tanzanian shillings.

In their design and implementation, such procedures sought to remake economic relations and the worth assigned to goods. The suite of monetary controls were formally distinct, but in practice, they overlapped and entwined to govern value in the country's jurisdiction.[168] They worked to limit the acquisition of resources, whether from a speculative future (in the case of credit restrictions) or abroad (in the case of exchange controls and import licenses). Converting wealth away from forms likely to circulate internationally (such as gold) into forms that could be corralled for state purposes (principally Ugandan shillings) helped Ugandan monetary authorities govern value across the territory.[169]

It was not merely the ability to pay that served as the means of ranking people and determining access to commodities; rather, the monetary regulations inherited and expanded by independent Uganda prioritized economic activity according to the logic of postcolonial developmentalism. Imports were categorized and ranked according to their expected contribution to economic production, particularly in export-oriented sectors or where they might substitute for imported goods. Citizens were similarly stratified according to the purpose of their applications: for example, in the context of severe scarcity, foreign exchange to fund education abroad was constricted in favor of the purchase of spare machine parts. By the 1970s, imports deemed to be luxuries were to receive limited or no credit from banks and few licenses from government, with the government overwhelmingly focused on securing the so-called essential commodities.[170] In other

---

[168] See the discussion in Mutibwa, *Bank of Uganda*, pp. 159ff.

[169] BoU GOV.807.1: Record of Meeting Between Minister of Finance and the Governor, December 11, 1970.

[170] A topic discussed at length in Chapter 4. For context, see Alicia Decker, "Idi Amin's Dirty War: Subversion, Sabotage, and the Battle to Keep Uganda Clean, 1971–1979," *International Journal of African Historical Studies* 43(3) (2010): 489–513; Richard Reid, *A History of Modern Uganda* (Cambridge University Press, 2017), pp. 216–238.

2.4 Governing the Frontiers of Value 135

words, one's standing as a citizen was refracted through international monetary imperatives.

Race and the Enforcement of Monetary Citizenship

The requirement to seek government approval for access to foreign money had surprisingly wide reaches, affecting ordinary people and often serving as a key interface for Ugandans to engage the state. Currency controls inclined the government to adopt a suspicious stance toward extraterritorial mobility. The Ugandan state did not fully ban foreign travel, so it was obliged to mediate between different value jurisdictions. As a result, the controlled conversion between national and foreign monies was also a key means for the racialization of citizenship in Uganda, most notably through the 1972 expulsion of Asian residents. Long suspected of earning money at the expense of Africans only to export it abroad, Asian merchants were the subject of popular resentment and rebuke across the postwar decades.[171] As the independent state encouraged the "Africanization" of the economy – revoking trade licenses, redirecting credit, and curtailing legal recognitions – the pressures only increased.[172] Among other commercial "sabotage," Idi Amin condemned "The Asians [because they] never gave loans to the farmers" of Uganda.[173] His "Economic War" claimed to put the economy into the hands of "true black Ugandans," but it was part of a longer history of racial capitalism shaping the unequal distribution of resources and political responses.[174]

Rather than any careful accounting, these bureaucratic and popular misgivings often worked through a combination of indistinct ideas and emblematic examples: while little was objectively known about the extent of exported wealth, iconic incidences came to stand for more general assumptions. For instance, in 1969, Uganda's monetary

---

[171] Edgar Curtis Taylor, "Asians and Africans in Ugandan Urban Life, 1959–1972," PhD dissertation, University of Michigan, 2016.
[172] Edgar Taylor, "Claiming Kabale: Racial Thought and Urban Governance in Uganda," *Journal of Eastern African Studies* 7(1) (2013): 143–163; Anneeth Kaur Hundle, "1970s Uganda: Past, Present, Future," *Journal of Asian and African Studies* 53(3) (2018): 455–475.
[173] "Speech at Uganda Farmers' Forum," in *Speeches* (Republic of Uganda, 1973).
[174] BoE OV75/12: "Uganda – The Economic War," March 7, 1973. On the economic war, see Decker, "An Accidental Liberation"; Derek Peterson, "Government Work in Idi Amin's Uganda," *Africa* 91(4) (2021): 620–640.

regulators were worried to learn of an "Asian by the name of Shah" who was refused entry to London at the discovery he had "a big heap of East African currency notes." The notes were in various denominations, hidden under a false bottom in his suitcase. It was only by "sheer coincidence" that this was found because the customs authorities thought he might be trafficking drugs. Denied his English sojourn, Mr. Shah was put on a plane back to Nairobi, only to abscond to India during a layover in Cairo, leaving his suitcase of money behind. In all, the seized money came to KSh. 156,600, TSh. 59,600, USh. 58,900, more than US $3,000, 20 Deutsche Marks, 50 Swiss francs, and £214 sterling in travelers cheques plus £60 sterling in notes. Mr. Shah was Kenyan, but this did not stop the Ugandan Embassy in Cairo writing to Kampala to note their concern that Uganda was likely losing a lot of "money through Asians and other non-citizens." This was probably accelerating as Uganda's Trade Licensing Act tried to transfer businesses from Asian to African traders. A more thorough inspection of Asian travelers should therefore be initiated.[175] The lack of specifics – from the suspect's full name to his rationale and source of funds – were not the cause for caution, but rather an impetus for further surveillance and policing.

Many of the general assumptions about race and mobility pivoted on ideas about Asian families and loyalties. Kinship and commerce were fused and strung across borders, from upcountry Uganda to Nairobi and across the Indian Ocean.[176] In the view of their critics, Asian economic returns circulated both too narrowly and too widely. They were too narrow because profits remained within racial, even familial circuits.[177] Writing to Idi Amin days after the initial expulsion order, the self-described "Natives of the Land, Ugandan Traders of

---

[175] BoU O.Gov.801.10: Embassy of Uganda to Secretary of Treasury, November 21, 1969.

[176] In a large literature, see Gijsbert Oonk, *Settled Strangers: Asian Business Elites in East Africa, 1800–2000* (SAGE, 2013); Gaurav Desai, *Commerce with the Universe: Africa, India, and the Afrasian Imagination* (Columbia University Press, 2016); Robert Gregory, *South Asians in East Africa: An Economic and Social History 1890–1980* (Westview Press, 1993).

[177] Amin made his frustrations about sexual and kinship norms explicit at a gathering of Asian elders in December 1971, telling them "African males have hardly been able to marry Asian girls" while "Asian men in this country are loving and living with African girls without unfavourable pressure from the parents of these girls." *Uganda's Economic War* (Ministry of Information and Broadcasting, 1975), pp. 18.

2.4 Governing the Frontiers of Value

Busoga District" condemned their Asian competition. "They live together ... They play together ... They do not speak our languages." Deals were done only among "their own relatives (Indian for Indian) thus retaining the entire industry in one large or small family." The privacy of familial dealings furthered misgivings as family firms eluded government scrutiny – commerce hidden behind the veil of domesticity.

These exclusionary networks were also too expansive, escaping the borders of the country. "All these so-called citizens have a HOME elsewhere," but they remain in Uganda to receive their undue rewards. Even those who die in Uganda showed their alien allegiances by having their ashes returned "back home and not thrown in the River Nile."[178] For these petitioners, cross-border family business and the ritual performances that accompanied diasporic belonging were troublesome. Such improperly scaled networks – too circumscribed and too expansive at the same time – invalidated their standing as Ugandans. From the perspective of credible citizenship, Uganda's Asians failed to put their profitable productivity to a collective use; indeed, they were often defined outside the national collective at all. As a result, even those Asians who had legal Ugandan citizenship found themselves expelled under the demands of a racialized economic nationalism.

Given their subterranean nature, it is impossible to know the extent of cross-border financial flows; scholars who interviewed 1,250 expelled heads of household in late 1973 estimated that "almost one-third of the expellees had some money and/or property outside Uganda at the time of expulsion, though not all of this was necessarily sent from Uganda."[179] Uncertainty encouraged speculation from a few examples, often homogenizing Ugandan Asians as uniformly wealthy, despite the considerable number who lacked meaningful domestic, let alone foreign, savings. By May 1966, the Ministry of Finance was complaining that money continued to be exported, despite exchange controls against sterling, with Asians the assumed culprit.[180] A couple of years later, the amount of remittances legally permitted was reduced

---

[178] JDA Trade & Industry 14/25: The Natives of the Land, Ugandan Traders of Busoga District to Idi Amin, August 8, 1972.

[179] Bert Adams and Mike Bristow, "The Politico-Economic Position of Ugandan Asians in the Colonial and Independent Eras," *Journal of Asian and African Studies* 13(3–4) (1978): 156.

[180] *Background to the Budget, 1966–67* (Ministry of Finance, 1966).

to stop the export of money under false pretenses (such as paying for education abroad). Yet, efforts to control these networks routinely faltered: in 1970, the government worried that the ability to travel with gold jewelry presented a "big loophole" to foreign exchange controls as Asian families translated Ugandan currency into ornaments only to convert them back into dollars or sterling abroad.[181]

The expulsion in the final months of 1972 tried to end the international networks through which Asian wealth was generated and mobility enabled. The Bank of Uganda's infrastructure was crucial to the expropriation and dispossession of Asian families. The government controlled not only the official source of foreign currency but also required banks to freeze accounts held by Asians and transfer them to the UCB. In fact, amid the systematic and opportunistic violence, the Asian expulsion also unfolded through a more enumerative logic. Decree 27 of 1972 required the declaration of assets by non-citizen Asians.[182] "Every departing Asian," it declared using the standard euphemism of the time, "shall declare his assets and liabilities and supply such other particulars and information relating to his property or business, if any, to the Minister."[183] Those subject to the decree were obliged to provide company articles of association; copies of accounts for the previous two years; title deeds, debentures, loan agreements, and other contracts; and a written notice nominating someone to act as their agent in the sale of these assets.

The dutiful recording of such information on a suite of bureaucratic forms was necessary to qualify for an "emigration treatment," the legal allowance of foreign currency for the expelled. For example, when Jayantilal Mulji Lakhani sought to transfer money out of the country from his Barclays account in 1972, he was obliged to provide a pile of paperwork. The centerpiece of this submission, "The Declaration of Assets and Liabilities of Foreigners Leaving Uganda Permanently," recorded the identification details for him and his family, his British nationality, his life insurance plan, and a list of household assets (glassware, kitchenware, steelware, and blankets coming to around USh. 3,000). His flight details – down to the class of travel and the

---

[181] BoU GOV.807.1: Meetings between Minister and Governor, 1970–1972.
[182] BoE OV75/11: The Declaration of Assets (Non-Citizen Asians) Decree 1972.
[183] "Uganda: Presidential Decrees on the Expulsion of the Asians," *International Legal Materials* 11(6) (1972): 1388–1391.

2.4 Governing the Frontiers of Value

cost of the tickets – were provided, too. Another form, from the East African Income Tax Department, certified he owed no taxes.[184]

This itemization was repeated thousands of times, allowing the state to reckon with the value to be seized. Initial promises to compensate the expelled property owners in return for declaring their assets quickly failed to materialize.[185] Instead, what wealth was previously the subject of intrigue and speculation was exposed and expropriated. In return, expelled Asians were issued a paltry but necessary amount of foreign currency to permit them to establish themselves in a new monetary jurisdiction. Phares Mutibwa notes that the resulting queues outside the Bank of Uganda began forming at 3:00 a.m.[186]

Some sought to subvert the process through smuggled passports.[187] Others tried to exchange their currency for gold, valuable property, or financial securities they could use outside Uganda.[188] Mamdani reports some Asians bought air tickets "to go ten or twenty times around the world," planning to get a refund when they left Uganda. "As rumours in the city had it, three million shillings (approximately £175,000) worth of tickets had been sold in a week" before authorities intervened.[189] Expelled Asians drove as many as 1,000 vehicles across the borders in the confusion, sometimes with the help of Kenyans or forged documents.[190] But, ultimately, the majority of their wealth remained behind, in seized assets and bank accounts that could not be converted to more mobile forms of value. Officially, this was to contribute to the national wealth, boosting the resources available to

---

[184] BoU 1179, CUR.104.2: Foreign Exchange, BOU00054, Emigration Treatment of Jayantilal Mulji Lakhani, September 1972.

[185] By the start of 1973, the government of Uganda referred to Asians "handing over" their businesses, rather than buying them. BoE OV75/12: "Uganda," January 4, 1973. By the end of 1973, Asian refugees in the UK registered assets worth £113 million with the Foreign and Commonwealth Office (though government recognized the incentive was to inflate such claims). Uganda's foreign reserves were perhaps £7–8 million total but under £1 million when short-term debts to the IMF were included in the calculation. They could, in other words, little afford to compensate the expelled Asians. BoE OV75/12: "Uganda," December 19, 1973.

[186] Mutibwa, *Bank of Uganda*, p. 264.

[187] BoU G.151.77. GOV.224: P. Wanyama, Special Branch Officer to Minister of Finance, May 19, 1975.

[188] BoU: Report on Operations of the Exchange Control Department for the Financial Year 1972/73.

[189] Mamdani, *From Citizen to Refugee*, pp. 20–21.

[190] BoU: Internal Auditor to Governor, January 20, 1973.

the state and autochthonous entrepreneurs. In reality, as Chapter 4 discusses further, state stewardship fell far short of collective purpose.

The Criminalization of Regional Transactional Geographies

While the Asian expulsion was a calamitous exercise of state violence, it took place as part of a wider effort that tried to change how value was governed. Two years earlier, thousands of Kenyan migrant workers were expelled by the Obote government.[191] In the final months of 1972, British businesses, too, were targeted, with some trade licenses not renewed and others expropriated. These included large firms like British American Tobacco, a host of tea growing estates, and smaller proprietors.[192] In December 1972, affected businesses were required to transfer their assets to the Uganda Commercial Bank, with strict rules limiting the export of capital.[193] Many other Ugandans were frustrated by currency controls and the hierarchies of worth they represented.

If the apogee of monetary exclusion was the Asian expulsion, the dynamics of monetary enclosure were present in the lives of Ugandan Africans, as well. Like many employees of Kakira Sugar Works, Amafuku Alphonse had family ties to Kenya. When his brother fell chronically ill in Nairobi, Alphonse was in "a really threatening situation," facing repeated trips to Nairobi to assist and the potential costs of relocating the nine family members to Uganda. The clock was ticking: what savings his brother had were nearly depleted and the family was facing starvation. "With the most highest honour and respect," he wrote to the Governor of the Bank of Uganda requesting KSh. 8,000 to cover his costs while in Kenya.[194]

In other words, despite the territoriality of the currency, Uganda's residents did not live territorial lives alone. Nor did they envision their economic lives as tied uniquely to one nation-state. Their trajectories, families, and aspirations were strung across national borders, making

---

[191] Ali A. Mazrui, "Casualties of an Underdeveloped Class Structure: The Expulsion of Luo Workers and Asian Bourgeoisie from Uganda," in William Shack and Elliott Skinner (eds.), *Strangers in African Societies* (University of California Press, 1979), pp. 261–279.
[192] BoE OV75/12: Barber to Gordon, February 16, 1973.
[193] BoE OV75/11: Telegram from Kampala to London, December 18, 1972.
[194] JDA Trade & Industry 18/17: Amafuku Alphonse of Kakira Sugar Works to Bank of Uganda, November 1, 1978.

2.4 Governing the Frontiers of Value 141

the geography of their transactions regional in nature. This was true for putative sons of the soil and strangers alike, and all had to therefore engage the state in its moneychanger posture. Untold numbers of applications for foreign exchange were submitted to the Bank of Uganda. Few are individually of note: they are for Kenyan shillings to receive medical attention in Nairobi, or purchase spare parts, or attend a secretarial course. In other cases, they are for British sterling to buy machinery, or Sudanese pounds to return home after a career in Uganda, or US dollars to settle a brother's debts in Yemen.[195]

Wary of a precarious balance of payments, the Bank of Uganda often needed to decline applications it deemed inessential and found itself the object of popular discontent as a result.[196] In the years after 1966, the Bank of Uganda promulgated stricter foreign exchange rules. In the words of one observer in 1969, the three countries seemed determined to "each tread the path of autarchy."[197] In 1972, as the economy buckled under the pressure of the Asian expulsion, the Exchange Control Act further limited traders and expatriate use of foreign currency, requiring its surrender to government control.[198] The next year, the foreign reserve was so paltry that the government twice suspended foreign exchange allocations even when requests came from licensed importers.[199] The national accounts were only salvaged by the combination of low imports and record export earnings, thanks to high prices for coffee.[200]

Such levers were not always effective, but they did oblige Ugandans to work through the state's bureaucratic protocols, filling out the required forms in triplicate and attaching a passport photo. The pragmatics of currency controls also obliged relations of dependency and hierarchy. Those who could convince their District Commissioner to support their petition stood a better chance than those unattached to officialdom. When Mr. Wulusimbi, of Kampala, wrote to Amin's Private Secretary to complain about his failures to receive foreign

---

[195] See the collections in KDA 743/2: Banking; JDA Trade & Industry 10/18: Foreign Currency.
[196] BoU: 78th Meeting of the Board of Directors, June 28, 1974. See also KDA 864: Clearance for Obtaining Foreign Exchange, July 15, 1977.
[197] BoE OV75/7: Visit to Mauritius, Tanzania, and Uganda, February 1969.
[198] BoE OV75/11: Uganda Statutory Instruments Nos. 130, 131, 132 of 1972, November 13, 1972.
[199] BoE OV75/12: P.N.M. to Tomkins, "Uganda," December 19, 1973.
[200] BoE OV75/13: Uganda Annual Review for 1973, British High Commissioner at Kampala, January 22, 1974.

exchange, he demonstrated his patriotism by enclosing a pamphlet he wrote: "Why You and Me are a Ugandan Economic Warrior."[201] Such displays of virtue tried to persuade the moneychanger state. Recall Zerubaberi Were's self-fashioning as a "progressive farmer" heeding the call of the government to access foreign exchange. In another case, an application from a medical worker needing a spare vehicle part in order to transport patients to hospital received a handwritten endorsement: "This is a deserving case. I recommend that he be awarded 6,000."[202]

For many others less able to maneuver the regulatory complexities, access to signs of value that could circulate beyond the borders of Uganda was notoriously fraught. The litany of procedures delineated between types of applicants, purposes, and amounts permitted, but the detail was likely to overwhelm and confuse, rather than clarify.[203] All the petitioners had the equivalent amount of money in Ugandan shillings, but their ability to convert between monies was blocked without the support of the state. The County Chief of Mwenge, Edward Gumisiriza, explained the replacement vehicle parts he needed from Kenya would "get my vehicle ready and serve my fellow countrymen, thus moving and explaining the government policies more effectively."[204] After the mother of his child married another man, John Byenkya needed to visit Kenya to collect his five-year-old son from a grandmother who could not afford to look after him.[205] Ocaba Wiy also had a family distributed across borders, needing access to 5,000 Kenyan shillings in order to collect his child with a Kenyan woman who he met while at Makerere University in Kampala.[206] Delays were common, even in cases when formal approval was issued, and as I discuss in Chapter 4, the alternatives were criminalized markets for foreign money and goods.

A twofold move served to interrupt these lives: money became a necessary means to access desired goods, while simultaneously, money

---

[201] BoU: Walusimbi Unit and Housing Exchange to J.E. Ekochu, August 27, 1974.
[202] JDA Trade & Industry 18/8: Foreign Exchange 1979. Senior Medical Assistant to Director of Foreign Exchange, June 12, 1979.
[203] See discussion in BoU GOV.807.1: Minutes of Meeting between Minister and Bank of Uganda.
[204] KDA 743/2: Application for 10,000/= Kenya Currency, March 9, 1978.
[205] KDA 743/2: Allocation of Foreign Exchange, January 13, 1978.
[206] KDA 743/2: Ocaba Wiy to Bank of Uganda, December 1977.

2.4 Governing the Frontiers of Value

was nationally circumscribed, invalid in other jurisdictions. In these cases, moral obligations were threatened not so much by money's absence; rather, it was about confinement within too narrow a regime of valuation. The path to a necessary surgery, a working vehicle, or a familial goal crossed the borders of the state, but not without being routed through the government's authority. In this way, the official government of value impeded popularly held commitments to how value should be circulated and to what end.

Policing the Borders of Money

As East Africa's currencies were progressively divorced – from the common currency of colonialism, through the freely exchangeable national currencies after 1966, to the imposition of exchange controls between the countries in 1970 – the borderlands became a more troubling geography for a monopoly on valuation. It was in the cross-border circuits of petty trade, familial exchange, and commodity smuggling that the state confronted the supersession of its monetary borders. Every regulatory change raised the specter of the borderlands: even a small tax change could lead to increased smuggling from Kenya (where taxes remained lower).[207] Residents of the borderlands could do so easily because of the difficulty of policing the borders and their easy conviviality with neighbors on the other side.[208]

In Uganda's northern frontier with Sudan, citizens of the two countries regarded "themselves as one and the same."[209] There and elsewhere, the border was rarely demarcated, meaning little signified – let alone enforced – the territorial division. As a result of the frontier's conviviality, Sudanese and Ugandan currencies moved easily between the populations. From the perspective of a state seeking to maintain a monetary reserve, this was troubling. An intelligence report from the region in early 1976 noted a net export of currency due to "Sudanese nationals along our borders [who] are always bringing into Uganda market items for sale such as sugar canes, potatoes, millet, beans, etc." The Ugandan shillings they were paid followed them back to Sudan,

---

[207] BoE OV75/7: "Government Finances," February/March 1969.
[208] On frontiers and conviviality, see Francis Nyamnjoh, "Incompleteness: Frontier Africa and the Currency of Conviviality," *Journal of Asian and African Studies* 52(3) (2017): 253–270.
[209] BoU 0, GOV.120.9: General Manager to Deputy Governor, August 18, 1970.

rather than being spent south of the border.[210] The need for correct denomination and nationality of money was at the core of negotiations between the two states, next to security and refugee concerns.[211]

There were, in other words, currency catchment zones, not all of which led Ugandan shillings to flow toward the nation-state. The trends were exacerbated not only by Uganda's dependence on foreign goods; it was also a result of the country's decades-old reliance on labor migration from neighboring countries.[212] Uganda's industrial hub of Jinja was just a few hours from the Kenyan border, attracting significant numbers of workers from the neighboring country. Following independence, complaints multiplied. "One cannot see the real justification for some of these firms teeming with non-Ugandans," wrote the Department of Labour to the District Commissioner in late 1964.[213] Even worse, these "non-Ugandan Africans … will always have one foot here and the other in their home state."[214] The Bank of Uganda General Manager noted with distaste that Kenyans "are mainly employed as semi-skilled workers in the industrial sector [of Uganda]. There appears to be a prejudice in quite a number of manufacturing industries that the Kenyans are more persistent and hardworking than the citizens, and consequently they are employed in large numbers."[215] These workers sent or carried their wages back to Kenya, draining Uganda of its national reserve. Further south, upon finishing working in Uganda's fields, considerable numbers of Tanzanians, Rwandese, and Burundian workers passed through the main border post into Tanzania. For the Bank of Uganda, this "deeprooted … labour mobility in East Africa is unfavourable to Uganda."[216] The trouble – from the perspective of an institution responsible for consolidating and growing its holdings of foreign

---

[210] BoU G.184.75, RES.306.1.D: Ag. PS Ministry of Internal Affairs to Secretary of Treasury, Secretary of Commerce and Governor, February 2, 1976.
[211] JDA Admin Central 4/4: Resolutions & Recommendations Uganda/Sudan Border Conference (n.d., but 1970s?).
[212] Michiel De Haas, "Moving beyond Colonial Control? Economic Forces and Shifting Migration from Ruanda-Urundi to Buganda, 1920–60," *Journal of African History* 60(3) (2019): 379–406.
[213] JDA Immigration 4/4: Naturalisation, Ugandanisation, and Census, 1952–1971. Labour Department to DC Busoga, November 18, 1964.
[214] JDA Immigration 4/4: D.C. Busoga to P.S. Ministry of Internal Affairs, October 17, 1964.
[215] BoU 0, GOV.120.9: General Manager to Governor, July 31, 1970.
[216] BoU 0, GOV.120.9: General Manager to Governor. "Border Posts," 1970.

2.4 Governing the Frontiers of Value 145

currency – was that the direction of money's movement was predominantly *out* of Uganda.

This became evident shortly after the Bank of Uganda opened outposts at the two busiest border crossings with Tanzania and Kenya. Shortly thereafter, the Bank of Uganda was surprised to document the volume of this movement: in June 1970, they were averaging 120 travelers amounting to USh. 15,000 to 20,000 daily. Moreover, goods were cheaper in Tanzania, meaning little money was spent in Ugandan shops or markets. The result in both cases was a drain on Uganda's reserve of Kenyan and Tanzanian currency. The Bank of Uganda issued approximately Shs. 400,000 to Tanzania in the first six weeks and Shs. 150,000 to Kenya in half as long. This was money that could be used by Ugandans to import tractors or receive medical care in Nairobi. Efforts to stem the tide were undermined by social relations that transcended the border. The "activities of black-market money exchangers," wrote the regulator, were responsible for facilitating the conversion between forms of value.[217] These brokers worked the particularities of the frontier's space to the benefit of their commercial conversions: buses traveling to Uganda would stop just a bit before the border. There, the bus operators would "grab every Tanzania shilling from the travelers" in exchange for their Ugandan equivalents. In the reverse direction, the police "constables are in collusion with some bus conductors and allow travelers to Tanzania (with Ugandan currency) to pass through and exchange their money at a commission ... some yards deep into Tanzania. The policemen at the barrier do nothing about this, under the pretext that the illegal money changers are in Tanzania."[218] The Kenyan and Tanzanian officials failed to cooperate across jurisdictions, not least because the two neighboring countries benefitted from the balance of exchanges in these regions.[219]

All in all, it was difficult to obtain a monopoly over how value was managed at the border. That the tedium of recording and requiring conversion of currency amounts below USh. 100 meant it was hard to enforce by border officials. The identities of travelers – particularly

---

[217] BoU 0, GOV.120.9: General Manager to Governor. "Border Posts," 1970.
[218] BoU 0, GOV.120.9: General Manager to Governor, June 25, 1970.
[219] The story was similar with Rwanda. BoU: Relations between Uganda and Rwanda, June 17, 1972.

women – were difficult to determine for lack of identity documents, so the same person could cross as many as ten times with money on their person.[220] Some locals simply waited for the outpost to close for the night before crossing, while other travelers did not declare "all the money they have on them for fear it would be robbed."[221] The result from the Bank of Uganda's perspective was not only a continued escape of value from their control but also an additional expense of running these outposts.[222]

2.5 Conclusion

The troubles on the borders reflect divergent geographies of exchange and loyalty. The state endeavored to monopolize the currency used within its borders, as well as control the conversion between Ugandan shillings and foreign money. Doing so required the flow of resources within families be severed. Citizens, however, did not so easily narrow their cross-border relationships and the transactional geographies they supported. Against the dictates of the Bank of Uganda, many Ugandans insisted they belonged to multiple economic communities. The state lacked the resources or the will to fully sever these regional ties. Officials tolerated the existence of "legitimate regular small trade within the border villages" but could not countenance "an element of currency dealing [that] had cropped up."[223] Delineating between the two was not, however, clear – particularly when it was a profusion of small, individual deals that amounted to a substantial threat to foreign reserves.

The imperatives of monetary governance had sometimes contradictory implications, and East Africans negotiated these in shifting, pluralistic ways. In place of a cultural nationalism, Uganda's independence technocrats designed a financial architecture that wove together a nation and financed a state. It reflected the insistence of late colonial subjects that they were productive contributors to not only their own

---

[220] BoU 0, GOV.120.9: Kibirango to General Manager, July 20, 1970.
[221] BoU 0, GOV.120.9: L. Kibirango to General Manager, July 20, 1970.
[222] BoU 0, GOV.120.9: General Manager to Governor, April 13, 1971.
[223] BoU 0, GOV.305.1: Exchange Controllers Meeting, BOU00236, 1974–1983: "Minutes of 14th EA Exchange Controllers Meeting at CBK," December 5, 1975.

2.5 Conclusion

welfare but also the nation's bottom line. Yet, credible citizenship traded social fraternity and solidarity for enterprising accumulation, and it required convincing the expatriate bankers that their interests aligned with what Mubiru called "the aspirations of a sovereign developing nation."[224] It provided a model only as long as the connivance of collective and individual advance held together. Already, this chapter has suggested some of the weaknesses that appeared throughout the 1970s, and Chapter 4 will examine them at much greater length. The next chapter, however, turns to Tanzania, where the nationalization of foreign banks in 1967 marked an assertive effort by the party-state to monopolize valuation of key assets.

---

[224] Joseph M. Mubiru, "Central banking with specila reference to developing countries (n.d. [but 1967?]). In practice, the bankers often disagreed, even to the point of "flaunting the authority" of the Bank of Uganda. DCO 11/2451: Local Director, Barclays Kampala to General Managers, London, July 10, 1968.

3 *Restricted Value*

Bank Nationalization and the Price of Decolonization in Tanzania

3.1 Introduction

Sir Frederic Seebohm was late. Nervously glancing at his watch, the chairman of Barclays Bank (Dominion, Colonial, and Overseas [DCO]) was anxious to get going. It was June 3, 1969, and he was meant to be on the road to the airport by 5:00 p.m. Yet, it was past 4:00 p.m., and he was still locked in negotiations with the Tanzanian Minister of Finance, Amir Jamal.[1]

It wasn't supposed to be this way. When Seebohm packed his bag and a special ceremonial pen in London a few days earlier, he thought it was for a signing ceremony, a polite dinner, and a cocktail reception. His trip was not meant to be a high-stakes negotiation with Tanzanian officials. For one thing, Seebohm did not involve himself in such matters: he directed one of the world's most important banks, overseeing hundreds of branches in dozens of countries, weaving together monetary geographies in ways the British empire could no longer do.

For another thing, these negotiations were meant to be done – finally. When the President of Tanzania, Julius Nyerere, suddenly nationalized the foreign banks in the country more than two years prior, it set Barclays on a lengthy – albeit intermittent – negotiation over compensation for their expropriated business. Seebohm had chimed in on the process – setting bottom lines for his staff and occasionally meeting with President Nyerere and Minister Jamal, but only to establish a foundation of conviviality and goodwill. He did not get into the specifics of asset valuation, pension liabilities, or the write-off of dubious debts.

But here he was, at risk of missing his flight, engaged in a last-minute dive into the minutiae of a deal he was most eager to seal. As far as he was concerned, it was most unwelcome and deeply unbecoming.

---

[1] Barclays (Dominion, Commonwealth and Overseas) Archive [hereafter DCO] 38/438: Mr. F. Seebohm Visit to Dar es Salaam, June 1–4, 1969.

3.1 Introduction

It showed the basic untrustworthiness of his counterparts: the deal was meant to be done, but they insisted on an eleventh-hour struggle over £35,000. Such a figure was not overly substantial; it represented less than 3 percent of the sum Barclays was due to receive. But it was a meaningful principle and opened the door to other troubles. Barclays would not simply roll over for what they thought was a last-minute ploy by the Tanzanian government.

Such principles mattered for British bankers. Across the world, postcolonial states were targeting the European multinationals who stayed on after empire officially ended. Since at least 1960, when Gamal Abdel Nasser nationalized the banks in Egypt, firms like Barclays worried about the contagious effects of individual acts. From Ghana to Burma and beyond, the stable business of British commerce was threatened by the untoward actions of radicals and nationalists. This made the outcome of Tanzania all the more important to Barclays' management.

Seebohm knew he could not stop any single act of nationalization. After all, such actions were legal as long as the government provided compensation.[2] Nationalizations were common in the postwar years, including in France and Italy. Even the Bank of England was nationalized in 1946 – not to mention the railways and other industries taken over by the Labour government after World War II. By 1962 the UN General Assembly resolved in favor of the right to expropriate foreign property.[3] What mattered was the question of compensation, but how exactly to assess the value of the nationalized business had consumed Seebohm's staff and their Tanzanian opponents since February 6, 1967.

On that day, Julius Nyerere had shocked British capitalists by beginning to summarily acquire part or all of dozens of major enterprises.

---

[2] Legal scholars of the era disagreed as to whether to distinguish between "expropriation" (usually defined as individual acts of seizure) and "nationalization" (focused on entire sectors or industries). Here, I use the terms interchangeably to refer to the compulsory and compensated takeover by government of private enterprises in the collective interest. See the discussion in A. W. Bradley, "Legal Aspects of the Nationalisations in Tanzania," *East African Law Journal* 3(3) (1967): 152. They also differed over whether compensation was always necessary, or whether it should be "adequate" (as preferred by capital-exporting countries) or "appropriate" (as favored by Third World nations). I am grateful to Toni Marzal for emphasizing this latter point.

[3] "Banking Confusion," *East African Standard*, February 8, 1967.

Figure 3.1 Julius Nyerere announcing the Arusha Declaration.
Courtesy of the Tanzania Information Services.

This included import and export firms, large retailers, and consumer goods companies. It also included all nine banks operating in Tanzania, including the three dominant British firms: Barclays DCO, Standard Bank, and National & Grindlays. The nationalizations became the centerpiece of the government's new guiding policy, the Arusha Declaration (see Figure 3.1).[4] Elaborating a vision for *ujamaa* (African socialism) and *kujitegemea* (self-reliance), the declaration deepened and accelerated existing efforts to remake the nation along lines that would free Tanzanians from subjugation and exploitation. While private business would remain in many sectors, the Arusha Declaration called for expanding the scope for cooperative and state enterprises. The "major means of production" – a list that ranged across land, transport, trade, industry, and banking – were to be

---

[4] See the manifold influences discussed in Paul Bjerk, "Agency and the Arusha Declaration: Nyerere, NUTA, and Political Discourse in Tanzania, 1966–67," *Journal of African History* (forthcoming).

3.1 Introduction

"under the control and ownership of the Peasants and Workers themselves through their Government and their Co-operatives."[5]

"Our independence is not yet complete," Nyerere told the crowds when announcing bank nationalization.[6] Bringing money under the direction of the government was a necessary first step in the larger action. With around 80 percent of bank holdings in 1967, the three large British banks dominated the country's financial sector. Because expatriate banks in Tanzania were, in practice, merely branches of their metropolitan offices, they were beholden to foreign interests. Their collusion and hostility to competition meant their managerial decisions reverberated throughout the country and made alternative models largely infeasible.[7] While the British banks expanded their upcountry branch networks during the 1950s boom years, they reversed course after independence in 1961. Little effort was expended on providing savings accounts to Africans, and Tanzanians remained frustrated about the paucity of lending.[8]

If this suited the needs of colonial capital, it was doubly troubling in independent Tanzania. First, commercial business practices did not align with the policy goals of the government. Lending decisions and branch networks were at odds with the aspirations of the ruling Tanzania African National Union (TANU). Moreover, the banks shuttled their profits out of the country to British shareholders and chose to overwhelmingly invest their customers' deposits and other surplus funds in London's capital markets.[9] Prior to 1967, foreign banks exported an estimated TSh. 29.1 million annually.[10] Folding

---

[5] "Public Ownership in Tanzania," by Julius Nyerere, reprinted in the *Arusha Declaration, and TANU's Policy of Socialism and Self-reliance* (Government Printer, 1967), pp. 21–25.

[6] "Tanzania Nationalises Banks," *East African Standard*, February 7, 1967.

[7] Mikael Selsjord, "Recent Developments in Commercial Banking in East Africa: A Statistical Analysis," *Economic & Statistical Review* (20) (1966): VIII–XXII.

[8] H. H. Binhammer, *The Development of a Financial Infrastructure in Tanzania* (East African Literature Bureau, 1975), pp. 39–40.

[9] John Loxley, "The Development of the Monetary and Financial System of the East African Currency Area, 1950 to 1964," PhD dissertation, University of Leeds, 1966; Julian Crossley and John Blandford, *The DCO Story: A History of Banking in Many Countries 1925–71* (Barclays Bank International Limited, 1975), p. 55.

[10] Insurance firms were estimated to do a further TSh. 19 million annually. Aart J. M. van der Laar, "Foreign Business and Capital Exports from Developing Countries: The Tanzanian Experience," in Lionel Cliffe and John Saul (eds.),

these banks into a new National Bank of Commerce (NBC) was to give Tanzania's government control over credit, able to invest in national priorities, rather than British profits.

The bank nationalization of 1967 was, therefore, emblematic of Tanzania's lengthy effort to wrest control of economic matters away from legacy arrangements. Freedom (*uhuru* in Kiswahili) was a watchword of popular and official discourse, and bank nationalizations were intended to liberate the economy from foreign dictate. As Amir Jamal put it, "The phase of political revolution is over. We have now entered the phase of economic revolution."[11] Banks – as financial enablers of all sorts of other commercial and government activity – were foundational to this pursuit of economic sovereignty. Without authority over interest rates, collateral requirements, and minimum deposit balances – without, in other words, control over the minutiae of finance – the aspirations to self-determination would flounder. As Nyerere put it while speaking to a large audience, governing money was more important than all the other sectors that the Arusha Declaration nationalized. While less visible and more arcane than the *ujamaa* villagization or urban culture that has attracted historians in recent years, monetary politics were fundamental to African socialism and self-reliance.[12] If they often remained in the domain of elite debate, they were also of public interest. In the days after February 6, farmers long excluded by expatriate banks clamored for credit from the nationalized banks. Even bank savings accounts took on a patriotic hue, as elderly citizens appeared at the branches with currency to deposit in new accounts.[13]

Socialism in Tanzania, vol. 1 (Nairobi: East African Publishing House, 1972), pp. 84–85.

[11] "The Economic Revolution: Assembly Passes Takeover Bills," *The Standard*, February 15, 1967.

[12] For recent assessments of villagization, see Schneider, *Government of Development: Peasants and Politicians in Postcolonial Tanzania* (Indiana University Press, 2014); Priya Lal, *African Socialism in Postcolonial Tanzania: Between the Village and the World* (Cambridge University Press, 2015); Felicitas Becker, *Politics of Poverty: Policy-Making and Development in Rural Tanzania* (Cambridge University Press, 2019). On urban history, see James Brennan, *Taifa: Making Nation and Race in Urban Tanzania* (Ohio University Press, 2012); Emily Callaci, *Street Archives and City Life: Popular Intellectuals in Postcolonial Tanzania* (Duke University Press, 2017); Emily Brownell, *Gone to Ground: A History of Environment and Infrastructure in Dar Es Salaam* (University of Pittsburgh Press, 2020).

[13] "Priority Now for Farmers – MPs," *The Standard*, February 15, 1967.

3.1 Introduction

Within three months of nationalization, bank deposits were 30 percent higher than a year before.[14]

A monopoly on banking offered Tanzania's leadership an important basis for both self-reliance and *ujamaa*. For many years, the banks in Tanzania colluded to limit competition among themselves.[15] Their Banking Agreement was a closely guarded document that meant banks did not differ in the prices they offered borrowers and depositors.[16] As a result, bank competition was limited to minor differences, such as the quality and location of their services.[17] Nationalization offered the government an opportunity to swap the price-fixing firms for state-mandated prices and priorities. A monopoly on valuation would keep more money in Tanzania, direct credit to public goals, and do so in more accessible, affordable ways. It would, thought TANU's leadership, turn banking into an infrastructure of national planning. Governing value on a territorial scale was not, however, a project of autarky, or what Nyerere sometimes critiqued as "isolationism." The TANU state valorized self-reliance as a new orientation to international engagement and commerce. Foreign banks would be nationalized to better control the conversion between Tanzanian and foreign money, and banking would be enrolled in the wider politics of race and nation, but international trade and expertise were still welcomed.

This chapter reconstructs the nationalization of banks through an analysis of the negotiations between Barclays Bank and the government of Tanzania, as well as the early workings of the state bank and allied institutions.[18] The corporate correspondence, transcripts of

---

[14] This is due both to limits on foreign transfers and increased citizen deposits. *The Standard*, May 4, 1967.

[15] The collusive agreement between the banks was "unparalleled" in its "strictness and the wideness of its scope" according to E.-J. Pauw, "Banking in East Africa," in Peter Marlin (ed.), *Financial Aspects of Development in East Africa* (Weltforum Verlag, 1970), p. 233.

[16] In 1963, Erwin Blumenthal's report publicized the secret agreement, leading to Standard Bank officials worrying the Tanganyikan government would ask for copies of it. BoE OV7/78: Standard Bank General Manager to Loynes, February 27, 1963. Even the next year, the East African Currency Board's boss lacked a copy of the document. BoE OV7/79: Loynes to H.D. Cayley, May 12, 1964.

[17] A point made by Amon Nsekela, "The Role of Commercial Banking in Building a Socialist Tanzania," *African Review* 4(1) (1974): 26.

[18] Barclays and Standard were generally in the same position, though Standard had a larger interest in Tanzania and sometimes approached negotiations with more intransigence. National & Grindlays was a smaller bank with limited bargaining power, leading to its earlier settlement with Tanzania.

negotiations, accounting records, and the personal diary of Frederic Seebohm provide detailed insights into a style of postcolonial politics often hidden from outside scrutiny. In addition to discussing why and how banking was harnessed to economic planning in socialist Tanzania, I emphasize a less obvious aspect of economic self-determination – namely, how the capacity to assign value was central to the exercise of sovereign power. Managing banking would give the state new power in this regard, but it first needed to establish the price owed to nationalized firms. At stake in the lengthy back-and-forth between government and corporation was how much the expropriated business was worth. Tanzania's leading technocrats – men like Minister of Finance Amir Jamal, NBC chairman Amon Nsekela, and Principal Secretary for the Treasury J. D. Namfua – drew upon the expertise of economists and accountants as they tried to reach a deal for compensating Barclays and others. The struggle for African socialism and self-reliance unfolded through decisions over how to calculate the value of businesses, money, and goods. In other words, national control of banking was routed through what Liliana Doganova calls the "political technology" of accounting.[19] Accounting was a stage on which competing monetary authorities struggled to determine worth.

The meetings and correspondence that began in February 1967 endeavored to find what Barclays' management called "a satisfactory basis for settling our claims for the value of the business."[20] What they demanded was agreement on a suitable *formula* for affixing the value of banking in Tanzania. Such a calculative practice would function not only to establish worth but to justify it, thereby legitimating the expenditure of limited foreign reserves as compensation. By turning to putatively impartial numerical calculations, Barclays' negotiators tried to represent the firm's worth in ways that would discipline divergent perspectives. Yet, rather than producing consensus, the negotiators found they spoke "different accounting language[s]."[21] Multiple formulas were proposed; myriad variables introduced, debated, and discarded. The protocols of valuation did not settle matters; they were

---

[19] Liliana Doganova, "Discounting the Future: A Political Technology," in Sandra Kemp and Jenny Andersson (eds.), *Futures* (Oxford University Press, 2021), pp. 379–394.
[20] DCO 80/5300: Enclosure 1 in Note for Seebohm, January 5, 1968.
[21] DCO 80/5301: Nationalisation in Tanzania, Talks in Dar es Salaam, January 1968.

3.1 Introduction

instead a genre of reasoning and communicating that brought together otherwise divergent interests and ideological commitments.[22] As Ballestero argues, pricing unfolds through "calculation grammars" that only partially direct the process.[23] I show how, eventually, accounting formula became placeholders to be backfilled for an agreed upon compensation *figure*. Economic valuation is never free from ethical and political influences, which means that tracing the specificities of valuation – its techniques and justifications – reveals more than the resulting quantities; valuation struggles are disputes over the qualitative values that matter in a given situation.[24]

It was not the case that valuation merely sought to assign price. More fundamentally, it was concerned with defining the economic object to be priced. What constituted the asset to be valued was very much at play, not a settled matter. Instead of a clearly defined commodity – a bag of wheat or a vehicle – the nationalization targeted a bundle of different assets, not all of which were necessarily linked into a coherent whole.[25] Rather, over the course of their negotiations, Barclays and the government differed over the partibility or unity of assets, their boundaries, and components.[26] As before, this involved the application of accounting protocols. It also involved the addition or removal of elements to the calculations: Barclays tried to eliminate assets that might prove beneficial to the new state bank or add variables that would improve the price received. Inversely, Tanzania refused to countenance certain assets that Barclays claimed were part of their business or insisted that other dynamics be included as part of the valuation. The bank to be nationalized, in other words, did not exist fully formed on February 6, 1967; it was rather the result of valuation over the course of more than two years.

---

[22] Classic studies of how objectivity is achieved through the socialization and institutionalization of calculation include Porter, *Trust in Numbers: The Pursuit of Objectivity in Science and Public Life* (Princeton University Press, 1995); Lorraine Daston and Peter Galison, *Objectivity* (Zone Books, 2007); and Norton M. Wise, *The Values of Precision* (Princeton University Press, 1997).
[23] Ballestero, "Ethics of a Formula," p. 265.
[24] Marion Fourcade, "Cents and Sensibility: Economic Valuation and the Nature of 'Nature'," *American Journal of Sociology* 116(6) (2011): 1721–1777.
[25] On assets, see Kean Birch and Fabian Muniesa, *Assetization: Turning Things into Assets in Technoscientific Capitalism* (MIT Press, 2020).
[26] On partibility, see Emma Park, "Intimacy & Estrangement: Safaricom, Divisibility, and the Making of the Corporate Nation-State," *Comparative Studies of South Asia, Africa, and the Middle East* 41(3) (2021): 423–440.

If the resulting enumeration was often dizzying in its technicalities, it was hardly lacking in political importance and emotional significance. As Barclays' Chairman Frederic Seebohm knew, getting the right number was crucial: too low and other countries might think it inexpensive to take over foreign businesses. Too high and Tanzania would be unable to afford the deal.[27] For their sake, Tanzania's negotiators were hemmed in by a complicated and shifting political arena, the requirements of the 1967 law authorizing the expropriation, and a measure of ill will toward the British banks who were anything but cooperative. This lack of shared ground inhibited an easy consensus on how to price the compensation owed to Barclays. Yet, neither did one side have a clear upper hand through which it could unilaterally enforce its accounting.[28] The result was therefore less a systematic accounting for assets and liabilities than an improvisational compromise between the adversaries. In practice, this was reflected by the move from irreconcilable differences concerning accounting formulas to a negotiated agreement about the final figure of settlement. The formulas would backfill a figure chosen for political and economic calculations.

In what follows, I suggest that controlling money and value required weaving together and working through aspects usually considered apart – from popular affect to calculative practices. Public and private, emotional and technical came together in the project of making postcolonial finance and the nation-state. I first turn to the immediate aftermath of the Arusha Declaration's nationalizations, as citizens enthusiastically took up the call, expatriates desperately tried to understand the implications, and TANU leadership endeavored to steer a new course. I place this within a wider context of efforts to liberate or control postcolonial economic policy before returning to the minutiae of the bank–government negotiations over valuation.

---

[27] In unprofitable or difficult countries, it could even be convenient to be nationalized, with banks able to use their capital elsewhere or adopt a less risky model of managing the bank on behalf of government. I am grateful to Justin Willis for emphasizing this.

[28] See the comparison between National & Grindlays, on the one hand, and Standard and Barclays, on the other, in Emmanuel Onah, Chinwe Okoyeuzu, and Chibuike Uche, "The Nationalisation of British Banks in Post-Colonial Tanzania: Did the Banks' Net Capital Export Position and Home Government Support Influence Compensation Negotiation Outcomes?" *Business History* 64 (6) (2022): 1088–1109.

3.2 Atmospherics of Nationalization

Barclays senior management in London learned something dramatic had occurred in Tanzania on the afternoon of February 6, 1967. A terse telegram was sent from their Dar es Salaam branch, reporting the immediate nationalization of their business in the country. "We are advised full compensation will be paid" and "government wishes all branches to continue normal business under present management."[29] Yet, the situation was anything but business as usual. Simultaneously, the Bank of Tanzania announced limits on foreign exchange transactions, including with Kenya and Uganda where currencies historically circulated freely. The Dar es Salaam telegram precipitated a cascade of communications as Barclays in Nairobi relayed the news around the world. Shortly thereafter, a flurry of inquiries – from Johannesburg and Lusaka, Tokyo and Switzerland – coursed across the cables as bankers, merchants, and diplomats tried to make sense of the situation.

In East Africa, the commercial classes were gripped by anxiety and dismay. The restrictions on foreign transactions brought international business "to a virtual standstill."[30] In Nairobi, many were dismayed, and confusion reigned as little communication was forthcoming from Tanzania. On the road between Arusha and Nairobi, officials checked for undeclared currency at a newly constructed border post in Namanga.[31] Dar es Salaam was awash in rumors. Police stood guard outside some bank branches, briefly refusing to allow employees to go home for the night.[32] Sensitive paperwork and foreign currency were not to escape government control. In Mwanza, there were reports that police were searching bank employees – even "the ladies' handbags" – as they left the building.[33] In Dar, one branch manager reportedly had his car inspected while leaving work, and police searched departing air travelers for large sums of money.[34] Bank staff were "bewildered" at the change in circumstances.[35] British expatriates projected an image

[29] Barclays 80/4658: Telegram from L.H.O. Dar es Salaam, February 6, 1967.
[30] "Banking Confusion," *East African Standard*, February 8, 1967.
[31] "Kenya's New Border Post," *The Standard*, February 16, 1967.
[32] The police stated this was only to prevent a run on the bank by nervous customers. UKNA FCO 31/52: Tanzania Nationalization of Banks, February 6, 1967.
[33] DCO 11/2398: Local Director to General Managers, February 9, 1967.
[34] "Tanzania Moves to Stop Cash Panic," *East African Standard*, February 8, 1967.
[35] DCO 11/2404: Tanzania, February 10, 1967.

of frustrated resolve but worried about themselves, their wives, and children: should they get them out of the country? For the many Asian bank employees, the news was even more disquieting. Without the protection of a foreign firm's procedures – and the British preference for using Asians as middle management – their standing was suddenly uncertain. How would they fare as state employees? Would they even be given the chance, or would they be subject to rapid Africanization?[36]

In contrast, many Tanzanians received the news with enthusiasm. State media reported that more than 100,000 people attended Nyerere's two-and-a-half-hour speech the day prior. There, he elaborated TANU's vision of socialism and self-reliance to a vocally supportive audience.[37] The President announced further rounds of nationalizations in subsequent daily speeches to large popular demonstrations.[38] Radio and newspapers amplified the exhilarating, revolutionary promises, with new actions revealed daily by Nyerere. In the months that followed, groups of Tanzanians took to city streets and rural roads to demonstrate their support for the new policies. TANU leaders encouraged the collective displays of nationalist energy. When a young enthusiast died on a march from Arusha to Dar es Salaam, he was turned into a national hero overnight. Nyerere, too, walked 138 miles from his home village to a TANU conference in Mwanza in October 1967, with the press amplifying the electric reaction of town residents to his arrival.[39] As Priya Lal relates, "marching or walking [was] a key element of Tanzania's socialist political culture" (see Figure 3.2). So too was writing, and the nationalist press carried

---

[36] On racial tensions in independent Tanzania, see Brennan, *Taifa*.
On Africanization in Tanzania, see Ronald Aminzade, *Race, Nation, and Citizenship in Postcolonial Africa* (Cambridge University Press, 2013), pp. 118–123; on banking Africanization elsewhere, Stephanie Decker, "Decolonising Barclays Bank DCO? Corporate Africanisation in Nigeria, 1945–69," *Journal of Imperial and Commonwealth History* 33(3) (2005): 419–440; Chibuike U. Uche, "British Government, British Businesses, and the Indigenization Exercise in Post-Independence Nigeria," *Business History Review* 86(4) (2012): 745–771.

[37] George Roberts, *Revolutionary State-Making: African Liberation and the Global Cold War, 1961–1974* (Cambridge University Press, 2021), p. 66.

[38] Cranford Pratt, *The Critical Phase in Tanzania: Nyerere and the Emergence of Socialist Strategy* (Cambridge University Press, 1976), p. 238.

[39] Andrew Coulson, *Tanzania: A Political Economy*, 2nd ed. (Oxford University Press, 2013), p. 223.

3.2 *Atmospherics of Nationalization* 159

Figure 3.2 Citizens from Tanga marching to State House in Dar es Salaam to support the Arusha Declaration.
Courtesy of Tanzania Information Services.

numerous letters from citizens in support of the Arusha Declaration.[40] Adherents like F. A. Mgendi enthusiastically declared his support for the Arusha Declaration's assault on "the most inhuman, ruthless foreign exploitation, domination, [and] oppression imposed upon the blacks."[41] Poets, musicians, and playwrights also "rallied behind the government's ambitious program to eliminate social inequality and evenly distribute the nation's resources."[42]

More immediately, bank managers in Tanzania watched with alarm as they faced the practical imperatives of opening their branches the

---

[40] Lal, *African Socialism in Postcolonial Tanzania*, p. 97.
[41] "Letters to the Editor," *The Nationalist*, January 18, 1968. On the meaning of exploitation, see James Brennan, "Blood Enemies: Exploitation and Urban Citizenship in the Nationalist Political Thought of Tanzania, 1958–75," *Journal of African History* 47(3) (2006): 389–413.
[42] Kelly Askew, *Performing the Nation: Swahili Music and Cultural Politics in Tanzania* (University of Chicago Press, 2002), p. 184.

next day. The British bankers huddled together at Standard Bank's Dar es Salaam branch on Tuesday, February 7, to determine their course of action. Wary of provoking the state – and its more enthusiastic supporters marching in the street – the expatriate bankers endeavored to carry on as best they could. That same day, the government hosted further meetings with all the banks, trying to work through the practicalities of new credit and payment procedures. It involved considerable logistical difficulties. In addition to the impossibility of international remittances, bankers were told to report any substantial customer withdrawals and government officials assumed responsibility for all new loan applications.[43] Government and the University of Dar es Salaam economists soon arrived at the banks to collect statistics and other information – a form of oversight Barclays found "very time-wasting."[44] In the view of Barclays' management, it all seemed "hopelessly impracticable."[45]

While they could not be seen to overtly undermine the effort, the British expatriates took certain steps to stymie the government action and protect their interests. Barclays local director, Ernest Elliot, acknowledged it was "necessary to be flexible and to assist" as required, but along with colleagues from National & Grindlays and Standard, he recognized that "the apparent success of nationalization would stimulate neighboring countries to follow the same pattern."[46] It was a threat to their business and one stimulated by what they thought to be the "idiotic speeches" of African politicians.[47] In response, they took a number of steps, starting with the imposition of new fees for anyone doing business with Tanzania in Uganda and Kenya.[48]

They also took steps to remove assets from Tanzanian control. As early as February 7, Barclays was "seeking to have destroyed" key documents housed in their newly nationalized branches.[49] While the bankers expressed outrage at their staff being searched – and in at

[43] DCO 80/4658: Elliot to General Managers, London, February 9, 1967.
[44] DCO 11/2398: Innes to Dyson, February 13, 1967.
[45] DCO 11/2398: Local Director Dar es Salaam to General Managers, London, February 7, 1967.
[46] DCO 80/4658: Note of Meeting held at Standard Bank, February 7, 1967.
[47] DCO 80/4658: Elliot to Dyson, March 23, 1967.
[48] James Mittelman, "Underdevelopment and Nationalisation: Banking in Tanzania," *Journal of Modern African Studies* 16(4) (1978): 605.
[49] DCO 80/4658: Crankshaw to Correspondents, February 7, 1967.

3.2 Atmospherics of Nationalization

least one case, denied an exit permit for Nairobi – the reality was the presence of police meant "in certain cases controlled documents cannot be destroyed or dispatched" to Nairobi. In these cases, British management held the documents "under their direct control."[50] The "pruning [of] appropriate confidential files" included documents serving as collateral for loans, travelers cheques, and telegraphic keys, and information about expatriate salaries.[51] It also included the "controlled, completely effective mutilation or destruction" of all forty-three copies of the Barclays Handbook "which constitute[d] a very valuable 'asset' for which we are likely to receive inadequate (if any) compensation."[52] This last action was particularly pernicious, not only because the handbooks set out bank policies and procedures. It was also exactly the sort of asset that the Tanzanian state had expropriated and for which Barclays would spend years arguing they were owed. Rather than surrendering it, Barclays staff pushed for immediate elimination: "The sooner the better. Why wait!"[53]

In addition to paperwork, the British banks were eager to remove another crucial asset from their Tanzanian businesses: expatriate staff. Bankers' claim to monetary authority and financial discretion had long rested on the assertion of a uniquely competent managerial class. As the embodiment of Britain's globally dominant banking industry, Barclays staff carried a sense of their essential importance to East African commerce. A refusal to assist the National Bank of Commerce was an effort to weaken it. This was all the more so because the technicalities of accounting and bank management were unevenly distributed in Tanzania. The colonial state had deprived Tanzanians of higher education, and the foreign banks invested little in training local staff. As a result, the managerial experience and expertise of banking were racially exclusive. In total, there were nearly sixty British expatriate staff working in Tanzania for Barclays, Standard, and National &

---

[50] DCO 11/2398: Innes to Dyson, February 13, 1967.

[51] DCO 80/4658: Telegram to Elliot, February 13, 1967; DCO 11/2398: Memo to Dyson, February 9, 1967. It also included "agency arrangements, exchange rates, [and] list of correspondents." DCO 80/243: "Instructions to Branches in Tanzania on Nationalisation."

[52] DCO 11/2404: Memorandum to General Managers, February 16, 1967.

[53] DCO 11/2404: Memorandum to the General Managers, February 16, 1967. These archival records belie what former bankers told James Mittelman during his research, "Underdevelopment and Nationalisation," p. 606.

Grindlays.[54] Tanzania recognized their utility to the nationalized successor, but government overtures to hire British staff or even pay one of the banks to manage the new enterprise were rejected, lest they gave "any impression that British banks are behind the new bank."[55] Outraged at their sudden subordination to the independent state, the bankers decided to rapidly withdraw their staff. A week after nationalization, Barclays London decided to begin removing staff from Tanzania as soon as practicable, starting with their families.[56] Such a move was likely to be controversial, and the UK Commonwealth Office advised the banks that it could damage their claim to compensation and prove detrimental to the already sour relations between the countries. It might even free up space for Chinese or Soviet replacements.[57] Nevertheless, on February 16, his London bosses instructed Ernest Elliot to "discreetly" begin the phased withdrawal of his staff in Tanzania. If government raised objections, he was to say the staff travel was due to previously scheduled holidays, courses, or new postings.[58] Despite fears that the government would impede this exodus – including by denying exit permits – by April 11, all but the Local Director had left Tanzania (and he was scheduled to depart a week later).[59]

Barclays called the exfiltrated employees "in effect refugees from Tanzania" and found them new postings in Zambia, Uganda, Kenya, or Britain.[60] But despite the considerable uncertainty facing Asian staff, only "British covenanted" staff received support emigrating. "You will appreciate," one early telegram put it, "that we cannot absorb Asians [into the] United Kingdom and difficulties could arise in other East African territories from immigration."[61] In practice, the legal category of "British covenanted" justified a racial sorting of employees, with whiteness warranting mobility and support not

[54] DCO 80/4658: Nationalisation of Banks in Tanzania, Notes of Meeting held February 9, 1967.
[55] DCO 11/2404: Telegram from Elliot, February 14, 1967; DCO 80/5300: Note of Conversation with Sir Julian, September 21, 1967.
[56] DCO 80/4658: Telegram to Elliot, Dar es Salaam, February 14, 1967.
[57] DCO 80/4658: Note of Telephone Call from Commonwealth Office, February 16, 1967; UKNA FCO 31/44: Tanzanian Nationalization of Banks, March 2, 1967.
[58] DCO 80/4658: Telegram to Elliot, February 16, 1967.
[59] DCO 80/4658: Dyson to de Loynes, April 11, 1967.
[60] DCO 80/4658: Telegram from Barclays Nairobi, February 17, 1967.
[61] DCO 80/4658: Telegram to Elliot, Dar es Salaam, February 8, 1967.

3.2 Atmospherics of Nationalization

guaranteed to minoritized staff. Instead, the British bankers merely asked the government to "retain all existing locally-employed staff including Asians and safeguard their pension rights."[62] Indeed, they had a dual interest in doing so: "grooming" the most senior Asians in each branch to take over allowed for a measure of competent transfer, seeming evidence that they did not purposefully undermine nationalization.[63] They also hoped that picking loyal employees to take over branch management would improve the bank's future prospects, however uncertain those may be.

Barclays and Standard were also in possession of a final bargaining chip: significant reserves of money owed to Tanzania.[64] Due to their long-standing preference for exporting capital from African countries, each bank held more than one million pounds sterling in their London accounts. The money actually belonged to depositors in Tanzania who entrusted the banks with their savings; however, faced with government nationalization, Barclays and Standard refused to release the funds. Rumors quickly made the rounds in Dar es Salaam, with reports that up to £4 million of Tanzanian money was being held in London.[65] When the Tanzanians requested this money, Barclays at first coyly replied that "it is not established that there are any balances in London which would have accrued to our former Tanzania branches."[66] Eventually, though, they forthrightly held out the return of these frozen balances as an inducement to settlement. The languishing reserves – which British diplomats called the "ransom" – were a stark reminder that political independence more than five years earlier had done little to undo the colonial geography of money.[67]

---

[62] DCO 80/4658: Nationalisation of Banks in Tanzania, Note of Meeting, February 9, 1967.
[63] DCO 80/4658: Dyson to de Loynes, April 11, 1967.
[64] This was not the case for National & Grindlays, a fact that encouraged them to settle before the other British banks. Onah et al., "The Nationalisation of British Banks," pp. 8–9. See the discussion in Crossley and Blandford, *The DCO Story*, pp. 267–269.
[65] DCO 80/4658: Note of Telephone Call from Commonwealth Office, February 16, 1967.
[66] DCO 80/4658: Barclays Telegram to National Bank of Commerce, March 2, 1967.
[67] UKNA FCO 31/55: Commonwealth Secretary's Visit to Africa Talking Points, October 1967.

3.3 "A Profound Shock": Making Sense of Nationalization

The Tanzanian decision seemed to many observers a sudden rupture. It was announced without any prior consultation. The laws authorizing the nationalizations were to follow in the coming weeks, meaning early responses lacked crucial details about what exactly was happening. Foreigners were gripped with the question of how to make sense of this turn of events and how to respond. British interests were preeminently affected, but Britain had no official representation in Tanzania between 1965 and 1968 due to the former's policy toward Rhodesia. They instead relied on rumors, news reports, and inquiries to allies on the ground.[68] In an era of brief telegrams and slower air mail, information could take days to arrive, only exacerbating the uncertainty and nerves. In some cases, delays or errors in translation from Kiswahili to English contributed to the miscommunication.[69]

One British official suggested the immediate cause of nationalization was the enormous flows of money, mainly by Asians, out of Tanzania.[70] This drain of currency was a constant concern that the British banks were seen to facilitate. The month prior, Joseph Nyerere – the Regional Commissioner for Mwanza and brother of the President – gave an incendiary speech at a Revolution Day rally, in part targeting Asians who sent money and diamonds abroad. What should be done to the man exporting value to India, he asked the crowd? "Kill him," the audience responded. And what should be done with their property? "Confiscate it."[71]

Other observers viewed the Arusha Declaration through Cold War lenses. One conservative journalist thought Nyerere was "being pushed to become an African Castro" due to Zanzibari influence. The nationalizations were "not honourable," and "tantamount to theft" due to Tanzania's likely inability to pay proper compensation.[72]

---

[68] More than two years later, British diplomats still struggled to understand why bank nationalization occurred. UKNA FCO 31/444: President Nyerere and the Nationalisation of the Banks, March 7, 1969.
[69] DCO 11/2398: The Tanzania Situation, East Africa & Mauritius Association, n. d.
[70] UKNA FCO 31/53: Hope-Jones to Dick, "Nationalisation in Tanzania," February 16, 1967.
[71] UKNA FCO 31/84: "Exchange Control Act Defaulters," *The Nationalist* January 16, 1967.
[72] "An African Castro?" *The Statist*, February 24, 1967.

3.3 "A Profound Shock": Making Sense of Nationalization 165

London's *Times* concurred, thinking mainland Tanzania was taking a "'great leap forward' on Sino-Zanzibari lines."[73] These writers looked to Zanzibar's earlier nationalizations, its revolutionary rhetoric, and closer ties to communist states as explanation for the Arusha Declaration. In contrast, the *Financial Times* correspondent told his readers that "last week's sudden fit of nationalization in Tanzania lies not in Dar es Salaam, the capital, but deep in the heart of the African bush." Announcing his recent return from ten weeks in one of "the remotest parts of Tanzania, cut off completely from urban Africa," Joe Rogaly argued this was less about socialism – by his calculation, less than 10 percent of the Arusha Declaration concerned the topic – but rather about self-reliance. In Rogaly's condescending explication, Nyerere "is not just copying Mao – this is the thought of a rural schoolmaster" for whom self-help and energetic labor were the key to national advance.[74]

Rogaly's efforts to divorce Tanzania from a red scare were of limited effectiveness. Racial and Cold War stereotypes shaped interpretations and responses to the nationalizations by many businessmen. For instance, Frederick Pedler, Deputy Chairman of the United Africa Company and Chairman of the East Africa & Mauritius Association, arrived in Dar es Salaam the day after the Arusha Declaration was published. He recoiled at the city's atmosphere. In his contemptuous missives to other foreign capitalists, he cast the entire exercise as "pathetic." Rather than popular enthusiasm, he saw only boredom on the faces of marching Tanzanians. Rather than Tanzanian initiative, he saw shadowy, outside influences:

Why so leftish? The Chinese, physically, are not seen. Nevertheless, Chinese money has been flowing into Tanzania, through a Pakistani bank. Yet I do not really think the ideological guidance has really come from Pekin. It is American (from Berkeley), Canadian, British (financed from our aid funds), and Scandinavian. The "Kommisars" posted to the nationalized banks are drawn from this brigade.

For Pedler, the Arusha Declaration was intelligible through a combination of Cold War dichotomies and the naivete of African politicians. Dismissing the left as dangerously misguided, he tried to remind

---
[73] "Green Guards in Tanzania," *The Times*, February 13, 1967.
[74] Joe Rogaly, "The Key to the Tanzanian Scene," *Financial Times*, February 14, 1967.

Tanzanian ministers of the risks of hostility to foreign business. "Private investment creates managers, and this is Africa's most vital need, even ahead of capital," he tried to tell them.[75] Yet, in the heady days after the declaration, few doors were open to him.

In a recent reconstruction of the Arusha Declaration, George Roberts emphasizes the adversarial factions and personalities of TANU elites. Rather than a cohesive vision that enrolled a unified nation, the policy reflected manifold influences and caused multiple fractures.[76] The wisdom of nationalization was the subject of frequent debate within TANU, with some cautioning against rapid or expansive action, while others urged even more intervention. These internal differences, personal relations, and shifting outcomes were of central concern to expatriate businesses making sense of the moment. They called upon sympathetic insiders, such as Edwin Mtei, the Governor of the Bank of Tanzania, who told them that nationalization was against his judgment and caught him off guard. He was so frustrated by the nationalizations that he tendered his resignation (though Nyerere rejected it and Mtei carried on in the role for years to come). "I am so sorry you have been so disappointed in us," he told one British interlocutor.[77] Amir Jamal, too, seemed suspicious of the moves but loyally fell in line with the policy.

The complete and immediate takeover of foreign banks caught Barclays off guard. Although they were preparing for government takeovers in other countries, Tanzania was not even on the list of potential sites.[78] According to Dirk Stikker, a director of the Royal Dutch Shell Group who met with Nyerere the morning of February 6, the President's goal with the Arusha Declaration was more modest than what was announced mere hours later. The aim, reportedly, was only a 50 percent government holding in foreign firms, especially in large industries. As for the banks, the goal was to nationalize them

---

[75] DCO 38/438: "Tanzania," by F.J. Pedler, United Africa Company, January 13, 1967.
[76] Roberts, *Revolutionary State-Making*, chapter 2. See also Issa Shivji et al., *Julius Nyerere: Development as Rebellion*, vol. 3 (Mkuki na Nyota, 2020), pp. 119–135.
[77] DCO 11/2398: Nationalization in Tanzania (Preliminary Report), February 1967.
[78] DCO 80/5299: Mogford to Truitt, May 28, 1969.

3.3 "A Profound Shock": Making Sense of Nationalization

over a protracted period of time.[79] Yet, by 3:30 p.m., Nyerere had summoned bank leadership to a meeting where he announced their immediate and complete expropriation.[80]

In the businessmen's view, the *volte face* was the result of two influences: leftist radicals and mental illness. On the one hand, they blamed the "small caucus" of Abdulrahman Mohamed Babu, Michael Kamaliza, and Oscar Kambona for redirecting Nyerere at the Cabinet meeting held at 11 a.m. that day. In the dichotomous framing of the era, these revolutionary "wild men" were a reckless influence on the more moderate TANU officials like Mtei and Jamal.[81] The radicals could carry the day, however, because Nyerere was in the throes of a "mid-summer madness." As John Innes, Barclays local director in Nairobi put it,

His sanity has always been suspect and various members of the Nyerere family have at times been in mental homes; it is now generally felt that he has had one of his brainstorms which has carried nationalization to its ultimate in an avalanche.[82]

Other foreign capitalists concurred, characterizing Nyerere's enthusiasm as borderline "hysterical and unbalanced."[83] The Deputy Chairman of Standard Bank thought it was wise to adopt a "paternal" approach, reminding TANU of foreign capital's importance.[84] Such allegations of child-like unreasoning, of course, have a long colonial genealogy, and Chapter 1 discussed how they refracted through the

---

[79] DCO 11/2398: Nationalization in Tanzania (Preliminary Report), February 1967; UKNA FCO 31/53: D.U. Stikker Meeting with Julius Nyerere, February 7, 1967.

[80] The President was joined by Amon Nsekela and Ministers Jamal, Babu, and Swai who, the British thought, "were clearly shaken." DCO 80/4658: Nationalisation of Banks, February 7, 1967.

[81] UKNA FCO 31/53: Nationalization in Tanzania, February 16, 1967. George Roberts notes these were partly Cold War fantasies, and Babu in particular spoke in favor of more cautious moves on nationalization. *Revolutionary State-Making*, pp. 75–76. For his part, Pratt suggests that Nyerere's suggestion of nationalization was "extremely popular" at TANU's NEC meeting, encouraging the President to bring it to Cabinet where "approval was easily secured." Nyerere was capitalizing on the moment, moving far faster than expected two weeks prior. Pratt, *The Critical Phase*, p. 238.

[82] DCO 11/2398: Innes to Dyson, February 13, 1967.

[83] DCO 11/2398: The Tanzania Situation (Part 3), East Africa & Mauritius Association, n.d. but late February 1967.

[84] UKNA FCO 31/52: Memorandum, February 8, 1967.

East African Currency Board.[85] Yet, the racialized denigration of Tanzania's leaders had an additional significance for expropriated capitalists. It helped explain why the foreign businesses could so quickly be cast aside, despite what they thought to be a sturdy place in Tanzania. As Barclays' Chairman Frederic Seebohm put it in his letter to Nyerere a couple weeks after the nationalization, "The sudden and expected announcement ... came as a profound shock to the banking and general business community." He regretted it came without prior discussion, and he lamented that fifty years of contribution to Tanzania's economic development was being overlooked.[86]

Adopting this rueful tone was a strategic decision of the chairmen of all three British banks. From the moment Nyerere informed the Dar es Salaam bankers of the nationalization, he had promised "full and fair compensation." As he readily told one journalist when discussing compensation, "We must pay the price for our policies."[87] As long as he did so, the act was widely understood in international law to be legal.[88] As Seebohm's predecessor, Sir Julian Crossley, reminded his banker colleagues they could not object to nationalization – only a lack of compensation.[89] Emphasizing the "sudden" nature of the decision, however, could shift the legal calculus ever so slightly: while most

---

[85] Johannes Fabian, *Out of Our Minds: Reason and Madness in the Exploration of Central Africa* (University of California Press, 2000); for their part, Britain's Canadian stand-in in Dar es Salaam thought Tanzania "on an emotional binge over Arusha Declaration," with Nyerere "untypically immoderate ... But if he is riding a tiger it is one he has himself helped to conjure up." UKNA FCO 31/52: McGill Telegram, February 9, 1967.

[86] DCO 11/2398: Seebohm to Nyerere, February 24, 1967. In addition to their core banking business, Barclays was proud of the Barclays Overseas Development Corporation (established 1946) which positioned the banks work as an explicit contribution to African development. The official history called it "a showpiece of good intent." Margaret Ackrill and Leslie Hannah, *Barclays: The Business of Banking 1690–1996* (Cambridge University Press, 2001), p. 281. See also Crossley and Blandford, *The DCO Story*, pp. 144–145; James Morris, "'Cultivating the African': Barclays DCO and the Decolonisation of Business Strategy in Kenya, 1950–78," *Journal of Imperial and Commonwealth History* 44(4) (2016): 649–671; Billy Frank, "The 'Private' Face of African Development Planning during the Second World War," in J. M. Hodge et al. (eds.), *Developing Africa* (Manchester University Press, 2017), pp. 111–132.

[87] UKNA FCO 31/73: "Why Tanzania Nationalised," Gemini News Service.

[88] It also followed the relevant Tanzanian law, the Foreign Investment (Protection) Act of 1963.

[89] DCO 80/5300: Note of Conversation with Sir Julian, September 21, 1967.

thought compensation only needed to be properly priced and prompt, some legal analysts had begun to argue it "must be agreed before nationalization actually takes place."[90] Although it was unlikely to carry the day – and Barclays was unsure it wanted to do anything but settle this amiably – depicting the Arusha Declaration as impulsive and uncoordinated combined a legal stratagem, a racial prejudice, and the bankers' emotional whiplash.

3.4 Decolonizing the Economy and Its Discontents

The late 1960s were a time of considerable debate about the status of property and multinational corporations. Political decolonization set the stage for lawyers, diplomats, and economists from formerly colonized countries to successfully justify the expansion of sovereign power into the domain of production, finance, and trade. Oil-producing states were especially effective in asserting the sovereign right to national resources.[91] By the 1970s, these various movements had crystallized into the New International Economic Order, which Adom Getachew characterizes as an effort to "finally overcome the economic dependencies that threatened to undermine postcolonial self-government."[92] Through his articulation of "African socialism and self-reliance," Julius Nyerere was an energetic diplomatic and intellectual force in this international sea change. *Ujamaa na kujitegemea* did not involve a complete divorce from the international system; rather it worked at multiple scales, from new international regimes to the level of the village and the family.[93] Both before and after 1967, the independent state endeavored to diversify its imports and exports, reduce its vulnerability to market volatility, expand the indigenous sources of managerial expertise, and provide for basic needs through domestic

---

[90] DCO 80/4568: APPI Memorandum, February 17, 1967; see also Bradley, "Legal Aspects"; Clarence Dias, "Tanzanian Nationalisations: 1967–1970," *Cornell International Law Journal* 4(1) (1970): 59–79.
[91] Christopher R. W. Dietrich, *Oil Revolution: Anticolonial Elites, Sovereign Rights, and the Economic Culture of Decolonization* (Cambridge University Press, 2017).
[92] Adom Getachew, *Worldmaking after Empire: The Rise and Fall of Self-Determination* (Princeton University Press, 2019), p. 144.
[93] Priya Lal, "Self-Reliance and the State: Multiple Meanings of Development in Early Post-Colonial Tanzania," *Africa* 82(2) (2012): 212–234.

production.[94] Neither politicians nor intellectuals were unified in how best to proceed, and the resulting policies and institutions reflected this diversity, as well as an experimental responsiveness to internal troubles and external disturbances.

It is a mistake to see *ujamaa* and *kujitegemea* as antagonistic to money or trade *tout court*. The nationalization of banks was intended to better control the circulation of money. It would do so by keeping more proceeds within the nation and by transforming the basis on which credit was issued. TANU leadership distinguished between banking in the service of profits versus banking in the service of people's needs. Foreign banks could only do the former, meaning widespread need was unmet by capitalist firms. The duration, cost, and allocation of credit were foremost among the critiques. Transferring assets and management from private to public enterprise was meant to change this. Few Africans received loans from banks, whether for commercial or consumptive purposes, because an insistence on collateral justified discriminating against would-be borrowers. Even after independence, opening a bank account required Africans to be accompanied by their employers, "usually Europeans and Asians."[95] Banks like Barclays overwhelmingly lent to export agricultural intermediaries, a form of finance that was lucrative, low-risk, and short term. Crop finance of this sort was an important earner of foreign exchange, but it did little to support nascent industries. For that, banks would need to put money to work on longer timelines, but they were loath to tie up their capital in uncertain initiatives when they could reliably receive a return in London's financial markets. As a result, surplus funds in Tanzania – including savings from its citizens – were invested in London, doing little to expand the local market.[96] Tanzania, in other words, lent money to Britain.[97]

Despite Barclays' management's "profound shock" at the perceived suddenness of the Arusha Declaration, the nationalizations of

---

[94] Thomas Biersteker, "Self-Reliance in Theory and Practice in Tanzanian Trade Relations," *International Organization* 34(2) (1980): 229–264.

[95] Idrian Resnick, *The Long Transition: Building Socialism in Tanzania* (Monthly Review Press, 1981), p. 76.

[96] John Loxley, "Structural Change in the Monetary System of Tanzania," in Lionel Cliffe and John Saul (eds.), *Socialism in Tanzania: Politics and Policies* (East African Publishing House, 1972).

[97] Selsjord calculated that on a regional basis, "East African banks had lent £5.7 million to banks abroad" in 1965/66. "Recent Developments," p. XVI.

3.4 Decolonizing the Economy and Its Discontents 171

1967 were far from the first effort to redirect money in the service of the people's needs. Banking had for years been the subject of political opprobrium and policy reform.[98] Customers, too, complained about inefficiencies and high costs.[99] In the 1950s, one joke about unjustified fees reinterpreted the Barclays (Dominion, Colonial, and Overseas) acronym as "Don't Come and Overdraw."[100] While the Barclays Overseas Development Corporation began after World War II issuing longer term loans, the bank's core business remained the same.[101] Legal restrictions on lending to Africans dating from the interwar era were repealed only in 1961. In the ensuing years, the state established a variety of new financial institutions, including the Tanganyika Co-operative Bank (est. 1962) to lend to agricultural cooperatives, the National Housing Corporation (1963) to support homebuilding, and the Tanzania Bank of Commerce (1965) to provide banking to the government and its enterprises. Many of these were hemmed in by expatriate banks: the Co-operative Bank worked as an intermediary for them, rather than as a competitor, and the Bank of Commerce was a joint operation of the government and private banks.[102]

The Bank of Tanzania Act of 1965 inaugurated the country's most important effort to control money and credit. The central bank that it authorized began operations the next year, including issuing a national currency.[103] In contrast to the East African shilling, a national currency gave the Tanzanian state a monopoly on legal tender in the country. The Bank of Tanzania also provided the state greater power over credit creation than the conservative Currency Board. The Bank of Tanzania was also authorized to establish important regulations,

---

[98] Clara Caselli, *The Banking System of Tanzania* (Milan, 1975).
[99] Pauw, "Banking in East Africa," p. 236.
[100] Crossley and Blandford, *The DCO Story*, p. 180.
[101] Brian Macdona, "Financing Development in Africa: The Role of the Commercial Banks and Their Overseas Investment Corporations," *African Affairs* 66(265) (1967): 324–328.
[102] Speaking at the end of 1963, Nsilo Swai complimented the British bankers for their role and pointed to the Co-operative Bank as "a fine example of the operation of our mixed economy." TNA CB/14/1 Speeches by Swai, November 15, 1963.
[103] Paul Bjerk, "A Preliminary History of the Bank of Tanzania," in Salvatory Nyanto (ed.), *A History of Post-Colonial Tanzania: Essays in Honor of Prof. Isaria N. Kimambo* (James Currey, forthcoming); Edwin Mtei, *From Goatheard to Governor: The Autobiography of Edwin Mtei* (Mkuki na Nyota, 2005), chapter 11.

Figure 3.3 Government bureaucrats attending a training course at the Tanzania Bank of Commerce where they are shown various foreign currencies in 1966.
Courtesy of Tanzania Information Services.

including minimum reserve requirements for commercial banks, access their internal credit information, and influence insurance policies. It also improved the scope for foreign exchange controls, first imposed in 1965. Such supervision was hardly radical – the legislation followed years of consultation with the Bank of England, the German Bundesbank, and the International Monetary Fund – but it still marked a significant departure from the *laissez-faire* of colonial banking.

While many of these initiatives were justified in the malleable idiom of *maendeleo* (development), they were often more directly concerned with defending and growing the reserve of foreign money held by the state (see Figure 3.3).[104] In some ways, there were considerable successes, including the ability to marshal more than double the expected

[104] On the meanings of *maendeleo*, see Emma Hunter, "A History of Maendeleo: The Concept of 'Development' in Tanganyika's Late Colonial Public Sphere," in Joseph M. Hodge, Gerald Hodl, and Martina Kopf (eds.), *Developing Africa: Concepts and Practices in Twentieth-Century Colonialism* (Manchester University Press, 2014), 87–108.

3.4 Decolonizing the Economy and Its Discontents 173

domestic financing during the First Five Year Plan (1964–1969).[105] Despite these developments, by 1967, the Tanzanian state was still limited in its command over the economy. A series of political crises in the prior years meant that only in 1966 was TANU leadership able to dedicate more time to development activities.[106] It remained endangered by enduring underdevelopment and periods of rapid capital flight. The price of the major export earner, sisal, declined dangerously after independence as synthetic replacements became commonplace. After 1966, the leading earners of foreign money – cotton and coffee – struggled to keep up with rising demand for imported goods.[107] The drain of capital from Tanzania was estimated to be 120 percent of the incoming investment between 1962 and 1966, severely curtailing state and commercial ambitions.

This year-over-year drain was exacerbated by periodic accelerations that threatened the state's limited reserve of foreign currencies with which to pay for imports and repay foreign loans. The TANU National Executive Committee (NEC) meeting that drafted the Arusha Declaration actually took place under the shadow of one such event. As Edwin Mtei told the party elite gathered in Arusha at the start of February, there were quite literally East African Airways planes "flying overhead carrying tonnes of Bank of Tanzania notes" that would require the central bank to dip into its "meagre foreign exchange." The problem was so bad, he explained, that bankers in Nairobi "did not even have to count the notes being airlifted to Nairobi because they were still in the manufacturers' cellophane packages of one million shillings." Were the situation not stopped, "we would soon be bankrupt as a nation, unable to implement the decisions we were making."[108] Mtei meant his provocation to quell the NEC's more ambitious ideas and to maintain the relatively liberal status quo that prevailed in the financial sector; however, the expatriate banks were decisive contributors to the outflow of capital from Tanzania, both by financing the import of expensive commodities and exporting their

---

[105] Shs. 1,037 million compared to the planned Shs. 450 million. John Loxley, "Financial Planning and Control in Tanzania," in *Towards Socialist Planning* (Tanzania Publishing House, 1972), pp. 47–48.
[106] Pratt, *The Critical Phase*, p. 183.
[107] M. J. H. Yaffey, *Balance of Payments Problems of a Developing Country: Tanzania* (Brill, 1970), chapter 3.
[108] Mtei, *From Goatherd*, p. 107.

own profits. While it is not possible to say how influential Mtei's warning was, it is clear the Arusha Declaration was driven in part by frustration about Tanzania's slow economic progress.[109] Anxiety about capital flight was long-standing, and better command of monetary resources was foundational to Tanzania's effort to plan its development and exert sovereign control over economic matters.[110]

Banks like Barclays were deeply aware of the risks of postcolonial policy autonomy. The *Financial Times* called nationalization an "occupational hazard" that threatened "significant parts of banks' empires." But rather than an existential threat, it was something many were learning "to live with" and "able to take in stride." Despite nationalizations in Egypt, Syria, Burma, and Tanzania, for instance, Barclays still had nearly 50 percent more branches than they did a decade prior.[111] Nevertheless, European capitalists and states saw the trend of postcolonial expropriations as a menace to be stopped. The British businesses and state worked in the period after February 1967 to contain the fallout from Tanzania's actions.

Although the UK government thought Tanzania would inevitably have to pay a "price in terms of lowered well-being and diminished prospects" for the nationalizations, the British were limited in their influence due to a lack of diplomatic presence in Dar es Salaam.[112] Instead, they had to work through the Canadian High Commission and were reticent to push too hard on this back-channel. What information they had often amounted to "market gossip."[113] Given the existing antagonisms between the former colony and metropole, immediate protest by Her Majesty's Government would likely backfire, perhaps driving Tanzania closer to the Chinese.[114] In any case, there was little the British government could do, despite initial pressure from private industry. In the weeks after February 6, the Commonwealth

---

[109] Coulson, *Political Economy*, p. 219f; Roberts, *Revolutionary State-Making*, p. 81.
[110] Nsekela, "The Role of Commercial Banking."
[111] C. Gordon Tether, "Overseas Banks and Their Occupational Hazard," *Financial Times*, February 15, 1967. For more on the bank's growth in the 1960s, see Ackrill and Hannah, *Barclays*, pp. 274–293.
[112] UKNA FCO 31/44: Nationalisation of Banks in Tanzania, n.d. [but March 1967].
[113] DCO 11/2398: Memorandum: Tanzania, February 10, 1967.
[114] UKNA FCO 31/52: Nationalization of Banks in Tanzania by Morrice James, February 8, 1967.

3.4 Decolonizing the Economy and Its Discontents 175

Office enumerated what leverage they had in terms of technical assistance and aid. There were hardly any loans, and withdrawing British civil servants and teachers from Tanzania was not altogether practical. Besides, an overly strong reaction could be less effective than more conciliatory approaches. Instead, they met frequently with British multinationals in London and offered what assistance they could. For instance, indignant questions in Parliament were arranged to "ventilate" the issue and encourage negative press coverage.[115] Other governments were leaned on, lest they helped the Tanzanians too much.[116] They also promised to liaise with the World Bank, both in order to limit any potential contagion and to consider its role as a mediator in negotiations to come.[117] For its part, the Bank of England divulged confidential information about Tanzania's sterling reserve balances to assist the UK's strategic response.[118]

Faced with waning state influence, multinational corporations arranged their own advocates. Two were especially active: the East Africa & Mauritius Association and the Association Internationale Pour La Promotion et la Protection Des Investments Prives en Territoiries Etrangers (APPI). The former was established in 1964 by mostly British firms with interests in the newly independent region.[119] It was intended to improve the position of individual firms, possibly forcing governments like Tanzania's to moderate events like these.[120] The latter was based in Geneva, with a membership of internationally influential directors from companies like Credit Suisse, Unilever, British American Tobacco, and Rio Tinto. APPI worked with some secrecy and members agreed to a "solidarity clause" in which negative acts toward one would bring the disapproval of all.[121]

---

[115] DCO 80/4658: Telegram to Innes, Nairobi, February 15, 1967.
[116] DCO 80/4658: Note for General Managers, March 17, 1967.
[117] DCO 80/4658: Memorandum: Tanzania, February 10, 1967.
[118] UKNA FCO 31/52: Annex: Nationalization of Banks in Tanzania, February 10, 1967.
[119] Julian Crossley (of Barclays) and F. J. Pedler (of the United Africa Company) helped found the East Africa Association, which added "Mauritius" to its name in 1967. In 1967, it had 120 members headquartered in ten North Atlantic countries. UKNA FCO 31/71: Aide Memoire, February 1967. On its history, see Poppy Cullen, "Adapting to Independence: The East Africa Association, Post-Colonial Business Networks and Economic Development," in Véronique Dimier and Sarah Stockwell (eds.), *The Business of Development in Post-Colonial Africa* (Palgrave Macmillan, 2020), pp. 69–97.
[120] DCO 11/2398: Note to Chairman, March 1, 1967.
[121] DCO 11/2398: APPI: Tanzania, for Mr. Dyson, March 10, 1967.

In the aftermath of February 1967, Barclays turned to these transnational networks to defend their property. These lobbying networks reflect what Quinn Slobodian characterizes as the "dogged commitment to ... dividing the public world of states from the private world of property."[122] The East Africa & Mauritius Association announced ten days after nationalization that they would send a delegation to Dar es Salaam to "show the flag."[123] Their internal meetings discussed how to punish or pressure Tanzania, and they decided to pressure neighboring countries to ensure "the Tanzania disease" did not spread.[124] In their view, the task was one of image management: "nationalization must not only not work in Tanzania but also be seen not to work." For this reason, companies should "take the strongest possible line in every one of their dealings," and international businesses must convince other countries of the folly taking place in Tanzania.[125] In Uganda, the leadership promised a continuation of the status quo, though the Governor of the Bank of Uganda, Joseph Mubiru, mused that Nyerere would "become either the greatest hero in Africa or be destroyed."[126] In Kenya, the political and commercial elite had more to lose from a closure of the Tanzanian market, and President Kenyatta was angry at the lack of notice from Nyerere. The Minister of Commerce & Industry Mwai Kibaki also allayed the concerns of the British businesses, promising they had no reason to fear contagion in Kenya. While Kenyatta was under pressure from the left, he was uninterested in nationalization. At most, he would further the Africanization of trade or encourage the provision of corporate equity to African investors.[127]

APPI produced extensive legal analysis of the Tanzanian situation, but nowhere was their desired outcome evidently secure. As one academic reported to Barclays, the Tanzanian law bore considerable

---

[122] Quinn Slobodian, *Globalists: The End of Empire and the Birth of Neoliberalism* (Harvard University Press, 2018), p. 140.
[123] DCO 11/2398: Meeting of the East Africa & Mauritius Association, February 16, 1967.
[124] DCO 80/4658: Chairmen's Meeting, February 22, 1967.
[125] DCO 11/2398: Meeting of the East Africa & Mauritius Association, February 16, 1967.
[126] DCO 11/2398: Nationalisation in Tanzania, East Africa & Mauritius Association, March 1, 1967.
[127] DCO 11/2398: East Africa & Mauritius Association Report on East Africa, February/March 1967; see also UKNA FCO 31/49: Reactions from Kenya to Tanzania Nationalization.

similarities to Britain's own actions under the Labour government after World War II.[128] Some lawyers even worried that Tanzania had a good claim on the balances Barclays froze in London, and a turn to the courts would backfire.[129] Ultimately, international law offered little consolation to the expropriated firms. Tanzania's actions were likely legal – as long as they compensated the banks.[130] What was left to Barclays was the task of ensuring they received the best price possible. The next section analyzes these negotiations, paying particular attention to how the struggle for economic sovereignty unfolded through calculative techniques and debates about the power to determine valuation.

3.5 Accounting for Value

The government of Tanzania insisted from the fateful afternoon of February 6, 1967 onward that they were committed to paying what Nyerere called "full and fair compensation." Doing so would categorize the action as a permissible nationalization, rather than an illegal confiscation.[131] However, from the start of the ordeal, those involved recognized the difficulty of finding an agreed definition for full and fair compensation. As a result, the negotiations often stalled for months at a time. After an initial series of meetings in the months after the Arusha Declaration, talks collapsed in the face of a yawning gap between proposed valuations for the nationalized business. In January 1968, constructive talks were held in Dar es Salaam, but a basis for compensation was still lacking. A year later, following a shift in valuation styles, the gap was smaller, but it still took until June 1969 for a deal to be signed.

The impasses and delays happened for numerous reasons. Telegrams were delayed, schedules were conflicting, and antagonisms smoldered. Barclays could afford to carry the loss of the Tanzania business for a

---

[128] DCO 11/2398: The Nationalisation Bills in Tanzania, 1967.
[129] DCO 80/5300: Memorandum to Mogford, February 28, 1967.
[130] For the legal transformations of this era, see Nicolás Perrone, *Investment Treaties and the Legal Imagination: How Foreign Investors Play by Their Own Rules* (Oxford University Press, 2021).
[131] While expatriates tended to speak of "prompt, adequate, and effective" compensation, they generally accepted this to be, in theory, what Tanzania promised in terms of "full and fair compensation." DCO 11/2398: Note on meeting at the House of Commons, March 15, 1967.

while. TANU, for its part, was in the throes of internal schisms. The Tanzanian state was overstretched and understaffed; amid urgent tasks facing government, parting ways with their limited foreign exchange had less appeal. A lack of foreign reserves meant Tanzania could ill afford to pay too much for all the nationalized firms. Within the state, some like Edwin Mtei earnestly desired a ready agreement, thinking it would boost confidence in Tanzania's currency. But he jostled with others who thought payment should be parsimonious. After all, had the British banks not already compensated themselves enough through a history of exorbitant profits exported to London?[132] As Nyerere put it with characteristic wit, "I did say full and fair compensation and I meant it, but I did not say prompt."[133]

Most important, though, were the shifting and competing interests and techniques for assigning worth. In the days after nationalization, the bankers in London began computing a range of valuations for their Tanzania businesses. Accountants gathered together assets and liabilities, profits and losses in order to begin their negotiations with Nyerere's government. The Egyptian and Burmese precedents could guide their financial reckoning, but the bank's calculus was anything but straightforward.[134] While they had a financial interest in a large payment, they recognized too high a number would carry certain risks. For one thing, it would make it less likely the government could afford compensation. There was also the matter of appearances: if Tanzania was pressured into a large payment, it would suggest to everyone – especially other countries – that Barclays was earning undue profits at the expense of Africans. The outrage could spread to Kenya, Uganda, and Zambia. On the other hand, if they settled for a small amount, other states might think nationalization was an affordable policy.[135] They needed a "suitable" compensation, one that would satisfy their bottom line and shareholders but also one to which Tanzania would agree. In the early days, they wanted a feasible number in order to not lose momentum. A deadlock would harden attitudes, making

---

[132] DCO 80/5301: Nationalisation Tanzania, Talks in Dar es Salaam, January 1968; also DCO 80/4658: Elliot to Dyson, March 20, 1967.
[133] DCO 80/5300: Note for File, September 18, 1967.
[134] On the Egyptian experience, see DCO 80/5300: Memorandum to the General Managers, February 18, 1967.
[135] DCO 80/5301: Economic and Legal Aspects of the Nationalisations in Tanzania, May 21, 1968.

3.5 Accounting for Value

settlement unlikely. The "impression will be that the Tanzanian government has got away with it and snapped up the business of the British Banks for nothing."[136]

The risks of future nationalizations weighed on Barclays in another important way. Whatever was agreed in Tanzania could serve as the basis for agreements with other countries. As a result, the British bankers insisted that before any specific settlement number was agreed, "the basis on which the compensation due to us should be computed."[137] In other words, compensation for the bankers was a matter of finding an accounting standard – what they called a "formula" – with which to calculate the amount of money Tanzania owed them. As a result, satisfying the goals of the Arusha Declaration hinged on the successful maneuvering of accounting protocols and asset valuations.

For its part, the Tanzanian government suggested the net assets of all nine nationalized banks only amounted to £900,000.[138] To guide their negotiations, they hired a Danish accountant, H. C. Steen Hansen, to navigate the technicalities of valuation. Steen Hansen was chosen, in part, because Denmark was unaffiliated in the dispute with Britain and, in part, because there was "no doubt that Danes were good capitalists who were also used to state enterprise."[139]

Within a matter of months, Steen Hansen and his colleagues found suitable calculations for most of the affected banks.[140] The only holdouts were Barclays, Standard, and National & Grindlays. Steen Hansen's involvement worried the British banks who were accustomed to being the principal source of banking expertise in Tanzania. They were loath to share their internal accounts with him, due in part to a history of misleading bookkeeping that lowered their tax obligations, it seemed.[141] When Steen Hansen initially suggested a fair price for

---

[136] DCO 80/5831: Compensation in Tanzania, August 3, 1967.
[137] DCO 80/5301: Letter to Steen Hansen, Compensation Claim, August 7, 1968.
[138] Jamal told MPs this when introducing the bank nationalization law. DCO 11/2398: Elliot to Dyson, February 15, 1967.
[139] DCO 80/5300: "Tanzania: How Arusha Works" by Basil Davidson, December 30, 1967.
[140] The National Bank of Pakistan had assets equal to liabilities, so no compensation was paid. The Bank of Baroda and Algemene Bank Nederland received small payments, reportedly leaving "satisfied" with the deal. DCO 80/5300: "Tanzania: How Arusha Works" by Basil Davidson, December 30, 1967; Dias, "Tanzanian Nationalizations," p. 68.
[141] Mittelman, "Underdevelopment and Nationalisation," p. 609.

compensation would be one or two years of profit, the bankers' worries only deepened: surely this was a hatchet job from a leftist amateur, not a competent or impartial arbiter.[142] Taking over Barclays Tanzania for one or two years' profits, they replied, was like buying a house for one- or two-years' rent. Their worry turned to frustration, though, when their inquiries in Copenhagen learned that Steen Hansen was a known Anglophile, "a right-wing man rather than left, and has a high reputation."[143] At best, Steen Hansen seemed to speak a "very different accounting language."[144] The banks tried to sideline Steen Hansen – dismissing his approach as a "theoretical argument" – and work directly with J. D. Namfua, Amon Nsekela, and other state officials.[145]

J. D. Namfua became the lead Tanzanian negotiator. A former official of the Tanganyika Federation of Labour, at the time, Namfua was serving as Principal Secretary for the Ministry of Finance. He was joined by Roland Brown, a former UK Labour candidate and legal advisor to Tanzania, and Reginald Green, an American economist advising government.[146] In responding to the bankers' claims, Namfua and colleagues pointed to the National Bank of Commerce Act of 1967. This law authorized the expropriation of the banks and called for the repossession of assets and liabilities "situated" in Tanzania. It required compensation to be paid based on their "net asset value," an accounting technique which simply subtracts liabilities from assets.[147] This was a common-enough accounting approach (known sometimes as the "book value" of a firm), but Barclays knew it did them no favors.[148] At the center of their concerns were the characteristics of their banking business. Unlike, say, a settler farm or

---

[142] The relationship with Steen Hansen was so soured that by May 1968, at a report of the Danish accountant's illness in Dar es Salaam, a Barclays official jotted "nothing trivial I hope" in the margins. DCO 80/5301: Extract from Report on Tanzania, May 1968.
[143] DCO 80/5831: Memorandum, August 10, 1967.
[144] DCO 80/5301: Nationalisation in Tanzania, Talks in Dar es Salaam, January 1968.
[145] DCO 80/5301: Ambrose to Steen Hansen, September 1, 1967.
[146] Green reflects on the valuation process in "A Guide to Acquisition & Initial Operation: Reflections from Tanzanian Experience, 1967–74," in Julio Faundez and Sol Picciotto, *The Nationalisation of Multinationals in Peripheral Economies* (Macmillan, 1978), pp. 17–70.
[147] DCO 11/2398: The National Bank of Commerce (Establishment and Vesting of Assets and Liability) Act, 1967.
[148] DCO 11/2398: Tanzania – Thoughts on Preliminary Study of Act, February 17, 1967.

3.5 Accounting for Value

a cement factory, the value of a bank was largely unconnected to any tangible assets.[149] Indeed, "the value of the physical assets of Barclays D.C.O. in Tanzania [was] less than their liabilities there."[150] This was partly due to the British predilection for investing very little in the (post) colonies. Instead, customer deposits and bank profits were invested in London. Even those tangible assets the bank did own in the country, such as their premises, were financed out of local deposits (which were liabilities the bank owed to those customers). The result was that "the compensation received on a net asset basis will be small," limited to items like furniture, motor vehicles, and stationery.[151] In other words, the strategy of exporting capital to London kept very few assets within the Tanzanian business. As Barclays' chairman put it, "this meant that our 50 years of development and profitable operations were virtually valueless from the point of view of compensation," at least, that is, if assets were calculated according to the law's formula.[152]

Other accounting standards would return different valuations. In the opening weeks, the three British banks decided to work together to enforce their perspective – namely that the worth of their business was fundamentally based on intangible assets, the most important of which were the closely linked notions of "goodwill" and "going concern."[153] When the government acquired Barclays' business, they acquired trained staff, customer relations, and other aspects that did not appear on a balance sheet. These were what accountants call "goodwill," and Barclays insisted they were "very real asset[s]" that must be included in any assessment of the expropriated business, even if they did not appear in their balance sheet.[154] Furthermore, they asserted it was reasonable to expect the expropriated business to continue on the solid

---

[149] One legal analyst characterized the assets for these purposes as "all rights under contracts and agreements, books of account and records, stock in trade, choses in action and all other rights, interests and claims in or to property." Bradley, "Legal Aspects," p. 154. See also Onah et al., "The Nationalisation of British Banks."
[150] DCO 80/5300: Opinion by Mann, September 20, 1967.
[151] DCO 80/4658: Memorandum: Compensation, February 14, 1967.
[152] DCO 80/5301: Seebohm Visit to Dar es Salaam, June 1–4, 1969.
[153] These were sometimes substituted for each other but often linked as alternative ways of framing the future expected returns. DCO 80/5301: Report by Williams, Negotiations in Dar es Salaam on Compensation, January 17–19, 1968.
[154] DCO 80/5301: Nationalisation Tanzania, Talks in Dar es Salaam, January 1968.

footing Barclays established. Government acquired a "going concern" with continuing revenue and relations, not a static commodity.

In their opening negotiating position, Barclays demanded £2,477,870, split between three components: £98,093 in unremitted profits between October 1966 and the date of nationalization, £207,483 for losses due to severance, and £2,172,294 for the value of the business as a going concern. The first two figures were relatively unimportant. One simply reflected prior earnings that were not exported to London before capital controls were installed. The other, Barclays confided internally, was included in order to have something to eliminate as part of negotiations. It was the third most substantial figure that shaped negotiations, and it was the formula for determining that figure that most concerned Barclays. For the bankers, the value of their business was a number best achieved through the projection of past profits into the future. More specifically, the three British banks agreed among themselves to average prior years' earnings and multiply them by a number of future years. This amounted to an artifice in multiple ways: How many years of prior earnings should be averaged? How many years into the future could such an average be expected to hold? On what basis should it be assumed past earnings predicted future earnings? Should their opening formulas not prove persuasive, they stood ready with "standby" claims that used a different method but gave nearly the same result.[155]

The invocation of "goodwill" was meant to justify these calculative compositions and facilitate a larger payment from the government. From their opening letter to Nyerere in February 1967, Barclays insisted that the first step in negotiations must be agreeing to a way of calculating the value of their business. Ultimately, this was an insistence that the government agree to a formula that would bequeath a larger valuation. In directing the negotiations through balance sheet calculations, however, the bankers tried to immunize their claims against accusations of self-interestedness. Their preferred accounting protocols, the banks argued, were "well understood and accepted in business circles throughout the world."[156] But the effort to enforce these standards failed to become generally agreed in this situation. Rather than achieving objectivity, the accounting standards remained matters for contestation between interested parties.[157]

[155] DCO 80/4685: Memorandum: Tanzania Compensation, May 8, 1967.
[156] DCO 805302: Reed to Namfua, February 15, 1969.
[157] Bruno Latour, "Why Has Critique Run out of Steam? From Matters of Fact to Matters of Concern," *Critical Inquiry* 30(2) (2004): 225–248.

3.5 Accounting for Value

"Goodwill" may have been offered as a technical term of art, but it was frequently interpreted as an ethical claim. Tanzania's negotiators argued "at length and heatedly" that there was no goodwill.[158] For one thing, the term was applicable only in cases of a willing buyer and willing seller – not compulsory expropriation.[159] Moreover, Barclays had squandered any goodwill it had by rapidly withdrawing its expatriate staff and freezing millions of Tanzanian deposits in London. Among other things, destroyed staff records impeded the work of the National Bank of Commerce.[160] In contrast, other banks withdrew their staff slowly to facilitate the adjustments. And whatever amity might have been salvaged was lost when Barclays submitted their opening claim – a figure Nyerere and colleagues found insultingly high.[161] Imbuing "goodwill" with ethical significance kept the technical accounting standard from overruling other considerations.

The question of a formula by which to value nationalized banks proved irresolvable in the first year after the Arusha Declaration. The middle of 1967 was spent exchanging letters and running numbers. The Ministry of Finance team successfully reached deals with a variety of other expatriate firms, including in December 1967 the third largest British bank, National & Grindlays.[162] The other two, however, risked becoming what Barclays hoped it would not: "a festering sore poisoning our relationships in the years ahead."[163] With progress stalled, both sides were deprived of wealth they were owed: the full and fair compensation to Barclays and the sterling equivalent of TSh. 40 million that remained unremitted in London.

---

[158] DCO 80/5301: Tanzania Nationalisation, talks in Dar es Salaam, January 1968.

[159] DCO 80/5300: Steen Hansen to Rodway, August 18, 1967. It was shared by legal analysts that suggested the significant transformation of a political context invalidated the sorts of value that might be claimed previously: "the legislative introduction of a socialist structure does not require compensation for every interest which is of economic value while the capitalist system continues." Bradley, "Legal Aspects," p. 166.

[160] Amon Nsekela, "Some Practical Problems of Nationalization," *Mbioni* 5(4) (1969): 25.

[161] DCO 11/2398: Notes on a Meeting at the House of Commons, March 15, 1967.

[162] DCO 80/5300: Notes of Conversation with National & Grindlays Bank, January 11, 1968; N&G did so because it was a smaller bank than Barclays and Standard, had a weaker bargaining positioning, and was in the process of becoming a specialized bank (rather than one with many overseas branches). See Mittelman, "Underdevelopment and Nationalisation," pp. 612–613.

[163] DCO 80/5831: Memorandum: Compensation in Tanzania, August 3, 1967.

This last fact was particularly upsetting. When the negotiating teams for Standard and Barclays met their counterparts in Dar es Salaam in January 1968, the Tanzanians scolded the British for abdicating their role as trusted stewards of depositors' cash. Adopting the rhetoric of more vocal nationalists, Tanzania's negotiators reminded Barclays and Standard of their years of large profits due to the virtual "cartel" that allowed colluding banks to "impose on the public what charges it liked."[164] They refused to adopt Barclays' preferred method of valuation, despite Barclays offering to extend repayment for up to fifteen years through the provision of a loan to Tanzania. For their part, the bankers thought little of the opposing side: Roland Brown was "living in a world of his own" on commercial matters; Reginald Green was "a theorist, with no experience of practical business"; and Steen Hansen "waffled away from time to time without contributing anything useful."[165] Namfua was pleasant but deferred to these advisors who held a strong line, refusing to countenance the claim by Barclays.

On the second day of meetings, the two banks offered concessions. They offered to waive their claims for administrative losses and severance costs (which, anyways, had been included in their opening bid with an eye to removing). They would also lower their asserted value of the business. For Barclays, this represented a figure £677,289 lower than the original, though internally they were willing to settle for as low as £1.4 million.[166] The Tanzanian team said they would consider the banks' formula of multiplying averaged prior profits by a certain number, but they refused to use only the past two years of returns. They insisted, in other words, that the formula's variables be open for negotiation: the proposal of using two years average profits was deemed for what it was, an artifact subject to negotiation. Instead, the Tanzanians said averaging five years of profit was a better judge of the banks' earnings. Their reasons were multiple: for one thing, 1966 was a bumper year in Tanzania more generally, and the banks' profits reflected that. For another, averaging five years' profits gave a

---

[164] DCO 80/5301: Report by Williams, Negotiations in Dar es Salaam on Compensation, January 17–19, 1968.
[165] DCO 80/5301: Nationalisation Tanzania, Talks in Dar es Salaam, January 1968.
[166] DCO 80/5301: Tanzania Nationalisation, talks in Dar es Salaam, Summary Report, January 1968.

"very unsatisfactory" number for the banks (around £60,000 compared to £142,000 when using the two-year average).[167] The banks protested that a five-year average obscured the upward trajectory in their growth, but the government refused to incorporate the additional variable of weighted averages.

The formula, in other words, proved unable to structure the negotiations. Rather than an objective instrument to shape the deal, it was impugned as partial, even misleading. Namfua and his team recognized accounting as a mutable device for establishing worth; they pried open the formula's component parts to proffer lower valuations. Over the course of the negotiations, it became clear that the accounting protocols did not live up to their promise of directing negotiations as intended. Nor could they persuasively justify the asserted valuation. The bankers tried to substitute new numbers in hopes of rescuing their desired compensation payment. They tried to pin the government to a specific multiplier, but such goals were elusive as long as Tanzania likewise saw formulas as a façade. "Whatever formulae were adopted," the Barclays accountants lamented, "Government would mold it to ensure that the resulting figure would approximate that which Government were prepared to pay."[168]

Lacking any other basis for agreement, the negotiations broke down. Nevertheless, the work of transforming banking in Tanzania continued. The next section examines that work before returning to the final round of discussions to establish the value of Barclays' business in Tanzania.

3.6 Banking, African Socialism, and Self-Reliance

Despite the stalled compensation negotiations, government officials in Tanzania hurried forward with the project of making banking work

---

[167] Barclays' profit figures were the following:
1962–38,000
1963–a small loss
1964–6,000
1965–114,000
1966–152,000.
DCO 80/5301: Tanzania Nationalisation, talks in Dar es Salaam, Summary Report, January 1968.

[168] DCO 80/5301: Report by Williams, Negotiations in Dar es Salaam on Compensation, January 17–19, 1968.

for *ujamaa* and *kujitegemea*. While the immediate aftermath of the nationalization was a chaotic administrative flurry and a commercial standstill, within a surprisingly short time, the new governmental bank began operating with some success. If Tanzania's opponents were betting on "quick collapse, they lost," noted one journalist.[169]

The state's goal was not the end of banking, but rather its repurposed expansion. As Amir Jamal said, nationalization was "to extend the monetary sector to people at the subsistence level." The government would do in fifteen years what the banks could not be expected to do in fifty years.[170] Maintaining confidence in the currency and banks was therefore an important task. Tanzania's critics hoped to shape public perception of the situation so the nationalization would flounder. In contrast, TANU was careful to insist the National Bank of Commerce would be run on "strictly commercial lines," free from interference.[171] Paul Bomani toured warehouses for major traders, telling journalists that commodity stocks were high and sufficient to weather any short-term difficulties.[172] Bank customers, too, were safe. "I myself have my money deposited with one of the nationalized banks," Nyerere assured citizens when announcing the takeover, going on to clarify that customer accounts remained theirs, while the institution was being acquired.[173] Such promises of continued commercial value were aimed not least at Tanzanians who TANU called upon to contribute to national productivity. Parastatal banking would form an infrastructure for this economic citizenship (see Figure 3.4).

The NBC was guided by its inaugural chairman Amon Nsekela. He was born in Mbeya Region and an early member of TANU. Over time, Nsekela rose from a schoolteacher and district officer under British rule to a wide variety of important roles in the independent state, including Principal Secretary in pivotal ministries and the secretary to the 1964–1965 Presidential Commission on the Establishment of a Democratic One-Party State.[174] From Nsekela's perspective,

---

[169] DCO 80/5300: "New Bank Weathers the Storm," September 1967.
[170] "Banks Take-Over Legalised," *East African Standard*, February 15, 1967.
[171] "Nationalised Banks Show Good Profit," *Times of Zambia*, September 11, 1967.
[172] "Bomani Explains Unrest," *The Standard*, May 9, 1967.
[173] "Tanzania Nationalizes Banks," *East African Standard*, February 7, 1967.
[174] Amon Nsekela, *Socialism and Social Accountability* (Kenya Literature Bureau, 1978), p. ix.

3.6 Banking, African Socialism, and Self-Reliance

Figure 3.4 An NBC customer deposits money in his account.
Courtesy of Tanzania Information Services.

British control had made colonies "mere appendages of Western industrialised economies," and nationalization was a necessary part of self-determination.[175] His appointment to run the NBC bespeaks its importance to the state, and he used the office to not only oversee the bank but to frequently address party members and citizens about the opportunities and challenges for banking after 1967.

Among the first tasks facing the NBC was to amalgamate the branches, staff, and balance sheets of the nine nationalized banks. The NBC also needed to establish ties with international banks to continue financing the import and export of commodities. This was a job Britain's multinational banks believed themselves uniquely equipped to provide: with an unparalleled global presence, they could transfer money around the world for their customers. At first, the Bank of Tanzania and NBC were overwhelmed by the volume of

---

[175] Amon Nsekela, "The Public Corporation as an Instrument of Economic Development in Africa," *Mbioni* 7(3) (1972): 5.

international transfers. Quickly, though, the Algemene Bank Nederland and Ottoman Bank offered to serve as international correspondents. Within a few weeks, the NBC had thirty-three foreign accounts, and twenty-five foreign banks offered them credit amounting to nearly £2.5 million. As the only bank in Tanzania, the NBC was too important to sideline. As one journalist put it, "The short-term crisis can be said to have ended finally on the day the British banks in Nairobi started doing business with the National Bank of Commerce."[176] By April 1967, new lending rules were established, and commercial activity was recovering.[177] Previously delayed international transfers were reported to be quick and efficient by September.[178] In the same month, the new bank reported making £300,000 in its first half-year.[179]

Finding suitable staff was another challenge for the NBC.[180] The 1,500 staff that remained sometimes displayed frustrating habits: while Nsekela thought there "was a wealth of talent in the middle and lower echelons," the history of managerial control instilled diffidence and a lack of confidence in taking on new tasks.[181] They also had loyalties to their former employers that could manifest as rivalries with their new co-workers: "A Barclays man always felt superior to a Standard man and vice versa," reported Amon Nsekela when reflecting on the NBC's travails.[182] As members of the conservative bourgeoisie targeted by the Arusha Declaration, Nsekela thought their hesitance understandable if troubling.

More generally, the new bank was stymied by the historic underinvestment in African banking staff and the intransigence of affected businesses. As discussed, British bank employees were welcomed to work for the new enterprise, but they preferred a rapid exodus. A Bank of England employee seconded to the Tanzanian central bank was rebuked for "conveying the impression that all his allegiance was to his new

---

[176] DCO 80/5300: "New Bank Weathers the Storm" clipping from September 1967.
[177] Dias, "Tanzanian Nationalizations," p. 74.
[178] DCO 80/5300: Tanganyika Portland Cement Co. by J.H. Cummins, September 7, 1967.
[179] "Nationalised Banks Show Good Profit," *Times of Zambia*, September 11, 1967.
[180] The reliance on expatriate management and expertise was a wider phenomenon. In 1968, 78 percent of senior parastatal posts were foreigners. Aminzade, *Race, Nation, and Citizenship*, pp. 173–181.
[181] Nsekela, "The Public Corporation," p. 19.
[182] Nsekela, "Some Practical Problems of Nationalization," pp. 21–22.

3.6 Banking, African Socialism, and Self-Reliance

masters" in Tanzania and warned off from working to help the National Bank of Commerce.[183] Instead, Tanzania began recruiting experienced bankers of other nationalities. In consulting with the banks, the British Commonwealth Office considered interfering behind the scenes with Tanzania's recruitment drive, and although "privately we might want to see the new bank get into a mess," it was decided that too much chaos would not serve British interests in East Africa. The National Bank of Commerce, the meeting in London concluded, "was quite free to recruit where it liked," though the British should not be too forthcoming with assistance.[184] Yet, whatever magnanimity the British claimed, those involved with staffing the NBC reported considerable pressure from Britain to impede Tanzania hiring suitable replacement bankers.[185]

Denmark, the Netherlands, and Sweden proved an especially important source of expertise, with perhaps a dozen bankers joining the NBC in its first year, including the first general manager, I. G. Konradsen.[186] In January 1968, he was replaced by a Frenchman, J. F. Eugene Gerbier. US and UK economists and statisticians in the Treasury and University of Dar es Salaam also worked closely with the bank on lending policy, foreign exchange management, and other financial accounts. More important to the day-to-day functioning of the NBC, though, were the branch employees who stepped into the void left by departing British staff. Many of these were of Asian heritage, and some reports suggested they were actually better than the young British staff who previously served as their bosses.[187] However, their salaries remained at levels they felt incommensurate with seniority, and many were fearful that Africanization would follow nationalization.[188]

---

[183] DCO 80/4658: Memorandum Tanzania, March 2, 1967.
[184] DCO 80/4658: Memorandum of Commonwealth Office meeting, March 22, 1967; the NBC general manager did, however, report a lack of open doors in Europe due to a perception of British interference. UKNA FCO 31/44: Letter to Hawker, March 17, 1967.
[185] TNA Accession 469: CCMCB/20/9 Tanzania National Bank of Commerce, 1965–67: Van Eeghen to A.J. Nsekela, April 6, 1967.
[186] The USSR offered banking experts, but non-aligned nationals were preferred. "Dane Chosen to Examine Firms in Tanzania," *The Times*, clipping in DCO 11/2398.
[187] Nsekela's first annual report said many of the Asian staff were "recruited directly in India by the former Banks." Non-citizen staff were 23 percent of total staff but around 50 percent of senior roles. "Chairman's Statement," in *NBC Annual Report* 1967/68, p. 7.
[188] DCO 80/5300: Letter from [illegible] Asian employee, Mwanza, December 12, 1967.

For their part, African bank staff sought to overcome their prior marginalization. The NBC established a training unit and began sending staff to the United States, Sweden, Pakistan, and elsewhere for banking courses. Yet given the breadth of roles needing educated Africans across Tanzania, banking still struggled to find suitable candidates. In 1961, only 480 Tanganyikan Africans had completed secondary school, and fewer than 100 had graduated university.[189] Unmaking this legacy was slow going, and banking had to compete with many other sectors in need of skilled manpower. The result exasperated Nsekela: in its first year of operation, the NBC was "allocated precisely one graduate!"[190]

The various banks coming under national control differed in organization and systems. Consolidating and standardizing their methods were time-consuming and difficult, but it also allowed for certain efficiencies. For instance, competing bank branches in Tanzanian towns could be trimmed to one, and by June 1968, fourteen duplicate branches were closed.[191] Expensive expatriate salaries could also be eliminated. As one senior official told a friendly journalist,

> For all practical purposes, from a national standpoint we were providing some £400,000 a year in foreign banking profits, as well as paying about £150,000 a year in expatriate banking staff salaries and management fees, and all this simply for the pleasure of having foreign banks manage our own money.[192]

Wrestling financial authority away from expatriate banks was at the core of socialism and self-reliance. One of the immediate actions of the government was to consolidate control over credit policy (see Figure 3.5). Starting the week of February 6, a Dar es Salaam committee met monthly to make decisions about overdrafts and loans. Its membership was a mix of TANU technocrats and expatriate advisors.[193] Depositors were guaranteed continued rights to withdraw

---

[189] Al Noor Kassum, *Africa's Winds of Change: Memoirs of an International Tanzanian* (I. B. Tauris, 2007), p. 40.

[190] He found it "utterly incompatible" with their importance. "Some Practical Problems of Nationalization," p. 34; On the push for African education vis-à-vis expatriates, see Pratt, *The Critical Phase*, pp. 129–134.

[191] Binhammer, *Financial Infrastructure*, p. 45.

[192] DCO 80/5300: "Tanzania: How Arusha Works" by Basil Davidson, December 30, 1967.

[193] *National Bank of Commerce, Reports & Accounts*, February 7 to June 30, 1967.

3.6 Banking, African Socialism, and Self-Reliance

Figure 3.5 The first meeting of the board of the National Bank of Commerce, shortly after nationalizations in 1967.
Courtesy of Tanzania Information Services.

their money, but overdrafts and loans were initially curtailed. In the turmoil of February and March 1967, this was especially important because skittish businesses would use bank credit for their day-to-day operations while secreting their savings and surplus out of the country. The committee was careful to limit this capital flight. Some borrowers, however, complained: short-term overdrafts "which used to be granted as matter of course" by bank managers now needed to wait for central approval. Large loans, too, were more difficult to receive, even for "unimpeachable customers."[194] Over time, the NBC decentralized to an extent: branch managers received common instructions and came together for training, but they had discretion over lending within a certain limit.[195]

On a longer time frame, the state would seek to change the characteristics of bank credit.[196] Amon Nsekela explained that the "creation

[194] Barclays 80/5300: "New Bank Weathers the Storm," September 1967.
[195] *National Bank of Commerce, Report and Accounts*, February 7 to June 30, 1967.
[196] Ann Seidman, *Comparative Development Strategies in East Africa* (East African Publishing House, 1972), pp. 240–248.

of a uniform lending policy" was a goal of the bank. In allusion to the racialized history of credit in Tanzania, the National Bank of Commerce Act directed it to conduct its business without discrimination.[197] The state enterprise also took meaningful, if modest, steps to move into more medium-term lending, rather than the short-term agricultural credit that predominated. He urged branch managers to not be so conservative in their lending: they should not maintain high branch liquidity for its own sake, but only if there were no viable lending opportunities.[198] Nsekela viewed the previous banks' policies as unsuitably biased. They were at odds with the production of an economy that served people's needs and liberated them from historical dependencies. Many citizens agreed, requesting the NBC expand their presence to areas previously neglected by expatriate banks. Members of Parliament quickly called for the state to expand credit for farmers – a demographic to which Barclays boasted it had previously "been able to avoid lending much."[199]

In contrast to British firms, the NBC would use "short-run profitability" as only one criterion for meeting this demand. Instead, "the social costs and benefits" would also be considered. This implied a remaking of the geography of banking, with more outreach to rural areas.[200] "We maintain that the regional distribution of credit could be improved," Nsekela wrote five months into the NBC's operations, and "we do not subscribe to the traditional view which regarded up-country branches merely as sources of surplus funds for use in urban centres."[201] Closing redundant branches facilitated opening nearly 50 new branches and 150 mobile agencies in the first half decade (see Figure 3.6).[202] And over time, Nsekela hoped, the NBC would become

---

[197] Bradley, "Legal Aspects," p. 156.
[198] UKNA FCO 31/48: Tanzania's Economy – Consequences of the Arusha Declaration, December 1967.
[199] DCO 11/2398: Local Director Dar es Salaam to General Managers, February 19, 1967.
[200] In this way, it followed the official preference for rural life in Tanzania. See the discussion in Brownell, *Gone to Ground* and Callaci, *Street Archives*.
[201] *National Bank of Commerce, Report and Accounts*, February 7 to June 30, 1967.
[202] Nsekela, "The Public Corporation," p. 20; Binhammer, *Financial Infrastructure*, p. 45.

3.6 Banking, African Socialism, and Self-Reliance

Figure 3.6 A newly constructed NBC branch in Arusha.
Courtesy of Tanzania Information Services.

like any other national utility – electricity, education, water, and health – for which "every Tanzanian will be yearning."[203]

Nationalization offered Tanzania's vanguard party-state a new means for producing citizens befitting *ujamaa* and *kujitegemea*. Amon Nsekela, for instance, thought the NBC served a pedagogical role, dispelling the "superstition and ignorance" that surrounds money.[204] Peasants and workers – the archetypal subjects of socialist Tanzania – were often exhorted to dedicate themselves to the hard work of self-reliance. The NBC also encouraged them to "save for a rainy day." This required overcoming people's ignorance about the security and purpose of banking, and encouraging them to see their personal savings as a national resource. By moving money out of "hundreds of thousands of little bundles or covered pots and pillows in the homes of many of our people," it would not only be kept safe,

---

[203] Nsekela, "The Public Corporation," p. 26.
[204] Amon Nsekela, "Leading Commercial Banking with Unity of Purpose," *Mbioni* 4(8) (1967): 24.

it would also consolidate these into a "general pool" from which loans could be made.[205] The official questions and answers appended to the Arusha Declaration explained that "We want our people to save so that the nation may have more money available for development," with the Post Office and banks praised as the path to self-reliance.[206]

The state undertook a "massive educational program to re-orient people's savings habits towards using national savings institutions in preference for hoarding cash in their pillows and under the ground."[207] Instead of leaving their money with the local shop or church, the NBC worked with schools, cooperatives, and trade unions to cultivate the "banking habit" and bring their services to people's doorstep. When rural cultivators panicked after a mobile bank drove off with their deposited money, educational efforts were redoubled (see Figure 3.7). The NBC operated a cinema van, published a Kiswahili newspaper, and sponsored radio shows such as "Benki Yako" (Your Bank) and "Weka Pesa Zako Benki" (Put your money in the bank). Bankers were directed to trade in their demeaning views of the masses and consider popular needs over their personal advancement.[208] Between 1967 and 1974, its proliferating presence pushed current accounts from 136,000 to 366,000, with overall customer deposits growing from TSh. 762.7 million to 1,812.6 million.[209]

Select groups of Tanzanians were targeted for commercial training as part of the state's goal of creating citizens who would meaningfully contribute to African socialism and self-reliance. In the Gerezani area of Dar es Salaam, for instance, the NBC provided loans to artisans working under the aegis of the National Small Industries Corporation – provided they attended lectures on bookkeeping, marketing, and the advantages of cooperatives.[210] Suitably functioning *ujamaa* villages,

[205] Amon Nsekela, "The Role of the National Bank of Commerce in Our Society," *Mbioni* 6(3) (1970): 32.
[206] *Arusha Declaration: Answers to Questions* (Government Printer, 1967).
[207] "Nationalised Banks Show Good Profit," *Times of Zambia*, September 11, 1967.
[208] Ngila Mwase, "Decision-Making in Tanzania's National Bank of Commerce: Controls and Participation Dichotomy," Economics Research Bureau Paper 75.9, 1975.
[209] James Mittelman, *Underdevelopment and the Transition to Socialism: Mozambique and Tanzania* (Academic Press, 1981), p. 181; Caselli, *The Banking System*, p. 225.
[210] Binhammer, *Financial Infrastructure*, pp. 46–47. On Gerezani, see Brownell, *Gone to Ground*, pp. 132–136.

3.6 Banking, African Socialism, and Self-Reliance

Figure 3.7 A mobile NBC agency serving customers.
Courtesy of Tanzania Information Services.

too, were promised priority access to credit, and the NBC endeavored to provide financial education so that each village would have at least one member with rudimentary accounting skills (see Figure 3.8).[211] As in the case of Uganda discussed in Chapter 2, this was about new sorts of citizens whose productivity would improve with access to new sorts of finance. But it also risked exacerbating inequalities as those already able to navigate and repay loans were prioritized.[212]

The most important form of lending in Tanzania was crop finance. It had been the preeminent line of work for Barclays and Standard and an ongoing source of frustration for government officials, cooperatives, and others. This lending was overwhelmingly short-term and seasonal, with large amounts of money issued to intermediary buyers of Tanzania's exported produce like cotton, coffee, and sisal.

---

[211] Amon Nsekela, "Social Accountability of a Public Enterprise," in *Socialism and Social Accountability* (Kenya Literature Bureau, 1978), p. 95.

[212] John Loxley, "Rural Credit and Socialism," in Lionel Cliffe (ed.), *Rural Cooperation in Tanzania* (Tanzania Publishing House, 1975), p. 280.

Figure 3.8 Villagers in Mugandu were awarded an NBC shield in recognition of their high levels of deposits with the bank in 1978.
Courtesy of Tanzania Information Services.

This finance was used to pay producers, and the banks were repaid when the crop exporters were, themselves, paid by metropolitan industry. The colonial model inherited by independent Tanzania financed much of this by the temporary import of capital from elsewhere.[213] While the Bank of Tanzania had already started assisting with the task, in 1966, more than half of the £7,000,000 needed for cotton alone was brought in by expatriate banks. Without this transnational capital, Tanzania faced an enormous strain on its resources for the export industries so fundamental to its economy. Rather remarkably, the NBC was able to work with the Bank of Tanzania to finance the 1967 agricultural season entirely from domestic resources.[214] And in the following years, domestic financing rose rapidly, thanks to the

---

[213] Loxley, "The Development of the Monetary and Financial System."
[214] *National Bank of Commerce, Report and Accounts*, February 7 to June 30, 1967.

3.7 From Formulas to Figures 197

central bank financing government activities and British banks no longer exporting their surpluses.[215] Government revenue for the financial year ending in June 1967 exceeded estimates by £4 million, allowing it to spend £8.5 million on development purposes. The public corporations were reaping "huge profits," with the National Insurance Corporation doubling in the year after its creation. In 1967–1968, the NBC also made a profit of TSh. 17.2 million, despite losing TSh. 12.1 million to the sudden devaluation of sterling.[216] In the next year, its profit was TSh. 31.2 million, and in 1973–1974, the figure was TSh. 91 million.[217]

3.7 From Formulas to Figures: The Vulgar Business of Bargaining

While much could be done by the NBC with compensation negotiations in abeyance, they were not irrelevant. The implications were made clear at the end of the January 1968 talks discussed earlier. Although the day and a half of detailed, sometimes bruising, meetings ended without agreement, the teams from Standard and Barclays were pleasantly surprised to be called into J. D. Namfua's office before they departed for the airport. Over more than an hour of friendly, informal chat, Namfua made clear that the debate about accounting formulas was overshadowed by the political milieu in Tanzania. For one, any settlement would need to be justified to the Cabinet and Parliament. For another, it would be essential that the compensation payment did not bankrupt the fledgling NBC (whose balance sheet was to carry the cost).

The easy atmosphere of this final meeting allowed for a crucial shift in the negotiations. Rather than a continued back-and-forth about net asset values, averaged profits, and rates of interest, the Barclays bankers cut to the chase, telling Namfua it seemed to them that the government had in mind a number they were willing to pay – somewhere around £700,000 for the Barclays' business. Namfua laughed at the frank speculation but said nothing specific. Instead, he asked that the banks might more easily make their accounts available to Steen

---

[215] W. Edmund Clark, *Socialist Development and Public Investment in Tanzania, 1964–1973* (University of Toronto Press, 1978), p. 185.
[216] Dias, "Tanzanian Nationalisations," p. 74.
[217] Mittelman, *Underdevelopment and the Transition to Socialism*, p. 177.

Hansen and informed them he would be in London in April 1968 – but hoped a deal was reached long before then.[218]

The conversation with Namfua allowed a door to open. While accounting formulas remained a key technique through which the sides reasoned and argued, they took a backseat to the ultimate compensation figure that would be paid. The shift from formulas to figures was explicitly noted by the bankers. In previous rounds, the final compensation figures were not entirely irrelevant; after all, the formulas were always summarized with a total figure of payment. But in the months to come, instead of figures following formulas, formulas would come to backfill intended settlement figures. In other words, accounting protocols, with their seemingly endless number of variables – What rate of interest? How many years averaged? Multiplied by what number? Weighted to what degree? – were manipulated with an eye to a mutually acceptable price for the expropriated businesses. Valuation, here, was no longer framed as the result of objectively given standards; rather, valuation was the result of commercial concerns and political pressures. There was even an aesthetic dimension to valuation, with certain numbers holding more symbolic significance than economic implication. In this way, it recalls an argument made by Martha Lampland about "provisional" or "false" numbers.[219] Rather than being stable referents or fixed representations, numbers may serve as expedient instruments. With divergent ideas about how to compute value and lacking clear lines of authority and command, accounting became a convenient path toward a desired result.

Nevertheless, the path from formulas to figures was neither straightforward nor quick. Despite Namfua's expressed wish to close the negotiations by April 1968, the months dragged on. The banks could not bring themselves to depart from their accounting predilections. Number crunching was, of course, a core concern of banking, and accountants had important positions in their negotiating team. A formula – even one designed to reach a certain figure – was also important for the bank's own purposes: they, too, had superiors that needed convincing in order to accept the ultimate figure.[220] Convincing accounting was an important persuasive technique within the bank.

---

[218] DCO 80/5301: Report by R.E. Williams, Negotiations in Dar es Salaam on Compensation, January 22, 1968.

[219] Martha Lampland, "False Numbers as Formalizing Practices," *Social Studies of Science* 40(3) (2010): 377–404.

[220] DCO 80/5302: Reed to Namfua, February 15, 1969.

3.7 From Formulas to Figures

A well-designed formula could also serve the bank's interests in any future nationalization.

So, when Barclays sent a new proposal to Namfua in April 1968, they again did so proposing to multiply averaged profits (for five years) by sixteen. In their view, it was a formula given approval by Steen Hansen and which considerably lessened the gap between the parties' positions.[221] They were wrong. Finally responding a few months later, Namfua expressed his frustration with the proposal. He acknowledged "a certain convenience in discussing valuation in terms of average profit multiplied by a factor."

However, if the factor proposed is not regarded as having any intrinsic merit, but is moved up or down by one side or the other in order to achieve a predetermined result, *we are not engaged in a process of valuation, but in the vulgar business of bargaining.*[222]

With confidence in his position, Namfua reminded the bankers in September 1968 that the law in Tanzania only called for compensation for the net value of assets. This, of course, was a position that weakened Barclays, and in their internal deliberations, they redoubled their strategy of speaking "in terms of figures, not formulas."[223]

An opportunity to discuss figures did not arise soon. For the rest of 1968, the negotiations stalled until Amir Jamal sent Frederic Seebohm a holiday greeting. On New Year's Day 1969, the Chairman of Barclays wrote to thank the Minister of Finance for the "beautiful Christmas card which I am keeping on my desk." More substantially, Seebohm welcomed the news that J. D. Namfua would be coming again to London. Detached from the day-to-day negotiations, the senior men could diplomatically facilitate momentum when valuation techniques created disruptions.

In preparation, the British bankers stepped more firmly away from accounting formulas. A year prior, Barclays had reduced their overall claim from £2,477,670 to £1,800,581. This was still much more than the £807,463 proposed by government.[224] In the past twelve months,

---

[221] DCO 80/5301: Letter to Namfua, April 17, 1968.
[222] DCO 80/5301: Namfua to General Manager, Barclays, September 23, 1968. Emphasis added.
[223] DCO 38/439: Note re: Tactics for Meeting with Namfua, January 7, 1969.
[224] This was the £700,000 to which Namfua had laughed in January 1968 plus £100,000 unremitted profits for the period directly before nationalization (which seemed almost certain to be included in any deal).

no one had really budged from these positions, so the bankers proposed to evenly split the difference of £1 million, resulting in a compensation claim around £1,300,000. They resolved to "go straight to the point ... and not haggle downward." In fact, by this time, they even doubted the utility of creating an artificial formula to justify the approach, for if another nationalization occurred elsewhere, "we could always pick the best formula emerging from the Tanzania settlement."[225] With this figure in mind, Barclays felt they might reach a deal. Any other components (the questions of pensions and bad debts, for instance) and the terms of repayment (a loan repaid over some number of years) would be easy to handle on the side.

When Namfua and his legal advisor Roland Brown came to London in January 1969, the new approach proved conducive – though a desire to conclude matters after two years certainly mattered, as well. Namfua made it clear the government would not consider paying more than £1,000,000 to Barclays. This was, he explained, a "public relations" issue, with the number taking on symbolic importance for the government and citizenry.[226] Yet, the mathematics of accounting offered the negotiators ways to represent the compensation to multiple audiences, internal and external. Barclays was eager for a larger number – closer to £1,300,000 – but could simultaneously cover costs already burdening Tanzania, therefore lowering the net cost to the state. As S. G. Mogford wrote to Namfua, the bankers took "considerable pains" to keep the "actual compensation figure" below the £1 million mark. They did so by assuming the cost of pensions for their former Tanzanian staff currently paid by government. The government, in that case, would be freed from an existing liability amount that, were it to be subtracted from £1,300,000, would bring Tanzania's total payment quite close to their professed upper limit. Tanzania would be able to present a number desired by their audiences, while Barclays could do the same. One deal, two figures. Because a price is composed – meaning it is made of various inputs and manipulations – the sum paid for

---

[225] DCO 38/439: Note re: Tactics for Meeting with Namfua, January 7, 1969.

[226] DCO 80/5302: Memorandum of Conversations with Namfua and Brown, January 1969. The symbolism may reflect Jamal's February 1967 statements to Parliament that the assets of all the banks only amounted to £900,000. UKNA FCO31/55: Notes of Interview between Steen Hansen and Reed, July 6, 1967.

3.7 From Formulas to Figures

compensation could be depicted in multiple ways, befitting both Barclays and the government.[227]

While the parties "intentionally spoke in terms of figures rather than formulas," the banks still needed a formula to "justify the basis of any agreement to our Board."[228] The ultimate formula was contrived to meet a prescribed result: ten times the average profit for the last four years (pensions excluded) plus the unremitted profits (minus items held in suspense outside Tanzania that are chargeable to its profit and loss account) brought the accountants to a total compensation payment of £1,305,549.[229] The resulting deal would see Tanzania pay that sum for "full and final settlement" plus £93,399 in unremitted profits, while Barclays would cover a pension cost of £241,951. Tanzania would pay 30 percent of the settlement immediately and accept a loan at 6 percent annual interest that they would subsequently repay for ten years, starting February 7, 1970.[230] It was not exactly below one million sterling, but rather close. Eager to maintain the momentum, Namfua accepted the slightly higher figure.[231] When combined with the return to Tanzania of the £687,745 balance blocked by Barclays in London, it might even seem a rather good deal.[232] It was certainly much better than the nearly £2.5 million Barclays initially demanded.

It was, in any case, a good enough deal for the Barclays chairman to write to Amir Jamal, asking for the Ministry to reserve a hotel room for the signing ceremonies in early June 1969.[233] Jamal and Seebohm had remained above the accounting fray – a diplomatic conviviality embodied in Christmas cards and cheery airmail. As a result, Seebohm had every reason to expect his two days in Dar es Salaam to be a "routine discussion of the wording of the document, followed by a dinner party, various courtesies, and a return home the following day."[234]

His expectations were, however, wrong.

---

[227] On the composition of prices, see Jane Guyer, *Legacies, Logics, Logistics: Essays in the Anthropology of the Platform Economy* (University of Chicago Press, 2016), chapter 10.
[228] DCO 80/5302: Mogford to Namfua, February 14, 1969.
[229] DCO 80/5302: Mogford to Namfua, February 14, 1969.
[230] DCO 80/5302: Agreement between Government of the United Republic of Tanzania and Barclays Bank DCO.
[231] Barclays 80/5302: Namfua to Mogford, May 21, 1969.
[232] DCO 80/5302: Agreement between Government of the United Republic of Tanzania and Barclays Bank DCO.
[233] DCO 80/5302: Seebohm to Amir Jamal, May 22, 1969.
[234] DCO 38/438: Seebohm Visit to Dar es Salaam, June 1–4, 1969.

3.8 Of Pensions and Pens, Parties and Planes: Closing the Deal at the Eleventh Hour

The unexpected twist to Seebohm's Tanzania visit – the surprise that would see him nervously looking at his watch, worried that his airplane would leave without him – was not immediately evident upon arrival in Dar es Salaam. Amon Nsekela and colleagues met Seebohm and his Assistant General Manager B. F. D. Daniels upon arrival, whisking them through customs and taking them to the city's premier hotel, as guests of the government. At lunch, they were joined by Amir Jamal, Roland Brown, and Reginald Green who were "all smiles and good nature."[235] Seebohm went for a rest, while his employee, Daniels, met with Namfua, Brown, and Green to run through any minor issues in the documents. At 4:00 p.m., the mood turned suddenly, as Daniels informed Seebohm that Namfua was refusing to accept the pension agreement, unless Barclays agreed to take on the liability in Tanzania shillings, rather than pounds sterling.

That such a demand was even possible reflected the transformations in monetary sovereignty enabled by independence. During colonial control, Tanzania's currency (the East African shilling) was held at par with sterling, meaning it moved in lockstep with the value of Britain's money. Indeed, the colonial currency was something of a geographically circumscribed simulacra of British pounds: a token with the same value as sterling but only acceptable within the East African region. When Tanzania established its own currency in 1965, it initially maintained equivalence to the sterling. As Britain was the largest trading partner, this provided considerable conveniences. It also was believed to enforce sound state finances, an essential component in maintaining confidence in the postcolonial money. Yet, in November 1967, Britain had finally capitulated to considerable pressure on its currency, devaluating it by nearly 15 percent. In contrast to prior decades, though, Tanzania was not automatically wedded to the new value of sterling. And, indeed, officials at the Bank of Tanzania and Ministry of Finance refused to follow the sterling downward. In other words, the postcolonial money-changer state provided new degrees of policy autonomy.

In the lobby of the Kilimanjaro Hotel in June 1969, Tanzania's departure from British currency valuation had more direct

---

[235] DCO 38/438: Seebohm Visit to Dar es Salaam, June 1–4, 1969.

3.8 Of Pensions and Pens, Parties and Planes

consequences. Overnight, Barclays would be on the hook for £35,000 more in pension costs, and any future deviations between British pounds and Tanzania shillings would exacerbate the situation.[236] So, at 5:00 p.m., negotiations about the bank's acceptance of pension liabilities resumed. However, they ended before any progress was made in order to attend a cocktail party that Amon Nsekela had arranged for his British guests, senior NBC staff, and some local businessmen. Some of the NBC staff formerly worked for Barclays, and Seebohm used the soirée to inquire after their subsequent experiences and worries about the future.

Quickly enough, though, Seebohm found himself in a corner with Amir Jamal, continuing to argue unsuccessfully before being joined by Roland Brown and Reginald Green. Seebohm's disbelief and distaste at his predicament is evident in his account of the situation:

Brown soon came out in his true colours – very left wing – and an enormous chip on his shoulders. Green, a young American, with no doubt a computer brain, remained facetious, smoking a filthy pipe with a broken stem patched up with tape, clothed in dirty white slacks and a psychedelic waistcoat and shabby jacket.[237]

The next morning started little better. Failing to receive the expected call from Amir Jamal, Seebohm and Daniels prepared a brief memorandum "stating perfectly clearly our position" and delivered it to the Ministry where officials "were all trying to work out some compromise." This only caused "consternation," so the bankers found their way to the British High Commissioner's house where they had prescheduled lunch with Jamal and Nsekela. A meal provided a respite, but for the duration of the afternoon, the parties "argued solidly and completely unavailingly." It was at that point that Seebohm began glancing at his watch, nervous about finding enough time to return to his hotel and catch his flight.

Once again, the trick was to split the difference. Seebohm's "half-hearted" suggestion in this regard was met with agreement by Jamal. Seebohm thought Namfua was upset, but Brown seemed relieved. The rest of the evening was a blur: first, Jamal "hauled" President Nyerere out of a conference to share the news. The President was "clearly

---

[236] For the bank's impression of how devaluation affected their claim, see DCO 80/5300: Memorandum to Mogford, November 24, 1967.
[237] DCO 38/438: Seebohm Visit to Dar es Salaam, June 1–4, 1969.

delighted" at the deal, expressing his fondness for Britain and desire for "many more English advisers and technicians." Parting ways, Seebohm rushed across town to the hotel to get his "gold Parker pen" and hurriedly read the amended agreement.[238] Quickly signing and exchanging pens, the representatives from Barclays said their "unsmiling" farewells before driving "like Jehu to the airport with only minutes to spare."

Unfortunately, there was no airplane. It was delayed in Nairobi for mechanical problems. If the trip felt like a comedy of errors, this last surprise offered a chance to regain composure and sociability. They were joined by Nsekela for a couple of whiskey sodas at the airport bar, chatting about future cooperation, credit limits, and advice for their old staff. Eventually, the two foreign bankers secured themselves a couple of first-class tickets on an Alitalia flight. On reaching London, Seebohm wrote, "tired but triumphant!"[239]

3.9 Conclusion: Liberating Value

In February 1969, two years after the banks were suddenly nationalized, the *Daily Telegraph* carried a brief story intended to scandalize its British readers. The report told of a reader who finally received a long-delayed payment they were owed from Tanzania. The cheque was issued by Tanzania's National Bank of Commerce and payable through the London branch of the Moscow Narodny Bank. "Evidently," wrote the anonymous journalist, "the Russians are profiting to the full from Tanzania's nationalization of the banks." The same cheque was endorsed as "not negotiable in Rhodesia or South Africa," earning the story its headline: "Restricted Value."[240]

The journalist's Cold War fantasies were outsized, but they were right to note the politicization of finance by independent Tanzania.[241] The prohibition on cashing the cheque to the benefit of white minority rule was only one way that money was made into a political instrument. For many Tanzanians, the transformation of money and credit

---

[238] Crossley and Blandford, *The DCO Story*, p. 269.
[239] DCO 38/438: Seebohm Visit to Dar es Salaam, June 1–4, 1969.
[240] "Restricted Value," *Daily Telegraph*, February 12, 1969.
[241] It is likely Narodny was only serving as an intermediary for the NBC (which lacked UK presence), but Zanzibar did maintain a substantial account at the Russian bank's London branch. Coulson, *Political Economy*, p. 242.

was an important national priority. Making credit an instrument of national sovereignty required changing its characteristics and governance. The legacy of colonial capitalism bequeathed a situation in which the banks were "remote controlled" by their London offices.[242] As I have suggested, what was at stake in nationalization was not the restriction of value, but rather the liberation of value from outside control. Rather than socialism and self-reliance auguring the end of money and finance, TANU leadership was apt to repurpose these as instruments for the pursuit of a monopoly on valuation.[243] The Tanzanian state aimed to govern value by using banking as an infrastructure to enable wider transformations in relations of production and exchange, as well as the nature of citizenship. For Nyerere and colleagues, this was an extension of political independence. As the President said while opening an expanded Tanzanian Breweries factory in February 1967, "an economic expression of nationalism is nothing new in the world." Indeed, it was common to capitalist, socialist, and communist countries, even if their particular approaches differed. For poor countries like Tanzania, who achieved political independence through "peaceful methods," the result was "economic dependency," unless they took steps to control the "major means of production, distribution, and exchange."[244] It was a long-standing aspiration to limit the export of capital and change the standards of creditworthiness imposed by expatriate banks. Before 1967, the establishment of the Tanganyika Co-operative Bank, the Tanzania Bank of Commerce, and the Bank of Tanzania each tried, in their own way, to marshal credit in the service of the nation and its citizens. By the time of the Arusha Declaration, however, they were perceived as partial measures, insufficient to carry forward African socialism and self-reliance. The ongoing influence of foreign banks and their intransigent refusal to put their capital to the service of popular needs marked them as an obstacle to the sovereign direction of wealth and well-being.

[242] DCO 80/4658: Interview with Steen Hansen by A. Hjorth Hansen, June 5, 1967.
[243] For a consideration of money in the Soviet Union, see Kristy Ironside, *A Full-Value Ruble: The Promise of Prosperity in the Postwar Soviet Union* (Harvard University Press, 2021); for its role in East Germany, see Jonathan Zatlin, *The Currency of Socialism: Money and Political Culture in East Germany* (Cambridge University Press, 2008).
[244] UKNA FCO 31/73: Nyerere Speech at Opening of Tanzania Breweries Extension, February 28, 1967.

As Felicitas Becker describes it, the government "sought to replace the decentralized decision-making mechanism of the market, mediated through self-regulating prices, with a system where crucial economic decisions, including prices, were made centrally."[245] In practice, governing value in the name of popular need was not a straightforward task after nationalization. Redirecting individual initiative to collective need did not happen overnight. The NBC was an important infrastructure of wider economic enterprise, though much of it remained directed at financing the export (rather than production) of crops.[246] Nor is this to say it was always popular: as early as 1966, farmers told government inquiries that the "very low prices" paid to them were "absurd."[247] The history is one of piecemeal initiatives, sometimes experimental and often reactive to changing circumstances. The oil crises after 1973 were important limits on the state's monopoly on valuation, and the party newspaper *The Nationalist* frequently carried complaints about government inaction on rising prices.[248] By 1967, officials from the NBC were regularly collecting retail prices of key commodities in shops and markets and feeding the information toward the National Price Control Advisory Board.[249] Some of this reflected a longstanding resentment of Asian shopkeeping practices, but their problems were practical. In their meetings, they reasoned through the economic rationale, political impediments, and even how the physical characteristics of different goods made them more or less prone to regulation.[250] But the extensive and uneven economic geography

---

[245] Becker, *Politics of Poverty*, pp. 181–182.
[246] Clark, *Socialist Development*, pp. 162–166. See also Mittelman, *Underdevelopment and the Transition to Socialism*, p. 179 and chapter 10.
[247] Quoted in Resnick, *Long Transition*, p. 67. Consider also the antagonisms between farmers, cooperatives, and centralized control over prices and marketing in James Giblin, *A History of the Excluded: Making Family a Refuge from State in Twentieth-Century Tanzania* (Ohio University Press, 2005), pp. 254–257.
[248] Brownell, *Gone to Ground*, pp. 149–181.
[249] TNA: Accession 523 E.20/23 Economic Control 1967–68: Central Statistical Bureau memo, May 1968.
[250] For instance, while cassava was "an essential commodity in some areas the lack of standard[ization] makes it not amenable to price control." TNA Accession 523 E.20/23 Economic Control 1967–68: Minutes of the First Meeting of the National Price Control Advisory Board, November 6, 1968.

3.9 Conclusion

frustrated early efforts, such as the co-operative shops originally endorsed by Nyerere and others.[251]

The State Trading Corporation was called upon to remake retail, displacing the Asian merchants seen as responsible for immoral pricing.[252] In 1973, the Regulation of Prices Act widened the scope for the state's monopoly on valuation for a huge range of commodities.[253] A special task force composed of Treasury and Bank of Tanzania officials, as well as representatives of major parastatal entities, compiled a list of items to be regulated, some 400 products deemed essential and popular across the country. They detailed the wholesale and retail prices, the cost of transporting such goods upcountry, and the various brands and sizes in which they were sold, all with an eye to establishing prices that were viable and fair, as well as designing a system "to discourage manipulation of prices by traders." It would not be a straightforward task, they knew: fluctuations in import costs, tensions with regional authorities, and the possibility of shortages were all known risks, so was the likelihood of retailers' subterfuge. Government inspectors were expensive and unreliable, so instead the state aimed for "a self-policing system" where consumers were authorized to enforce official prices.[254] Thus, all would "be required to display, conspicuously, gazette prices in their shops and must also put [on] price tags."[255] By March 1974, the legal prices for more than 1,000 items were stipulated by the National Price Commission (NPC). In doing so, it joined other government agencies that set prices for water, electricity, and transportation, as well as those for export agriculture and essential food crops.[256] Yet, especially for portable goods sold near enough to Tanzania's borders, price

---

[251] TNA Accession 523: E.20/23 Economic Controls, 1967–68: Board Paper No.7/67, Nyerere Address October 17, 1967.

[252] Aminzade, *Race, Nation, and Citizenship*, pp. 220–230. Resnick, *Long Transition*, pp. 224–273.

[253] Joseph Semboja and S. M. H. Rugumisa, "Price Control in the Management of an Economic Crisis: The National Price Commission in Tanzania," *African Studies Review* 31(1) (1988): 47–65.

[254] TNA Accession 523: E.20/23 Economic Control, 1967–68: O. Mwambungu, "Price Controls on Goods & Services," 1967.

[255] "The Report of the Special Task Force on Price Control" (Tanzania Treasury, March–April 1973), https://opendocs.ids.ac.uk/opendocs/handle/20.500.12413/6331.

[256] Alan Whitworth, "Price Controls Techniques in Poor Countries: The Tanzanian Case," *World Development* 10(6) (1982): 481.

Figure 3.9 Amon Nsekela addresses the opening of a bank branch manager seminar (held in the former Standard Bank branch of Dar es Salaam).
Courtesy of Tanzania Information Services.

standardization was undermined by smugglers.[257] When such illegal diversions challenged the state's initiative, it did not hesitate to use exceptional powers against the so-called saboteurs (including 500 foreign exchange operators detained without trial in 1975–1976).[258]

This expansion of a monopoly on valuation was a monumental effort to use government loans, price controls, and other regulations to enforce a more egalitarian distribution. By the end of 1974, perhaps up to 85 percent of large- and medium-scale economic activity was in the public sector.[259] The NBC undergirded much of it, though Amon Nsekela came to regret their limited efficacy (see Figure 3.9). Decisions

[257] Jamal suggested adjusting prices near borders to minimize the prevailing price differences. AR/MISR/157/9: Amir Jamal to Paul Bomani, "Standardization of Prices," December 19, 1970.
[258] Reginald Green, "The Economics of Disintegration: Tanzania, 1982–83" (1983), p. 5. https://opendocs.ids.ac.uk/opendocs/handle/20.500.12413/4775. This foreshadowed the larger economic crimes campaigns of the 1980s discussed in Aminzade, *Race, Nation, and Citizenship*, pp. 230–234.
[259] Green, "A Guide to Acquisition," p. 19.

taken elsewhere in the state threatened the bank's solvency. In February 1969, Nsekela wrote to Amir Jamal, the Minister of Finance, that "nearly all our Branch Managers" were reporting fears among their Asian clients – who constituted about 60 percent of the banks' trader customers – that their trade licenses would not be renewed. Were that to be the case, the collateral held by the bank on these loans (mostly retail properties and stock) would collapse, putting the NBC "in a very tricky situation."[260] Moreover, as loans were used to keep afloat parastatals and agricultural cooperatives, the NBC came to bear the burden of others' inefficiencies and troubles – not all of which were above board.[261] He expressed frustration at the unrealistic expectations placed on the bank.[262] He lamented the lack of meaningful change to banking from the capitalist to the socialist era. In his view, within a properly socialist Tanzania, the work of the NBC would be almost unrecognizable from that undertaken previously. Instead of branch managers exercising discretion over loan applications, they would take their orders from the country's comprehensive economic plan. Credit would be allocated according to the direction of the plan, meaning the NBC would largely be reduced to drawing up financial plans and ensuring they are followed within state enterprises. Rather than lending, "the control function becomes paramount," with all transactions checked for conformity with the economic plan.

Yet when the bank chairman spoke to a group of TANU Youth League cadres in November 1973, he was disappointed to note the NBC was far from that ideal. Important changes had been made: each bank branch had Workers' Councils that helped direct its activities, it could give preferential interest rates to nationally strategic sectors, and it was planning to lend to the newly invigorated *ujamaa* village initiative. Perhaps most significantly, a detailed credit plan was designed to cover all parastatals. Yet, troubles persisted. Authoritarian branch managers sometimes mistreated staff, and women in the Head Office were particularly upset at their treatment as "second class citizens."[263]

---

[260] AR/MISR/157/7: Nsekela to Jamal, "Trade Licenses," February 25, 1969.
[261] On the STC's reliance on NBC credit, see Coulson, *Political Economy*, pp. 340–341. Bjerk rightly notes that the Bank of Tanzania was a critical support for this, too. "A Preliminary History."
[262] Nsekela, "Some Practical Problems of Nationalization," p. 20.
[263] Nsekela, "The Public Corporation," p. 25.

Rural credit continued to predominate.[264] Moreover, the parastatals who were NBC's main customers still worked closely with foreign capitalists, and comprehensive socialist planning of productive activity was lacking in Tanzania.[265] As a result, there was little scope to radically transform banking, making the NBC's work a series of half measures. It was, Nsekela told the audience, "midway between behaving like a capitalist bank and a socialist bank" and the speed of continued transformation largely rested outside the NBC's immediate control.[266] The result, in other words, was at best a partial liberation of value.

[264] Mittelman, *Underdevelopment and the Transition to Socialism*, p. 205 lamented that "Tinkering with the rural credit machinery cannot change the essential aspects of this system," including its capture by local elite.

[265] On Tanzanian parastatals' accommodation of multinational corporations, see I. G. Shivji, "Capitalism Unlimited: Public Corporations in Partnership with Multinational Corporations," *African Review* 3(3) (1973): 359–381.

[266] Amon Nsekela, "The Role of Commercial Banking in Building a Socialist Tanzania," in *Socialism and Social Accountability* (Kenya Literature Bureau, 1978), p. 107.

4 | *Crimes against Economy*
The Economy of Accusation in 1970s Uganda

4.1 Introduction

On April 21, 1976, officers Okucu and Ekuma left the police station to walk the streets of Jinja, Uganda's second most important commercial town. Purposefully slipped into Okucu's pocket was a ten-shilling note with serial number A/29 334493. Dressed in plain clothes, they poked their heads into shops, inquiring as to supplies and prices – seemingly innocuous customers hankering for a deal. At a shop staffed by a young woman, Harriet Biryeri, they found the sort of deal they wanted: handing over their ten shillings for what the court later learned was 450 grams of unsliced white bread, the officers departed the shop only to return a moment later to arrest the cashier. Carefully retrieving their money from the till, they hauled the "young offender" and the unsliced loaf off to jail.

Ms. Biryeri's case would be heard two months later, in front of the Economic Crimes Tribunal. Confronted with the testimony of the officers, there was little she could do beside plead guilty to the crime of overcharging for a controlled commodity. Instead of the legally prescribed price of 3 shillings and 40 pence, Biryeri partook in what, at that time, was a commonplace but illegal act of exchange: accepting more money than officially allowed in a sale. A 1975 Presidential Decree established the Economic Crimes Tribunal, tasked with policing hoarding, overcharging, smuggling, and other malfeasance. Such crimes were punishable by death, and across Uganda, thousands were hauled before the special courts, confronted by cameras, crowds, and evidence of their improper market behavior (see Figure 4.1).

For Major Erifazi, the chairman of the Economic Crimes Tribunal sitting that day in Jinja, justice would not be met merely by a declaration of guilt. Instead, it required adjourning the court and marching with those gathered to the store a few blocks away. There, the crowd confronted Mrs. Batambuze, the owner, whose absence on the day of

Figure 4.1 An unnamed woman photographed before the Economic Crimes Tribunal in 1975.
Courtesy of the Uganda Broadcasting Corporation.

4.1 Introduction

the crime saved her from conviction. It did not, however, mean she walked away from the sting operation unscathed. Her pleas for mercy held little sway for Major Erifazi, who ordered her property seized, doors locked, and trading license cancelled. As for the ten shillings, the court returned it to the police, and the bread was officially ordered to be destroyed.[1]

Economic sovereignty, I demonstrated in Chapter 2, required the regulation of commercial temporalities and geographies. Currency was circumscribed to the national territory, agricultural and labor rhythms were realigned through lending, and the nation was pulled toward a modernizing horizon. Erstwhile colonial subjects were refashioned as credible citizens – people whose merit was revealed through industrious contributions to the national economy. But by the second decade of independence, as this chapter details, the economic model groaned under a combination of domestic misrule and international turbulence. Price inflation, commodity shortages, and diminished production ruled the day. The prices offered to farmers did not keep up with inflation, and even if they had, agricultural finance and transport broke down. In turn, farmers refused to cultivate or sell cotton, coffee, or other exports. As wages stalled, workers absconded to grow food on their land. Factories lacked supplies and machinery. Goods stood motionless, unable to be profitably sold. Loans went unpaid. For many Ugandans, delays came to dominate life, as distances – to work, school, or shop – suddenly seemed further than a few years prior.

Commercial profitability and state efforts to govern the economy stalled. Those places most important to Uganda's economy – Buganda's cotton fields, Jinja's factories, or the Kilembe copper mine – no longer reliably produced export value. Money, work, and trade escaped regulation as Ugandans invented new ways to provide for themselves. Subsistence farming displaced export crops, unlicensed hawkers challenged tax-paying shops, and smugglers perforated the fiscal borders of the nation. These sorts of practices were more difficult for the moneychanger state to capture, intermediate, or redirect. Because of this, they were an affront to the state's claim to economic sovereignty.

---

[1] Jinja District Archive (JDA) Justice, Law, Order & Security 64/23: Economic Crimes Tribunal, 1975–1979. Case No. BT/20 of 1976, the Republic of Uganda versus Harriet Biryeri, 1976.

In response, large swaths of everyday life were criminalized, with cases like Biryeri and Batambuze reflecting the state's desperate effort to govern value. Three activities proved extraordinarily bedeviling to the state: smuggling (known as *magendo*), hoarding, and overcharging. Some connected to the Amin state relied on impunity and illegality to quickly accumulate riches through magendo. The Kiswahili epithet *mafuta mingi* was used to describe the resulting lifestyle: decadent and conspicuous. But magendo was also generalized throughout the population, and the subsequent legal responses tried to stem the existential threat of declining export revenues and rising import costs. After seizing power in a 1971 coup, Idi Amin's claim to legitimacy relied on the promise of economic transformation, and his officials energetically went about promulgating new property regimes, reforming trade rules, and encouraging agrarian production.[2] He called this an "Economic War."[3] The 1972 expulsion of Uganda's Asian population – vilified as alien exploiters – was a part of this thoroughgoing campaign to empower Uganda's African population.[4] The considerable scholarly attention it has received, however, tends to divorce it from regulatory dramas that placed many others in the crosshairs. This chapter suggests it is better seen in the wider tapestry of economic governance in the 1970s.

To do so, it attends especially to the sorts of allegations that coursed through public and private life as bureaucrats and police, farmers and workers, families and neighbors tried to rectify an economic order gone awry. If, among other things, Asians were accused of shuttling money out of the country to the detriment of native Ugandans, many others were blamed for misdeeds that similarly scuttled Uganda's fortunes. Peasant farmers were cast as unproductive, bureaucrats as

---

[2] On Idi Amin, see Mark Leopold, *Idi Amin: The Story of Africa's Icon of Evil* (Yale University Press, 2021); Alicia Decker, *In Idi Amin's Shadow: Women, Gender, and Militarism in Uganda* (Ohio University Press, 2014).

[3] *Uganda's Economic War*. Ministry of Information and Broadcasting, 1975. See the discussion in Richard Reid, *A History of Modern Uganda* (Cambridge University Press, 2017), pp. 236–238.

[4] For recent considerations of the expulsion, see Anneeth Kaur Hundle, "Insecurities of Expulsion: Emergent Citizenship Formations and Political Practices in Postcolonial Uganda," *Comparative Studies of South Asia, Africa and the Middle East* 39(1) (2019): 8–23; Edgar Taylor, "Claiming Kabale: Racial Thought and Urban Governance in Uganda," *Journal of Eastern African Studies* 7(1) (2013): 143–163.

4.1 Introduction

corrupt, and fathers as negligent. Ugandans deployed these allegations to call to account those deemed responsible for shortages. The 1975 Presidential Decree that ensnared Biryeri, Batambuze, and others authorized a prominent mode of state accusation – namely, indictment. It generated innumerable police investigations and arrests. Very quickly, specialized courts were filled with citizens indicted for mispricing bread, hoarding cooking oil, and smuggling coffee. These legal accusations were accompanied by a nearly constant stream of condemnation and denunciation in state media.[5] Newspapers inveighed against economic criminality, and chiefs took to radio to condemn farmers for insufficiently producing export crops. As a result, in the 1970s, few could position themselves as credible contributors to the nation, even as they were obliged to do so to justify their standing in the nation.

Accusations did not only emerge from officialdom. As shortages and illegalities became commonplace, Ugandans were liable to denounce each other.[6] What, exactly, was to blame for their economic woes was not entirely clear. Generalized misgivings were channeled into more targeted suspicions of neighbors, colleagues, and traders. These were circulated through petitions, letters, and personal appeals.[7] Bosses were reported for embezzling public funds, schoolmasters were said to be hoarding supplies, and shopkeepers were decried for refusing to sell at official prices. Many allegations were forwarded to local officials; some were addressed directly to Idi Amin. The accused were obliged to defend themselves, marshalling what evidence they could to persuade others of their propriety. For instance, Y. K. Makur, a primary school headmaster, wrote to the Toro District Commissioner

---

[5] Derek Peterson and Edgar Taylor, "Rethinking the State in Idi Amin's Uganda: The Politics of Exhortation," *Journal of Eastern African Studies* 7(1) (2013): 58–82.

[6] Such allegations were not entirely new. For instance, Baganda have accused others of using "sorcery to deplete the fertility of their neighbor's land" since the 1920s, Christine Obbo, "The Effects of Land Tenure Change upon Women in East African Smallholder Agriculture," Land Tenure Center Paper 124 (University of Wisconsin-Madison, 1985), p. 60.

[7] On postcolonial letters and petitions, see Nana Osei-Opare, "If You Trouble a Hungry Snake, You Will Force It to Bite You," *Journal of African History* 62(1) (2021): 59–78; Daniel Branch, "Public Letters and the Culture of Politics in Kenya, c.1960–75," *Journal of Eastern African Studies* 15(2) (2021): 339–357; Rohit De and Robert Travers, "Petitioning and Political Cultures in South Asia," *Modern Asian Studies* 53(1) (2019): 1–20.

to deny reports against his family and ask for an official investigation to settle the matter: "We have fear of the bad people who have no exact truth."[8] Yet, truth was hard to come by, and accusations often devolved into a flurry of mutual recriminations.

Oftentimes, the complaints were directed at government officers who were failing to meet their obligations. Both local and national governments were called to account by citizens who were exasperated by the shortages of the era. They blamed bureaucrats for incompetence or neglect, demanding a rightful share.[9] Insufficient imports of spare parts meant goods languished, unable to reach their destination. Doctors could not make their rounds; commuters could not reach their work.

Shelves stood empty, depriving households of sugar, salt, and cooking fat. For Ugandans, the dearth of what was known as "essential commodities" was not so much a threat to survival nor was it a mere inconvenience. Rather, people were upset by the way shortages impeded domestic rhythms and social life. Weddings could not take place without oil in which to cook the food; without sugar, ordinary consumption – the afternoon respite of tea or a kindness offered to guests – was likewise offended. Scarcity, in other words, interfered with respectability and hospitality. And because the state claimed a monopoly over wide swaths of the economy, it was to the government that many citizens appealed.

The situation was all the more galling because the 1970s were defined not by absolute absence. Rather, the economy was one of relative deprivation. Ugandans recognized that some people could acquire essential commodities, while they could not. Sometimes the trouble was one of timeliness: Teachers, agricultural extension officers, and government employees complained they could not wait in line for goods without neglecting their professional duties. For other Ugandans, the obstacles were a lack of meaningful connections: only those with reliable contacts in the state or subterranean networks could count on acquiring what spare commodities did exist. For many others, the whole matter was exceedingly complex, with goods available according to plans and dictates they could not fathom. To be sure, there was considerable scarcity, and some goods were truly absent

---

[8] Kabarole District Archive (KDA) 401: Y.K. Makur to District Commissioner, Toro, June 8, 1971.
[9] James Ferguson, *Give a Man a Fish: Reflections on the New Politics of Distribution* (Duke University Press, 2015).

4.1 Introduction

from Uganda, but what animated – even incensed – people was the unequal access to the sort of commodities that made possible a decent life and respectable status.

As the state's monopoly on valuation waned under pressure from alternative practices and ethics, competing ideas about worth came to the fore and occasioned conflicts over distribution, hierarchy, and labor. This chapter analyzes the resulting *economy of accusation*, in which material paucity encouraged the exchange of recrimination and allegation.[10] I use this term to attend to how the macroeconomic transformations of the 1970s intersected with social habits and popular ethics. Impediments to consumption and difficulties with production encouraged resentments, and the ensuing allegations gave rise to habits of suspicion and discretion. They also produced popular cultures of petition and appeal that remade the boundaries of belonging and changed state procedures. The anxieties undergirding this opprobrium differed – racialized antipathy targeting Asian merchants, for instance, or the imperative of revenue generation sanctioning the Economic Crimes Tribunal – but together they generated a milieu in which all were susceptible to denunciation.[11] By drawing on citizen complaints, media reports, government correspondence, and legal records, I show how popular and state accusations tried to discipline commodities and citizens in the postcolony.

The allegations were a way to make claims against wayward Ugandans, whether through the compulsion of law, the force of moral suasion, or the threat of violence. As the promises of prior years – that commercial well-being could be merged with national progress – faltered, the economy of accusation rose in prominence. The material firmament of mid-century developmentalism eroded, yet the

---

[10] "Accusation" has most commonly been approached historically in regard to totalitarian settings, e.g., Sheila Fitzpatrick and Robert Gellately, "Introduction to the Practices of Denunciation in Modern European History," *Journal of Modern History* 68(4) (1996): 747–767. Anthropologists emphasize a more diverse range of interpersonal and emotional settings for accusations. Geoffrey Hughes, Megnaa Mehtta, Chiara Bresciani, and Stuart Strange, "Ugly Emotions and the Politics of Accusation," *Cambridge Journal of Anthropology* 37(2) (2019): 1–20.

[11] Louisa Lombard emphasizes the role of denunciation amid unstable sovereignty in "Denouncing Sovereignty: Claims to Liberty in Northeastern Central African Republic," *Comparative Studies in Society and History* 60(4) (2018): 1066–1095.

expectations of economic liberty associated with postcolonial citizenship did not collapse. Ugandans still expected the rights to produce and transact, and they continued to demand the state play its part – especially in allocating essential commodities, distributing productive assets, and advancing credit. Where it could not, citizens took matters into their own hands through smuggling or other criminalized acts. For its part, the state continued to demand popular acquiescence to its economic model, including a monopoly on currency and on international trade. This chapter shows how economic life was transformed in this critical era, and it demonstrates how Ugandans maneuvered in multiple registers to meet their ideas about proper life, even amid considerable hardship.

These notions of economic citizenship coursed through government correspondence, shaped media reports, and animated protest about matters of taxation, farming, and shopkeeping. Some positioned themselves as the proper national subjects – racially African and native to the land. Others defined themselves as taxpayers or adopted the status of "Common Man." The ability to contribute to the nation's progress was another means by which Ugandans demonstrated virtue. In contrast to arguments about the hollowness of African citizenship and statecraft, this chapter shows the enduring strategies of claiming value through the distribution of goods and the allocation of opportunity – even in situations of widespread illegality.[12]

Attending to allegations, indictments, and petitions in their various forms reveals the ethical sensibilities that were offended by economic volatility and shortage. For instance, weaknesses in state distribution of essential commodities rankled popular presumptions about worthiness, launching thousands of demands for sugar and salt. In other cases, implicit theories about the relationship between productive labor and deservingness were tested by commodity shortages: Cotton and coffee farmers – who "generate the foreign exchange of the country" – could not buy materials from shops due to the distances from their rural plots. This, insisted the Governor for Western Province, required government reform.[13] Still others demonstrate conflicting ideas about whether individual identity should affect consumption: Residents of

[12] A corrective also offered by Paul Nugent, "States and Social Contracts in Africa," *New Left Review* II(63) (2010): 35–68.
[13] KDA 402/1: Alex Owor to Marketing Manager, National Textiles Board, June 6, 1977.

Bugoye sub-county complained that the wholesaler for sugar, textile, and hoes was causing the common man to suffer because "he uses a lot of nepotism, going as far as first looking at somebody's face to see" whose brother or sister they are. Customers, these petitioners insisted, should be free from the logics of kinship and clan.[14]

The chapter begins by depicting the shortages that defined much of the 1970s, arguing that it eventually came to threaten economic sovereignty and citizens' ideas of decency. I trace the everyday negotiation of paucity and indignity, as well as popular demands for policing the economy. The result unsettles a dichotomous framework of "society" against "the state," suggesting instead a pluralistic and opportunistic engagement across Uganda.

4.2 Unmaking the Economy in the 1970s

At independence in 1962, Uganda's economic prospects were widely heralded, and in subsequent years, indicators around growth and export earnings were often encouraging. Yet, like many other economies, by the mid-1970s, shortage and a sense of decline set in. Some of the immediate causes came from beyond Uganda's borders: the 1973 oil crisis reverberated across the continent, adding inordinate strain to Uganda's balance of payments. Declining profitability and legitimation crises in the United States led to an inversion of the postwar model, so that by the latter half of the 1970s, the United States was no longer exporting capital, but rather draining it from all other regions, starving places like East Africa of investment.[15]

Other causes of Uganda's woes were more proximate. In many cases, the lack of production could be traced to the expulsion of Asian commercial expertise, capital, and relations in 1972. Significant chaos lay in its wake.[16] Consider the property seized from Asians. The Departed Asians Property Custodian Board was responsible for distributing the expropriated shops, factories, plantations, and private homes to Ugandan Africans. Mrs. Batambuze – the Jinja shopkeeper whose premises were seized by the Economic Crimes Tribunal

---

[14] KDA 654/2: The People of Bugoye Sub-County to the District Commissioner, Rwenzori, September 19, 1975.
[15] Giovanni Arrighi, "The African Crisis," *New Left Review* II(15) (2002): 21–22.
[16] Michael Twaddle (ed.), *Expulsion of a Minority: Essays on Ugandan Asians* (Athlone Press, 1975).

in 1976 due to Biryeri's overcharging for bread – was allocated the shop after its owners were expelled in 1972.[17] She was one of many who received property seized by the state. The expropriation also produced opportunity for venality, and the scramble for property involved considerable underhanded dealing and confusion. Even when not overtly compromised, the exercise stumbled over itself, mired in confusion and clientelism, incapacity, and conflict.[18] As a result, many shops and industries lay dormant, with energies instead directed at mutual recriminations.[19]

The distribution of expropriated property also led to innumerable private dramas. The resulting economy of accusations could be deadly. In the small town of Nyenga, some kilometers outside Jinja, was a jaggery mill, where sugarcane was processed. The mill was built and operated by an Asian family who purchased the land from its African owner, only to be expelled in 1972. The Custodian Board allocated it to two men who, despite being "great friends ... failed to run the affairs of the jaggery jointly." As a result, it was allocated to a new owner, but not before one of the first recipients removed an engine, boilers, and various other industrial equipment. What followed involved undelivered jaggery, defrauded creditors, mysterious and sudden deaths, unnamed colonels allegedly assigning the property to new owners, and "a very difficult man" who was known to have "bewitched Amisi Naki and also organized murderers who came and cut up Juma Kilimunganda recently."[20] As a result, the mill did not function for four years, until another man began maintaining the site, cutting the grass, reinstalling equipment, and paying a watchman. Unfortunately, his efforts were for naught: as the District Commissioner informed him, he lacked official allocation rights to the mill and would be best advised to stop until the Custodian Board formally opened applications for the property.[21]

---

[17] JDA Justice, Law, Order & Security 64/23: Case No. BT/20 of 1976.
[18] JDA Trade & Industry 16/4: Abandoned Shops, 1979–1984.
[19] Anneeth Kaur Hundle, "1970s: Uganda: Past, Present, Future," *Journal of Asian and African Studies* 53(3) (2018): 467–471.
[20] Witchcraft is an especially potent form of allegation in the region. See the recent summary by Adam Ashforth, "Witchcraft," in Gaurav Desai and Adeline Masqueilier (eds.), *Critical Terms for the Study of Africa* (University of Chicago Press, 2018), pp. 365–380.
[21] JDA Admin. Complaints & Petitions 4/4: District Commissioner Jinja to Provincial Executive Secretary, November 5, 1976.

Even in less-fraught circumstances, the upheaval after 1972 tested the production and circulation of goods. In daily life, this manifest as slowdowns, interruptions, and a near-constant hunt for the spare parts and fuel that would get lorries and buses back on the road.[22] Distances that needed to be traversed – from fields to factory, from home to office – became yawning gaps as transport was unavailable. Many of the small shops staffed by Asian merchants, including those in rural areas, lay empty. Where a new owner was assigned, they often lacked the credit and social relations to reliably acquire goods. Once convenient purchases of household items now required traveling upward of twenty miles only to find those goods sold out.[23] Transactional territories cracked apart, with goods sitting immobilized and trade stalled as problems at sugar mills in the east paralyzed soda factories in the west.[24]

As the decade progressed, the coffee and cotton production that was so crucial to Uganda also changed. The reliable production of export crops depended upon a confluence of state financing and domestic labor. A fundamental challenge of peasant production is temporal dissonance: money is needed to plant and maintain the crop, as well as sometimes pay temporary laborers to harvest it, yet few peasants have cash before harvest. In Uganda, the state deployed a cascade of credit through parastatal firms and cooperative societies that advanced money to farmers on the expectation it would be repaid after harvest.[25] State firms like the Uganda Commercial Bank would lend to regional cooperative societies who would disperse funds at the "primary societies," a network of sites for buying and initially processing crops. Loans were repaid from the proceeds a few months later. These cooperatives were not historically under direct control by government but were required to sell their members' crops up the chain to the Coffee Marketing Board (est. 1963), the Lint Marketing Board

---

[22] For a discussion in Tanzania, see Emily Brownell, *Gone to Ground: A History of Environment and Infrastructure in Dar Es Salaam* (University of Pittsburgh Press, 2020).

[23] JDA Trade & Industry 14/25: Application for Appointment as an Agent of STC, December 15, 1972.

[24] KDA 402/1: Provincial Governor to Manager, Foods & Beverages, March 7, 1977.

[25] Diana Hunt, *Credit for Agricultural Development: A Case Study of Uganda* (East African Publishing House, 1975).

(est. 1959), and the Produce Marketing Board (est. 1968).[26] In some years, this worked well: by 1966, agrarian lending had grown to include three hundred cooperative societies, with "defaults so low as to be almost negligible."[27] This successful alignment required inducing farmers with an appropriate price for the cotton and coffee, as well as maintaining logistical networks. Yet, over the course of the 1970s, the price paid to farmers was unsatisfactory and transport unreliable.[28] As a result, farmers refused to sell their crops.

Finance also suffered. Banks were hesitant to issue loans to cooperative societies that would pass them on to farmers. Many loans were misappropriated, leaving no money to buy crops. In other cases, farmers took credit but sold their crops through other channels, making it hard for the cooperatives to recover debts.[29] For five years beginning in 1974, the Kalungani Growers Co-operative Society failed to recover loans due to embezzlement. At another cooperative society money meant for buying cotton was instead used to buy coffee, in the hopes of making a quick profit on coffee and then buying cotton.[30] Across the country, administrators desperate to ensure a reliable supply of export crops tried to enforce proper fiduciary standards, yet more often they failed to pay farmers as promised. The effect was to invert the intended financial relationship by making farmers the creditors of the cooperatives and, ultimately, the state. After years of exhorting farmers to "double production," the state's status as debtor, not creditor, was "a very embarrassing situation."[31] It also had knock on effects, as farmers were unable to repay any personal loans they

[26] Crawford Young, Neal Sherman, and Tim Rose, *Cooperatives & Development: Agricultural Politics in Ghana and Uganda* (University of Wisconsin Press, 1981), pp. 16–17, 63–65.
[27] *Work for Progress: Uganda's Second Five-Year Plan, 1966–1971* (Government of Uganda, 1966), p. 60.
[28] In the first four years of the decade, coffee farmers were paid an average of 17 percent of the international price for coffee; at its nadir in 1977, the figure was 6 percent. See Godfrey Asiimwe, "From Monopoly Marketing to Coffee Magendo: Responses to Policy Recklessness and Extraction in Uganda, 1971–79," *Journal of Eastern African Studies* 7(1) (2013): 107–109.
[29] Diana Hunt earlier estimated only 50 percent of loans were used for their intended purposes and notes the social contagion of default. *Credit for Agricultural Development*, pp. 196ff.
[30] JDA Justice, Law, Order & Security 13/17 Security Matters, 1975–1979. Report to Superintendent of Police and Prisons, South Busoga, September 6, 1976.
[31] KDA 628/2: Provincial Governor to Minister of Co-operatives & Marketing, July 31, 1978.

4.2 Unmaking the Economy in the 1970s

may have taken and could ill afford to pay their taxes.[32] The difficulties facing Uganda were not the abstractions of finance but the technicalities of money: cooperatives lacked enforcement of proper accounting standards, and there were no trucks to move currency.[33]

As a result, the circulation of capital ground to a halt. The General Secretary of the Uganda Co-operative Savings & Credit Union – a bank for farmer cooperatives – was incensed by the problem. D. B. Mutahigwa told his staff at the start of a new year that they must "rededicate" themselves to the union and reject "the temptation that may lead us to the lazy performances, abstinence from duties, and procrastination." His condemnation was motivated by the Union's stark financial standing. The last year had not been good: limited loan repayment meant low income for the organization and a lack of funding for the next year. They had to bring a message of collective purpose to the "ungrateful" cooperatives, whose delinquent officials "play a selfish role." If bank staff were to justify their salaries, it would require meeting higher standards of efficiency and morality, thus refusing "such gains that may be connected with *Mafuta Mingi* or *Magendo* styles," he warned, using terms associated with illegal trade.[34] Mutahigwa's pleading and preaching was an effort to embed financial credit within a morality of collective effort. In his appeals to forego "personal pleasures" in favor of "dedicated service," he called for a way of valuing crops that merged the interest of cooperative members and the nation – what I have described, following Weber, as domination by virtue of a constellation of interests.

Yet, these sorts of accusations and exhortations were often insufficient to turn the tide. Personal rectitude faced an uphill battle when confronted with declining prices and widespread infrastructural breakdown. Even when coffee and cotton were sold as intended, the crops could often go no further due to a lack of transportation. Given the spatial dispersal of cotton and coffee growing – not concentrated on plantations, but rather distributed to innumerable domestic farms – the trouble of transport was all the more acute.[35] Coffee delivered to

---

[32] KDA 244/4: Cotton & Coffee Marketing in Mwenge and Kyake, June 10, 1971.
[33] JDA Agriculture 24/2: Ministry of Co-operatives and Marketing to All Unions, December 15, 1977.
[34] JDA Finance 20/22 Uganda Co-operative Savings & Credit Union, 1978–1983. General Secretary Briefing to the Staff Meeting, August 3, 1978.
[35] KDA 628/2: Increased Cotton Production, 1975/76 Season, August 5, 1975.

Busoga's largest cooperative in November 1976 was still in the storehouse a year later due to lack of lorries. The inability to sell coffee onward for export meant the cooperatives were unable to pay farmers on time.[36] Hiring vehicles was expensive, further limiting the small margins available to growers. When vehicles were available, the gunny bags that held coffee were in short supply. Coffee languishing in storehouses was the target of theft by opportunists who would bring it across the border for private sale.[37]

The County Chief of Kibale in Toro begged the government to provide "any good competent transport company." Forty-one miles from Fort Portal and nearly twice that to Mbarara, work was delayed since the collapse of Kibale's Pamoja Transport Company. This is "our constant disease," Amini Keresi wrote to his superiors on the occasion of an expected visit by Idi Amin in 1976.[38] Yet, the importation of spare parts and new vehicles was a significant strain on Uganda's diminishing foreign exchange reserve.[39] Old vehicles and tractors lay "rotting" on the ground "because there are no parts for them."[40] For the vehicles that did work, fuel was hard to come by and expensive. Not long after, in Bunyoro, the delivery service for cotton seeds was only allowed 150 liters of diesel per day, yet this was insufficient for even a single trip to the main towns of Hoima and Masindi; as a result, the entire region was not receiving cotton seed.[41] With the ideal cotton planting period soon to end, the laggardly pace of distribution risked upsetting the imperative of agricultural rhythms and therefore setting back the district's citizens for months to come.

These material and financial infrastructures were a crucial part of the valuation practices of the state. Without them, agricultural products could not be converted into, first, Uganda shillings paid to farmers

---

[36] JDA Agriculture 24/2: Buyala Growers Co-operative Society to Uganda Advisory Board of Trade, November 14, 1977.
[37] JDA Agriculture 50/15 Month Reports, 1974–1977: October Monthly Report for Jinja District, Department of Co-operative Development, November 11, 1977.
[38] KDA 480/2: County Chief, Kibale to D.C. Toro, July 5, 1976.
[39] KDA 402/1: Applications to Purchase New Lorries with Trailers and Pick-ups, January 28, 1977.
[40] KDA 628/2: Memorandum on Problems Affecting Industries in Western Province, February 24, 1976.
[41] KDA 628/2: Cotton Seed Dressing and Distribution 1976/77, Planting Season, July 15, 1976.

and, then, foreign currency earned by the state. The absence of the former encouraged Uganda's farmers to pursue alternative tactics. Among them was the simple refusal to sell to the state. In late 1976, the Western Province government was consumed with efforts to acquire coffee beans. People "are still having heaps and heaps of unbought coffee in their houses," wrote Steve Mulebeki in South Bunyoro district. "I would be very grateful for any constructive comments/action accordingly on this particular subject matter."[42] On the other side of the country, the walls of coffee storehouses were starting to crack due to the amount of unsold beans accumulating.[43] Chiefs compiled lists of farmers with unbought coffee, yet farmers pointed the finger at the Kakumiro Growers' Co-operative, where illegal buyers caused the troubles.[44] These buyers – alleged to be cooperative society officers – used crop financing to buy coffee at Shs. 1.50 and then sell it to the government at the official price of Shs. 2.50. They could do so because "there is just too much coffee even from past seasons."

For its part, the Kakumiro Growers' Co-operative replied with a range of contrary claims. To excuse themselves, the management blamed a litany of common troubles: its coffee processing facility relied on an old engine that was constantly breaking down. Some of their vehicles lacked spare parts and tires, and they were without gunny bags. The Uganda Commercial Bank refused to finance the union due to a shortfall in the prior year. If there was illegality, it was not in their ranks, wrote the manager, P. K. Ndungu, but among the local coffee societies from whom they purchased. The farmer outcry against Kakumiro Growers' Co-operative Union, he pleaded, was nothing less than a sham allegation from these illegal buyers who were upset the Union would not launder their proceeds.[45] Such accusations and counterclaims flowed back and forth in official correspondence, variously trying to compel action by others and defend against official recriminations. The result was a further impediment to the smooth

---

[42] KDA 628/2: Steve Mulebeki to District Co-operative Officer, January 4, 1977.
[43] JDA Agriculture 53/2: Economic Crops 1960–1978: Provincial Co-operative Officer Busoga to Ministry of Co-operatives and Marketing, July 1, 1976.
[44] KDA 628/2: D.G. Waimaga to District Commissioner, January 5, 1977; KDA 628/2: Provincial Commissioner for Co-operative Development to Supervising Manager, Kakumiro G.C., January 14, 1977.
[45] KDA 628/2: Kakumiro Growers' Co-operative Union to Provincial Commissioner for Co-operative Development, January 14, 1977.

operation of Uganda's export economy. Over time, this dissolution of productive networks and the resulting mistrust would even threaten the economic sovereignty of Uganda.

4.3 The Fate Economic Sovereignty

Whatever the cause of the Kakumiro's crisis, it was not a problem confined to the district. In the words of the Assistant District Commissioner, it was "a national problem."[46] As the marketing system slowed and alternative channels proliferated, farmers across Uganda turned away from the state. The proliferation of illegal coffee brokers could mimic and replace the state. In many cases, they even adopted the measurement scales, vehicles, and personnel of the official trade, thereby obscuring the truth of the transactions.[47] The effect was to deprive authorities of their fiscal foundation. This combined with diminished production. Coffee began dropping in 1970, while cotton's decline started in 1972. The decline of cotton not only undermined "our highest foreign exchange earner," complained Governor Owor in a Western Province Planning Committee meeting in May 1977. It also limited domestic production of oils, soaps, textiles, and other industries for which cotton was an input.[48] In response, his office tried to increase the price paid to growers and streamline marketing procedures.

Uganda's citizens made it clear to the state that the status of the export industry was discouraging their involvement. Cocoa farmers in South Bunyoro flooded government offices to complain they were only paid "on paper" – issued receipts for their produce on the promise of future cash payment.[49] When government tried to pay maize farmers less than the promised USh. 3 per kilo, they rejected the offer. An exasperated Gulam Gafabusa of Bweyale told the government supervisor he would "pour [his 700 bags of maize] on the road so that everybody can see what the Government is doing for the People."

---

[46] KDA 628/2: D.G. Waimaga to District Commissioner, January 5, 1977.
[47] JDA Finance 21/1: District Co-operative Officer Jinja to District Commissioner, Jinja, August 9, 1976.
[48] KDA 402/1: Minutes of the Provincial Planning Committee Meeting, May 11, 1977.
[49] KDA 612/4: Ag. District Commissioner, South Bunyoro to Provincial Governor, January 10, 1979.

Mrs. Okullu of nearby Kigumba town said she would do likewise, turning the food into a roadblock: "I will find out later whether there is Government in this Country or not." Others decided to brew maize into alcohol, rather than sell it as directed.[50] Ugandans confronted more draconian valuation practices with a combination of resentment and refusal, undoing the constellation of interests on which economic sovereignty and citizenship depended.

The government was not only starved of foreign currency earnings, it also lost its ability to limit the expenditure of foreign currency. By the start of 1974, foreign exchange control offenses were becoming "very common."[51] In response, it began an increasingly frantic effort to corral and control currency.[52] For the official stewards of the foreign money, the matter was one of national vitality. "If the country is not to perish," wrote the Bank of Uganda's directors, it was essential to "break the vicious circle" Uganda faced by exporting more and lowering foreign currency expenses.[53] The accumulation of international currencies became a national hymn, led from ministerial heights. "Our task is noble," lectured Minister Justus Byagacaire in February 1974.

Let us pray to Almighty God to give us His Grace and Blessings so that we succeed in playing our part fully and effectively in building better and healthier Ugandans and in earning Uganda foreign exchange through the sale of coffee, cotton, tobacco, and other crops and animal products.[54]

Other-worldly appeals were matched by this-worldly demands. There were perennial campaigns to increase the production of cotton,

---

[50] KDA 628/2: Area Marketing Supervisor to Produce Marketing Board, May 29, 1978.
[51] BoU 0, GOV.305.1: Minutes of EA Exchange Controllers Meeting on 18 January 1974.
[52] For a similar period in Ghana, see Bianca Murillo, *Market Encounters: Consumer Cultures in Twentieth-Century Ghana* (Ohio University Press, 2017), chapter 5. Prosecution of price, trade, and currency control violations also occurred in Biafra and postwar Nigeria, but "in a way that created more confusion than clarity." Samuel Fury Childs Daly, *History of the Republic of Biafra: Law, Crime, and the Nigerian Civil War* (Cambridge University Press, 2020), p. 140.
[53] Bank of Uganda, Minutes of the Eighty-First Meeting of the Board of Directors, December 6, 1974.
[54] JDA Agriculture 36/4 Lectures and Talks, 1969–1974: Speech by Hon. Justus Byagacaire, February 4, 1974.

coffee, and other lucrative crops. Chiefs and agricultural officers went from farm to farm checking how many crops were planted, and if they were spaced and maintained appropriately. Each chief was required to keep a record of all able-bodied people in his area and to check that they were, in fact, growing cotton.[55] Sub-counties and parishes deemed lacking were singled out for further actions, including the replacement of food crops with export crops.[56] Farmers were required to clear bush to plant cotton, despite a lack of hoes and sometimes even seeds.[57] Tighter surveillance of farm activities was used to both demand more production and estimate what was being sold illegally.[58] The enforcement of agricultural standards and domestic labor was coupled with a nationwide campaign to enforce ethical standards. Promises of insecticide, tools, and financing were coupled with appeals to "have national pride" and "inculcate in ourselves a spirit of self-help and self-reliance."[59] As Derek Peterson writes, the government was trying to "curate the economy."[60]

Scholars of Uganda in the 1970s have emphasized the moralizing government rhetoric, and these official exhortations are a prominent example of the wider economy of accusation.[61] Official reprimand coursed across the newspapers and radio, warning against the "evil practice" of smuggling.[62] The Uganda Broadcasting Corporation staged photographs of alleged smugglers, hoarders, and overchargers.[63] Broadcasts warned the public against partaking in such transactions. Shopkeepers was castigated for not paying their rent, women were chastised for impropriety, and the unemployed were cast as nefarious figures. Yet, this was not uniquely an urban phenomenon.

---

[55] KDA 612/4: Checking on Growing of Cotton, July 11, 1977.
[56] KDA 628/2: Double Cotton Campaign, September 8, 1976.
[57] KDA 628/2: P.B. Kawima to Provincial Governor, September 20, 1976.
[58] KDA 628/2: Memorandum Based at [sic] Stopping Coffee Being Smuggled, October 19, 1976.
[59] KDA 628/2: Report on Double Cotton Production Follow Up Safari, October 6, 1976.
[60] Derek Peterson, "Government Work in Idi Amin's Uganda," *Africa* 91(4) (2021): 623.
[61] See Decker, *In Idi Amin's Shadow*; Peterson and Taylor, "Rethinking the State in Idi Amin's Uganda."
[62] KDA 271: Ministry of Information & Broadcasting, Uganda News, July 4, 1977.
[63] Derek Peterson and Richard Vokes, *The Unseen Archive of Idi Amin* (Prestel, 2021).

The colonial structure of rural governance adopted by the independent state was put to its old task of forcefully redirecting peasant priorities.

The local government demanded an ever more urgent pace of work: "every year must have its own speed [and] this year must have great[er] speed than the previous year," said the chief in Kibaale.[64] Cotton would be picked, coffee weeded, and drinking curtailed. County chiefs could amplify their own policing by sending requests to the Uganda Broadcasting Corporation's district news roundup. Chiefs like Amini Keresi turned to vernacular radio broadcasts to convey the message. The public, he said in a transcript meant for broadcast in five languages, must "put much effort on digging ... [for] that is where most of our wealth comes from." To his *askaris*, he broadcast a message to "work like red ants and also to avoid corruption."[65] The local government in Kibaale did so in Rutooro and English, publicizing recent instances of overcharging for fabric, moving bicycle tires across district lines, and hiding essential commodities. Such announcements not only tried to command economic life but also to position local officials as the frontline of national priorities.[66] In his demands on people's labor and behavior, Keresi did not merely enforce a particular notion of morality; he stood as the local face of a national effort to govern value. Without the chiefly imposition upon farmers to dig and harvest, the government would lack the financial basis on which to operate. Unable to draw reliably on future earnings, they required a more thoroughgoing pressure on the everyday rhythms of families.

Bureaucrats took to the street to get a handle on these intermediate traders. Over the course of 1976–1977, Vincent Mayiga, Mbale's Provincial Commissioner for Commerce, kept up a steady stream of monthly reports to his superiors. Despite the frequent inscrutability of the commodity market, he reported on the state of shops across his jurisdiction. If only goods would move through appointed agents, he thought, the "sky-rocketing" prices would reduce.[67] Bureaucrats like Mayiga maintained a fastidious attention to prices and availability. He followed up allegations about illegal transactions and reported

---

[64] KDA 270: Amini Keresi to Information Officer, Toro, February 8, 1978.
[65] KDA 270: Amini Keresi to Information Officer, Toro, January 26, 1978.
[66] KDA 270: Office of the County Chief to District Information Officer, November 8, 1976.
[67] JDA Justice, Law, Order & Security 13/17: Provincial Commissioner for Commerce, Mbale to P.S. Ministry of Commerce, November 25, 1977.

popular complaints about overcharging or absent goods. He ran out of stationery and struggled with his own lack of transportation.[68] Shopkeepers who kept their stores well stocked were noted for their hard work, but he also suspected they were taking advantage of their proximity to the border with Kenya. He shared the good news when maize meal and matches were abundant, but his dispatches mostly document volatility, inflation, and absence.[69]

The street-level documentation of men like Mayiga fed into government demands on citizens. The Minister of Commerce, for instance, called licensed importers together in 1978 to express his dissatisfaction with the state of the sector. It was not merely that some were hoarding, overcharging, and smuggling goods "thus causing artificial shortages in the country." Even when goods were distributed, they reflected an inequitable geography of availability. Some licensed importers sold only in Central Province; distributors of manufactured goods would sell directly outside factory gates, rather than ship them elsewhere. The Minister sternly warned that commodities must "also reach the remotest areas of the country." Staff in these firms misallocated foreign exchange and were "unapproachable," working only in the morning hours to the detriment of those who come from upcountry. The state's idiom pointed to a sense of national collectivity that was being contravened by improper and iniquitous distribution agents. "You are, no doubt, aware," decried one circular, "that kerosene is purchased with foreign exchange earned by the people. It is therefore your onus [and] responsibility to ensure that kerosene bought is equitably distributed to them."[70]

In the starkest terms, economic criminality brought into question one's membership in the nation. While the categories of smuggling, hoarding, and overcharging achieved greater judicial importance in the years after the Asian expulsion, a similar set of concerns animated that moment. Asians were blamed for the illicit movement of wealth across borders, a refusal to sell to Africans, and the deceitful manipulation of prices and measurement. When the same actions continued after the expulsion, some officials rehearsed these racialized tropes. In an excoriating address

---

[68] On the dedication of bureaucrats during the Amin years, see Peterson, "Government Work in Idi Amin's Uganda," pp. 620–640.

[69] See the collection in JDA Justice, Law, Order & Security 13/17 Trade Development Department, Monthly Report, 1974–1978.

[70] JDA Trade & Industry 11/5: Minister of Provincial Administrations to all District Commissioners, April 5, 1978.

to licensed traders of cement, iron sheets, and beverages, the Provincial Governor of Busoga condemned their overcharging and hoarding. The public's complaints about a lack of goods was a result of the traders "who go rumouring" that the government is to blame all the while having the goods "in plenty hidden some place." Contravening the mandatory circulation of commodities proved not only that the traders have "no love for the development of your country" but also that they are the "true enemies of Uganda and are by virtue of this, foreigners who have been forced to stay here." Coming only a few violent years after the Ugandan state made clear its exceptional power over who belongs and who does not, this rhetoric was a significant threat. For those who did not discern the character of his condemnation, he made it quite clear: "You seem to be African Indians in Uganda." Through their illegal transactions and practices of valuation, these traders showed they did not deserve the rights of citizenship.[71] Even worse, their actions were humiliating the rest of Ugandans, dogged by the question of whether "we are incapable of sustaining our own country?"[72]

The government tried to turn this shame back toward economic middlemen, castigating them for their disruptive wrongdoing, yet such efforts to rule through persuasion or threat usually fell short (see Figure 4.2). Instead, the state frequently reorganized commercial distribution in an effort to clamp down on economic crimes. The plans could be quite detailed – down to how many retailers for each commodity on which streets in Jinja.[73] Malpractices were to be eliminated through a combination of new bureaucratic protocols and institutions. A profusion of paperwork – signed and stamped, sometimes in triplicate – was designed to secure the movement of commodities against unwanted redirection. Counting money and things was hard; making accountable citizens was harder still.

Parastatal organizations were dissolved and reconstituted, restaffed and reorganized along new axes of responsibility and command. In some cases, new entities provided *mafuta mingi* latitude for more

---

[71] Others used a similar idiom, speaking of Ugandan retailers as "far worse than the Patels" at hoarding. DCO 80/4490: Mr. Duncan's Visit to Uganda, September 1974.

[72] JDA Administration Central 5/21 Speeches: Provincial Governor, Busoga to Agents, January 15, 1976.

[73] JDA Trade & Industry 23/3: Minutes of the Meeting on Essential Commodities, April 7, 1975.

Figure 4.2 Governor of Central Province Nasur Abdullah addresses agents for essential commodities in 1975.
Courtesy of the Uganda Broadcasting Corporation.

predation.[74] In other cases, distribution licenses could be revoked and reassigned, raising the question of backroom deals but rarely providing evidence for such suspicions.[75] Ministers speculated that only by "flooding the home market with goods" through short-term loans would shortages and malpractices abate.[76] Many Ugandan bureaucrats recognized *magendo* as a problem that could be ameliorated best through improved services, not expanded policing. Busoga's cooperative officer set aside his frustration at cotton smuggling to Kenya to note that giving the growers and ginnery a lorry would mean they had less need to travel to Kenya.[77] In his view, it was better to create shared interests than antagonisms.

---

[74] For instance, in April 1978 a new method was promulgated for kerosene agents; the new agents were well-connected to the state. JDA Trade & Industry 11/5: Minister of Provincial Administrations to all DCs, April 5, 1978.

[75] JDA Trade & Industry 23/3: Provincial Governor, Busoga to Trade Development Officer, September 11, 1975.

[76] KDA 638: Minutes of the Minister of Commerce's Meeting with Direct Importers, September 25, 1975.

[77] JDA Agriculture 53/2: Provincial Co-operative Officer Busoga to Ministry of Co-operatives and Marketing, July 1, 1976.

4.3 The Fate Economic Sovereignty

Overall, the state's pressure was of waning efficacy. Agricultural officers needed to frequently visit farmers' plots in order to maintain the pressure but lacked the fuel to keep up these tours.[78] Government rallies attracted up to 2,000 attendees, yet it was unclear if this signaled any change in motivation given the range of impediments facing farmers – from a lack of hoes to deteriorating roads and threats from wild animals.[79] Instead, a turn to subsistence farming provided families a means of social reproduction unbeholden to outside predation. Farming even increased in cities as wage economies faltered.[80] Increased time farming food crops led to employee absenteeism.[81] Commercial traders turned to farming and cattle rearing – activities less about their exchange value than their use value.[82] Access to productive land, especially in rural areas, meant there was little malnutrition in rural areas during the 1970s.[83] This focus on subsistence came at the cost of exports.[84] Cotton was uprooted and coffee neglected. Such agrarian disobedience provoked the ire of an official decree in 1977, threatening hefty fines and imprisonment for any person who did not maintain their "coffee *shamba* in a cleanly cultivated condition and free from bananas, perennial grasses and weeds."[85]

The malfeasance and impunity of Amin's ruling circle put different parts of the state under enormous pressure. The Uganda Commercial

---

[78] JDA Trade & Industry 15/4: Ag. Provincial Commissioner for Agriculture, Busoga to D.C. Jinja, July 14, 1976; JDA Admin Central 5/9: Annual Report 1975 Provincial Commissioner for Commerce, Busoga.

[79] KDA 628/2: Report on Double Cotton Production Follow Up Safari by the Governor of Western Province.

[80] Daniel Maxwell, "Urban Agriculture: Unplanned Responses to the Economic Crisis," in Holger Bernt Hansen and Michael Twaddle (eds.), *Developing Uganda* (James Currey, 1998), pp. 98–108.

[81] KDA 463: Mbaire to Kifuko, July 19, 1978; KDA 402/1: Minutes of the Provincial Governor with this Staff, March 10, 1977.

[82] JDA Admin Central 5/9: Annual Report 1975, Provincial Commissioner for Commerce, Ministry of Commerce, Busoga.

[83] Holger Hansen, "Uganda in the 1970s: A Decade of Paradoxes and Ambiguities," *Journal of Eastern African Studies* 7(1) (2013): 98.

[84] It may have also come at the cost of women's agrarian autonomy, as men's movement from export to subsistence crops further diminished what control and income women previously had from growing and selling food. Pernille Sorensen, "Commercialization of Food Crops in Busoga, Uganda, and the Renegotiation of Gender," *Gender & Society* 10(5) (1996): 608–628.

[85] Government of Uganda, "The Coffee Production Decree," 1977.

Bank, for instance, was required to assume USh. 600 million in bad loans by 1978 – its own balance sheet ruined to keep other entities running. When the General Manager complained, he was fired. The Bank of Uganda was also obliged to issue loans to government departments whose own revenue collapsed at the same time their spending soared. In effect, it became an ever more important arbiter of wealth, with concomitant demands that its staff depart from proper protocol. Women working at the currency center in Gulu were abducted by soldiers in March 1977, perhaps as part of a robbery.[86] Men from the Office of the President would call the central bank headquarters, demanding a million shillings in cash be issued to them outside regulated channels; in other cases, foreign exchange was demanded without any corresponding domestic currency.[87] It was, in the words of technocratic reformers in 1979, "an orgy of financial indiscipline," but the central bank was hardly alone as state offices became for many an instrument of accumulation.[88]

In effect, a constellation of interests on which economic sovereignty depended was fracturing as Ugandans revalued their time and labor, investing in subsistence and other activities not amenable to state mediation. Yet for several reasons, the disquiet of the era did not lead Ugandans to merely retreat to family farms. While many had access to land, it was by no means universal. Even when families could survive without dependence on drastically eroded wages, they were dissatisfied with the state of affairs. The expectations of the independence era – that political sovereignty would permit the consumptive and commercial liberties of economic sovereignty – were not easily let go. More specifically, some crucial household goods could not be grown or found; Ugandans called these "essential commodities," and their relative paucity stood as stark reminders of the failures of self-rule.[89]

---

[86] BoU G.184.75: Banking Department: Governor Obel to Colonel Mondo, March 10, 1977.

[87] BoU G.60.67, GOV.104.1: Foreign Exchange Reserve Management, 1977–1982: Treasury Officer to General Manager, July 28, 1975; Governor to General Manager, November 12, 1975.

[88] Commonwealth Team of Experts, *The Rehabilitation of the Economy of Uganda*, vol. 2 (Marlborough House, 1979), pp. 273–275.

[89] Alicia Decker, "An Accidental Liberation: Ugandan Women on the Front Lines in Idi Amin's Economic War," *Women's History Review* 22(65) (2013): 961–964.

While many took matters into their own hands, turning to illegal transactions to purchase the essential commodities of sugar, salt, soap, and cooking oil, others turned to the state officials responsible for their supply. In other words, not only did the state place demands on Ugandans' labor and production, but as the crises of the 1970s compounded, Ugandans increased their demands on the state. The prevalence of the unsanctioned economy did not reflect the wholesale rejection of the state's prerogatives; rather, it was up to bureaucrats to rectify the commercial disarray. Citizens called for an end to economic irregularity, despite the risks that state enforcement would rebound onto those obliged to partake in illegality. In the sections that follow, I examine how everyday ethics of consumption, respectability, and hospitality combined with broader expectations about economic opportunity to fuel widespread calls for the state to reassert its sovereign command over the situation.

4.4 Economic Life in the Shadow of Absence

In October 1973, R. W. Kasozi wrote to the government on behalf of the registered trade unions. Kasozi and his colleagues found themselves in need. Spending most of their days in "the field" meant they had little time to "run back into town and find sugar still being sold to the public." In ordinary circumstances, their work presented little obstacle to necessary errands, yet these were no ordinary times. "It must have also come to your notice," he wrote, "that people leave their villages early in the morning hours and invade the Jinja town, for nothing but sugar." What sugar was available flew off the shelves, meaning trade union staff were confronted by empty shops when they finished work. Some were even prioritizing sugar over their professional duties. "Our minds having been diverted to hunting for sugar, the organization work is being hampered and this is indeed detrimental to the interests of our members to whom we are obligated to serve." If the trade unions around Jinja were to carry on, they would need 200 kilograms of sugar delivered at regular intervals.[90]

The predicament of trade union organizers was, in part, a problem of labor time. As queues became commonplace, snaking around street corners in the hope of getting scarce goods, those unable to wait stood

---

[90] JDA Trade & Industry 17/15: R.W. Kasozi to Regional Labour Officer, Ministry of Labour, October 22, 1973.

little chance of securing their share.[91] When Kasozi wrote of villagers "invading" Jinja to queue for sugar, he suggested a more general resentment by wage workers who found their incomes insufficient in an economy that demanded timeliness, not merely money.[92] They spent the day waiting in a queue only to come back "empty handed, disappointed, and tired."[93] For these constituents, consumption was a competitive affair, with their own deprivation standing in contrast to the acquisitions of less deserving others. Rather than absent, commodities like sugar had a spectral, fleeting presence – available momentarily, or through exclusionary channels. The result was all the more affecting. Not only did it conjure envy and resentment, but the transitory availability of goods compelled more laborious efforts to buy them.

One result was that Ugandans implored bureaucrats to meet their obligations, drawing on hierarchical idioms about duties and rights. These were not abstract entitlements but concrete relations that were historically salient and could further specific notions of what was proper and desirable.[94] For instance, when B. O. Lumonya, the Commissioner for Education in Busoga Province, wrote to the Governor seeking sugar for teachers, his request was deferential, emphasizing the appreciation and gratitude of the deprived. "I am sorry for bothering you on school matters," Lumonya hesitated, but "as the father of the Province," it was to the Governor that he must turn.[95] In practice, access to commodities was not a right inhering on the basis of citizenship alone; instead, applicants needed to justify the

---

[91] On time poverty, see Ato Quayson, *Oxford Street, Accra: Street Life and the Itineraries of Transnationalism* (Duke University Press, 2014). On queuing, see Caroline Humphrey, *The Unmaking of Soviet Life: Everyday Economies after Socialism* (Cornell University Press, 2002), p. 46f; Katherine Verdery, *What Was Socialism, and What Comes Next?* (Princeton University Press, 1996), pp. 46–50.

[92] In other cases, it was rural Ugandans who suffered: when shops were only open in the morning, they may not arrive "all the way from up-country" in time to secure some stock. KDA 638 Minutes of the Minister of Commerce's Meeting with Direct Importers, September 25, 1975.

[93] KDA 744/1: BAN Rukara to Manager, Food & Beverages, October 20, 1975.

[94] Akin to Carol Summers, "Radical Rudeness: Ugandan Social Critiques in the 1940s," *Journal of Social History* 39(3) (2006): 741–770. For a recent ethnographic assessment of dependence, see China Scherz, *Having People, Having Heart: Charity, Sustainable Development, and Problems of Dependence in Central Uganda* (University of Chicago Press, 2014).

[95] JDA Trade & Industry 17/15: Essential Commodities for Teachers Teaching in Jinja Municipality Primary Schools, October 1, 1975.

4.4 Economic Life in the Shadow of Absence

basis for their legitimacy through a combination of rightful dependency and productive worth. Kasozi, for instance, did not make his claim on behalf of his rights as an economic citizen of Uganda in general, but rather as a contributor to the well-being of a specific constituency: trade union members based in Jinja. The scarcity of goods meant an equitable distribution of commodities was untenable, so Ugandans positioned themselves as especially worthy – as figurative sons, productive union organizers, and so forth. In the process, they differentiated citizenship through their own idioms of claims-making.[96]

These petitions were often alert to Ugandans' ability to vote with their feet. Teachers threatened to leave the classroom if the government did not divert sugar, salt, and soap to schools.[97] Three hundred workers at the Toro Growers' Co-operative Union could not travel the 22 kilometers to the nearest shops "to line up when goods are available," so appealed for a special allocation.[98] Without it, they would not appear for work. Absconding workers threatened far more than their bosses' bottom line. By 1975, as the country's output groaned to a halt, queuing was seen as a threat to the entire nation. Council staff in Jinja were promised special deliveries in order to focus on their work.[99] The Governor of Western Province, Alex Owor, took up the plight of tea estate workers, imploring the General Manager of Uganda Foods and Beverages to provide "special incentives" to workers in the form of 5,000 bars of soap, 50 bags of sugar, and 50 tins of cooking oil. "Government is very much concerned with the shortage of labour," he explained, leading to "a considerable amount of loss in terms of foreign exchange."[100] The trouble was urgent: tea harvesting "is a non-stop type of job" because it is most valuable if the leaves are picked when green. Without more workers, the plants would

---

[96] Themes central to Frederick Cooper, *Citizenship, Inequality, and Difference* (Princeton University Press, 2018).

[97] JDA Trade & Industry 17/15: Local Business Applications & Reports, 1972–1975; Provincial Commissioner for Education to Provincial Governor, Busoga, October 1, 1975.

[98] KDA 654/1: Essential Commodities for Workers, Toro Growers' Co-operative Union, April 11, 1978.

[99] JDA Trade & Industry 23/3: Town Clerk, Jinja to Provincial Executive Secretary, Busoga, June 19, 1975.

[100] KDA 651/2: Alex Owor to General Manager, Foods & Beverages, February 10, 1977.

decay, earning less as a result. Soap, sugar, and salt were key to morale and an "inducement to workers for double production."[101]

Citizen petitions reveal a diverse range of priorities. Some followed the logic of the nation, claiming that queuing would "waste indefinite and valuable time which we would otherwise put to the public disposal."[102] Military reservists complained they had not received sugar, salt, and cloth for three months. They were concentrating on doubling agricultural production – "dedicated to our service" – but needed the state to rectify this "malpractice."[103] For his part, Governor Owor negotiated dearth by categorizing and ranking citizens: productive contributors to the foreign exchange reserve were prioritized over others.[104] One university professor recalls that by 1974, "society was graded into status groups" with the elites entitled to receive "without struggle and at normal prices, so much rice, so much sugar, etc. per week." Ugandans less attached to the state, however, were left to their own devices.[105] The logics of prioritized access also obliged recipients to be sufficiently appreciative: without gratitude, one could suddenly be detached from the networks of allocation. For example, Rashid Kwebiiha invoked the ire of the County Chief after complaining about the paltry amount of sugar he received. Docking his allocation for ingratitude, the Chief cautioned him further: "If you cannot accept that free offer, then you will have helped the rest who have never even seen half a kg."[106] Here, the decentralized despotism adopted by the postcolonial state showed its distributive force and its demand for acquiescence.[107] It also reveals the zero-sum sensibility of the time: sugar in one man's tea was responsible for depriving another. As a result, a sense of entitlement merged with the necessity of supplication.

[101] KDA 628/2: Provincial Executive Secretary to Minister of Industry & Power, February 24, 1976.
[102] KDA 744/1: Kagaba & Nyakabwa, Advocates to D.C. Toro, September 22, 1975.
[103] KDA 654: Dominic Mayanja to Governor, Western Province, October 19, 1977.
[104] KDA 628/2: Memorandum on Problems Affecting Industries in Western Province, February 24, 1976.
[105] Semakula Kiwanuka, *Amin and the Tragedy of Uganda* (Weltforum Verlag, 1979), pp. 95–96.
[106] KDA 654: County Chief to Rashid Kwebiiha, December 4, 1975.
[107] On decentralized despotism, see Mahmood Mamdani, *Citizen & Subject: Contemporary Africa and the Legacy of Late Colonialism* (Princeton University Press, 1996), chapter five.

4.5 The Ethics of Essential Commodities

The intermittent availability of commodities threatened to unmake the rhythms of production on which the nation depended. The local government could make some changes, such as selling essential commodities on the weekends when teachers could buy, but this was of only marginal importance.[108] Medical staff in Western Province appealed for essential commodities after going "many weeks in every month" without sugar or soap. Sometimes sugar and salt were available at the hospital, but there was no soap or cooking oil. Their working hours stopped them from queuing at shops "lest services are dislocated to the disadvantage of the public."[109] The staff of the Kyembogo Tractor Hire Service also found themselves in the wrong place when shelves were stocked. Penning a letter to the District Commission for Toro, they positioned themselves as fruitful contributors to agricultural productivity in need of sugar, salt, soap, and hoes. "We cannot leave work when sugar etc. [are] supplied in the town, as we are in the field operating. Sir, could you be so kind enough to get us the above mentioned" commodities?[110]

4.5 The Ethics of Essential Commodities

The absence of essential commodities was not only an impediment to national productivity; it also interfered with the pursuit of social standing and ethical life. What Ugandans called "essential commodities" were conduits for fulfilling a good life. Far from inert implements of survival, they were objects of meaningful significance in the raising of children, the hosting of guests, and the fashioning of oneself.[111] In interviews about the period and across the archival sources, "sugar" stands out as the most salient absence, followed shortly by salt, soap, and cooking oil. Other goods – bicycles and hoes, for instance – were also difficult to acquire in the 1970s but did not reach the same status.[112] In the idiom of the time, "essential commodities" were not

---

[108] KDA 744/1: Kalyebara to Headmaster & Staff, July 2, 1975.
[109] KDA 744/1: Provincial Commissioner for Health, Western Province to Chairman, Essential Commodity Allocation Commission, August 1975.
[110] KDA 744/1: Kyembogo Tractor Hire Service Unit to D.C., Toro, July 31, 1975.
[111] Timothy Burke, *Lifebuoy Men, Lux Women: Commodification, Consumption, and Cleanliness in Modern Zimbabwe* (Duke University Press, 2005).
[112] And because subsistence was generally secure, it was not basic food items that had such significance either. Compare to bread in settings such as the Soviet

so much those essential for life as they were essential for a bare minimum of the *good* life. After all, you can drink tea without sugar. From the perspective of many, however, you cannot drink tea without sugar in a dignified manner.

Sugar, salt, soap, and cooking oil were essential commodities because their absence deprived Ugandans of respectability. Piled into hot tea, sugar is not merely a desired flavor but also a constitutive part of domestic rhythms, including hospitality. What calories it provides are coupled with its symbolic role in social life. While improvised substitutes were possible – pounded sugarcane for sweetener, or papaya leaves for washing clothes – these were hardly sufficient.[113] The performance of respectability by individuals and households often hinges on the availability of tea with a heaping addition of sugar.[114] As a letter from the Lira District Teachers' Association in 1979 – complaining of the "meagre" quantity of sugar they received – made clear, its absence during the past decade was an affront to notions of fairness, an impediment to appropriate decorum, and unbecoming their professional stature.[115] This fell along gendered lines.[116] For husbands and fathers, the inability to secure essential commodities was especially unnerving. Teachers at the Nyakagongo Primary School bemoaned that the portion of sugar they received was "inadequate for a family man."[117] For women, the decline of male wages was an even greater pressure. They were less able to position themselves as contributors to the nation or draw on institutional connections, yet their obligations to provide for children remained.

Union and Egypt. Humphrey, *The Unmaking of Soviet Life*; Jessica Barnes, *Staple Security: Bread and Wheat in Egypt* (Duke University Press, 2022).

[113] Emmanuel Katongole, *A Future for Africa: Critical Essays in Christian Social Imagination* (Wipf & Stock Publishers, 2017), p. 17.

[114] There is a colonial genealogy to this, as notions of civilization denigrated and displaced some sites and practices of consumption in favor of others.
In Buganda, the elite traded historic mutuality with dependents for more socially circumscribed teatime rituals with British patrons. In other cases, Christianity discouraged existing forms of alcohol in favor of more docile drinks, including tea with sugar. Summers, "Radical Rudeness," pp. 748–749.

[115] Lira District Archives (LDA) Box 501: Moses Otyek-Akeny to Minister of Commerce, November 20, 1979. I appreciate Derek Peterson sharing this letter with me and discussing the importance of sugar to notions of respectability.

[116] Decker, *In Idi Amin's Shadow*, chapter 4.

[117] KDA 744/1: Nyakagongo Primary School Staff to Saza Chief, June 25, 1975.

4.5 The Ethics of Essential Commodities

As a result, many expanded their market activities.[118] Others took to magendo or formed relations with men who could access networks of value and goods distribution.

If the absence of essential commodities was an impediment to everyday notions of ethics, it was an even greater challenge at special occasions. By April 1976, the national distributor was besieged by "members of the public who always come for commodities claiming that they are [a] funeral right."[119] Saving money to provide for wedding guests was difficult enough during these years; for those that could accumulate some cash, the inability to purchase sugar, salt, soap, and oil was even more troubling.[120] In the days leading up to his son's wedding, a Mr. Yusufu of Jinja appeared in the office of the Provincial Governor bearing both the wedding invitations and a letter of introduction from his District Commissioner. With this documentary accoutrement, Yusufu hoped to acquire beer, flour, cigarettes, and rice to host his guests.[121] Solomon Kasaija-Atwooki faced particular pressure from his born-again in-laws who would not partake in the usual homemade alcohol but instead wished for tea with plenty of sugar and an additional bag of sugar as part of the bride price.[122] Even otherwise influential Ugandans could not count on securing the goods necessary for a fitting wedding. Senior State Attorney Henry Tungakwo Araali failed to purchase beer from inadequately supplied agents. Scrambling in the weeks before his June 1977 wedding, he wrote directly to Uganda Breweries, beseeching their manager that his "humble request will meet with your utmost sympathy."[123]

---

[118] Nakanyike Musisi, "Baganda Women's Night Market Activities," in Felix K. Ekechi and Bessie House-Midamba (eds.), *African Market Women and Economic Power: The Role of Women in African Economic Development* (Greenwood Press, 2005), pp. 132–140.

[119] JDA Trade & Industry 9/17: Foods & Beverages Monthly Report for April 1976.

[120] KDA 654: Letter from Benjamin Bogere, Jr. re: Michael Mpuro Ibanda, May 8, 1978.

[121] JDA Trade & Industry 11/17: Request for Commodities, March 20, 1978.

[122] KDA 654: Solomon Kasaija-Atwooki to General Manager, National Sugar Works, June 7, 1978. Christine Obbo writes of the "conspicuous consumption displayed at Church weddings" where tea and, in the 1950s, soft drinks became expected performances of prestige. *African Women: Their Struggle for Economic Independence* (Zed Books, 1980), pp. 37–38.

[123] KDA 654: Application for the Purchase of Beer, May 30, 1977.

Rites of initiation like weddings and funerals are prototypical moments for the circulation and redistribution of wealth and property; government monopoly obliged Ugandans to incorporate the state in these rituals. Consider John Baptist Musana, who requested to purchase 200 cases of beer, gin, and soda after "having decided to have a Holy Marriage on Catholic Centenary day." This proud occasion would take place at the Nalugi Parish and his father-in-law's home. "The donation of the wedding," he explained, would occur on October 1, 1978, with contributions from his wife's family, his own clan, and his best friends. But,

the donors are anxious to see that this request is approved in a fatherly manner, before or as soon as after the above mentioned date. It will enable me to be buying few by few cases from the money which will be donated generously towards the wedding.

Please, he asked the Provincial Governor, would you meet my request "with fatherly consideration to enable me to have a colourful, peaceful, brotherly wedding, on the most important day in Uganda for my faith?"[124] Men like Musana did not only forge new families at weddings; scarcity also obliged them to cast the state as an additional father figure.[125]

In an economy where many retained land from which to produce subsistence crops, the category "essential commodities" named the sorts of purchases deemed crucial to the maintenance of a decent meal, a proper visit, and a respectable wedding. The widespread absence of essential commodities contributed to a sense of moral decline. Lacking the means to respectable consumption and sociality, Ugandans turned to a variety of tactics. If some adopted the bureaucratic protocol to hail the state as a fatherly patron, and others drew on personal connections, still others turned to activities deemed criminal by a state desperate to orchestrate the production and circulation of value. This could rankle others, however, and many Ugandans welcomed, even demanded, more policing of the economy. The following section elaborates how these competing itineraries unmade the economic rhythms of the 1960s.

---

[124] KDA 654: John Baptist Musana to Provincial Governor, September 1, 1978.
[125] Cf. Michael Schatzberg, *Political Legitimacy in Middle Africa: Father, Family, Food* (Indiana University Press, 2001).

4.6 Popular Demands for Economic Policing

Facing an unaccountable commercial world – with commodities slipping out of controlled channels into illegible, exclusionary circuits – citizens called on the state to discipline the market. They cast a suspicious eye on neighbors and the movement of goods. There was widespread consensus that the essential commodity shortages were due to hoarding and smuggling. Even if this behavior usually escaped observation, absence was its own sort of evidence: when goods were not available, it was presumed they were being sold illicitly. Complaints against "notorious traders" would pile up, spurring investigation and sometimes administrative responses.[126]

Many complaints blamed merchants. In 1972, residents of Kicwamba Gomborra complained that they "shoulder expensive prices from traders, butchers, and shopkeepers." In addition to overcharging for substandard meat, the accused shopkeepers contravened regulations for measuring sugar, using old scales instead of the newer kilogram standards. Such deceit not only impoverished consumers but meant they could not buy goods to which they should have access.[127] A stream of such complaints about economic crimes reached government offices in the 1970s. Fifteen residents of Muhokya Busongora reported a Mr. Joseph Wagiraga for misappropriating USh. 2,800 and 98 bags of cement, leading to his arrest.[128] "The People of Budondo" wrote a secret letter accusing a merchant of "stealing the government's money" by renting out rooms in a property acquired from the Custodian Board.[129] They begged the local government to "send some spies to find out the truth." Elsewhere, town residents eagerly noticed when delivery trucks appeared and were appalled to learn a few hours later that shopkeepers claimed no goods actually arrived. This gap between what they saw and what they were told demanded explanation and fueled intrigue.

---

[126] JDA Trade & Industry 23/3: Commissioner for Commerce, Mbale to D.C. South Busoga, September 18, 1975.
[127] KDA 401/1: Expensive Selling of Meat and Sugar, August 27, 1972.
[128] KDA 401: Mr. Joseph Wagiraga Shs. 2,800 and 98 Bags of Cement, June 3, 1971.
[129] JDA Admin Complaints & Petitions 4/4: People of Budondo to District Commissioner, Jinja District, May 19, 1977.

In few cases could allegations be proven, but suspicion and accusation had their own efficacy, spurring Ugandans to further retreat from spaces of public scrutiny and to preemptively guard against unwanted trouble. To wit, the manager of one Jinja firm rushed to report the "dubious sale" of kerosene at his factory, casting blame on a staff member in an effort to insulate the company from reproach.[130] Traders in Kibaale County closed up shop when soldiers from nearby barracks began checking prices and demanding evidence of where they acquired the goods.[131] The effect of such discretion and secrecy was to make an already uncertain commercial realm even less perceptible.

Ugandans volunteered their services to stop smuggling. A group of former soldiers tried to parlay their prior "intelligence work" and "high training in investigations" into a new commission with the military. In a letter seeking an audience with Idi Amin, they laid out their plan. As the "eyes and ears of the government," they could help stop "subversive" economic crimes through "special duties on borders and boundaries." Such an offer was not without their own purpose; enlisting as soldiers in the Economic War was a way to display their outstanding virtues as citizens. The same soldiers had earlier applied to the Economic War Allocation Committee for a maize mill and, before that, for a tea estate. "To get a bank loan of sufficient money to run a business or buy a lorry would be another topic to discuss with Amin," they wrote.[132]

Some demands for economic policing were born of competitive spirits. Mahmood Mamdani traced the roots of the Asian expulsion to the maneuvering of the African petit bourgeoisie.[133] Facing the commercial dominance of Asian capitalists, the petit bourgeoisie harnessed state power to advance their own aspirations.[134] The dynamics of this racial capitalism were on full display in a lengthy letter sent to Idi Amin by "The Native of the Land, Ugandan Traders of Busoga District" at the start of August 1972. "You promised ACTION,

---

[130] JDA Trade & Industry 23/3: Area Manager of National Water & Sewerage Corporation to Ag. Provincial Executive Secretary, Busoga Province, August 9, 1976.
[131] KDA 466: Behavior of Some Soldiers of Kabamba Army Unit, May 2, 1974.
[132] KDA 480/2: Permission to Visit H.E. Amin, November 30, 1976.
[133] Mahmood Mamdani, *Politics and Class Formation in Uganda* (Monthly Review, 1976).
[134] For prior efforts to "Africanize" the economy, see Taylor, "Claiming Kabale."

4.6 Popular Demands for Economic Policing   245

and ... so also, ACTION we PROMISE in return." Expressing their affection and love for the new military government and its boss, the missive detailed an incredible range of demands that would help the "African Ugandan Traders." They argued that the government was responsible for ending their marginalization at the hands of "noncitizen trickster[s]," suggesting rent controls and preferential government tenders, commercial training and access to loans. It was to the citizen – depicted as autochthonous and productive – that the government was responsible, and the traders happily positioned themselves in a relationship of dependence to the sovereign. Mimicking the Lord's Prayer, they entreated Amin: "Your Excellency, relieve us from evils of Exploitation in Trade, preserve us in Commerce and Industry, and deliver us into the Fruits of INDEPENDENCE and everlasting PROSPERITY."[135]

The demands for economic policing, including the Economic Crimes Tribunal, was not limited to racialized struggles. It also existed between African merchants. In 1976, the Kagadi Traders Committee blew the whistle on the wholesale distribution agent for textiles, personally naming his three "black market agents" who were busy selling fabric at inflated prices. Such malfeasance took place under cover of darkness so in the morning, you would find no textiles in the shops. While shelves of upstanding shopkeepers were empty, the three illicit merchants were always supplied with "rolls and rolls" of printed textiles. "Do these people make [the fabric] themselves? Help us. They are milking us terribly."[136] Others complemented their accusations and complaints with detailed lists of suggested reforms. A twenty-six page memorandum submitted to Idi Amin by African traders decried nepotism, "briefcase businessmen," and the usual slate of economic criminality. They asked for further training, the exclusion of unlicensed competitors, reformed commodity distribution protocols, and changes to the government's pricing formulae.[137]

---

[135] JDA Trade & Industry 14/25: Traders of Busoga District to Amin, August 8, 1972.
[136] KDA 641/2: Kagadi Traders Committee to Governor Western Province, January 2, 1976.
[137] JDA Trade & Industry 23/3: Traders' Memorandum submitted to H.E Amin on Commercial and Related Economic Activities in Uganda [n.d. but 1976–1977?].

Throughout these complaints, Ugandans revealed an expectation that government could install an ethical regime of commodity distribution. Fair prices were those set by the state, even if few were unable to avoid buying goods at magendo prices during the 1970s. Allocation was to be decided on logics other than those of a marketplace, where ability to pay determines who can purchase a good; rather, Ugandans thought commodities like sugar and salt should be available to all and more specialized goods – say, bicycles or spare vehicle parts – should be sold to those who would use them for productive purposes, such as roaming agricultural extension agents or coffee transporters. Even Kagadi's jealously competitive traders reflected an ethic of equitable distribution, upset that the textile distributor was giving preferential buying rights to some shopkeepers and not others. They believed the only way to fix the textile system was "to appoint a reliable government agent."[138] Under his watchful eye, the wholesale textiles could be opened in the presence of all traders, instead of secretly distributed at night.

4.7 In the Matter of Economic Crimes

By and large, citizens' complaints called for the reformation – not the dissolution – of the state's government of value. As a result, the Ugandan state tried various means to contain wealth within its auspices. Parastatal organizations were formed in response to shortages and replaced when the problems persisted. Commodity allocation committees drew up lists of goods and recipients, issuing paperwork in triplicate to account for their distribution. District-level officials patrolled shops and reported on-the-ground conditions to their superiors. However, much to the frustration of the state, production and trade continued to elude their grasp. Worldwide inflation, the oil embargo, and investors' preferences deprived the state of meaningful control over economic dynamics. Ugandans, for their part, invented novel ways of creating value on their own terms. The examples are myriad, with few initiatives reaching significant scale on their own; rather, a profusion of unsanctioned behaviors accumulated to tremendous consequence. Indeed, the criminalized trade even shifted the economic geography of Uganda as the population of smaller border

[138] KDA 641/2: Kagadi Traders Committee to Governor, Western Province, January 2, 1976.

Figure 4.3 Domestic goods seized as evidence at an Economic Crimes Tribunal in 1975.
Courtesy of Uganda Broadcasting Corporation.

towns grew faster in the 1970s than larger urban areas like Jinja or Kampala. In a time of misrule, the presence of military and police made the latter insecure; in an era of shortage, the proximity to neighboring countries and farmland made the former advantageous. Smuggling proceeds financed new buildings in relatively smaller settlements, where they were less likely to attract unwanted attention.[139]

Taken on their own, smuggling, hoarding, and overcharging subverted different elements of the state monopoly on valuation (see Figure 4.3). "Smuggling" was the label for the circuits that transgressed sovereign territory, "hoarding" speaks to criminalized temporalities of trade, and "over-charging" names transactions that dissent from official measures of value. In practice, they often occurred in the very same transaction: coffee that was not sold to the marketing board (thus forming a criminal hoard) would later be smuggled to Kenya, where it was sold at a price much higher than allowed in Uganda.

---

[139] Edward Mugabi, "The Development of Towns in Uganda, 1970–1980: Political Change, the Decline of a Nation's Capital, and the Spread of Small Towns," Working Paper No. 39 (UCL Development Planning Unit, n.d.).

Criminalized transactions also turned the official signs and techniques of the currency regime against their intended purposes or moved them into avenues outside government control. For instance, staff at the Lugazi Sugar Factory were blamed for their part in an elaborate smuggling operation that came to light when their associate, Patrick Kisawe, was intercepted at the Entebbe International Airport. In Kisawe's possession was an overdraft cheque worth USh. 4,000 issued to the factory by the Uganda Commercial Bank. Under interrogation, he admitted that he intended to cash it in Nairobi where he would buy tins of Avon makeup for resale in Uganda. He hoped to make USh. 17,000 from the exercise. Kisawe's scheme depended on misusing bank credit and subverting the foreign exchange controls. Because Lugazi Sugar Factory qualified for access to foreign currency, the money-like token of the overdraft cheque could evade the strictures placed on ordinary currency.[140]

Magendo also found valuable niches in commercial sectors that were necessarily international. One method involved foreign airlines mispricing air tickets and paying the difference in foreign currency.[141] This "led to tickets being negotiated for foreign exchange outside Uganda thus creating a racket of illegal trade in air tickets."[142] Here, too, a certain form of value – namely, the air ticket – replaced Ugandan currency due to its enhanced mobility and fungibility. Such conversions between value forms were the site of considerable creative repurposing and, in turn, state policing. In May 1974, the management of the East African Posts and Telecommunications Corporation "discovered to its dismay that the general public were using its money order service fraudulently to transmit large amounts of money to Kenya for trade purposes." As a result, they had to suspend the service, but the amount of money that had been authorized before the duplicity was caught was so large that the Bank of Uganda protested it could not possibly transmit it to Kenya.[143] Eighteen months earlier, spot checks

---

[140] BoU GOV.807.1: Onago Obel, Governor, to Secretary of the Treasury, January 22, 1975.
[141] BoU GOV.305.1: Draft Minutes of 13th EA Exchange Controllers Meeting on 30 December 1974.
[142] BoU G.60.67, GOV.104.1: Memo from Director of Banks Supervision to Governor, February 5, 1976.
[143] BoU 2121, GOV.104.16: EAP&T Regional Director for Uganda to PS, Ministry of Transport & Communications, July 24, 1975.

of registered mail found numerous bank drafts, travelers' cheques, trade bills of exchange, and foreign currency notes evading government oversight.[144] This was a matter of collective concern, argued the Amin state, for foreign exchange balances "are the national assets of the countries who have built them up."[145]

Through these acts, Ugandans unmade the controlled conversion between monies on which the state depended. Currency controls that limited the translation between domestic and foreign currency were especially targeted (see Figure 4.4). Exchange control forms were often forged. Unauthorized people were found with specimen signatures from the Bank of Uganda, the Uganda Advisory Board of Trade, and copies of various exchange control paperwork already marked by the security machine.[146] The Bank of Uganda's machines for protecting against fraud broke down frequently, inhibiting proper accounting and security procedures.[147] In 1978, it had to shut down foreign exchange operations for nearly two months after they discovered fraudulent transfers being made from their system for as much as 40 million shillings.[148] As the public invented new methods of subversion, the outward signs and tokens of value – such as currency notes and cheques – risked losing the referential security by which they could be reasonably expected to actually maintain their worth.[149] This encouraged a turn away from the national currency and contributed to the debasement of economic sovereignty.

For the state, this was deeply troubling, not least because these activities undermined confidence in the monetary systems. Writing in May 1976, the Governor of the Bank of Uganda noted that it was "unfortunate that members of the public today seem to be overly sensitive and overly cautious about the Uganda currency. The root of

[144] BoU: Kibirango to Governor, October 23, 1972. Remittances Through Registered Mail.
[145] *Achievements of the Government of Uganda during the First Year of the Second Republic* (Kampala, 1972).
[146] BoU G.151.77. GOV.224: E. Rukyalekere to Governor, December 4, 1975.
[147] BoU G.184.75, RES.306.1.D: General Manager to Governor on 13 August 1976.
[148] BoU GOV.418.1: Foreign Exchange Allocation-Misc, BOU00034, 1979.
[149] For relevant, if opposed, discussions of money and reference see Andrew Apter, *The Pan-African Nation: Oil and the Spectacle of Culture in Nigeria* (University of Chicago Press, 2005); Bill Maurer, *Mutual Life, Limited: Islamic Banking, Alternative Currencies, Lateral Reason* (Princeton University Press, 2005).

Figure 4.4 An unnamed Kenyan pictured with the Kenyan currency he is accused of illegally exchanging for Ugandan shillings in 1975.
Courtesy of the Uganda Broadcasting Corporation.

this evil is truly the general loss of trust in the value of the currency." The result was that members of the public closely inspected money they received. When the state issued replacement notes without fully informing the public, it led to a bout of vigilante justice. People using the new notes were beaten up, leading to only more "hoarding of coins" and hesitance around notes, worried the Governor.[150]

One of the reasons Amin gave when overthrowing the Obote government was the "ever-increasing cost of living." In the following

---

[150] BoU G.184.75, RES.306.1.D: Governor to Minister of Internal Affairs, May 15, 1976.

4.7 In the Matter of Economic Crimes 251

years, his government tried multiple tactics to corral value within official circuits, including stripping traders of their licenses if they hoarded or overcharged. From bread to petrol and beyond, the stuff of everyday life was subject to an expanding range of regulations. On the first anniversary of the coup, Amin announced the establishment of a new Price Control Unit focused on "surveillance and control over consumer prices," as well as receiving consumer complaints. Local production would be promoted, official inquiries into the National Trading Corporation would be launched, and wholesale trade would be brought within the ambit of price controls.[151] When the Ugandan state established the Economic Crimes Tribunal in 1975, it reflected less a sea change than a more muscular, coercive effort to ensure it could intermediate the trade of not only coffee and cotton but also a range of other goods (see Figure 4.5).

This was not a wholesale invention of the Amin state; in fact, it drew on the colonial regulations.[152] Nor was the Economic Crimes Tribunal an empty shell over reckless, arbitrary violence, though that did characterize some of the era.[153] Rather, as I discuss, the Tribunal worked through certain bureaucratic and legal formalities. The result was that when the Tribunal turned accusations into indictments, the defendants had certain entitlement and room for maneuver. Some cases were rejected for insufficient evidence or because the defendants amended their wrongs privately. To be sure, the exercise of the law was often indiscriminate and coercive: many citizens were harangued and punished, often excessively.[154] Those close to the regime enjoyed impunity

---

[151] *Speeches by His Excellency the President, General Idi Amin Dada* (Government Printer, 1973).

[152] In 1940, the colonial territories began more expansive commodity and price controls. Profiteering, hoarding, and speculation were policed to conserve foreign exchange and ensure the availability of goods. After the end of hostilities, the administration of production, trade, and consumption remained to further economic modernization. David Killingray and Richard Rathbone (eds.), *Africa and the Second World War* (Palgrave Macmillan, 1986); Gardner Thompson, *Governing Uganda: British Colonial Rule and Its Legacy* (Fountain Publishers, 2003), chapter 10.

[153] A point about legal cultures amidst conflict that I draw from Samuel Fury Childs Daly, "The Survival Con: Fraud and Forgery in the Republic of Biafra, 1967–70," *Journal of African History* 58(1) (2017): 129–144.

[154] In practice, executions by order of the Economic Crimes Tribunal were perhaps not as common as they might have been. After a flurry of heavily publicized state executions in 1973 (i.e., before the Economic Crimes Tribunal), the Amin

Figure 4.5 Smuggled paraffin seized near the Uganda-Zaire border in 1978. Courtesy of the Uganda Broadcasting Corporation.

compared to the more marginal actions of the masses. Yet, the Tribunal cases I analyze are a reminder that not all accusations worked alike, and those routed through the court had dynamics of their own.

Western Province was typical of how this unfolded. At the start of 1976, Governor Owor called together a dozen security officials in Fort Portal to express his concern about "magendo prices." Police and soldiers were contributing to the malpractice by making purchases at these inflated prices; worse, they had not sufficiently enforced the laws to stop the situation. In response, the security forces promised to "do

state relied more on unofficial murder than juridical death. "Amin Orders Public Executions to Crush Rebellions," *Daily Monitor*, August 15, 2015.

4.7 In the Matter of Economic Crimes 253

some homework on the price list of controlled commodities" and begin more regular patrols to check on shop prices.[155]

Similar actions were undertaken across the country, though the police often struggled with their mandate. County chiefs felt powerless without armed patrols to support them.[156] Even then, success was not guaranteed. In the fishing communities of Lake Victoria, government officials were stymied trying to stop smugglers because word of their arrival preceded them, leading to canoes rushing away toward Kenyan jurisdiction.[157] When police did maintain the element of surprise it could still result in frantic boat chases across the inland sea. Police in South Busoga, for instance, believed Lugala, a village on the lake, was "the main gate of smugglers" to Kenya. Hiring a canoe one early morning in 1976, they set out to intercept the illegal cotton trade. Only after a vigorous pursuit – and threatening to shoot – did the suspects stop their boat. Onboard were ten sacks of cotton and five passengers who came from the same village where, to the police's frustration, chiefs did nothing to stop smuggling. The police arrested them, unmoved by their pleas that they needed to smuggle in order to buy essential commodities.[158]

Men like these were hauled before the Economic Crimes Tribunal. While hoarding, overcharging, and smuggling were the primary concerns, over time the types of actions classified as economic crimes grew. Patrick Mugisha was charged with theft while working as a petrol attendant. Corporal Okello was remanded for misappropriating money from arrested prisoners. Frederick Seronjogi and two accomplices were arrested for stealing 87 pounds of mercury from Kilembe Mines. Mr. Kiiza was charged with using an official rifle for private business.[159] The Economic Crimes Tribunal, in other words, came to subsume existing forms of criminal law, as theft, embezzlement, and public corruption were framed as primarily offenses against a national economy. The special Tribunal was designed as an exceptional judicial

---

[155] KDA 563/4: Governors Address to Members of Security Forces, January 29, 1976.
[156] JDA Justice, Law, Order & Security 13/17: County Chief's Office Bunya to D.C. South Busoga, April 2, 1979.
[157] JDA Justice, Law, Order & Security 13/17: Report Concerning Lolwe Island in Sigulu, Gombolola Bukooli County, June 17, 1975.
[158] JDA Justice, Law, Order & Security 13/17: Office of the Superintendent of Police/Prisons to D.C. South Busoga, February 4, 1976.
[159] These cases are available in KDA 39.

forum for handling an enormous range of cases, testament to the divide between popular economic life and sanctioned practices of valuation.[160]

Thousands of Ugandans were punished at the hands of the Tribunal, but it was not merely a venue for show trials. The Department of Public Prosecutions investigated cases and made recommendations about moving forward with prosecutions. Accused economic criminals were freed for insufficient evidence, police malpractice, a lack of witnesses statements, privately amending their wrongs, and other reasons. For instance, in November 1977, the case against Peter Kiiza and eight other defendants was dropped. Kiiza and his colleagues were at the time employed by the North Bunyoro District Administration. When the vehicle they were driving broke down, they allegedly removed seventeen rolls of textiles they were carrying. Rather than being made into school uniforms, the government employees were accused of personally profiting from the underhanded deal. Yet, upon their arrest they were able to collect the equivalent cost of the textiles (a sum of USh. 9,180), reimburse the District Administration, and satisfy the District Commissioner. Noting this course of events, the Senior State Attorney struck a pragmatic note, recommending the case be dropped on the grounds of insufficient evidence.[161]

Other cases display a sense of judicial evenhandedness. Laurentso Takwamu and Olive Kabadeya stood accused in May 1978 of smuggling coffee to Zaire. The State Attorney thought there was insufficient evidence on record to sustain the charge. The accused testified they were only carrying coffee from their uncle's farm to their father who would sell it for money for school uniforms.[162] Similarly, a case against Sesiria Mbambu was dropped. While, she too was alleged by the local chief to be taking Ugandan coffee to Zaire, she insisted that she was only traveling to a primary society that had cash, as hers was unable to buy her crop and "she wanted the money very badly." Mbambu's story was plausible, encouraging the state attorney to drop the case.[163] These court records provide evidence of the limitations of

---

[160] For comparison, see Rohit De, *A People's Constitution: The Everyday Life of Law in the Indian Republic* (Princeton University Press, 2018), chapter two.
[161] KDA 39: Masindi Police Criminal Case No. CRB. 673/77.
[162] KDA 39: Uganda versus Laurentso Takwamu and Olive Kabadeya, May 17, 1978.
[163] KDA 39: Uganda versus Sesiria Mbambu, July 13, 1978.

4.7 In the Matter of Economic Crimes

governing through accusation, even in the form of a legal indictment. Allegations were often based on flimsy evidence and compromised loyalties; the accused had room to rebuff the contentions, including within the exceptional tribunals.

The prosecutorial decisions could combine impressionistic and pragmatic reasoning with legal technicalities and an economic sensibility. They may also reflect less above board influence, given the stakes involved. James Batekateka was arrested for overcharging while serving as a distribution agent for Nile Breweries in April 1978. Accused of selling beer and whiskey above the allowed prices, Batekateka was let go because the state had failed to follow its own regulatory protocols. As the prosecutor explained, the prices Batekateka charged were simply out of date, and the Minister of Commerce had failed to issue signed statutory instruments updating the new prices. Moreover, the prosecutor stated that the USh. 100 "transport charge" the accused was adding to every crate of beer did not, precisely, contravene the law: as a surcharge and not a price increase, such a margin was not officially illegal under the Economic Crimes Tribunal Decree.[164]

Or, consider John Bukenya, whose arrest in December 1977 was by any measure bad luck. The owner of a taxi plying the road between Fort Portal and Kyenjojo, Bukenya was arrested with a jerry can and pipe next to his vehicle when the District Commissioner for Toro just happened to drive by. Bukenya had paid for the fuel in his taxi and explained that the siphoning was only to assist a neighbor who needed enough to get his car to the petrol station. Instead, the 2–3 liters of petrol was seized as evidence, along with the vehicle and the pipe. Yet, it was not clear any crime had been committed, at least not according to Julious Ajudriga, the police officer in charge of the case. The District Commissioner who made the arrest was responding to a radio announcement by Brigadier Isack Maliyamungu that promised severe penalties for anyone who siphoned petrol and then went to another petrol station to refill it. Yet, as far as Ajudriga could tell, there was no "signed decree" criminalizing such an act.[165] Without this formality, was a crime committed?

---

[164] KDA 39: Uganda versus James Batekateka, August 15, 1978.
[165] KDA 39: Memo by Julious Ajudriga at Fort Portal Police Station, December 31, 1977.

4.8 Negotiating the Economy of Accusation

The suspicions of the era ensnared many who insisted on their innocence. Jonathan Mukasa was one Ugandan who pleaded for understanding after being arrested for hoarding in September 1973. "I strongly support the Government in punishing hoarders of commodities," he patriotically announced. A licensed transporter and shopkeeper in Jinja, Mukasa was found by police at 5:30 a.m. with 200 tins of cooking oil in his storehouse. His protests, however, fell on deaf ears as his shop, goods, and lorry were seized and his good name was sullied on a radio broadcast. He addressed his lengthy plea for justice to every office that might help: from the President and the Minister of Commerce and Industry to the local trade development officer and the oil mill from which he received the consignment. The 200 tins were, indeed, not meant to be in his store, but his lorry developed mechanical issues on the way from the mill to the State Trading Corporation Depot. Laden with 400 tins of cooking fat, there was no way to winch the vehicle up for inspection without removing half the load. As Mukasa emphasized, he was an exemplary credible citizen, transporting for multiple years not only for the oil mill but also the Tororo Cement Factory, the State Trading Corporation, and others. The provincial veterinarian even trusted him so much that he would give Mukasa money to go buy goods on his behalf.

Mukasa's petition is filled with details that speak to his good character and collective contribution, from the invoices and signatures he collected to the years of unblemished service. Never in these years had he lost even a single tin of cooking oil – and certainly no untoward behavior was occurring the night of September 14. Instead, he clarified, the hour was late and moving the tins into his shop – a mere six meters from where the truck broke down – was protecting the goods from thieves while the repairs were done. If anyone jeopardized the essential commodities, it was the arresting officer who refused to listen to him and tried to drive the lorry with the reloaded tins, losing control of the vehicle as it "roared backwards through the streets [as] men jumped off the lorry for their lives." What more evidence could be needed that he was not hoarding, but protecting, these goods? Closing his case, he reasserted his patriotism – "The basis for our Government is God and God is just. So I hope that justice in this matter will prevail" – but linked it to a clientalistic dependency on the goodwill of his superiors,

4.8 Negotiating the Economy of Accusation 257

clarifying that he was not blaming them "for this harsh action" since they were likely not receiving accurate information.[166]

As this case suggests, what exactly constituted a hoard was not a settled matter.[167] In Bugembe district, administrators thought the chances of women "indulging in hoarding were very slim" and therefore preferred to license them for trade.[168] In Mukasa's view, it was also an issue of good character and intention: since his truck was being repaired, there was no intention to criminally contain the cooking oil. The local government sometimes agreed: when it faced transport troubles and was unable to quickly distribute cigarettes, officials in Western Uganda assured citizens that those kept in the store for some time "are not intended for hoarding."[169] When farmers refused to sell their maize, the Produce Marketing Board surmised that their motives were "mainly speculative," in hopes of higher prices during "lean times."[170] For police unwilling or able to ascertain intentionality, the mere act of removing goods from circulation was taken as a sign of hoarding. Immobilizing goods *and* hiding the immobility was even more heinous. Bar owners were condemned for the "dirty practice" of only exposing a couple cases of beer to customers. While they would blame suppliers for not bringing sufficient supplies, the reality was that they "keep the rest for MAGENDO business."[171] Some goods were more amenable to hoarding than others. Cooking oil had a sizable profit margin and would last, if suitably hidden from view. Coffee beans needed to be carefully dried to endure past normal marketing season. Maize, in contrast, "is terribly perishable in that it can easily go to waste and get spoilt by weevil, etc. unless fumigated, an exercise which, with due respect, may be beyond the competence of reach of most farmers."[172]

---

[166] JDA Trade & Industry 23/3: Jonathan Mukasa to Minister of Commerce & Industry, September 30.
[167] Gustav Peebles, "Rehabilitating the Hoard: The Social Dynamics of Unbanking in Africa and Beyond," *Africa* 84(4) (2014): 595–613.
[168] JDA Trade & Industry 23/3: Minutes of a Meeting in Bugembe District.
[169] KDA 744: Provincial Executive Secretary, Western Province. Distribution of Cigarettes, June 17, 1975.
[170] JDA Trade & Industry 23/3: Produce Marketing Board to all Governors, May 7, 1976.
[171] KDA 744: Meeting of Distributors and Bar Owners held on 24 November 1975.
[172] JDA Trade & Industry 23/3: M.D. of Produce Marketing Board to all Governors, May 7, 1976.

An elaborate micropolitics of display developed in the 1970s, as many Ugandans tried to hide their actions from prying eyes and the police tried to require visibility.[173] Escalating accusations encouraged discretionary habits. Chief Keresi of Kibale eagerly announced on radio the arrest of Joseph Rupiyazita for "hoarding" 74 hand hoes in an underground pit outside his house.[174] This dance between sequestration and display could lead to rather strange episodes, such as that of an elderly woman, Valentina Tibananuka of Bunyangabu.[175] Tibananuka spent nearly three years trying to get approved for a shop license, receiving approval from some offices but waiting for the District Commissioner. After more than two years of inquiring, completing forms, and offering to pay the requisite fees, she crossed into economic criminality by putting her goods on a ladder. As she insisted in her petition, this was only to air them out after being spoiled in boxes for so long, unable to be sold. The Chief, however, seized her goods, asserting that displayed goods were equivalent to a sale, even though she asserted "he did not see me nor catch anyone buying any single good from my house."[176]

The management of appearances was not merely an arbitrary enforcement of power by local chiefs. Nor was it reducible to a fiscal imperative for commercial surveillance. Properly deployed, it was meant to produce an ethical economic citizenship. The Trade Development Officer toured Busoga reminding traders that "Price tags must be clearly shown on goods for customers to see."[177] Price tags served to discipline the shopkeepers, objectively announcing the value of goods to impede discriminatory pricing.[178] Receipts, also, were a

---

[173] It was not only visibility that the state required. In an effort to stop unlicensed traders competing with shops, it was illegal for any person to "sell or offer or expose for sale anything in a market" without permission. Here, the risk was "hawkers" whose own mobility and display of goods would undermine the more easily policed and taxed shops. KDA 654/2: Office of the Assistant District Commissioner to All Chiefs, Kagadi Sub-District, September 5, 1975.

[174] KDA 244/4: County Chief Kibale to Information Officer, Toro, October 29, 1975.

[175] On sequestration and display, see Elizabeth Ferry, "'Deep in the Earth a Shining Substance': Sequestration and Display in Gold Mining and Central Banks," *Journal of Cultural Economy* 14(4) (2021): 416–434.

[176] KDA 612/1: Valentina Tibananuka to District Commissioner, May 25, 1972.

[177] JDA Trade & Industry 14/25: Office of the District TTDO to All Traders in Busoga District, February 2, 1973.

[178] On the "discursive authority" of price tags, see Quayson, *Oxford Street*, p. 24.

technology for enforcing the monopoly on valuation, required to be issued for all sales.[179] In Uganda, this was a particularly salient concern, given a history of racialized resentment toward Asian vendors who, it was felt, offered unfair and fluctuating prices.[180] In contrast, the independent state demanded commercial uniformity in which price tags, receipts, and official valuation removed the scope for improper discretion. Here, economic citizenship was animated by the indignity of relative scarcity and the anxiety that others could transact while oneself was deprived. It demanded standardization and equality in the price of commodities.

4.9 Conclusion

A few months after Harriet Biryeri sold expensive bread to the undercover police, Mrs. Batambuze was back in her shop at No.47/49 Main Street, Jinja. Unsatisfied with the decision of Major Erifazi to suddenly close the doors and revoke her license, Batambuze had petitioned His Excellency the President. It was not her fault, she told Idi Amin, that the young girl she employed contravened the pricing rules. Batambuze had given her instructions to charge proper prices, but Biryeri acted contrary to her boss's desires. For this, the employee was appropriately cautioned by the Tribunal. Yet, it seemed unjust that Section 19(4) of the Economic Crimes Tribunal Decree – which permitted allocated businesses to be repossessed from guilty persons – would apply to the shopkeeper who was neither guilty nor accused. And Idi Amin agreed, warning Batambuze against economic criminality but reissuing her right to the shop.

Many others did not receive such indulgences from Uganda's military leader. While Amin relished the opportunity to engage citizens as a charismatic and beneficent patron, this highly personalized style of rule went hand-in-hand with arbitrary command and violence. Those connected to the state enjoyed impunity and extracted enormous wealth. An earlier generation of observers focused on the dichotomous dynamics, seizing on the notion of *mafuta mingi* to emphasize the divide

---

[179] On the regulatory powers of receipts, see Gustav Peebles, *The Euro & Its Rivals: Currency & the Construction of a Transnational City* (Indiana University Press, 2011), chapter 3.

[180] Vali Jamal, "Asians in Uganda, 1880–1972: Inequality and Expulsion," *The Economic History Review* 29(4) (1976): 609.

between Amin's circle and the rest of Ugandans.[181] There is some truth to this: those from the northwest of the country – connected by language, kinship, religion, and soldiering – flaunted official rules from the pinnacle of a predatory regime. For many others, a turn to criminalized activity was an act of desperation – a dangerous means of survival undertaken for provisions, not profit. But there were manifold ties between *mafuta mingi* and petty participants, whether in the distribution of goods or patron–client relations. Women, for instance, could adopt their styles and find partners to variously garner respect, security, or autonomy.[182] There were also *magendo* participants who fit less neatly in such a dichotomy. More ambitious brokers created their own import–export business, buying crops in Uganda and then bulk importing commodities to Uganda for sale on the black market.[183] Some people were protected by only local government and did not reach national *mafuta mingi* levels. Moreover, in those volatile years, one's rank and relation to power could rise or fall quickly.

Negotiating this regime required Ugandans to adopt a repertoire of economic and political tactics that scholars often presume to be distinct. Confronted with shortages, Ugandans deployed an idiom of citizenship that engaged bureaucracy through its protocols. Forms were completed, stamped, and signed. Petitions were drafted, addressed, and copied to multiple offices. Announcements were followed, and lists were drawn together. They did so because bureaucrats did, indeed, receive, read, and respond to many of these entreaties. Commodity distribution committees met, assigned responsibilities, and followed up on protests. They did so in a context of considerable material lack, often due to no fault of their own: an unforgiving international trade regime and skyrocketing oil prices were only two forces that consigned 1970s Uganda to economic shortage. But the limited ability to harness goods and wealth for their own purposes, let alone the constrained ability of the state to monopolize

---

[181] Nelson Kasfir, "State, Magendo, and Class Formation in Uganda," *Journal of Commonwealth & Comparative Politics* 21(3) (1983): 84–103; Reginald Green, *Magendo in the Political Economy of Uganda* (Institute for Development Studies, 1981); Mahmood Mamdani, *Imperialism and Fascism in Uganda* (Heinemann Educational Books, 1983), pp. 51–54.

[182] Decker, "Accidental Liberation"; Obbo, *African Women*.

[183] Asiimwe, "From Monopoly Marketing to Coffee Magendo," pp. 116–117.

valuation, encouraged additional tactics. Smuggling, hoarding, and overcharging were rightly seen in some cases to be exploitative, especially when undertaken by those protected by high-ranking government posts. Yet, in many cases, the accusations and violence against economic criminals belied the fact that such actions were sensible and necessary means of providing for oneself and one's family. A *magendo* trip across the border, or a hidden reserve of coffee, or planting potatoes in place of cotton was anathema to the fiscal imperatives of the Ugandan state. They were central, however, to popular ethics of subsistence and respectability.

It is tempting to see the crisis of postcolonial statecraft – especially in a violent setting like 1970s Uganda – as a case of "domination without hegemony."[184] Lacking the cultural power to direct the labor and trade, the state relied on coercion. Yet, this risks too Manichean a reading. For one, men like Chief Keresi or Mbale's Provincial Commissioner for Commerce, Vincent Mayiga, were engaged in brokering between the central institutions of economic sovereignty and its everyday manifestations in currency, receipts, and price tags. It was through their scalar enterprises that a monopoly on valuation was maintained, or not. For another, not only did the state's agents pursue a variety of tactics alongside domination, from institutional reform to persuasive rhetoric, citizens also relied on pluralistic registers of behavior. Turning away from the state's regulatory controls did not herald an end to expectations placed on the state nor to the repertoires citizens had for drawing on the state's resources. Faced with shortages that impeded their pursuit of valued lives, citizens demanded a return to organized channels of commodity production and distribution. They pioneered a version of what Partha Chatterjee calls "political society" where non-elite populations, often engaged in some forms of criminalized behavior, "pick their way through … uncertain terrain" to compel the government.[185] In the very moment of hegemonic decline, citizens redoubled their deployment of its idioms and demonstrated enduring commitments to the idea that the state was responsible for governing value. They submitted accusations and reported malfeasance, calling upon hierarchical relations of duty and entitlement that

---

[184] Ranajit Guha, *Dominance without Hegemony: History and Power in Colonial India* (Harvard University Press, 1998).

[185] Partha Chatterjee, *The Politics of the Governed: Popular Politics in Most of the World* (Columbia University Press, 2004), p. 40.

stood in tension with more horizontal forms of allegiance and less statist modes of provisioning. If the criminalization of popular economies threatened the livelihoods and lives of many, it was from a compromised position – both entreaty and flight – that citizens negotiated the government of value. This pluralism – both compliant and subversive – would become a hallmark of East African citizenship, laced with ambiguities to which the book's final chapter turns.

5 | *Magendo*
Arbitrage and Ambiguity on an East African Frontier

5.1 Introduction

Sometime in 1976, the proprietor of a shop at the Kenya–Uganda border town of Lwakhakha painted a new sign on his building: *Mambo Bado*. In the rolling hills below Mount Elgon, Lwakhakha is a relatively remote post, much less trafficked than Busia and Malaba to the south. At the time, the area lacked paved roads and electricity. Those seeking waged labor or higher education had to migrate many hours away, to agricultural plantations or urban centers. Yet in a crucial way, the area was tightly integrated into extensive networks, namely through the smallholder cultivation of coffee. And it was this power of coffee to call forth and bring near exciting and exotic novelties to which this sign gestured: *Things Are Still to Come.*

In fact, things had already started coming to this frontier, and few residents had reason to believe it would cease anytime soon. Due to a spike in the world price and a surplus in Uganda, the area south of Mount Elgon became a massive transit zone for coffee. Price differentials between Uganda and Kenya made coffee trade an enormously profitable exercise. One village, in particular, became iconic: Chepkube. Only a couple of hours from Lwakhakha, Chepkube was a difficult day's walk from the nearest substantial towns, Mbale and Tororo in Uganda and Bungoma in Kenya. Yet, for a number of years, it became a destination for fortune-seekers, the source of enormous wealth, and the subject of a popular song and novel. For those in Chepkube and its environs, this trade, known by the Swahili word *magendo*, was filled with new opportunities, riches, and commodities. As the shop sign suggests, it opened the horizon for smallholders to imagine building novel, still undefined, futures for themselves and their families. The traders' frenzy sparked new social practices, as small-scale cultivators became commercial middlemen. In the ensuing few years, magendo bequeathed a spectacular binge economy, with Chepkube's residents enjoying newfound wealth and consumption.

Yet, the revaluation of coffee and the newfound permissiveness existed uneasily with inherited ideas about protocol and morality. Magendo challenged prevailing ethics through its specific, material techniques and temporalities of arbitrage. In the narratives of residents who participated in it, magendo was characterized by the sudden proximity of once distant commodities, currency, and people; furthermore, domestic space gave way to the wild, and night became day. Such conceptual and experiential inversions not only heralded the danger of matter out of place but also ushered in previously foreclosed opportunities of wealth, respectability, and privilege. This twofold ambiguity – of peril and profit – was part and parcel of a more general erosion of prevailing norms and forms of authority as magendo undermined existing ideas of propriety, respectability, and morality. As a result, by the time the trade ended a few years later, residents of this corner of Kenya were left with deep ambivalence about that which had come and gone.

The argument of this chapter is twofold. First, it elaborates the concept of the government of value by more fully depicting how a community in rural East Africa understood, debated, and regulated the production and distribution of wealth and regard. In prior chapters, the independent and colonial states have loomed large, as bureaucratic ideas and fiscal imperatives shaped what was defined as valuable and how it would be governed. East African citizens and subjects sometimes aligned with these notions; in other cases, they objected, resisted, or went about their lives with little regard for the state's would-be monopoly on valuation. What motivated popular or non-state ideas about value has, however, somewhat receded from view, in part due to the documentary evidence used. This chapter builds from ethnographic fieldwork around Mount Elgon, on the Kenya–Uganda border, to explain how some East Africans imagined the proper production and arrangement of value. In doing so, it also illustrates the theory of value and valuation undergirding the book as a whole.[1] What people around Mount Elgon thought of as valuable was not reducible to money, but nor was it domain purified from commercial concerns. Rather, properly understood, value rested on the

---

[1] Terence Turner, "Marxian Value Theory: An Anthropological Perspective," *Anthropological Theory* 8(1) (2008): 43–56; David Graeber, "It Is Value That Brings Universes into Being," *HAU: Journal of Ethnographic Theory* 3(2) (2013): 219–243.

careful arrangement among social relations, and between people and things. These social hierarchies and material interdependencies were mediated by labor undertaken, property accumulated, and respect earned on extended timelines. Yet, this locally hegemonic notion of value – of the proper relationship between moral virtues and material resources – was not only internally contested by those excluded from its rewards, or anxious to reap more quickly than they sowed. It was also vulnerable to changes arriving from outside – not least of which was the prevailing price of coffee. It is not that the state was unimportant – after all, the price differentials between Uganda and Kenya in part reflected state policy – but the method adopted here better reveals the competitive realm of valuation. The ensuing dramas of *magendo* – the ethical challenges, the existential risks – paint in relief locally salient ideas about value, standing at a distance from officialdom.

The second argument of the chapter returns to the idea of economic citizenship. Prior chapters have discussed the formation and unmaking of a constellation of interests between citizens and states. Claims to commercial rights merged with developmental planning to sediment a legal and cultural relationship focused on productivism, especially the cultivation of export value. State legitimacy rested in part on the credible advancement of individual commercial opportunity and the lamination of that onto broader notions of a collective improvement. Where the state was incapable or unwilling to do so, or when its extractive and disciplinary side was overbearing, citizens pursued a wide variety of livelihoods, sometimes at odds with official dictate.

This chapter deepens this later angle of economic citizenship through the concept of "arbitrage." While typically defined as an economic action premised on the price differentials between market jurisdictions, here I argue that arbitrage provides a way of understanding the relationship between East Africans and their states as opportunistic, strategic, and pluralistic. In contrast to a monopoly, citizenship has often been multiple, and it is the interplay and movement between ways of belonging that provides important avenues for East Africans' own ideas about aspiration and achievement.

Such an argument can be fruitfully placed alongside Albert Hirschman's classic typology of how people relate to polities.[2] In *Exit*,

---

[2] Albert Hirschman, *Exit, Voice, and Loyalty: Responses to Decline in Firms, Organizations and States* (Harvard University Press, 1981).

Voice, and Loyalty, Hirschman explored how citizenship is manifest in three registers: through faithful devotion to ideals (even when officials do not live up to them), through the articulation of grievances that demand changes, or through "the exit option" which threatens to drain states of their citizens. African historians have long explored these various modalities, not least of which is "exit."[3] In Bayart's analysis of postcolonial states, "escape" was "one of the constituent strategies" for popular politics.[4] In studies of the Uganda–Kenya borderlands, it has also proved influential: Stephen Bunker's important study of Gisu peasant politics in the foothills of Mount Elgon in eastern Uganda emphasized how the "the exit option" allowed coffee farmers to credibly threaten the state.[5] By "exit option," Bunker meant that Gisu cultivators could refuse to cultivate coffee in favor of subsistence crops, or they could sell their coffee in nearby Kenya, thereby depriving the state of a critical source of revenue. Bagisu combined "exit" with astute organization and vocal claims-making to achieve significant economic and political standing in both the Protectorate and independent state. Bunker's study ended before the Amin era on which I focus, though certainly many of the same dynamics characterize those years. If anything, smuggling coffee became more important for Gisu farmers because neither loyalty nor voice could be pursued very fruitfully during the repressive and violent 1970s.

However, interpreting coffee smuggling as "exit" is misleading. For one thing, unlike a turn to subsistence farming, smugglers did not forego income from coffee cultivation. Moreover, there was not a significant exit of Gisu people: residents of eastern Uganda did not *en masse* migrate from their home areas and the jurisdiction of their citizenship.[6] The coffee they ferried to Kenya did escape the official

---

[3] The ability to depart from undesired political hierarchies is crucial to the "land rich, people poor" dichotomy that has structured much comparative work in African economic history. In a related vein, A. I. Asiwaju emphasized how colonial subjects migrated as a form protest against European control.
"Migrations as Revolt: The Example of the Ivory Coast and the Upper Volta before 1945," *Journal of African History* 17(4) (1976): 577–594.

[4] Jean-François Bayart, *The State in Africa: The Politics of the Belly*, 2nd ed. (Polity Press, 2009), pp. 252–259.

[5] Stephen Bunker, *Peasants Against the State: The Politics of Market Control in Bugisu, Uganda, 1900–1983* (University of Chicago Press, 1991).

[6] Authorities in western Kenya noted throughout the 1970s fluctuating numbers of Ugandan refugees, but the number was relatively low and stays were often temporary, not least because the Kenyan government was unsupportive of mass relocations to their territory.

5.1 Introduction

export infrastructures, depriving the Ugandan state of revenue and subverting the controlled conversion between currencies. Yet, the huge numbers of smugglers were not oriented toward exit; indeed, the ongoing viability of smuggling was essentially premised on remaining within Uganda. It was by moving back-and-forth across the frontier that coffee would become valuable; likewise, it was by purchasing other commodities in Kenya that households in Uganda could be provisioned. Smuggling allowed them to keep their income, citizenship, and residence. As such, smuggling is best seen outside Hirschman's typology: not loyalty, voice, nor exit.

Instead, smuggling was a way of arbitraging citizenship, a pluralistic style of engaging and spanning multiple networks of affiliation, jurisdictions, and territories. Anthropologists have argued that arbitrage is an expansive notion. It is good to think with, "an interpretive framework that is widely deployable to various phenomena, economic and otherwise."[7] The arbitrage at the heart of magendo was premised on the cultivation of difference. Most centrally, coffee smugglers capitalized on the price differentials between market jurisdictions – evading the Ugandan monopoly on valuation in favor of Kenya's circumstances. Yet, this was but one way that residents of the Uganda–Kenya borderlands exploited, and sometimes produced, differences.[8] In the following discussion, I detail additional market practices and technologies used to construct price differentials, reminiscent of Jane Guyer's attention to the difference produced – including through "more or less deliberate interference" – by the translation between different currencies and commodities.[9] Sometimes, this required special tools; sometimes, it required deceit. In these cases, the marginal gains of magendo relied on the manipulation of appearances, leading to

---

[7] Hirokazu Miyazaki, *Arbitraging Japan: Dreams of Capitalism at the End of Finance* (University of California Press, 2013), p. 36.

[8] Anthropologists have emphasized the "messiness and hard work involved in making, translating suturing, converting, and linking" across heterogeneity. This is not an intermediary status to be overcome; rather, the variegated field of action was both the means and ends of arbitrage. Laura Bear et al., "Gens: A Feminist Manifesto for the Study of Capitalism," *Cultural Anthropology* (2015), www.culanth.org/fieldsights/652-gens-a-feminist-manifesto-for-the-study-of-capitalism.

[9] Jane Guyer, *Legacies, Logics, Logistics: Essays in the Anthropology of the Platform Economy* (University of Chicago Press, 2016), p. 80. More generally, see Jane Guyer, *Marginal Gains: Monetary Transactions in Atlantic Africa* (University of Chicago Press, 2004).

evident surfaces belying the quality of their underlying substance. I show how coffee beans, weapons, and food entered an economy of (mis)representation through which deceit and fraud served to produce a new form of profit. As a result, it called on participants to deploy a finely tuned repertoire for assessing and judging quality and value.

Magendo arbitrage, in other words, worked through the cultivation and capitalization on the disjuncture of jurisdiction, of measurement, and of appearance. Residents of the borderlands experienced these practices as morally fraught. Arbitrage is particularly apt to generate social instability and ethical quandaries because its pursuit depends on a variety of shifts through which difference is cultivated. That is, relatively stable assumptions and background conditions on which social, economic, and political relations are grounded become matters of concern, liable to change, fluctuation, or even collapse. Putative equilibria are shown to be mere conventions rather than matters of fact. The capacity to manipulate such evaluative schema, however, is not evenly distributed, with the result that the rewards of arbitrage often lead to an unsettling of received notions and mores about the appropriate acquisition and distribution of wealth. In these cases, arbitrage is often difficult to analytically separate from speculation, let alone the resulting types of social discord and the moral opprobrium directed at it.[10] The resulting assessments of this economic activity are rarely uniform; instead, arbitrage generates an ambiguous mix of desire and disdain. Based on oral histories and fieldwork on both sides of the border, I analyze the culturally salient idioms through which moral ambiguity was expressed and interpreted.

In what follows, I foreground the types of ethical reasoning and moral anxiety that emerged in the Uganda–Kenya frontier during the coffee boom of the second half of the 1970s. I focus predominantly on people identifying as Bagisu and Babukusu, communities on either side of the border that recognize a commonality captured by the encompassing ethnonym Bamasaba (meaning "people of Masaba," a term for Mount Elgon). I first provide a brief discussion of the colonial and postcolonial monopoly on the valuation of coffee, showing how Bagisu farmers interacted with the state regulations in Uganda. The bulk of the

[10] Hirokazu Miyazaki, "Between Arbitrage and Speculation: An Economy of Belief and Doubt," *Economy and Society* 36(3) (2007): 396–415; Jean Comaroff and John L. Comaroff, "Alien-Nation: Zombies, Immigrants, and Millennial Capitalism," *South Atlantic Quarterly* 101(4) (2002): 779–805.

chapter focuses on the magendo period 1976–1978, and although "magendo" is used to refer to small-scale cross-border trade outside of those years, my use of the term refers specifically to those years that residents readily recognize as the apotheosis of magendo. I explain the specific arbitrage techniques through which magendo unfolded before examining the ethical ambiguities that ensued. The argument emerges from fieldwork on both sides of the border south of Mount Elgon, but the social dynamics were concentrated in Kenya for reasons I explain.

5.2 A Monopoly on the Valuation of Coffee

As discussed in prior chapters, the economic model of East African states depended on the controlled conversion between crops, commodities, and currencies. Agrarian producers were responsible for cultivating crops like coffee which were then exported by government marketing boards. These institutions acquired revenue by paying the farmers less than they received internationally. They also paid farmers in a national currency but received payment from foreign buyers in sterling, dollars, and other international currencies. This second feature – what I have glossed as the moneychanger state – was just as important, but required extensive policing to control the conversion between monies. While certain elements were novelties – like the central banks and territorial currencies – to a considerable degree, Kenya, Tanzania, and Uganda reproduced the colonial economic model, not least in their continued reliance on export agriculture.

Uganda is exemplary. While coffee varietals have long been grown in the Great Lakes region, it was through incorporation into colonial states and international capitalism that coffee gained newfound value as a source of cash income.[11] For the first quarter of the twentieth century, Ugandan agrarian policy was a tortured back-and-forth between the interests of a nascent European planter population, the Asian commercial class, the colonial administration, and African elites and peasants.[12] Between 1914 and 1922, African coffee cultivation expanded little. In subsequent years, however, the Protectorate

---

[11] For a discussion in northwest Tanzania, see Brad Weiss, *Sacred Trees, Bitter Harvests: Globalizing Coffee in Northwest Tanzania* (Heinemann, 2003).

[12] van Zwanenberg with King, *An Economic History of Kenya and Uganda, 1800–1970* (Macmillan Press, 1975); Mahmood Mamdani, *Politics and Class Formation in Uganda* (Monthly Review Press, 1976); E. A. Brett, *Colonialism*

government invested in nurseries and outreach by new specialists; coffee soon joined cotton as Uganda's most important export crops.[13] Buganda was especially important in sheer volume, but its lowland ecology only supported Robusta coffee. In eastern Uganda, the volcanic soil, substantial rainfall, and higher altitude around Mount Elgon could support the more lucrative Arabica varietal. In response, the Bagisu residents invested considerably in the crop, with the number of acres dedicated to coffee growing from 400 in 1922 to 4,000 in 1934. Following the Second World War, "coffee receipts leaped upwards, giving the Uganda economy perhaps the greatest single boost which it had ever experienced."[14] In turn, peasant producers could buy new commodities including bicycles, vehicles, radios, and processed foods. Some cultivators even achieved considerable wealth, rising above their neighbors.

The Protectorate government endeavored to closely orchestrate how coffee was grown and sold. It privileged Asian middlemen and European exporters to the detriment of African commercial involvement.[15] By 1932, coffee processing in Uganda was only permitted in licensed facilities.[16] From 1943, the government dictated the price paid to farmers, allowing it to extract a significant difference between the producer price and the value on the world market. It justified this in the name of stable incomes, developmental investment, and the funding of a Price Assistance Fund (that would supplement incomes when the world price fell).[17] The Protectorate's monopoly on the valuation of coffee meant that "by the end of 1953 the farmers of Uganda had involuntarily contributed nearly £30 million to price assistance funds and about £22 million to development projects of various kinds, in

and Underdevelopment in East Africa: The Politics of Economic Change, 1919–1939 (NOK Publishers, 1973).

[13] See also chapter 1 of Godfrey Asiimwe, "The Impact of Post-Colonial Policy Shifts in Coffee Marketing at the Local Level in Uganda: A Case Study of Mukono District, 1962–1998" (Institute of Social Studies, 2002).

[14] C. C. Wrigley, *Crops and Wealth in Uganda: A Short Agrarian History* (East African Institute of Social Research, 1959), pp. 40–80.

[15] Vali Jamal, "Asians in Uganda, 1880–1972: Inequality and Expulsion," *The Economic History Review* 29(4) (1976): 602–616.

[16] van Zwanenberg with King, *An Economic History*, pp. 202–210; G. B. Masefield, "Agricultural Change in Uganda, 1945–1960," *Food Research Institute Studies* 3(2) (1962): 107f.

[17] J. J. Oloya, *Some Aspects of Economic Development with Special Reference to East Africa* (East African Literature Bureau, 1968), pp. 43–78.

5.2 A Monopoly on the Valuation of Coffee 271

addition to about £30 million paid in export duties."[18] It was a remarkable exertion of the state's power to determine and regulate value.

These policies generated considerable animus across the Protectorate. Historians have been especially attentive to the resulting troubles in Buganda, but in Bugisu, too, cultivators around Mount Elgon carried out a lengthy struggle for increased control over the fruits of their labor.[19] In the 1920s, they began withholding coffee from the market to protest the policies of the Bugisu Native Administration (BNA) and its chiefly functionaries. In 1927, the BNA exerted more control, particularly over the quality of coffee that would be accepted, leading to collusion among brokers and depressed prices to farmers. This was further institutionalized in the 1932 Native Produce Marketing Ordinance that, by 1936, gave exclusive marketing rights for all Bugisu coffee to the BNA. Resentment of this arrangement focused on low prices, falsified weights, and classification of Gisu coffee as low quality.[20] Gisu civil servants and peasants articulated their dissatisfaction throughout the decades and demanded more control over their position in the market.[21] The decade after the Second World War led to a series of organizational shuffles, but the strength of Gisu organization was enough to win a unified cooperative union that grew to be "by far the richest, strongest, and politically most active of Uganda's cooperatives."[22] Throughout, the ability to deprive the state of revenue by smuggling or subsistence cultivation proved an effective part of Gisu politics.

The resulting Bugisu Cooperative Union (BCU) merged ethnic aspirations for regional autonomy with economic betterment, a form of masculine "economic nationalism" in Pamela Khanakwa's words.[23] Its members asserted their prerogatives and interests against a central state

---

[18] Wrigley, *Crops and Wealth*, p. 70.
[19] For a recent statement on Buganda's agrarian politics, see Aaron Windel, *Cooperative Rule: Community Development in Britain's Late Empire* (University of California Press, 2022).
[20] See the history in Bunker, *Peasants Against the State*, pp. 42–59.
[21] On the dual marketing system, see chapter 1 of Asiimwe, "The Impact of Post-Colonial Policy Shifts."
[22] Bunker, *Peasants Against the State*, p. 22.
[23] Pamela Khanakwa, "Reinventing *Imbalu* and Forcible Circumcision: Gisu Political Identity and the Fight for Mbale in Late Colonial Uganda," *Journal of African History* 59(3) (2018): 367.

that was dependent upon and desirous of the wealth resulting from their agrarian labor. Nevertheless, as Stephen Bunker showed in his study of the BCU, the politics of coffee at various times pitted chiefs, civil servants, politicians, and smallholders against each other in a jostling for position, alliance, and income. At the end of the 1950s, eastern Uganda experienced protests and violence over questions of taxation and district boundaries, though coffee policies were never far from people's minds.[24] Foremost among the concerns were the terms on which coffee would be qualitatively evaluated and quantitatively priced. When farmers felt the arrangements did not align with their interests, they threatened to carry their coffee to Kenya or simply store the beans for a future where they would not be mistreated.

A similar set of fiscal imperatives and justifications shaped policies after independence. Intermediating coffee remained at the core of the state's financial viability, not least in the context of growing state expenditure. The determination of crop prices also took on an electoral significance as the government tried to appeal to the pocketbooks of voting farmers. As a result of paying higher rates in election years, by 1966–1967 the Price Assistance Fund was depleted.[25] This gave the state fewer resources to supplement any decline in world prices and exacerbated the importance of capturing revenue through export institutions. This interest in appropriating more revenue from peasants limited the hard-earned autonomy of the BCU, not least after Milton Obote's Uganda People's Congress centralized power through a new constitution in 1967. The elimination of opposition parties and the expansion of state regulation left the BCU in a more precarious position. A new Ministry of Marketing and Co-operatives set about eliminating coffee industrialists and rerouting all coffee through state-directed channels. By 1970–1971, BCU was required to sell all its coffee to the Coffee Marketing Board (CMB) at prices of the latter's choosing. CMB's politicization irritated many who found it biased and an instrument of UPC power.[26] The UPC set prices within the Cabinet, with farmers paid whatever residual amount was left after meeting

---

[24] Protectorate of Uganda, *Report of the Commission of Inquiry into the Disturbances in Uganda during April 1949* (Entebbe, 1950).
[25] van Zwanenberg with King, *Economic History*, p. 223.
[26] See Asiimwe, "The Impact of Post-Colonial Policy Shifts," pp. 97–101; Bunker, *Peasants Against the State*, p. 199f.

5.2 A Monopoly on the Valuation of Coffee

government revenue needs, the costs of the CMB and cooperatives, and "especially its needs for foreign exchange."[27] The result was a very narrow coterie arbitrating the value of coffee, constrained on the one hand by international market fluctuations and on the other by domestic political pressures.

After the 1971 coup, the Amin state did little intentionally to undo this monopoly on valuation, but institutional efficiency did falter. Whatever constellation of interests that previously kept farmers within the state's asserted monopoly – whereby the CMB was the sole buyer and exporter of coffee – had disappeared by the mid-1970s. In part, this reflects the illegitimacy of the government regime, but it also reflects the shifting market circumstances in which coffee growers existed. When Brazil's coffee was spoiled by frost first in 1973 and again more substantially in 1975, international prices soared; prices to Ugandan farmers, however, did not. As a result, smallholders either refused to bring their product to market or took the more daring path of magendo, selling their coffee across the border.[28] As a result, the BCU's supplies dwindled, prompting its officials and those from government to complain bitterly of a lack of coffee delivery. By the end of 1976, the Assistant District Commissioner held a meeting lamenting that the BCU had only received 500 tons of coffee compared to the 2,000 tons received in the same period the year prior. The Gisu farmers in attendance replied stoically, explaining that until official prices improved and essential commodities were available in shops, it made little sense to sell to the BCU. Yet, without the autonomy to determine prices, BCU officials could do nothing to compete with the "smuggling racket."[29] The result was a transformation of Chepkube, a well-positioned village just across the border in Kenya.

---

[27] Robert Bates, *Open-Economy Politics: The Political Economy of the World Coffee Trade* (Princeton University Press, 1997), pp. 166–167.

[28] On the Ugandan experience with magendo, see Godfrey B. Asiimwe, "From Monopoly Marketing to Coffee Magendo: Responses to Policy Recklessness and Extraction in Uganda, 1971–79," *Journal of Eastern African Studies* 7(1) (2013): 104–124; Nelson Kasfir, "State, Magendo, and Class Formation in Uganda," *Journal of Commonwealth & Comparative Politics* 21(3) (1983): 84–103; Reginald Green, *Magendo in the Political Economy of Uganda* (Institute for Development Studies, 1981).

[29] Bugisu Cooperative Union (BCU) Archive: "Report on Tour to Coffee Societies in the District," December 15, 1976.

5.3 Arbitrage and the Cultivation of Difference

For residents of Chepkube, the magendo era during the second half of the 1970s still elicits considerable excitement – memories marked with measures of amazement and hints of nostalgia. They recall it as a time when "black gold" allowed the fame of their small village to spread across East Africa, even the world.[30] One singer wrote a popular song whose catchy tune spread word across the radio waves. A novelist wrote a ribald, rollicking novel, *Black Gold of Chepkube*, which dramatizes the indulgences and risks of the trade.[31]

Residents mentioned the song and novel when trying to convey how remarkable the period was, but they also gestured around their homes, pointing to the durable property some were able to acquire from that period. Foremost in narratives of why Chepkube became such a renowned site was the presence of influential Kenyan politicians who used local buyers or their own kin when they "did not want to be seen" at Chepkube. Chepkube, I was told, came to be known as "Nairobi B," a nickname whose overstatement served to mark the sense of extraordinary commercial standing from that time.[32] "There were," my Ugandan host, Joseph, emphasized, "almost all tribes there."[33] A Kenyan teacher I know said similarly, "People came from everywhere – Kikuyu, Somali, even Gusii – and left money in Chepkube."[34] One government report went further, suggesting the trade attracted people from as far away as "Zambia and even Singapore," with the population growing from 300 to 20,000 in a matter of months.[35]

In a country and locality often riven by ethnic strife, magendo stands out in people's minds. While Babukusu predominate in the area around Chepkube, there is no pretense of ethnic uniformity, and the long-term presence of Teso and first-comer status of Sabaot is acknowledged. At various points – notably 1963 and 1991 – violent conflicts

---

[30] KRC HB/16/125: Annual Report for 1977, District Revenue Officer, Bungoma District.
[31] Wamugunda Geteria, *Black Gold of Chepkube* (Heinemann Kenya, 1988).
[32] Further south, the resulting construction boom in the border town of Busia led to a shortage of cement, corrugated iron sheets, and nails, as homes and shops were erected "to cater for the need of smugglers." KRC HB/16/122: Busia District Revenue Affairs Annual Report, 1978.
[33] J.W., February 2017.   [34] V.S., May 2017.
[35] KRC AGB 1/27: Bungoma District Annual Report 1976.

over land and representation have occurred between these groups.[36] The magendo era was different:

People were excited, and then *friendly*. Because the Sabaot, the Bukusu, and the Teso were friendly, because they were enjoying this, this transaction. The Ugandans bring coffee, they buy, sell. People were kind to each other. People were enjoying it.[37]

The boom also attracted new commodities to Chepkube. Merchants from Kitale and Bungoma brought clothes, pots, beer, whiskey, and more. Residents were flush with cash, leading to tailors sewing special pockets into oversized jackets. Kikuyu and Somali buyers were particularly able to mobilize significant capital. "We could see people coming with bags *full* of money ... You could see someone walk in with a *huuuuge* handbag, carrying about ten million shillings cash," conveyed one man who traveled there to observe. I spoke to two brothers who started buying mattresses from Bungoma and selling them for a 50 percent markup in Chepkube. The Kenyan teacher, Victor, emphasized the novel opportunities: "bicycles went up to Chepkube – brand *new*!" And the District Revenue Officer noted a sharp spike in radio buyers.[38] As far away as Central Province, thatched roofs were replaced by iron sheets.[39]

Illegal border trade was not new to the area. To the extent this era was exceptional, it was a matter of degree and direction rather than of kind. In the 1960s, for instance, it was more common for agricultural commodities to flow *towards* Uganda. In the year of independence, the Government of Kenya reported the arrival of "a cancer that hitherto was unknown in this District. This is illegal coffee sales across the Kenya–Uganda border." They estimated 200 tons of coffee were carried to Uganda "on basket loads, in sacks on bicycles, on buses, and occasionally during the night on vehicles."[40] At that time, the

---

[36] Gabrielle Lynch, "The Wars of Who Belongs Where: The Unstable Politics of Autochthony on Kenya's Mt Elgon," *Ethnopolitics* 10(3–4) (2011): 391–410; Daniel Branch, "Public Letters and the Culture of Politics in Kenya, c.1960–75," *Journal of Eastern African Studies* 15(2) (2021): 339–357.
[37] C.S., November 2016.
[38] KRC HB/16/124: Monthly Report of District Revenue Officer, Bungoma District, September 1977.
[39] Duncan Ndegwa, *Walking in Kenyatta Struggles* (Kenya Leadership Institute, 2011).
[40] KRC HB/16/86: Bungoma District Annual Report, 1963.

Ugandan export bodies not only paid more than in Kenya; they also paid cash on delivery in contrast to the long delayed payments from the Kenya Planters Cooperative Union. Some Kenyans acquired hand-processing machines that allowed them to clean the beans at home before traveling to Uganda, foregoing the usual work of their cooperatives. Much the same held for maize: in 1963, Kenyans took an estimated 50,000 bags to Uganda, where they received Shs. 10 more per bag.[41] Financially hard-pressed in the period after harvest but before payment, Kenyans took advantage of arbitrage to remain Kenyan while opportunistically engaging Uganda's monopoly on valuation. As late as 1972, the state worried that "favorable 'cash on delivery' terms" in Uganda served to "lure" Kenyan crops away.[42]

Panya Routes through the Forest

In 1976, the source of Chepkube's newfound magnetism was, of course, the arrival of Ugandan coffee. The village was well placed geographically to serve as a transit zone for coffee, much of which had been unsold since 1973 when international embargoes on exports limited normal channels of trade from Idi Amin's Uganda.[43] Instead, coffee poured out of seams in Uganda's territory, and the eastern frontier was a hub of magendo. Security reports made frequent mention of magendo, despite being unable to document its true extent, and official organs demanded it cease.[44] Sometimes, it was deemed a well-organized exercise, with a "gang" of up to 200 people coming together with *pangas* and spears to buy and transport coffee to Kenya. Often, it was simply individual initiative by families in need.[45] In 1976 the Bugisu Cooperative Union (BCU) organized a series of meetings with its coffee farming members, most of whom denied taking part but raised a series of complaints revealing why such a trade would occur: delayed payments, low prices, and the unavailability of "essential

---

[41] KRC HB/16/86: Bungoma District Annual Report, 1963.
[42] KRC HB/16/87: Monthly Report for October 1972, Bungoma District.
[43] Asiimwe, "From Monopoly Marketing to Coffee Magendo," pp. 104–124.
[44] See the voluminous correspondence in Mbale District Archive MBL/9/14; further afield, see Jinja District Archive (JDA) Justice, Law, Order & Security 13/17: "Smuggling of Cotton to Kenya," February 4, 1976.
[45] Mbale District Archives MBL/9/14: Meeting held at Bugisu Co-operative Union, July 25, 1978.

5.3 Arbitrage and the Cultivation of Difference 277

commodities like sugar, soap, salt, etc."[46] From the perspective of the Provincial Commissioner on the Kenyan side, the next year was "an all-time high mark and such places as Lwakhakha, Chepkube, and Sio Port were household names in smuggling circles."[47] The matter even reached the records of the Central Bank of Kenya, albeit in the manner of an open secret, with the 1978 Annual Report noting "the record surplus in the balance of payments, and the highest ever accumulation of foreign exchange reserves" thanks to buoyant coffee exports.[48]

Successfully bringing coffee to Kenya required careful negotiation of the landscape, often turning to areas previously unused, even proscribed. Bob Nakileza recalls "carrying heaps and heaps of [coffee] through the thick and dark forest, and open alpine moorlands of Masaba mountain ... I toured the dark and open ecosystems of the mountain, believably where my ancestors live."[49] Participants from both sides of the border emphasize how far coffee came over steep mountain paths to reach Chepkube, up to 100 kilometers on foot. "They would avoid towns, moving and dodging." While bicycles or donkeys were available in some instances, the routes were dangerous due to Ugandan police patrols. The simpler the locomotion, the safer. Roads were liable to interception, so instead arbitrageurs took to *panya* ("rat") routes through the thick forests of Mount Elgon. Such panya routes required local knowledge that subverted the formalities of the law.[50]

Despite their use, Ugandans ferrying coffee through the frontier region were at risk because the Amin government was antagonistic to citizens' magendo.[51] Tensions at the border were often high.[52]

---

[46] BCU Archive, Minutes of the Committee Meeting, November 23, 1976.
[47] KRC HB/16/73: Western Province Annual Report, 1978, p. 2.
[48] *Annual Report* (Nairobi: Central Bank of Kenya, 1978), p. 5.
[49] Bob Nakileza, "A True Story of Coffees Magendo through Mount Elgon (Uganda)," *Etudes rurales* (2007): 131–136.
[50] As in the case analyzed by Brad Weiss in Tanzania, the difference between types of roads has less to do with the paving or vehicle used; rather, different names correspond to different ideas about the character of movement on the route. Brad Weiss, "'Buying Her Grave': Money, Movement and Aids in North-West Tanzania," *Africa* 63(1) (1993): 19–35.
[51] State elite had their own smuggling operations, though. Mahmood Mamdani, *Imperialism and Fascism in Uganda* (Africa World Press, 1984).
[52] Generally, see Godfrey P. Okoth, "Intermittent Tensions in Uganda-Kenya Relations: Historical Perspectives," *Transafrican Journal of History* 21 (1992): 69–92.

In September 1977, Uganda's paramilitary State Research Bureau shot at two Kenyans in a Peugeot 404 Station Wagon, loaded with smuggled oil and diesel. A few days later, a Kenyan mob beat up two Ugandan soldiers shopping across the border in Kenya.[53] During a Kenyan national holiday the next month, Uganda Army aircraft flew low over Busia town, panicking Kenyans who thought they were going to be "bombed by Amin."[54] In November, Amin toured Uganda's Eastern Province, touting five years of his "Economic War" and calling for discipline and cooperation with the security forces to stop smuggling. The next month, Ugandan soldiers shot dead two Kenyans accused of coffee smuggling on Sigulu Island in Lake Victoria.[55]

Many other Ugandans were subject to state violence. Ugandan soldiers and police plied the area, sometimes escorting their preferred smugglers.[56] So too did civilian bandits who would pretend to be soldiers. "They would have gun-like tools," Joseph told me one day while walking across his fields, "and when they see people coming ... they go and take cover and they come up like they want to shoot them. So people throw their coffee and run away, and the [fake soldiers] collect their coffee and go and sell." The young men who perpetrated these thefts hoped to sell the coffee themselves. "These people they were not using guns," but only pieces of wood designed to look like guns, so when the deceit was discovered, some traders attacked and killed the thieves.

Magendo, then, relied on the successful manipulation of appearances: while some civilians dressed up like soldiers, in other cases,

---

[53] KRC HB/27/143: Western Province Intelligence Committee, September 27, 1977. See also KRC HB/27/5/6: Provincial and District Security Committee Correspondence. (Although this is a Kakamega Records Centre file, I was provided access at the KNA in Nairobi, where it was being held in 2016–2017.)

[54] Subsequent inquiries suggested this was an accidental navigation during routine training, but Kenyans were already worried by Amin's claim the prior year to large swaths of Kenyan territory. On territory, see KRC AGB/1/127; for the incident, see KRC HB/27/143: Western Province Intelligence Committee, No. 10 of 1977.

[55] KRC HB/27/143: Western Province Intelligence Committee, Report No. 1 of 1978.

[56] The involvement of Ugandan military elite in smuggling is a focus of Green, "Magendo in the Political Economy" and Kasfir, "State, Magendo, and Class Formation." See also Gérard Prunier, "Le Magendo: Essai sur quelques aspects marginaux des echanges commerciaux en Afrique orentale," *Politique Africaine* 9 (1983): 53–62.

5.3 Arbitrage and the Cultivation of Difference 279

Ugandan soldiers "mostly dressed in civilian clothes."[57] Arbitrageurs sought invisibility, while others misrepresented the outward signs of authority. The skillful presentation of self was also crucial if you were caught, because "it was your luck and how you are using your words when you meet soldiers." Others adopted a more aggressive dissimulation. Ugandan soldiers (*askari*) were hungry and poor, so intercepted travelers would feed them poisoned food. Others captured swarms of bees in a pot and released them if caught. Having covered themselves in paraffin, they could lie down and wait as the *askaris* ran away.

Panya routes through the forest were part of a more general reliance on undomesticated space. One Chepkube farmer noted his surprise at this abnormality: "Anyway, even people were sleeping in the forest! There were these people who used to use the forest routes. People went as far as waiting for coffee in the forest. There was even a market in the forest." The transposition of spaces of production and domesticity for the wilds of the forest was all the more unsettling because the forest represents a space associated with danger, immorality, and secret knowledge.[58] "Forests," in the moral geography of my interlocutors on both sides of the border, were spaces unfit for habitation.[59]

Yet, Chepkube became a locus of magendo during this period precisely for its proximity to these relatively ungovernable areas. Though not without its dangers, the river crossing at Chepkube is relatively easy to ford, and downed trees provide what one man called "local bridges."[60] These geographic affordances allowed residents to insert themselves within the trade. While Ugandans were safe in Kenya – often rejoicing upon crossing the river – they could not remain for long. Even if they could pass as Kenyan by speaking Lubukusu and

---

[57] KRC HB/27/214: Minutes of the District Commissioners' Meeting, August 19, 1976.
[58] For example, Gunter Wagner reports that the carefully guarded medicines of the rare rain magician were gathered "in the forest belt on the slopes of Mount Elgon" and hidden carefully. "To perform his rain-magic, he takes his paraphernalia to a secret spot in the forest where he builds a small arbour." Wagner, *The Bantu of North Kavirondo: Volume 1* (Oxford University Press, 1949), p. 148.
[59] This is sometimes tied to an ethnic chauvinism that denigrates those who make their livelihoods hunting and gathering in the forest. For a sense of the political tribalism in the area, see Lynch, "The Wars of Who Belongs Where," pp. 391–410; Claire Médard, "Elected Leaders, Militias and Prophets: Violence in Mount Elgon (2006–2008)," *Les Cahiers d'Afrique de l'Est* (2009): 339–361.
[60] R.C., November 2016.

Kiswahili, Kenyan police would check for ID cards or a distinctive scar left by vaccination in their country. If caught, they would be arrested and deported.[61] As a result, they were sometimes beholden to Kenyan intermediaries and rarely could partake for long in the forms of expenditure I discuss in the following text.

This impermanence allowed Kenyan residents of the frontier to mediate exchange between the brief visits of Ugandans and the bulk exporters of magendo coffee from Kenya. Incorporating locals facilitated the trade by drawing on the cultural infrastructure of the border.[62] Locals could wait around for coffee arriving through panya routes that visitors would be unlikely to find. They could also speak to arriving Ugandans in their mutually intelligible languages, rather than Swahili or English (let alone Kikuyu or Somali), which would be less familiar.

Frontier Repertoires: Relatedness across Difference

The populations demarcated as Kenyan or Ugandan in the region around Mount Elgon recognize a long, shared history. Wekesa speaks of a "fluid cultural zone" on which the border has been imposed.[63] The Bagisu of Uganda and Babukusu of Kenya speak of a common history of origin, migration, and settlement. Their languages are mutually intelligible, and kinship networks often extend across the border. In both countries, they are known for their similar cultural practices.[64] During this time, families circulate with increased vigor across the

---

[61] Beyond the immediate border area, there were roadblocks, requiring "all lots of letters, all lots of documentation in order to go to Kenya and come back. But if you did not have documentation, you would be arrested and end up in prison, and their prisons were really unfriendly, and people feared them so much." J.W., February 2017. A Ugandan politician – himself married to a Kenyan – explained that the pressure from the government of Kenya could even make one's cross-border family hesitant to provide too much help to Ugandan kin. "We were so mistreated!" he lamented. There were "Kenyan robbers! But you cannot report them. Where do you report them? You are illegal in that country." J.M., February 2017.

[62] I am grateful for discussions with Peter Wafula Wekesa on this point.

[63] Peter Wafula Wekesa, "Magendo and Survivalism: Babukusu-Bagisu Relations and Economic Ingenuity on the Kenya-Uganda Border 1962–1980," in Dereje Feyissa and Markus Höhne (eds.), *Borders & Borderlands as Resources in the Horn of Africa* (Boydell & Brewer, 2010), pp. 151–167.

[64] The biennial circumcision ceremonies happened in 1976, coinciding with the first wave of magendo. KRC HB/27/214: Minutes of the District Commissioners' Meeting, August 19, 1976.

5.3 Arbitrage and the Cultivation of Difference 281

territorial border, moving food for feasts and dramatizing their affinity. There is, in other words, a transactional territory, with the circulation of people and goods crossing state boundaries. It is these ties that lead some to speak of "Bamasaba," a term encompassing both Babukusu and Bagisu.[65] Yet it would be a mistake to overstate the unity of a population distributed across hills and valleys, maintaining pluralism in place of a more muscular ethnic patriotism.[66]

Instead of a uniform identity and territory, the frontier area was characterized by relatedness across difference. Residents had recourse to a latent repertoire of affinity that could be activated during the magendo era.[67] For Bamasaba, mutually intelligible language, the assertion of ethnic and kin-based solidarities, and shared histories of coffee cultivation provided a repertoire on which the exceptional arbitrage economy could function.[68] Yet it was precisely the fact that these repertoires facilitated exchange across disjuncture that made magendo so exceptional. Without the differential prices due to the distinct economic jurisdictions of Uganda and Kenya, arbitrage would not have occurred.

Consider the trajectory of Josiah. When my Ugandan host introduced me to his countryman, a farmer and trader, it was because of Josiah's reputation as one of the first to begin the magendo business. Josiah could do so because he was already working with a relative of his, a prominent man in Kitale, a town on the eastern edge of Mount Elgon in Kenya. In 1969, this relative asked him to surreptitiously bring Kenyan coffee to the Bugisu Cooperative Union in Uganda for sale, where the price was better. In the middle of the 1970s, he reversed course, acquiring Ugandan beans for Kenyan buyers. As before, his

---

[65] Kinship and exchange knit together other linguistic groups, too. During the magendo era, there was an influx of cattle from Uganda as Samia and Teso people "received cattle from their relatives who are Kenya citizens residing in Uganda." KRC HB/27/214: Minutes of the District Commissioners' Meeting, August 19, 1976.

[66] Julie MacArthur, *Cartography and the Political Imagination: Mapping Community in Colonial Kenya* (Ohio University Press, 2016).

[67] Francis Nyamnjoh, "Incompleteness: Frontier Africa and the Currency of Conviviality," *Journal of Asian and African Studies* 52(3) (2017): 253–270.

[68] As one government report put it when noting a rise in reported smuggling, "Perhaps the source of such rumours was based on the fact that the people living along the Kenya/Uganda border had so much in common with each other that they were engaged in barter market." KRC HB/16/161: Western Province Annual Report 1972.

circuit depended on a combination of kinship and connections to local notables. He set up shop on the Kenya side of the border with another relative and began moving coffee for sale to a Kenyan politician. He used a relative's home on the periphery of Chepkube to store coffee and opened a store in the market to sell soap, sugar, and other commodities.

Josiah was ambitious and, unlike many other locals, unsatisfied with being a middleman confined to Chepkube. He skipped the Kikuyu and Somalis coming to Chepkube and went up the commodity chain, directed by his existing contacts further afield. He was able to do so because he had enough capital to acquire lorries, but also because, in his opinion, Ugandans liked selling to a compatriot. Thus, Josiah did particularly well during magendo – eventually buying vehicles, land, and educating his children – because he was both closely embedded in the networks of kin and culture at the frontier and also able to form more distant commercial relations. The relative paucity of people able to maneuver across such differences is precisely what made his arbitrage lucrative. Business was booming, and he recalls moving 100 sacks of coffee per day, perhaps for up to KSh. 3,000 per sack.

His prominence did not go unnoticed, and when Amin sent "people to Kenya in the night to hijack him," he narrowly escaped. As he explained to me, his Kenyan colleagues helped him get back into business, with new capital and a portable safe to hide his proceeds. Fearful of returning to Uganda, he adopted the stance of an exile, and the Kenyan police, recognizing his importance to the trade, acquired an ID card for him "almost in a day."[69] Josiah, then, demonstrates how the ability to straddle different jurisdictions that remain apart, rather than homogenized, was foundational to magendo arbitrage. He also illustrates key dynamics of arbitrage citizenship, such as not fully exiting a jurisdiction but moving between Uganda and Kenya, with meaningful economic and political implications.

Measure for Mismeasure

If the movement of coffee between territorial jurisdictions was the fundamental form of arbitrage during magendo, more subtle differences were cultivated and crossed by participants. These tactics sought

---

[69] J.M., February 2017.

5.3 Arbitrage and the Cultivation of Difference

to maneuver between distinct evaluative schema through which exchange was mediated and to manage relationships between the surface appearance and enduring quality of goods. As Jane Guyer has influentially argued, the conversion between different techniques of measurement is a critical part of African economic repertoires.[70] Brad Weiss, too, has emphasized "the different strategic possibilities of measurement and quantification upon which the coffee trade depends."[71] Magendo shed the state's enforced metrology, whereby price per kilo was determined through marketing boards. At Chepkube, the translation between accounting by volume, by weight, and by Kenyan Shillings offered skillful traders an opportunity to exploit additional magendo margins. This required perceptive cultivation and management of difference, iterated over many individual transactions.

Ugandans arrived on the Kenyan side of the Malaba River with partially filled bags of coffee. These *gunia* – the iconic gunny sacks of the region – contained between 10–50 kilograms of dried coffee. Local Kenyans, who had the luxury of time and identification documents, would be waiting to greet these sellers with something like the going price. Unlike in the official coffee purchases in Uganda, there was no central authority to determine prices. Those closest to the river might offer a slightly lower price, hoping exhausted Ugandans would be happy to part with their coffee before traveling the final distance to Chepkube's market. Ugandans that reached Chepkube's market would find a bustling scene with innumerable potential buyers. Their coffee was scooped from their half-filled bags and deposited in the buyer's gunny sacks. Each scoop was counted and Ugandans received payment accordingly.[72]

The humble implement for scooping coffee was formative for magendo. Despite its simplicity, the *gorogoro*, as it is known, is a particularly noteworthy "market device."[73] A gorogoro, Kenyans will tell you, is a "two kilogram tin," most often repurposed from its original use as the container for popular store-bought cooking fats of

---

[70] Guyer, *Marginal Gains*. [71] Weiss, *Sacred Trees*, p. 169.
[72] At a high-point in December 1976, coffee was sold for KSh. 80 to 120 per *gorogoro*. KRC HB/27/334: Minutes of the Bugisu/Bungoma Border Liaison Meeting, December 2, 1976.
[73] As Michel Callon and colleagues explain, a market device is a material or discursive device that intervenes and formats economic behavior. Michel Callon, Yuval Millo, and Fabian Muniesa (eds.), *Market Devices* (Wiley-Blackwell, 2007).

the time, such as Kimbo or Cowboy. At the time, cooking fats were one of the most common commodities purchased by rural households, and the sturdy containers in which they came provided a convenient afterlife. Like the commodity it once held, the gorogoro is standardized, providing a shared marketplace metric. In everyday speech, this standard is "two kilograms," a figure arising from the gorogoros' original label: 2 kilograms of cooking fat. However, the commonality of an empty gorogoro is *not* weight; after all, the density of coffee (or whatever else is being measured) is different than cooking fat. Instead, the standard offered through the gorogoro is the uniform *volume*. Thus, while residents of Chepkube routinely referred to "two kilograms of coffee," as measured by the gorogoro, this was not a reference to weight, but rather to the standardized unit of volume provided by the empty cooking fat tin.

This presumed correspondence between weight and volume matters because the interplay between scales of measurement provided subtle forms of arbitrage. Scooping coffee out of arriving gunny sacks with a gorogoro standardized the variable amounts of beans brought from Uganda. As Ugandans were paid per gorogoro of dried beans, it also served as a means of commensurating between a volumetric scale and a different unit of accounting: Kenyan shillings. In the chain of magendo, the ability to enforce or evade such standardized commensuration – the construction of equivalence across difference – were tactics of arbitrage; the movement between fixed or variable relationships of weight, volume, and shillings were pivotal in the acquisition of marginal gains.

This was because magendo was characterized by one-off transactions. While some, like Josiah, had enduring commercial relationships, the vast majority of purchases were between individuals who did not know each other: "There was nothing like trust."[74] Traders took advantage of this through various means of inserting an additional margin on top of the prevailing price differences. Gorogoros, for example, not only enumerated coffee; they were also used to detect impurities. Participants re-enacted for me how they would hold the full containers at eye level and pour the dried beans into their own gunny sacks, looking for rocks, sand, fruit, or other less valuable fillers.[75]

---

[74] P.M., November 2016.
[75] On this deception in Bukoba, see Weiss, *Sacred Trees*, pp. 186–187; cf. *debe* containers p. 172.

5.3 Arbitrage and the Cultivation of Difference

Yet, those coming from elsewhere in Kenya to purchase from Chepkube did not match the discerning caution of locals in this initial purchase. When they arrived from Nairobi with lorries, they did not measure in gorogoros; rather, they purchased gunny sacks by the dozens. Chepkube's residents, often with a laugh or wry smile, explained to me some of the "funny, funny" tricks people would use, such as filling space with rocks. By the time such deception was discovered in Nairobi or Mombasa, it was hardly worth the time to follow up. More generally, the extraordinary magendo era stood in contrast to the more discerning valuation practices of the state export bodies. The official regime of cooperative societies and marketing boards graded the quality of farmers' crops. At Chepkube, there was very little in the way of sorting and ranking: it was "just wash and sell," a farmer from the Ugandan side told me.[76]

In some cases, precautions were taken. Over time, some gravity scales – from which a gunny sack could be hung and weighed – arrived in Chepkube, allowing buyers from elsewhere to pay per kilogram, rather than per gunny sack. Local arbitrageurs developed new tactics to produce a difference, most notably through soaking dried coffee beans in water overnight "to bulk them." The plumper beans would then receive a cursory drying in the sun of only their exterior. In these cases, the density of coffee (and, to a lesser degree, its volume) again became a variable, as a surface-level dehydration could conceal the moistened coffee within. The presumed material fixity of coffee was transformed into a plasticity subject to manipulation. The aim of these scalar maneuvers was to insert (or detect) a small disjuncture between the worth of goods offered and the price received.

The introduction and maintenance of these forms of scalar variation would, eventually, be converted into currency. In the frontier zone, however, money took on particular characteristics. With the value of their currency plummeting, Ugandans faced a stark reality: even though they could receive a more valuable currency through magendo, Kenyan shillings lacked broad-based validity in their home country. The result was that magendo in Chepkube was conducted in Kenyan shillings. "Ugandan currency was not even worth it."[77] Scooped by the gorogoro, coffee was then priced in Kenyan shillings, with these notes quickly exchanged for commodities. For Ugandans, therefore, Kenyan

[76] E.M., February 2017. [77] C.S., November 2017.

currency operated akin to a trade currency, incorporating them into temporary exchange with Kenyan coffee buyers and commodity sellers. It provided a technique of valuation, mediating between coffee and commodities, but did not serve as an enduring store of value.[78] Instead, Ugandans translated the arbitrage value of their coffee into manufactured goods that were portable and perduring. In the process, they subverted the controlled conversion between currencies on which the Ugandan state depended.

5.4 Magendo and Moral Ambiguity

Throughout my fieldwork, laughter frequently accompanied stories of the excesses of the trade, subtly acknowledging the unequal opportunism. It served to hold together contradictions – namely that the attractiveness of unbridled margins existed alongside recognition that Ugandans received the short end of the exchange. Laughter represented a sort of admission, not so much of guilt as of immoderation, excess, and the ethical ambiguity surrounding them.[79] The moral ambivalence around magendo did not arise from the illegality of the trade. Cross-border exchange was a long-standing practice for residents of this East African frontier, and the territorialization of economies and state morality exerted a weak force on their ideas about legitimate commerce.

Instead, the disquiet of the period was the result of a transformation in the accessibility of wealth and, in turn, the erosion of forms of authority and behavior through which ethical life was ordered.[80] Rather than its relationship to the law, magendo challenged people's ideas about the temporality of wealth, gendered and generational hierarchies, and the gap between surface and substance. In this way, it resembles de Boeck's analysis of cross-border diamond trade in Zaire, where social critiques of accumulation and expenditure were less about prohibited movement than the redirection of wealth towards

---

[78] Cf. Bill Maurer, "The Anthropology of Money," *Annual Review of Anthropology* 35(1) (2006): 20–21.

[79] Rihan Yeh, "Visas, Jokes, and Contraband: Citizenship and Sovereignty at the Mexico–U.S. Border," *Comparative Studies in Society and History* 59(1) (2017): 154–182.

[80] Cf. Simon Schama, *The Embarrassment of Riches: An Interpretation of Dutch Culture in the Golden Age* (Vintage Books, 1988).

5.4 Magendo and Moral Ambiguity

socially sanctioned patterns of self-making and collectivity.[81] Magendo's cultivation of difference – in terms of jurisdiction, but also measurement and appearance – provided the basis for excessive proceeds, where wealth was available in a manner "unsanctioned" by the prevailing social hierarchies of Bukusu society.[82]

The cultivation and capitalization on disjunctures of jurisdiction, of measurement, and of appearance was widely pursued, yet the resulting wealth from this arbitrage did much to challenge social norms and conceptual schema of frontier residents. The rest of this chapter examines the implications of this. An undisciplined "binge economy" replaced the perceived orderly arrangement between men and women, seniors and juniors, production and consumption. A sense that generational and gendered expectations and hierarchies were dissolving accompanied the inversion of conceptual and perceptual schema. Three particular inversions arose throughout my conversations with residents: what was once distant became local as space was compressed; anticipated temporalities vanished in the frenzy of trade; and distinctions between the productive and domestic spheres and their ungoverned, wild complements dissolved. The following sections analyze these in more depth. The idioms and tropes through which this was expressed reveal a sense of peril regarding the magendo era, but such an unease was never far from its cause: the enthusiastic embrace of magendo's opportunities. Thus, memories of the period are ambiguous, with contradictions often held together by an ironic laughter.

Binge Economy: Money and People Out of Time

While Ugandans returned home with the commodities of social reproduction (salt, clothes, pots), Kenyans turned their spending toward consumption. Binge economies can occur for many reasons – the discovery of new exports, say, or speculative frenzies – but around Mount Elgon, it was arbitrage that formed the basis for dramatic accrual and dissipation of wealth. Arbitrage also allowed participants to capture and redirect value in unprecedented ways. In Wilk's

---

[81] Filip de Boeck, "Domesticating Diamonds and Dollars: Identity, Expenditure and Sharing in Southwestern Zaire (1984–1997)," *Development and Change* 29 (4) (1998): 777–810.
[82] Janet Roitman, *Fiscal Disobedience: An Anthropology of Economic Regulation in Central Africa* (Princeton University Press, 2004), p. 79.

conceptualization, binge economies are typical of extractive frontiers "on the margins of the capitalist world system."[83] They are marked by excessive, seemingly irrational, expenditure where what counts is less the stability of one's pocketbook than one's ability to spend as quickly as possible. Performances of one's detachment from money demonstrate daring and *joie de vivre*. In Chepkube, too, competitive gift giving emerged as a common form of conviviality:

> People were very generous! A lot of drinking. Bars opened from nowhere. They would say, okay, I have a lot of money, I want to buy you a beer; you are my friend. Stand up! You stand up. I would pile crates of beer – Tusker, Pilsner – up to your height, and that's yours![84]

Where previously only locally brewed alcohol was available, brand name beer and even whiskey arrived from distant factories. Chepkube's market used to operate only one day a week, with a single bull slaughtered for sale, but during this period, upwards of ten heads of cattle were butchered daily and "by 10 p.m., there was no meat left!"

Such consumptive possibilities are remembered with relish, but they also manifest an unsettled order of age, gender, and rank. Throughout East Africa, alcohol and meat are symbolically charged goods.[85] Bukusu men historically demonstrated their worth through the quality of their homebrewed beer and their generosity in its distribution. Only elderly men (and sometimes women) could enjoy beer drinking as a regular pastime; younger folks only enjoyed it at special events or as a reward for labor.[86] These restrictions on consumption – and attempts to subvert them – are constitutive of the contested claims to authority of senior men. Notions and practices of drinking are, therefore, practical enactments of hierarchical and exclusive social relations. Transformations in access – due to commodification, regulation, or economic change – can unsettle norms of respect and power. In the case of magendo, novel consumptive possibilities were part of a more general disordering of people's relations, wealth, and temporalities. When I asked if magendo was organized, perhaps by elders, one man

---

[83] Richard Wilk, "Poverty and Excess in Binge Economies," *Economic Anthropology* 1(1) (2014): 66–79.

[84] V.S., October 2016.

[85] Justin Willis, *Potent Brews: Social History of Alcohol in East Africa, 1850–1999* (Ohio University Press, 2002).

[86] Wagner, *The Bantu of North Kavirondo: Volume 1*, pp. 68–79.

5.4 Magendo and Moral Ambiguity

shook his head, "No, there was no organization. Anyone would work on his own."[87]

The binge economy of Chepkube was characterized by a presentism in which urgent trade captured everyone's attention. The focus on the moment led many to discount the possibility the trade would end. As one Kenyan bureaucrat noted, "from the point of view of many active smugglers of all ranks ... it seemed as if the exercise would remain perpetual."[88] I was told of multiple civil servants who traded their secure careers for the present opportunities. Josiah was so flush with cash and so confident that present conditions would prevail that he paid for two years of rent upfront.[89] In other cases, tenants paid for five years of rent in one go.[90] The immediacy with which wealth was available militated against all other activities. There was no time to spare. Big buyers coming from afar would rent hotel rooms in the closest urban centers of Bungoma or further south. Others "just broke some branches [for] a makeshift camp" and "slept in the bushes to buy the coffee." Such arrangements belied the weight Bukusu communities have historically given to a proper home, seeing deficient housing as a sign of indolence.[91] Yet, during the coffee boom, no attention was given to such basic concerns. Walking one day near the river that divides the two countries, my friend stopped and pointed: "It was like a refugee camp here." Government ministers and their wives – even Margaret Kenyatta, I was assured – turned to such rudimentary quarters. Naively assuming the former mayor of Nairobi and daughter of the country's founding President could afford it, I asked, why not have a house built here? The answer was immediate and followed by hearty laughter at the incongruous, even Carnivalesque, logic of the time: "Who's going to build? Where are you going to get the labor?"

---

[87] C.S., November 2016.
[88] KRC HB/16/125: Annual Report for 1977, District Revenue Officer, Bungoma.
[89] J.M. February 2017.
[90] KRC DF/13/11: Bungoma District Annual Report, 1978.
[91] "The Vugusu, in fact, have a proverb saying that 'as regards a house nobody can be poor for a long time', meaning that poor housing conditions can easily be remedied. If a person lives in a very ramshackle, dilapidated hut—a thing only rarely to be seen—this is due less to poverty than to indolence, or to the owner's poor state of health and his failure to maintain the usual kinship and neighbourly relations, from which he should be able to obtain the necessary help." Gunter Wagner, *The Bantu of North Kavirondo: Volume 2* (Oxford University Press, 1956) p. 2.

The velocity of money also accelerated.[92] Some big buyers received substantial advances from banks, permitting them to turn a larger profit. If you were a well-connected Kenyan "overnight, you came and got 10 million shillings [in cash from the bank], you go and buy, take it, and by the time you reach Nairobi, or before, someone is buying it to take it to Mombasa. You pay it [the loan] back and go back again." Such stories illustrate the rapidity and repetition with which buyers scrambled for access to cash to buy arriving coffee. I was told of a senior government official and confidant of the President whose wife spent time in Chepkube. The minister "used his position" to get all the cash from the main bank branch in Bungoma. "People needed cash to buy coffee at Chepkube, so the bank even ran out of cash, failing to pay teachers because of it."[93] The Nairobi headquarters had to airlift cash to ameliorate the shortage. Others turned to cooperative agricultural societies, using their collectively held cash as an advance to purchase magendo coffee. In both these stories, collective futures (of children's education and farmer cooperation) are mortgaged for immediate gains.

Moralizing observers often condemn a lack of orientation toward the future, the inability to do anything but "live for the moment."[94] Many residents of Chepkube offer a similar reflection on the period. Amid the dramatic consumption, few invested in productive assets.[95] "People were busy," one former teacher told me. "Even our own coffee farms could not be managed. Because people were interested in getting *easy* money, quick money, only a few managed their farms." While few at the time resisted the attraction of magendo's immediacy, with the benefit of hindsight, some see "easy money" as a significant mistake.[96]

---

[92] This is often associated with moral danger. Maurice Bloch and Jonathan Parry (eds.), *Money and the Morality of Exchange* (Cambridge University Press, 1989), pp. 24–30.

[93] V.S., May 2017.

[94] On orientations to the future, see the introduction to Mike McGovern, *A Socialist Peace?: Explaining the Absence of War in an African Country* (University of Chicago Press, 2018); Sophie Day, Euthymios Papataxiarchēs, and Michael Stewart, *Lilies of the Field: Marginal People Who Live for the Moment* (Westview Press, 1999).

[95] Some bought automobiles, but lacked, I was told, "the knowledge of how to maintain a vehicle." Immobile vehicles stood as a testament, years later, to the period's over-exuberance.

[96] For related phenomena near and far, see Parker MacDonald Shipton, *Bitter Money: Cultural Economy and Some African Meanings of Forbidden*

5.4 Magendo and Moral Ambiguity

The "people who were getting money in an easy way," others told me, "it has ruined their lives. Because they have now had to learn to struggle for their lives by farming [or] doing businesses." In their reckoning, meaningful value was durable, and it took time and sweat to accumulate.[97] Only over time was it possible to gain the value that was born through the experience and productivity of discipline; this required converting quicker money into more enduring forms of value, such as land.[98] Wealth *out of time* – that is, money realized without the normal perquisites of self-restraint and collective effort – was likely to run out in no time.

The exigencies that characterized magendo upended existing temporal rhythms. Instead of the year being marked by discrete periods of coffee harvesting and marketing, the calendar was now completely dominated by the coffee trade. The buildup of coffee supplies in Uganda meant there were arrivals throughout the entire year. Moreover, Chepkube's weekly schedule was usually punctuated by a single market day. During magendo, "There was no market *day*." Instead, it was "every day. Morning. Night. It was full!" Domestic time was overridden by the pursuit of profit. Magendo was a 24 hour, 7 days a week affair. "Every hour people were operating; night and day were just the same."[99] Because Ugandans could best elude their country's soldiers at night, much of the business was conducted after the sun set. Despite the night, the Kenyan side was illuminated; there was no electricity in the area, but paraffin pressure lamps were common. "When you come from very far, you find this place was very clear, like daylight! And the business was working day and night, not stopping! No sleeping!"[100]

The productivity of the night still animates residents. One elderly gentleman exclaimed "Chepkube used to be like Cabinda in Angola – during even night, lights!"[101] A friend sitting quietly until this point

---

Commodities (American Anthropological Association, 1989); Heinzpeter Znoj, "Hot Money and War Debts: Transactional Regimes in Southwestern Sumatra," *Comparative Studies in Society and History* 40(2) (1998): 193–222.

[97] Suzette Heald, *Controlling Anger: The Sociology of Gisu Violence* (James Currey, 1989).

[98] Sibel Kusimba, "Money, Mobile Money and Rituals in Western Kenya: The Contingency Fund and the Thirteenth Cow," *African Studies Review* 61(2) (2018): 158–182.

[99] S.B., November 2016. [100] J.C., November 2016.

[101] E.C., November 2016.

chimed in, "like Dubai, with people buying. That is how Chepkube looked." In both cases, the references to petro-state profligacy – the flares of Cabinda's rigs and the ostentatious glare of Dubai's malls – seemed the best parallel for the transformation of their village. "People were not feeling any exhaustion at all," I was assured, because they were making profit. "He went about all day and night and tomorrow you will see him still on the same business." The rewiring of biorhythms, the fueling of superhuman energy – such was the sense of the time.

Arbitrage, Gender, and Generation

The trade attracted women, too. In both Uganda and Kenya, women have historically turned to commercial trade as means of securing their own incomes and a degree of self-sufficiency. Just as commonly, men have viewed these activities with paternalistic concern. Men around Chepkube told me of "reckless women [who] abandoned their responsibilities" to the household. "Even women, they were not staying in their homes. They had also become another problem," laughed one man suggestively. "As their husbands went, they also went. Perhaps they also came home late, just to sleep. The next morning, they had gone to look for money – because everyone was chasing money!" Women brewed beer and cooked meat for the crowds, both potentially suspect activities marked by masculine sociality and indulgence.

This concern reflects a more general anxiety of the time about the proper source of authority and the governance of value. For Bukusu communities, proper standing as an adult – with its rights and duties – does not emerge in a single moment but rather from an extended performance of rectitude. Moreover, it requires the formation and maintenance of suitable relations with others. Rites of initiation – male circumcision, marriage, and childbirth – are particularly intensive opportunities to demonstrate character and also make evident networks of mutual obligation and entrustment.[102] These rites, ideas,

---

[102] Jean la Fontaine, "The Power of Rights," *Man* 12(3/4) (1977): 421–437. On Bagisu circumcision, see Pamela Khanakwa, "Male Circumcision among the Bagisu of Eastern Uganda: Practices and Conceptualisations," in Axel Fleisch and Rhiannon Stephens (eds.), *Doing Conceptual History in Africa* (Berghahn Books, 2016), pp. 115–137.

5.4 Magendo and Moral Ambiguity

and arrangements secure a particular distribution of resources and regard, and are shaped by ideas about the proper timing and sources of accumulation.

In the communities around Mount Elgon, the authority of senior men over their juniors and women oriented productive activity and domestic life. As Wagner asserted based on research between 1934–1938, "The authority of seniors over their juniors, the principle of seniority, prevails in all social relations."[103] However, the manners in which these gerontocratic arrangements apportion and control access to wealth and respectability are not without their limits and tensions. This local government of value, in other words, is subject to contestation along certain axes. Local social orders and the ethical ideas accompanying them place people within complementary and opposed roles (e.g., husband and wife; father and son) and reinforce behavior that is befitting their role, even as it challenges other roles. Heald's work in the 1960s on the Uganda side of the border emphasized the countervailing pressure against senior men from the "aggressive individualism" cultivated in young men who endeavor to "win economic independence from [their] father[s]."[104] This leads to a "strong pattern of intergenerational conflict" in which the transmission of property is eminently important.[105] Such discontent often coalesces around the timing of initiation, where sons receive a part of their inheritance, despite the father being relatively young himself at that time. It is common to hear boys in the area pester their fathers to be initiated, with the fathers demurring in part to delay providing the land and cattle necessary for his son's autonomy. Increased land scarcity in the twentieth century only exacerbated the tension. Importantly, the object of frustration here is the patriarch – not the patriarchy. The antagonism reveals, in other words, a mutual investment in seniority, despite the limited resources through which to achieve proper adulthood.[106]

[103] Wagner, *The Bantu of North Kavirondo: Volume 1*, p. 77.
[104] Heald, *Controlling Anger*.
[105] Suzette Heald, *Manhood and Morality: Sex, Violence, and Ritual in Gisu Society* (Routledge, 1999), p. 77. A more recent study of Bukusu rites similarly notes this tension, with elders "endors[ing] the importance of long-term and often collective investments, assets, and inheritances," such as land, compared to others who may prioritize "short-term moneys." Kusimba, "Money, Mobile Money and Rituals," p. 3.
[106] Likewise, complementary but opposed roles are evident in the unfolding of courtship and marriage. Young men have every reason to favor earlier

It is in this context that magendo wealth is significant. *Prime facie*, the resources available through magendo offered a means for accumulation that avoided competition between generations. Magendo during this period provided economic advancement that did not come at the cost of one's father, explaining the permissiveness with which it is greeted. Yet, the shared schema and expectations about wealth were, eventually, thrown into relief and challenged during the binge economy. This was not least because of the quickening of the extended schedules through which the life course historically unfolded and the narrowing of the relations necessary to uphold them.

For example, the regulatory function of marriage – through which individuals enter into a more senior, mature role and through which property is redistributed across generations and families – was tested by arbitrage wealth. As Peter, a neighbor of my host, put it to me, magendo "was spoiling people, particularly the younger generation. Marriage was a problem. Someone could marry five wives because he has money, [yet] he could not support all of them" after magendo ended. Ritual time accelerated, and with it the stature achieved through maturity was debased. Whereas the sequencing of marriage, including the transfer of thirteen cattle, was typically drawn out over a longer period, newly enriched men could skip such time. The performance of ongoing entrustment signaled by the non-repayment of debt was cut short, suggesting impertinence.[107] "Even some [of my age mates] got married when they were very young, because they were thinking, it was their only chance to get married," said one man who was initiated in 1978.[108]

---

marriage; it affords them new privileges, respect, and labor. Their fathers, however, have less incentive to rush and may hesitate over the necessary bride wealth. Conversely, fathers of girls are eager to favor earlier marriage. Brides-to-be may move more slowly, unsure of the restrictions placed on them in their new home. This sort of temporal antagonism is not resolved through the fiat of fathers but rather through myriad, subtle negotiations that concern families everywhere. (Failing that, of course, impatient couples could choose to elope.) Wagner, *The Bantu of North Kavirondo: Volume 1*, p. 434. For a comparative discussion in Maragoli, see Kenda Mutongi, *Worries of the Heart: Widows, Family, and Community in Kenya* (University of Chicago Press, 2007), pp. 118–127.

[107] Parker Shipton, *The Nature of Entrustment: Intimacy, Exchange, and the Sacred in Africa* (Yale University Press, 2007).

[108] P.M., November 2016.

5.4 Magendo and Moral Ambiguity

In these cases, it wasn't so much that ideals had changed – marriage was still the goal, after all – but rather the proper temporality eroded. Other marriages fell apart, only to be reconstituted otherwise: "during magendo, it was easy for someone to leave his wife, or to leave her husband because when they come here, from Mbale there in Uganda, and another one comes from Kakamega, they meet here, [and] that one from Mbale will leave her husband and go with this man from Kakamega. Marriage was very simple."[109] Temporal acceleration is often noted as a dynamic of industrialized economies, yet here it was agrarian circuits that quickened the pace of social life.[110] For the frontier residents I know, it is through the idioms and examples of kinship and initiation that such dynamics are expressed.

In addition to the perceived impatience of young men and imprudence of women, another index of gerontocratic impotence figures prominently in memories of the time: even children were involved in the trade. Children stopped attending school to collect fallen coffee beans in the market. "A boy, a girl, sometimes 12 years, 10 years, sometimes maybe 8 years, even as young as 6, 7," Victor, the teacher, told me,

So, the little girl or little boy would pick and put them in a two kilo tin of Kimbo, cooking fat, fill it, and when it is full say, Sir, can you buy it? They bargained, okay, I'll give you twenty [or] I'll give you ten. That was a lot of money; for sugar, a kilo might have been three shillings at that time.

Magendo invited children into the disposition of their seniors, bargaining as any other adult would.[111] Pupils stopped attending school because "discipline and hierarchy collapsed. Both teacher and student engaged in the same business, so in this sense they were equal." One man mimicked the act of bending over and picking up individual coffee cherries spilled on the ground: "even little children, of Standard 3 or Standard 4, had money in their pockets!" With their money, they could acquire material trappings beyond their age. "They even bought new shoes!" one man told me who remained scandalized by the memory of typically barefooted children donning footwear.[112]

---

[109] P.M., November 2016.
[110] For a discussion, the "intensifications of capitalist time," see Laura Bear, "Time as Technique," *Annual Review of Anthropology* 45(1) (2016): 487–502.
[111] Cf. George Paul Meiu, *Ethno-Erotic Economies: Sexuality, Money, and Belonging in Kenya* (University of Chicago Press, 2017).
[112] V.S., October 2016.

Other schools were empty, with neither teachers nor students bothering to attend. The economic logic seemed clear: teachers may have been paid 4,000 shillings a month, one man recalled, but in magendo you could get 20,000 in a day; even 10,000 in a couple of hours. In the exuberance of magendo, protracted avenues for the production of valuable futures – labor and education – were traded for the immediacy of arbitrage. Some were worried: as schools emptied, an illiterate generation loomed. But as paternal authority waned, there was little that could be done against the allure of arbitrage. "It got us worried. We had to complain. But even if you complained, what would you do? The child leaves you and goes to look for this business."[113]

For senior men, the situation was disconcerting – even existentially threatening. "There was no respect because everyone was rich by that time," said one former subchief. For whom, I clarified? "For elders! If you now have a child having, I mean, more than, let me say, 100,000. And you have no money [as an elder], he overlooks you! What do you do for him? He can even buy you."[114] The broad accessibility of the trade and its resulting wealth undermined the hierarchies through which juniors and seniors related, value was apportioned, and values practiced. In the views of senior men, uncontrolled access to money permitted their social juniors to bypass not only proper authority but also the patient cultivation of responsibility.

Economies of Misrepresentation

I have suggested that the management of appearance was a central concern during magendo, but over time a wider economy of misrepresentation took hold. Representations during magendo often misled, whether through the peeling apart of surface appearance and underlying substance, or the case of Kenyan government elite managing their image while still partaking.[115] These forms of deceit did not always

---

[113] C.S., November 2016.   [114] J.C., November 2016.

[115] There is an echo of Apter's argument about a postcolonial condition of "semiotic suspension, in which signs, stripped of their referential moorings, are almost literally up for grabs." Andrew Apter, *The Pan-African Nation: Oil and the Spectacle of Culture in Nigeria* (University of Chicago Press, 2005), p. 283. But in contrast to Apter's view of a generalized epistemological rupture, the case here points to specific registers in which socially salient inversions were experience (e.g., night and day, domestic and wild). Cf. Achille Mbembe, *On the Postcolony* (University of California Press, 2001).

5.4 Magendo and Moral Ambiguity

rankle participants' moral intuition: as studies of fake goods make clear, "everyday dissimulation [is] a social modality" that is not merely defined by resentment and objection.[116] Opacity, deception, and pretext were often negotiated, rather than uniformly rejected.

Yet, not all magendo duplicity was met with ambiguous laughter, and over time some acts did provoke indignation and condemnation. For example, dishonest butchers sold meat unfit for consumption. "There was a time when there were very many dogs," a Chepkube farmer told me. "Then, all of a sudden: there was not a single dog!" Unscrupulous vendors, he thought, "were selling dogs at night, maybe from midnight when there was no more meat, to 2 a.m." Another confirmed this rumor, emphasizing that the timing of magendo was central to the impropriety: "That one happened, because as I said, people used to do this business at night, then at night people could do anything." No matter how illuminated, the night was a time of risk and danger. He continued, pointing to the intrusion of undomesticated spaces and their products into domestic consumption: "Yes, we had people from the forest who could come with elephant meat, perhaps antelope meat. At night, people could eat anything. You had to be very careful to not eat things at night. But they were sold mostly to those who came at night to buy, because they were tired, hungry, and they could land on certain meat." Inoculating oneself against these dangers, he suggested, was particularly difficult for new arrivals that lacked the careful disposition Chepkube demanded in those days.

Mambo Kwisha

The most dramatic incident of the magendo era – indeed, its denouement in the view of some – arose from the realization that counterfeit Kenyan shillings were being used to buy coffee. By September 1978, the Kenyan state was fretting about the large number of fake KSh. 100 notes circulating in both Uganda and Kenya. When two traders in Busia were arrested with KSh. 7,000 in fake notes others "dumped their horde into pit latrines," lest they meet a similar fate.[117] The next

---

[116] Sasha Newell, "Ethnography in a Shell Game: Turtles All the Way Down in Abidjan," *Cultural Anthropology* 34(3) (2019): 300. See also Guyer, *Marginal Gains*, pp. 86–91.
[117] KRC HB/27/210: Circulation of Counterfeit Kenya Currency, September 12, 1978.

month, Kenyan police proudly reported to their superiors that their anti-smuggling operations netted dozens of unlicensed bags of coffee in homes and shops, though many suspects absconded to Uganda before being arrested.[118] Officials feared that without these crackdowns, the magendo of the border would threaten all of Kenya:

> The counterfeit job is so good that even bank tellers are likely to accept the money as genuine ... Unless the situation is normalised, a stage might come where even genuine Kenya money in the KShs100/– may not be accepted by traders. It might even be advisable to change the currency lest the country be flooded by these fake currency which is likely to affect the economy of the country.[119]

Counterfeiting also troubled Chepkube. As my interlocutors put it, Kikuyu and Somali bulk buyers were in a scramble to acquire as much coffee in Chepkube as they could. This compelled some unscrupulous buyers to bring counterfeit Kenyan shillings to the frontier, slipped into bundles of genuine currency – an act blamed on Somalis. With such free money, these individuals could afford to outbid their competitors. The same quality that made cash attractive – its immediacy and lack of records – made recuperation unlikely. This angered participants, not least because it cut them off from the consumptive networks into which they had so eagerly entered. For some, it was experienced as a return to poverty.

In fact, many blame the fraud for the ultimate end of the binge economy. When word went out that the Somalis had been defrauding the sellers, "the Kikuyus complained and started beating the Somalis." Armed with pangas, spears, stones, and other implements, the incident turned into a daylong conflagration, with other participants joining in the assault. Those present remember the day well. "It was a very big confusion. People died."[120] Kenyan police did not arrive for hours because instead of keeping the peace in busy Chepkube, they were under orders to remain in their post in distant Malakisi. In the meantime, perhaps as many as seven or eight people died, mostly Somalis.[121]

---

[118] KRC DF/16/20: Anti-Smuggling Operation on 31 October 1978.
[119] Fraudulent dollars also crossed into Uganda: BoU G.184.75: Banking Department: General Manager to Governor, August 29, 1978.
[120] J.C., November 2016.
[121] One government report notes a violent incident with deaths and forty injured, leading to a ban on non-local residents. KRC AGB/1/127 Bungoma District Annual Report 1976. Another mentions the murder of a Somali woman trader and money-changer who had lived in the areas for twelve years. KRC DF/16/

In their place, the very same gerontocratic authority sidelined by magendo restored order. "The center of all the fighting was here, at this junction," I was told as we sat drinking soda overlooking the border river. "I remember two people who tried to stop the fighting: my late father and the late R.M. These ones carried spears, and held up spears." My friend adopted a look of stoic resolve and mimicked the act of holding a spear above his head, pointing straight up. "They were not scared of the stones being thrown in the middle. And it was stopped. So when the police came, everything was in control." His age-mate, sitting near us, chimed in, explaining that these men were highly respected elders: "They were the ones who kept the peace."[122] The police, failing to find anyone willing to testify, returned to their base and let the elders' solution suffice.

For others, it was not counterfeit money and the enfeebled local gerontocracy that ended magendo. Rather, it took the paternal authority of "the elder state" to bring arbitrage to heel: residents of Chepkube recall the death of Jomo Kenyatta and the assumption of Daniel arap Moi as the change that ended the trade.[123] "If Kenyatta could [still] be on the throne," said one former subchief, "I think things would continue because his own family were the ones here, they were having trucks here, buying." Nationally, Jomo Kenyatta and his family are remembered as acquisitive, even indulgent. This permissiveness is subtly contrasted with Moi, a well-known teetotaler and churchgoer, untempted by earthly pleasures.[124] By the time he was forced aside in 2002 after twenty-four years in power, Moi had solidified a reputation for authoritarian control that was presaged, frontier residents suggest, in his closure of arbitrage. For my interlocutors, Moi's rectitude in

---

20: "Murder Incident," from G.H. Mwangi, District Commissioner, Bungoma, September 20, 1977.

[122] J.C., November 2016.

[123] On the "elder state," see Paul Ocobock, *An Uncertain Age: The Politics of Manhood in Kenya* (Ohio University Press, 2017). Two Kenyan intellectuals with whom I spoke, however, disagree with Moi's role. Magendo, in their view, ended before Kenyatta's death, due to a combination of political machinations and economic changes (most notably the recovery of Brazilian coffee harvests). The archival record suggests it waxed and waned throughout the late 1970s and early 1980s, but the major coffee trade diminished by 1979.

[124] On Moi, including his "renowned sobriety," Gabrielle Lynch, *I Say to You: Ethnic Politics and the Kalenjin in Kenya* (University of Chicago Press, 2011). See also Keguro Macharia, "Loving Moi," Popula, https://popula.com/2018/08/20/loving-moi/.

moral matters is juxtaposed with the ethical ambiguities of magendo; the austerity of this famous arbiter of order stands against the exuberance of the period. It is his rule that serves to curtail the drunkenness, school-leaving, and disrespect for elders associated with magendo. The crack down on magendo also reflects the internecine struggle between elite Kenyan commercial and political interests: Moi's chief rival in the succession battle, Njoroge Mungai, in part financed his efforts through the export of Ugandan coffee. The undoing of those networks was part of a more general shift, after 1978, of economic power away from the Kenyatta circle towards Moi and his allies.[125]

Only with the change of power in Nairobi did a new Provincial Commissioner – a Born Again Christian from the Coast, I was told – arrive in Western Kenya. This man went to Lwakhakha, the small border post south of Chepkube, and found the iconic shop sign declaring *Mambo Bado* – *things are yet to come*. Ordering his officials to bring paint and rub off those optimistic words he scrawled a new slogan, *Mambo Kwisha* – *things are finished*! In this symbolic act, he concretized the closure of magendo, declaring an end to its open orientation to the future and consigning its extraordinary dynamics to the past.[126]

The government records from this time suggest the change in power did lead to more policing.[127] Officials were also concerned about the outflow of "essential commodities" to Uganda, as coffee smugglers bought sugar, salt, and other goods from Kenya before returning home.[128] Moreover, there was the risk of the "total collapse of the co-operatives" in Bungoma District, as Kenyans focused on brokering – not growing – coffee.[129] The Kenya Planters Cooperative Union was being starved of properly marketed coffee and raised the alarm that "the country was losing in terms of foreign exchange in that some of

---

[125] Daniel Branch, *Kenya: Between Hope and Despair, 1963–2012* (Yale University Press, 2013), pp. 121–139; Joseph Karimi and Philip Ochieng, *The Kenyatta Succession* (Transafrica, 1980).

[126] As a result of a Presidential order to stop smuggling, no shops or kiosks were allowed along the border except at authorized locations. KRC AUD/1/4: "Construction of Kiosks and Shops near Border Points," November 25, 1978.

[127] KRC DF/16/20: Anti-Smuggling Operation on 31 October 1978.

[128] KRC AUS/1/5: Provincial Price Control Office, Annual Report for 1978.

[129] Kenyan co-operatives also became the target of theft by those wishing to sell coffee in illegal channels. KRC DF/13/11: Bungoma District Annual Report, 1978.

5.4 Magendo and Moral Ambiguity

the coffee dealers did not deposit in Kenya their earnings."[130] Yet, stopping the trade was not easy. Kenyan police were often involved in magendo, finding their own constellation of interests with smugglers outside the law.[131]

For the residents I came to know, the sudden and conclusive end to the exceptional era was coupled with troubling afterlives. Residents note that as life returned to something like normalcy, there were effects that endured beyond *mambo kwisha*. One man laughed, explaining that people caught up on lost sleep and "became dormant."[132] They slowly returned to their neglected farms, but without access to durable stores of value or productive assets, "people became poor, or back to what they were before."[133] The market activity subsided – described by some as a "depression" – and, indeed, the number of trade and driving licenses fell as magendo subsided.[134] Outbreaks of cholera and tuberculosis are attributed to the cramped, unsanitary conditions of the time; others think venereal diseases and pregnancies increased as a result of promiscuity. Cattle rustling, too, grew into a significant problem. After magendo, "people had nothing. The younger ones ventured into stealing."[135] Guns, from Ugandan soldiers or purchased with coffee proceeds, heightened the danger of this activity. "First, people became poor. Then they started stealing."[136] Such competitive, zero-sum violence stands in stark contrast to the egalitarian, inclusive ethos of magendo.

---

[130] KRC HB/27/214: Minutes of the District Commissioners' Meeting, April 18, 1977. In reality, the export from Kenya of Ugandan coffee led to a surge in foreign exchange earnings.

[131] The new District Commissioner in Bungoma thought they needed to wipe the slate clean to remove the habits produced during the magendo era, telling his superior that because the police were used to getting bribes, they left the smugglers alone. He recommended all who served in the area since 1975 be transferred elsewhere. "There is no other way. They are used to heavy tipping and it has become a way of life as far as they are concerned." KRC DF/16/20: D.C. S.K. Tororey to Provincial Commissioner, "Smuggling," August 31, 1979.

[132] E.C., November 2016.   [133] C.S., November 2016.
[134] KRC B/16/125: Monthly Report, March 1979.   [135] J.C., November 2016.
[136] This claim is usually ethnicized, even if only implicitly, with Babukusu blaming Sabaot for cattle rustling. Kenyan officials also note an uptick in crime as "an after-effect of the coffee smuggling when people who were used to large sums of money in the illicit trade now turned to acts of thuggery to earn a living." KRC DF/13/10: Bungoma Annual Report, 1977.

Elsewhere, magendo profits were invested more productively. One intellectual and dissident during the Moi era told me that the magendo windfall capitalized a generation of Kenyan owned banks in the 1980s: it "got channeled into speculative economic sectors [like] banking, insurance," he said, naming two of Kenya's most prominent financiers in the 1980–1990s.[137] More prosaically, a former teacher told me of a visit once to Nairobi, where he came across warehouses named Chepkube. He thought,

"how is this name being used? We went into the details and we learned that the money they got from here they had invested in putting up storage houses in Nairobi. A few of us [from Chepkube], that knew the benefit of the money, they bought land in other places, they put up buildings in big town."[138]

But for those without the wherewithal to invest elsewhere, magendo "went like a dream."[139]

5.5 Conclusion

The government of value is nowhere a unitary project; when states have asserted a right to legitimately monopolize how value is defined and distributed, they have done so in a busy field characterized by competing and shifting ideas and protocols for production and circulation. One of the goals of this chapter is to better elaborate how some communities in East Africa have understood value. The Babukusu people who anchor this chapter had certain ideas and practices that arranged people and things according to what they deemed worthwhile and feasible. In their reckoning, the investment of time and energy in the cultivation of both crops and social relationships was both an ethical and material imperative. By no means was this unchanging nor was it consensual. It served certain interests better than others, and when new opportunities – waged labor in distant locales, or coffee arbitrage from Uganda – arrived, dissatisfaction with the hegemonic arrangements were revealed. Laborious, extended work was traded for quick rewards; the supervision and authority of senior men was subverted in favor of self-directed opportunities. Yet, by and large,

---

[137] A.O., October 2016. [138] C.S., November 2016.
[139] V.S., October 2016.

5.5 Conclusion

Babukusu shared a perception of how durable value was to be achieved in the foothills of Mount Elgon. It was this shared culture that was strained by the exuberance of magendo. The ethics, temporalities, and hierarchies of Chepkube's gerontocratic order saw their material bases erode: wealth was accessible without laborious production, marriages could occur without extensive contributions from kin, and social juniors could partake in typically senior behavior. Arbitrage is particularly apt to generate such conundrums for when it is pursued widely, it relies on a subversion of the orderly arrangement of people, timelines, appearances, and standards.

Nevertheless, those East Africans involved in magendo – whether in the case discussed here or elsewhere – also reflected an investment in ethical and material practices that were often at odds with states' interests and ideas about governing value. As I discussed earlier in the book, a constellation of interests did often align the productive activities of coffee farmers and marketing boards. Yet, providing for one's family and future was not always achievable through participation in the export earning regimes of postcolonial states. States demanded alternative ideas about commodification, work, and authority. Subsistence and smuggling provided two broadly available repertoires for escaping the state's monopoly on valuation, though in neither case was it an outright exit. Instead, what was more common is the partial disembedding and movement between economic jurisdictions, what I have termed arbitrage citizenship. Residents of the regional borderlands were especially well positioned to do so thanks to their histories of relatedness across difference. Shared rites, common vernaculars, and histories of intermarriage provided the basis for a pluralistic practice of belonging, not uniquely subordinated to the state.

Conclusion
A Neoliberal Government of Value

C.1 A Disappointed *Mwananchi*

One Saturday in early December 1978, a Kenyan man entered a shop in Wamono, not far from the Ugandan border. Noah Waliuba was shopping for salt in his area market. While conditions were nowhere near as dire as they were a few kilometers away in Uganda, many household commodities were not easy to come by in western Kenya, either. Goods like salt were being taken to Uganda, often by the same people who came across the border with coffee. Moreover, Kenyan shopkeepers were keen to sell to Ugandans, rather than their countrymen. Ugandans were desperate for essential commodities, and thanks to lucrative coffee smuggling, they also had enough cash to buy at inflated prices.

The result for men like Waliuba was deeply frustrating. As he put it at the end of that month in a letter to the District Commissioner in Bungoma, traders were "exploit[ing] the common man" by refusing to sell salt in the legally prescribed prices and amounts.[1] The trouble began when he entered the shop at plot No. 3, encountering a "small girl holding a child as well as selling or attending to customers." In reply to his request to purchase salt, the unnamed girl gestured to a bowl on the counter holding salt and some "vaseline tops," evidently intended to measure the commodity. Waliuba refused the offer and insisted he receive the usual form of salt: "a complete packet worth one (1/–)" shilling. His disagreement evidently attracted the shop owner, a Mr. Wekesa, who hurried over to reiterate that the salt was not being sold that way. "I told him," Waliuba wrote,

> that I wanted a packet and not in bits. He told me that I was not the right person to buy salt from his shop because he bought that salt to sell to people in bits. I asked him why I was not the right person and yet I am one of the customers.

---

[1] KRC HB/1/48: "Complaint Against Police and a Trader," December 21, 1978.

It initially seemed that his protest was effective for Wekesa handed over "a packet worth Shs. 1/–" and Waliuba offered a five shilling note in return. Yet, the buyer's satisfaction was short-lived, quickly souring to surprise and anger as the shopkeeper returned only Shs. 2/50 in change. "I asked him," Waliuba explained to the District Commissioner, "how much he was charging for the packet, [and] he replied that 'You have seen how much I have given you [in change, so] why should you ask'?"

Clearly incensed by this rhetorical question, Waliuba turned to a group of men sitting on the verandah, showing them the packet of salt he received despite being charged Shs. 2/50. Shouting that this was "magendo," Waliuba refused to let the matter go, despite the shopkeeper's offer to return his money and instead "sell his salt to other right people." Instead, the betrayed customer crossed the market to report the issue to Chief Wafula, who was standing outside another establishment with, it turned out, some plainclothes policemen. Taking them back to the shop, it was, in fact, the shopkeeper who cried foul, saying Waliuba "forced him to sell the salt otherwise he was not willing to do so." Mindful of the governmental rules about pricing, the Kenyan police wrote the shopkeeper a summons for "overcharging" and confiscated the salt as an exhibit.

Yet, if Waliuba expected justice, his faith was quickly disturbed. Shortly after sunset that same day, the victimized consumer began hearing "rumours from people on the same market" that the case was already closed. When he went to investigate the next day, Chief Wafula professed ignorance but promised to follow up on these rumours. Not content to wait and see, the aggrieved Waliuba travelled to the police station, more than 15 kilometers away. There, his troubles only deepened, as he learned the case was never registered with the station (as was official practice). Facing a bureaucratic wall of inaction, Waliuba did not return home quietly. For one, neither his salt nor his Shs. 2/50 had been returned to him. Moreover, these actions offended his own sensibilities as well as the highest orders of the land. As he told the District Commissioner, "overcharging cases in North Malakisi Location and in magendo way are alarming despite our beloved President of the Republic of Kenya calling to stamp out magendo." It was evident to Waliuba that "people in authority" are "encouraging Traders" to continue this illegal trade. His petition requested an end to this and assistance in recovering his salt or money.

The issues offending Waliuba were multiple, from the proper enforcement of the law to the degradation of national morality. Yet, the lens through which these were experienced was the framework of price. For the shopkeeper, price was mutable, a number set in relationship not only to official guidelines but also the opportunities from arbitrage across the Uganda–Kenya border. For Waliuba, this gap between the official precepts of valuation and the shopkeeper's practices was untoward, a clear offense against both law and morality. It was, ultimately, a matter of political significance, and he did not hesitate to call upon the state's own rhetoric and coercive powers to enforce a particular economic ethic. In his view, the pluralization of affiliation and loyalty emblematic of – but not confined to – borderlands were problems to be solved. Yet, it is clear that for others, such economic variation was itself the basis for virtue: getting a better price for salt could be the means to marry, build a home, educate children, and repay social obligations.

As discussed throughout this book, the question of price was not a concern for Noah Waliuba alone. Colonial officials regulated weights and measures; their price inspectors rooted around in African markets, complaining to supervisors that over-charging and mis-measurement were "worse than it could [possibly] be explained."[2] The prices paid for agricultural produce were long-running sources of disquiet, argument, and struggle in East Africa. By the postwar years, colonial administrators were fixing prices for key export commodities. They lamented that "[t]he African market does not in fact have one market price but several" and resolved to "eliminate variations [through] strict control."[3] Their postcolonial successors adopted similar ideologies and practices, as many citizens expected them to. How exactly goods would be priced – what protocols and ethics of valuation would be applied – were the concerns of statecraft and citizenship. This included the exchange rate for currencies and the cost of corporate compensation, as well as much more. Fed up with shortages, by the 1980s Tanzanians cynically spoke of "party prices" to name black market prices, thereby blaming the party-state for their role in spurring the

---

[2] TNA Box 30 File 9, 15/2 Moshi Price Control: Assistant Price Inspector to Director of Economic Control, Tanganyika, August 3, 1948.

[3] BoE OV7/82: "The Problems of Price Collection in African Markets," by L.W. Clarke, Nairobi, June 20, 1955.

criminalized economy.[4] In Kenya and Uganda, too, valuation elicited such interest because it merged the moral and the commercial, the political and the economic, the individual and the collective.

While the government of value worked best when interests were, more or less, aligned, it was never purely a consensual project of collective prosperity. Interests, after all, may be the result of limited alternatives. Even in its most agreeable registers, a monopoly on valuation favored certain regions and populations while requiring the subordination and marginalization of others. For a monopoly on valuation to cohere, it had to be legitimate in the eyes of many distinct audiences. Never, in other words, was the question of price merely a question of number. The problematic of price was, instead, a constellation of concerns over the relationship between people and things, the distribution of respect and resources, and relations of command and autonomy.[5] The value assigned to a commodity implicated far more than a single transaction; it implicated values as frameworks of legitimacy. For instance, among other things, the price of coffee beans tied together domestic political considerations, expectations about gendered farm labor, and the preferences of European consumers. For its part, the purchase of salt had ramifications for one's standing as a provider of family nutrition and a respectable host – not to mention the taste of one's evening meal.

Waliuba signed his letter to the District Commissioner as a "disappointed *mwananchi*," using a Swahili term most often translated as "citizen" (pl. *wananchi*). However, the word has an affective salience that is only partially captured in the legal-political register of this English language equivalent. As Emma Hunter writes in her discussion of the term in Tanzania, "The figure of the *mwananchi* was a moral construction as much as a political one."[6] In contrast to more neutral language, Tanzanians used *mwananchi* (literally, "son of the country") to invoke a "patriotic citizenship." It was linked to a notion of nation-building, in which all were called by the party-state to

---

[4] Brian van Arkadie, "Economic Strategy and Structural Adjustment in Tanzania," PSD Occasional Paper No. 18 (World Bank, 1995), p. 19.
[5] Jane Guyer, *Legacies, Logics, Logistics: Essays in the Anthropology of the Platform Economy* (University of Chicago Press, 2016), chapter 10.
[6] Emma Hunter, *Political Thought and the Public Sphere in Tanzania: Freedom, Democracy and Citizenship in the Era of Decolonization* (Cambridge University Press, 2015), pp. 194–195.

contribute.[7] In Kenya, "*wananchi*" was often deployed as a critique of the state and elites connected to it. As an idiom it positioned the "common man" or "the people" against the wealthy and politicians (who were often the same): when dissident politicians formed the Kenyan People's Union in 1966 to challenge the ruling party, they did so through the issuance of the *Wananchi Declaration*. Their proviso condemned the way President Jomo Kenyatta and his circle were adopting the expensive indulgences of the former colonial power and overseeing an economy that continued to marginalize ordinary people. For farmers, workers, and students, too, identification with *wananchi* provided a rhetorical wedge between the masses and the elite.[8]

However, an oppositional discourse is not necessarily a position of outright rejection. When Noah Waliuba called himself a "disappointed *mwananchi*" he was calling the state to account, not repudiating it. He was demanding it fulfill its duties toward citizens, as well as the hopes he and others had invested in the government of value. His disappointment stemmed from not merely the gap between pricing policy and practice. It also arose from the historical investment of ordinary people and the state alike in a project of making production, trade, and consumption function anew. This was a hope born of colonial subjection, popular struggle, and political promises. It was

---

[7] This had a complicated relationship to (in)equality: in everyday address it could perform a classless egalitarianism, but in practice new hierarchies emerged in the independence years, not least as TANU deployed the term. In addition, the idiom came to have racialized connotations. Carol M. M. Scotton, "Some Swahili Political Words," *Journal of Modern African Studies* 3(4) (1965): 531–533; Emma Hunter, "Dutiful Subjects, Patriotic Citizens, and the Concept of 'Good Citizenship' in Twentieth-Century Tanzania," *The Historical Journal* 56(1) (2013): 247–277.

[8] Indeed, it is still used that way, incorporated into otherwise English-language texts due to the affective significance of the Swahili term. Patrick Gathara, for instance, contrasts *wananchi* with *wenyenchi* (itself a term that could be translated as "citizens" or "countrymen" but in the context is better understood to reflect a valance closer to "owners of the country"): "This state, which preys on wananchi for the benefit of wenyenchi, has not been fundamentally reformed since independence." Patrick Gathara, "Abusive Governing Elites," *The Star*, April 1, 2016, www.the-star.co.ke/opinion/columnists/2016-04-01-abusive-governing-elites/. A feminine – and ethnicized – equivalent to "common man," *wanjiku*, is of a more recent vintage in Kenya. In Uganda, the idiom of "common man" circulated among non-elites and in Obote's ideological project. On the latter, see James Mittelman, *Ideology and Politics in Uganda from Obote to Amin* (Cornell University Press, 1975).

also born of the institutional and infrastructural legacies that made a monopoly on the valuation of key commodities seem both sensible and feasible to mid-century East Africans. And, yet, in his disappointment, Waliuba confronted alternative ideas and practices about how value might be assigned: whether through ever-more subdivided "bits" of salt, or through deals with police under cover of darkness. Shouting to passersby that "magendo" was taking place, hailing the nearby chief, or petitioning the District Commissioner were means of containing these alternatives, but they were hardly guaranteed success in the fractured and shifting ground of governing value in late-1970s East Africa. The intransigent alternative valuation practices that Waliuba decried were not routed through the official protocols of the state, nor were they legitimated in the idiom of citizenship. As a result, a disappointed *mwananchi* was emblematic of something broader: the disappointment of economic sovereignty and citizenship.

C.2 Making Economies after Empire

While decolonization has most often been understood as principally a political occurrence, it was nowhere disconnected from questions of production, exchange, and consumption. The production of new sorts of people and identities – namely, citizens – was thoroughly entangled with the production of things. In other words, it is at best misleading to claim, as Mamdani does, that "The first question at independence is not 'how do we distribute wealth?' but 'who belongs?'"[9] To assert the primacy of something called "the political" is to follow the abstractions of liberal ideas.[10] Rather than categorically distinct, the political, the economic, and the sociocultural are an integrated terrain of contestation.[11]

As a result, in East Africa, decolonization unfolded through institutions and ideologies that used political independence as a fulcrum for more thoroughgoing changes in who would determine how wealth would be produced and managed. The government of value was, in part, an inheritance from British administration but it also reflected the

---

[9] Mahmood Mamdani, *Neither Settlers nor Native: The Making and Unmaking of Permanent Minorities* (Harvard University Press, 2020), p. 34.
[10] Ellen Meiksins Wood, "The Separation of the Economic and the Political in Capitalism," *New Left Review* I(127) (1981): 77.
[11] Terence Turner, "Marxian Value Theory: An anthropological perspective," *Anthropological Theory* 8(1) (2008): 43–56.

imposition of the Bretton Woods system and African aspirations for development and well-being. I have focused especially on the role of central banks, national currencies, and savings and loans. These monetary infrastructures promised to channel resources to productive enclaves and corridors, but they would do so by consolidating foreign monies within their control. The collection of cash savings, the sale of financial instruments, and the export of crops worked to build a store of foreign value that could be leveraged to maintain and expand national wealth. The immobilization of foreign reserves was deemed necessary for wider progress, and it was part of an effort to escape the short-term seasonality of East African finances in favor of more reliable medium-term futures.[12] These financial instruments also promised to remake the sorts of people who populated East Africa, aligning citizens' personal interests toward the collective. They were intended to reorganize the geography of belonging, with loyalties directed toward national governments, rather than transnational transactional territories. The postcolonial states would govern authoritatively, but not through cultural or juridical power alone; rather, the desires and interests of citizens – for credit, for accumulation, for status – were routed through economic institutions and infrastructures. Marketing boards, national currencies, and state banks were formative of statecraft. As the Central Bank of Kenya's first governor put it after ten years at the helm, "Kenya moved into independence with people, and hope, but little foreign exchange."[13] Those residents unable to squeeze a bit more export value from the soil, or unwilling to transfer their wealth to the stewardship of the nation-state, were abandoned, demeaned, or coerced.

This was, at best, a paradoxical form of self-determination, as the inequities at home had their correlate in the enduring international power of Euro-American monies. Long after formal independence, decisions taken at the Bank of England could encourage the mass export of East African money, with little African states could do to impede currency smuggling.[14] If a national currency became the

---

[12] In this way, a national currency is akin to large infrastructures projecting a future. Timothy Mitchell, "Infrastructures Work on Time," *E-Flux* (January 2020).

[13] Duncan Ndegwa, *The Kenya Shilling: Within and Across the Frontiers* (Nairobi, 1977), p. 9.

[14] For instance, the devaluation of sterling in 1967 increased the arbitrage earnings for currency smugglers, with suitcases full of Kenyan shillings making their way to British banks. KNA AE/12/1: Devaluation of Sterling, May 5, 1968. More generally, see KNA ACW/1/589: Exchange Control Investigations 1970–76.

cornerstone for postcolonial polities, it was a foundation haunted by the importance of foreign trade and currency, as well as the firms that dominated them. Postcolonial states and their central banks were deeply constrained in their ability to change expatriate banks' prices and procedures, and nationalization occurred when ambitions pursued through less dramatic means were frustrated.[15] The lexicon of "sovereignty," "self-determination," and "self-reliance" may suggest independence, even isolation, but in practice the project could never be one of autarky. Across the twentieth century – whether it be the Soviets or black radicals, Nehru or Nyerere – self-determination was always concerned with remaking and managing interdependencies (unequal as they may be), not severing connections.[16]

Paths not taken – such as East African Federation – might have resulted in different formations. For one, if the common currency was maintained and initial plans for uniform crop marketing rules across the region were enacted, some of the arbitrage across the borders of Tanzania, Kenya, and Uganda would have diminished. The economic rationale for federation – namely that a larger market and shared infrastructures would further development – may have provided a larger internal market and more substantial resources; yet, it likely would have also exasperated the inequalities within the region.[17] The inequalities and divergent loyalties in the region would require careful and responsive management, both from politicians in a federal capital and the technocrats in an East African central bank. The risk, of course, is that a larger polity would be unable to rise to the occasion. And insofar as the goal would be to continue redirecting the commercial value produced by farmers – many of them women who

---

[15] DCO 11/2451: Minutes of Meeting of the Uganda Bankers Association, September 24, 1968.
[16] Even during the height of what was called Soviet economic isolation, the accumulation of "hard currency" was an essential of the Stalinist state. Elena Osokina, *Stalin's Quest for Gold: The Torgsin Hard-Currency Shops and Soviet Industrialization* (Cornell University Press, 2021). Others recent work emphasizing the interconnections of the USSR include Elizabeth Banks, Robyn d'Avignon, and Asif Siddiqi, "The African-Soviet Modern," *Comparative Studies of South Asia, Africa & the Middle East* 41(1) (2021): 2–10; Oscar Sanchez-Sibony, "Capitalism's Fellow Traveller," *Comparative Studies in Society & History* 56(2) (2014): 290–319. On African American cooperative economies, see Jessica Gordon Nembhard, *Collective Courage: A History of African American Cooperative Economic Thought and Practice* (Penn State University Press, 2014).
[17] TNA Acc.469: CIC 9/023 "The Economics of East African Federation, 1963."

were simultaneously tasked with domestic care and subsistence production – the alternative futures would offer little solace.

A focus on these alternatives should not occlude the meaningful successes from the perspectives of the time. Tanzania had substantial gains in literacy, life expectancy, real incomes, and other measures between 1961–1977.[18] Each of the countries experienced periods of meaningful economic growth.[19] These depended on several trends, not least of which was the calibrated interplay between export crops, domestic currencies, and foreign capital.[20] Yet, at the end of the 1970s, the ability of East African states to monopolize the valuation of key goods like foreign exchange or coffee was severely limited. The obstacles arose from multiple sources. Bureaucrats misused or mismanaged the official channels. Citizens found that official protocols no longer aligned with their own interests and ethics. As they activated alternative circuits of trade and affiliation to diversify away from a reliance on state channels, it furthered the troubles facing states.

At the core of their dilemma, though, was the lack of control over key prices. Declining terms of trade, the shock of the energy crisis, and the end of the gold standard placed East Africa under extraordinary economic pressure. In the mid-1950s, coffee was second only to petroleum in terms of its value as an international commodity; subsequent decades, though, saw global competition and overproduction undermine the prices paid to East Africans.[21] Important export goods also declined in their relative value: in 1965, for instance, 17.25 tons of sisal could purchase a tractor; a decade later, it took nearly 66 tons to do

---

[18] *Basic Needs in Danger* (International Labor Organization, 1982), quoted in Reginald Green, "The Economics of Disintegration: Tanzania, 1982–83" (1983), https://opendocs.ids.ac.uk/opendocs/handle/20.500.12413/4775.

[19] Morton Jerven, *Economic Growth and Measurement Reconsidered* (Oxford University Press, 2014).

[20] In his own reflections on the ten years after the Arusha Declaration, Julius Nyerere acknowledged the mix results of African socialism and self-reliance. But "without hesitation" he thought the nationalisation of the banks maintained Tanzania's wealth within its borders. Between 1967–76, he reported that the National Bank of Commerce had a net profit of TSh. 557.3 million, even after paying compensation to the nationalised firms. "A 'mrija', through which our little wealth was being sucked, has been cut," he wrote, using the emotive language of elites using a 'straw' to drain collective vitality. Julius K. Nyerere, *The Arusha Declaration: Ten Years After* (Government of Tanzania, 1977): 7–8.

[21] J. W. F. Rowe, *The World's Coffee* (Her Majesty's Stationery Office, 1963), p. 19.

C.2 Making Economies after Empire 313

the same.[22] Other critical goods responded to pricing power from outside of East Africa altogether: with the geopolitical realignment of oil producing states in the 1970s, energy prices spiked across Kenya, Tanzania, and Uganda. The cost of borrowing money also skyrocketed after the United States abandoned the gold standard. The effect on foreign reserve holdings could be catastrophic; Tanzania was successfully adding to its foreign exchange reserves in the years before 1973: an 80 percent increase in 1972 and another 30 percent more in 1973. However, "[t]hese reserves melted away almost overnight" thanks to decisions taken in Washington, DC.[23] Stalled production and global inflation only further subjected East Africans to prices over which they had little power. In the next decade, shortages of foreign exchange would depress by around half what manufacturing output Tanzania did have.[24] Even in good years, the lack of power over crucial prices meant East Africans had difficulty planning ahead.

In other words, if the government of value tried to turn political sovereignty into the power to shape prices, by the end of the 1970s, it was very clear that in many ways the region was a price taker – a form of political and economic subordination but there was some scope for maneuver. Tanzania, for instance, reached barter agreements with sympathetic countries to exchange oil and other commodities for Tanzanian agriculture.[25] Such barter limited the immaterial but objective power of capitalist markets by incorporating transnational solidarities and political negotiations.

There was also some effort to reform international exchange so that postcolonial states were not subordinated to valuations from abroad over which they had little control. Commitment was not uniform across the region. Uganda's turmoil provided little space for international involvement. The long-serving boss of the Central Bank of Kenya did think the IMF was unsuitable and saw an "urgent need for a new international monetary order," but other state elites had little appetite for challenging the status quo.[26] In contrast, Tanzanian officials were

---

[22] Joshua Grace, *African Motors: Technology, Gender, and the History of Development* (Duke University Press, 2021), p. 226.
[23] Michael Lofchie, "Agrarian Crisis and Economic Liberalisation in Tanzania," *Journal of Modern African Studies* 16(3) (1978): 454–455. Critical perspectives within the government are given in AR/MISR/156/7: "Recent Trends in the Tanzanian Economy and the Alternatives Before Us" (1975).
[24] Reginald Green, "The Economics of Disintegration: Tanzania, 1982–83" (1983), p. 1, https://opendocs.ids.ac.uk/opendocs/handle/20.500.12413/4775.
[25] Grace, *African Motors*, p. 217.   [26] Ndegwa, *The Kenya Shilling*, p. 23.

often at the forefront of these movements. As discussed in Chapter 3, the New International Economic Order (NIEO) was an energetic series of demands that key economic channels were governed in ways that were not to the detriment of postcolonial states. In addition to calling for reforms to trade regimes, national resource sovereignty, and the transfer of technology, the 1974 Program of Action ratified by the UN General Assembly made clear the importance of monetary matters. It called for international measures to limit debt burdens, as well as check inflation and exchange rate depreciations that were eroding the laboriously accumulated foreign reserves of developing countries.[27]

In the ensuing years, though, the troubles only multiplied. In response, Julius Nyerere and Michael Manley, Jamaica's Prime Minister, convened a 1980 conference on the "International Monetary System and the New International Order." With support from Swedish and other donors, the meeting brought together forty participants from around the world for four days of reflection and planning, including discussions of Jamaica and Tanzania's recent experiences negotiating with the International Monetary Fund (IMF). Among the participants were the economists and policy advisors Norman Girvan (of Jamaica), Justinian Rweyemamu (of Tanzania), and Ismail-Sabri Abdalla (of Egypt). They provided detailed assessments of the current international monetary regime, the place of poor countries within it, and how it might be reformed.

The result was the Arusha Initiative, which called for a new international monetary order to replace the "broken down" Bretton Woods system inaugurated in 1944.[28] Whatever the strengths and weaknesses of that earlier model, it now lay in ruins, and the ad hoc jumble that succeeded it was characterized by "inflationary and speculative disorders."[29] The Arusha Initiative's founding declaration decried the conditions demanded by the IMF, dismissing the institution's claims to scientific objectivity and neutrality as misguided and impotent in the face of global capitalism. For Rweyemamu, the trouble was that a better "international money constitute[d] an international 'collective good'" but there was currently a lack of institutional architecture to support it. What was needed was a "world central bank" to "issue legitimate

---

[27] *Programme of Action on the Establishment of a New International Economic Order* (UN General Assembly, 1974).
[28] "Editorial Note," *Development Dialogue* (2) (1980): 3.
[29] "The Arusha Initiative: A Call for a United Nations Conference on International Money and Finance," *Development Dialogue*(2) (1980): 11.

international money." This new entity would be responsible to all national central banks and their citizens, unlike the international financial institutions that currently played the role of lender of last resort. In his view, such a system could provide better purchasing power and stability to all countries, as well as inducing harmony between national economies.[30] It would, in other words, provide for a constellation of interests among countries. Yet, both the economists and politicians involved in the Arusha Initiative recognized the enormity of the task at hand: while a more equitable and stable global government of value may have been possible, the current system was not to everyone's detriment. The prevailing "monetary disorder," the resolution argued, "serves those very institutions – the transnational enterprises and banks – which have dominated monetary reform efforts since the demise of the Bretton Woods system."[31] They had no doubt that meaningful reform – the sort which permit a modicum of self-determination in the Third World – was a political as much as an economic challenge.

C.3 A Neoliberal Government of Value: "Getting the Prices Right"

The Arusha Initiative is emblematic of political and economic reasoning that became increasingly rare in the decade that followed. Rather than muting the power of the IMF or changing its purpose, the use of international financial levers to compel postcolonial states only increased. The role of the IMF grew, as did the breadth of conditions attached to its emergency financial support. Julius Nyerere famously resisted the demands of the Bretton Woods institutions, decrying "IMF meddling" in Tanzania's "price control machinery."[32] He clashed with Edwin Mtei, the founding boss of the Bank of Tanzania, who made clear his allegiances to more orthodox monetary management as early as 1967.[33] The disagreements were multiple, but preeminent was the government's monopoly on the valuation of its currency. The IMF demanded the Bank of Tanzania further reduce its fixed exchange rate, believing it would make exports more

---

[30] Justinian Rweyemamu, "Restructuring the International Monetary System," *Development Dialogue*(2) (1980): 75–91.
[31] "The Arusha Initiative," pp. 15–16.
[32] Julius Nyerere, "No to IMF Meddling," *Development Dialogue* (2) (1980): 7–8.
[33] Issa Shivji, *Julius Nyerere: Development as Rebellion*, vol. 3 (Mkuki na Nyota, 2020), pp. 276–293.

competitive. Nyerere thought this a short-sighted, even cruel, condition for budget support. As Mtei recalls, the President told him "I will devalue the shilling over my dead body."[34] Perhaps no statement better encapsulates the importance of the moneychanger state to postcolonial sovereignty, and perhaps no fact so neatly captures the decline of that model as Nyerere's resignation in 1985 as he found it impossible to continue his resistance.[35]

The detailed histories of structural adjustment and neoliberalism remain to be written for East Africa but in Uganda and Kenya, too, this period inaugurated a profound transformation in how value was governed. Very often, the target of structural reforms were precisely those goods previously subject to a monopoly of valuation by postcolonial states. In the decade after 1985, the Tanzanian currency fell from 17 to over 520 per dollar.[36] In Kenya, agreements with foreign financiers in the 1980s committed the government to devalue the currency, reduce bank lending, and increase the prices offered to farmers.[37] The Moi government, however, equivocated and it was only after a crescendo of financial and political crises that economic liberalization gathered speed in 1992. Import licenses and price controls were eliminated, currency controls removed, and privatization begun.

In Uganda, after returning to government office following Amin's ouster, Jack Ssentongo upbraided Bank of Uganda management in mid-1979: "He charged that several millionaires were created directly through the allocation of foreign exchange when the majority of Ugandans were suffering in the villages." Turning Uganda around would require not only their honesty but also convincing the public

---

[34] Paul Bjerk, "A Preliminary History of the Bank of Tanzania," in Salvatory S. Nyanto (ed.) *A History of Post-Colonial Tanzania: Essays in Honor of Prof. Isaria N. Kimambo* (James Currey, forthcoming). Additional complexities facing the moneychanger state in the 1970s are in TNA Acc.600 FA/A/30/22 Exchange Control 1965–79.

[35] It is notable that when the CFA was massively devalued in 1994 the French authorities did so against the strenuous demands of African leadership. Fanny Pigeaud and Ndongo Samba Sylla, *Africa's Last Colonial Currency: The CFA Franc Story* (Pluto Press, 2021), pp. 67–71.

[36] Tony Waters, "Beyond Structural Adjustment: State and Market in a Rural Tanzanian Village," *African Studies Review* 40(2) (1997): 59.

[37] Maria Nzomo, "Democracy, Gender, Equity, and Development in Africa, with Special Reference to Kenya," in J. Nyang'oro and T. Shaw (eds.), *Beyond Structural Adjustment in Africa* (Praeger Publishers, 1992), pp. 99–119.

of the central bank's honesty.[38] Such a task would have to wait as political strife meant it was only after the National Resistance Movement seized power in 1986 that international institutions had a viable interlocutor. Yet, the pressure they placed on the NRM government was only effective with time. In part, this reflected the ideological opposition of key NRM officeholders; in part, it reflected the institutional disarray that confronted the new administration. For instance, when the economist Ezra Sabiti Suruma returned from an academic job in the United States to become the Bank of Uganda's new director of research, he was shocked at the lack of "accountability and very weak managerial capacity" in the central bank. For the first half of 1987, Suruma was holed up in the Nile Mansion Hotel, often "bewildered and helpless" in the face of foreign exchange shortages and excess money supply. The major banks were insolvent and inflation approached 350 percent. While he worked closely with World Bank and IMF teams to reform the Bank of Uganda's internal systems and dispense emergency balance of payments support, superiors in the government resisted the considerable pressure to liberalize the exchange rate. NRM officials thought that "if it allowed the population to hold foreign currencies, the government would go broke." Only in 1990 did the IMF prevail as the Exchange Control Act of 1964 was repealed and private foreign exchange bureaus took over the central bank's erstwhile role in the moneychanger state.[39]

In other words, the controlled conversion of the moneychanger state was successively delegated to market exchange. But just as the postcolonial government of value relied on more than currency controls, so too did neoliberalism take aim at more than foreign exchange regimes. Two elements are worth emphasizing. First is that neoliberalism was not an epochal rupture, nor a unidirectional shift from state control to market society. Structural adjustment did not emerge fully formed; rather, it unfolded in fits and starts, contested by both popular and

---

[38] The Deputy Governor disagreed, saying that foreign exchange allocation had been removed from their power and given over to a Cabinet Sub-Committee during Amin's later years. BoU GOV.305.3, Memorandum, BOU00197, Management Meetings, 1979: Address by A.J.P.M. Ssentongo, July 4, 1979.
[39] Ezra Sabiti Suruma, *Advancing the Ugandan Economy: A Personal Account* (Brookings Institution Press, 2014).

elite interests and expectations.[40] Second is that this was as much a matter of ideas as it was a shift in practice. While the subversion of a state monopoly on valuation was common enough in the prior decades, the 1980s marked a significant transformation in ideas about how value *should* be governed. As I have argued in the prior chapters, and as Noah Waliuba's petition reiterates, even when official command over value was limited in practice, there were prevailing ideas about what role the government should have in financing, marketing, and pricing. Shopkeepers subdividing salt and overcharging for goods reflected widespread practices, but they lacked much in the way of justification that could be voiced, let alone accepted as legitimate. What neoliberalism did, in part, was change the languages, ideas, and expectations about how value would be legitimately governed.

Neoliberal advocates did so, by promulgating a different theory of what constitutes a legitimate basis for valuation. Neoliberalism began as an intellectual movement committed to protecting private property and capital from the perceived predations of governments. Government responsiveness to citizens' redistributive demands were especially feared. Decolonization multiplied the number of sovereign states who might interfere with capitalist markets; it also diversified the ideological field in which ideas about exchange, redistribution, and property were debated. In response, neoliberal policy entrepreneurs turned to international law and conservative constitutionalism that would insulate markets from redistributive claims-making.[41]

The neoliberal vision was shaped by a theory of valuation that was equally moral and material. For Friedrich Hayek, the proper establishment of prices was essential not only to economic flourishing but to political freedom. He viewed with antipathy social democratic and socialist economic planners who marshalled national accounting

---

[40] In some of its original formulations, "structural adjustment" was in fact a demand of lower income countries; only subsequently were the language and some of the techniques appropriated by what Johanna Bockman calls a "capitalist counterrevolution." "The Struggle over Structural Adjustment: Socialist Revolution versus Capitalist Counterrevolution in Yugoslavia and the World," *History of Political Economy* 51(S1) (2019): 254–276.

[41] Quinn Slobodian, *Globalists: The End of Empire and the Birth of Neoliberalism* (Harvard University Press, 2018); Philip Mirowski, "Defining Neoliberalism," in Philip Mirowski and Dieter Plehwe (eds.), *The Road from Mont Pèlerin: The Making of the Neoliberal Thought Collective* (Harvard University Press, 2015).

C.3 Neoliberal Government of Value

statistics, advances in computing, and regulatory institutions to manage or replace markets. In his view, this was ultimately based on a "pretence of knowledge" – namely that government plans could gather and organize enough information to properly govern production and distribution.[42] He influentially developed an argument that the only virtuous means for establishing the worth of something was through the unplanned interaction between competing firms setting prices and private buyers agreeing to that valuation. "Prices," in this view, were "signals" that conveyed the value of a good and the values of people who paid for that good. In Hayek's articulation, markets coordinated dispersed pockets of knowledge that were discovered and sorted in ways no planner could ever possibly achieve. Rather than states governing prices, prices should govern people. As he put it in one interview, "The function of prices is to tell people what they ought to do."[43] In this approach, prices were signals that communicated where investments should be made, what work should be done, and what goods should be purchased. If planners set prices – with whatever purpose – it impeded the ability of private entrepreneurs and buyers from establishing how to allocate capital and direct labor. The combination of communication and command that prices represented for Hayek was constantly under threat from those who would use the instruments of statecraft to subsidize, inflate, or otherwise recast the value of things.

It is this intellectual artifice that accounts for the rhetorical proviso of structural adjustment: "get the prices right." By the 1980s, "price" took on a mythological role within the World Bank and IMF. Scholars often point to the 1981 Berg Report as a turning point. It targeted domestic policies, calling for currency devaluation, reduction in urban wages, and the liberalization of trade regimes to boost export competitiveness.[44] Yet, the neoliberal government of value did not arrive overnight. It was the 1983 *World Development Report*, a World Bank document, that sedimented the official ideology for much of what was to come. Produced under the close supervision of the neoliberal economist Anne Krueger, the program it outlined was based on the

---

[42] Friedrich von Hayek, "The Pretence of Knowledge," Lecture to the memory of Alfred Nobel, 1974.
[43] Quoted in Slobodian, *Globalists*, p. 233.
[44] John Loxley, "The Berg Report and the Model of Accumulation in Sub-Saharan Africa," *Review of African Political Economy* 27/28 (1983): 197–204.

Hayekian theory in which "price distortions" from government regulations interfered with the proper value of things.[45] In this view, African policymakers systematically manipulated the prices of currency, credit, crops, and other commodities in ways that exacerbated rural poverty, undermined productivity, and stymied economic growth.

Critiques of government involvement were not new. On the left, Giovanni Arrighi and John Saul warned against postcolonial elite profligacy that came at the expense of rural producers, but worried that a different model was constrained by global capitalist dynamics.[46] On the right, P. T. Bauer argued against state marketing boards since the late colonial period.[47] Already by 1975, the World Bank was using its influence in Kenya to "strongly favor incentives, particularly price signals, as the appropriate means for regulating the behavior of the private sector." It argued Kenya lacked the sort of "honest, sensitive, flexible bureaucracy" necessary for anything but governing through "the price system."[48]

Over the course of the next decade, crisis and capitalist reaction allowed these ideas to gain traction. Deepak Lal, for instance, published an influential jeremiad against development planning and price controls in 1983 under the auspices of England's neoliberal think tank, the Institute of Economic Affairs. Like Bauer, Lal participated in the conclaves organized by Hayek and his circle, and proper pricing protocols were at the core of his argument.[49] As he put it, citing Hayek, economic planning "throws sand into one of the most useful ...

---

[45] Howard Stein, *Beyond the World Bank Agenda: An Institutional Approach to Development* (University of Chicago Press, 2008).

[46] Giovanni Arrighi and John Saul, *Essays on the Political Economy of Africa* (Monthly Review Press, 1973). Reginald Green, the Tanzanian government financial advisor, was also alert to the "unfortunate" "tendency of most [currency] control systems ... to multiply over time, creating cumbersome, overlapping, and self-contradictory mazes riddled with loopholes." "Political Independence and the National Economy: An Essay in the Political Economy of Decolonisation," in Christopher Allen and R. W. Johnson (eds.), *African Perspectives* (Cambridge University Press, 1970), p. 303.

[47] P. T. Bauer, *West African Trade: A Study of Competition, Oligopoly, and Monopoly in a Changing Economy* (Cambridge University Press, 1954).

[48] *Kenya: Into the Second Decade* (World Bank, 1975), p. xiii; 264–292.

[49] Dieter Plehwe, "The Origins of the Neoliberal Economic Development Discourse," in Mirowski and Plehwe, *The Road from Mont Pèlerin*.

C.3 Neoliberal Government of Value

mechanisms for transmitting information, as well as for coordinating the actions of a myriad of interdependent market participants."[50]

By the 1980s, among the most influential voices in development policy circles were Michael Lipton and Robert Bates.[51] Lipton was the progenitor of "urban bias" theory that posited postcolonial states extracted from rural producers to the benefit of urban consumers.[52] Drawing mostly on research in India, Lipton advocated policies – such as overvalued currencies and government marketing boards – that he saw as unfairly exploiting rural people. He downplayed conflict between labor and capital, or between foreign and national interests, to point the finger at a conflict between rural and urban interests.

Bates further popularized this theory, especially through his work on African economies. He argued that political decisions about marketing boards, currency controls, and related institutions suppressed the prices farmers received and, therefore, the amount of agricultural output they produced.[53] What Bates called the "price-setting game" played by African bureaucrats was at the root of the continent's deteriorating fortunes.[54] They underpaid farmers and expanded parastatal organization because, this theory argued, it was politically worthwhile to intervene on behalf of urban residents who would otherwise pose a risk to the continued power of a ruling government. By influencing the price of key commodities, African policymakers muddied the waters of efficient capital and labor allocation.

The neoliberal ideas moved between books and reports, loan conditions and policy statements. Advocates like Bates stepped out of the classroom as consultants who, for instance, provided guidance on how

---

[50] Deepak Lal, *The Poverty of "Development Economics"*, 2nd ed. (Institute for Economic Affairs, 1997), p. 132.
[51] See the discussion in Gareth Jones and Stuart Corbridge, "The Continuing Debate about Urban Bias," *Progress in Development Studies* 10(1) (2010): 1–18.
[52] Michael Lipton, *Why Poor People Stay Poor: A Study of Urban Bias in World Development* (Temple Smith, 1977).
[53] Howard Stein and Ernest Wilson, "The Political Economy of Robert Bates: A Critical Reading of Rational Choice in Africa," *World Development* 21(6) (1993): 1035–1053.
[54] Robert Bates, *Markets and States in Tropical Africa: The Political Basis of Agricultural Policies* (University of California Press, 1981).

to decentralize the coffee industry in Uganda.[55] At the World Bank, Anne Krueger directed a five-volume study of 18 countries' agricultural policies to further bolster the neoliberal case. As its adherents captured the reins of power in not only the World Bank and IMF, but also government in Britain, the United States, and Germany, the ideas were coupled with geopolitical and financial muscle. In the case of Tanzania, the connection was explicit: shortly after Ronald Reagan was elected, the U.S. government sent Nyerere a copy of Milton Friedman's coauthored *Free to Choose*.[56] The structural adjustment loans that followed tried to undo the institutions that obscured the supposedly "proper" value of things, including removing subsidies, lowering barriers to trade, liberalizing exchange rates, and purging price controls. Six African countries, including Kenya, received a version of structural adjustment lending between 1980–1983, and a further twenty-one followed by 1989.[57]

While there is little doubt marketing boards and fixed exchange rates were formative institutions, these critiques are remarkable for what they exclude.[58] For one, the supposed barrier between town and country was hardly impermeable as remittances and circular migration were common. Often, the actual policy bias was in favor of rural elites, as rich farmers "actively established their class dominance and secured political power" by pushing urban administrators to serve the interests of large landholders.[59] Just as importantly, scholars like Robert Bates depicted price-making as something only African states did; the extraordinary costs of being subordinated to the foreign dictation of energy, credit, and other prices received at most a passing mention in their writing. The economic utility of harnessing rural surplus for development transformation was, likewise, dismissed. And the historical variety of reasons for governing markets and prices fade through a single-minded focus on cynical political machinations.

The idea that prices should only be set by private firms was a radical argument in a world where government involvement was the

---

[55] Robert Bates et al., *The Reorganization of the Marketing and Processing of Crops in Uganda: Report to the Ministry of Cooperatives and Marketing* (University of California, 1981).
[56] Shivji, *Julius Nyerere*, p. 278.   [57] Stein, *Beyond the World Bank*.
[58] Vali Jamal and John Weeks, *Africa Misunderstood* (Macmillan, 1993).
[59] T. J. Byres, "Of Neo-Populist Pipe-Dreams," *The Journal of Peasant Studies* 6(2) (1979): 210–244.

C.3 Neoliberal Government of Value   323

norm – not merely in the global South but in Euro-America, too. Coming from the World Bank – which previously advised governments on crop price setting and planning – it was also a *volte face*.[60] It is worth emphasizing that African states were in many ways not exceptional in the 1960–1970s. The Bretton Woods agreement made fixed exchange rates for national currencies the norm. Liberal North Atlantic states had extensive price controls during World War II, and most continued to intervene in systemically important sectors – oil and the cost of credit, preeminently but not exclusively – in the subsequent decades.[61] And of course, actually existing socialist and communist regimes severely limited the scope of pricing.[62] While East African states never produced the extensive social welfare that neoliberalism targeted in the North Atlantic, their mediation of currencies and intervention in commodity markets did reflect a widely shared history of states governing value.[63]

At its most pronounced, the vision of structural adjustment amounted to a repudiation of the prevailing government of value. In place of the existing monopolies on valuation, neoliberalism envisioned a transformed role for the state. Carried through to its intended ends, adjusted states surrendered direct power over currency exchange rates and delegated the pricing of export crops to merchants. This changed who would have the capacity to determine worth. By foregrounding valuation as a style of governing, we more clearly see that the putatively *economic* model of neoliberalism was also an implicit political theory. It is not correct to think there was a

---

[60] Loxley, "The Berg Report," p. 199.
[61] For wartime price controls, see Isabella Weber, *How China Escaped Shock Therapy: The Market Reform Debate* (Taylor & Francis Group, 2021), chapter 2. On central bank credit controls in France, see Eric Monnet, *Controlling Credit: Central Banking and the Planned Economy in Postwar France* (Cambridge University Press, 2019). For US credit policy, see Sarah Quinn, _American Bonds: How Credit Markets Shaped a Nation_ (Princeton University Press, 2019).
[62] Generally see Johanna Bockman, "The Long Road to 1989: Neoclassical Economics, Alternative Socialisms, and the Advent of Neoliberalism," *Radical History Review* 112. On Maoist price controls, see Weber, *How China Escaped Shock Therapy*, chapter 4. The "Soviet price system" was subject to enormous scrutiny, but for a recent discussion, see Xenia Cherkaev, *Gleaning for Communism: The Soviet Socialist Household in Theory and Practice* (Cornell University Press, 2023).
[63] On the austerity of social provisioning, see Emma Park, *Infrastructures of Attachments: Austerity, Sovereignty, and Expertise in Kenya* (Duke University Press, 2024).

straightforward "retreat of the state" in favor of "the market." Instead, there was a reorganization of bureaucratic power and purpose that simultaneously tried to enforce structural adjustment, secure elite positions, and respond to popular demands. In this approach, the legitimate role of African states was to secure market exchange and capital accumulation from untoward interference by workers, civil servants, or others who would distort the price of goods. As Olukoshi and Mkandawire recognized, this could often be accomplished only through authoritarian imposition and violence.[64]

At least in part, this was because neoliberals have such a narrow theory of *values*, reducing people to individual utility maximization and thus eliding other ethical commitments that motivate action. It was also cavalier for the universality of its application: neoliberal proponents rejected the view that poor countries required carefully contextualized economic approaches. They also rejected that a monopoly on valuation should be limited in scope: while currency and key exports were the focus of East African statecraft, these states did not govern all valuable activity according to a single rationale. In contrast, the neoliberal ethos that triumphed called for a singular approach premised on the governance of value through private firms fixing prices.[65]

The role of the citizen was likewise transformed. I have argued that what was at stake was not the "social citizenship" that prevailed in industrialized welfare states. Waged employment was limited in most postcolonial settings, so sick pay, pensions, and health insurance did not become generalized. Instead, what prevailed were ideas about the right to transact, to open businesses, to receive loans, and to work the land. Credible citizenship made a virtue of productive output, and it limited the ability of East Africans to make claims on collective wealth. Yet, men like Waliuba could still feel confident in the legitimacy of their right to certain goods at certain prices. What changed with neoliberalism was, in part, the ability to justify such claims-making:

---

[64] Adebayo Olukoshi and Thandika Mkandawire, *Between Liberalisation and Oppression: The Politics of Structural Adjustment in Africa* (Codesria, 1996). In other cases, it was routed through decidedly non-market logics. Nicolas van de Walle, *African Economies and the Politics of Permanent Crisis, 1979–1999* (Cambridge University Press, 2001).

[65] Thandika Mkandawire, "The Spread of Economic Doctrines and Policymaking in Postcolonial Africa," *African Studies Review* 57(1) (2014): 171–198.

these sorts of petitions were placed outside the bounds of legitimate grievance.

While unfamiliar with Hayek or Bates, Waliuba also wanted to "get prices right," but he pursued this as a citizen, not merely a consumer. He invoked his status as *mwananchi* to call obdurate traders and delinquent bureaucrats to account. His goal was not to tie the hands of regulators nor to partake in some market free of their influence. Rather, he wanted the state and its agents to follow through on the government of value, shaping market exchange in line with popular ethics about what constituted a fair price and proper distribution of commodities. It is notable that Waliuba was writing from rural Kenya; in contrast to the overly simplified model of "urban bias," it is not the case that urbanites were the only consumers with an interest in affordable goods, including foodstuffs. To be sure, any given price implies a broader distributional regime, with relative winners and losers. But there were more salient identities and antagonisms that the dichotomy promulgated by "urban bias" theory.

With the gradual ascendency of neoliberalism, divisions such as class or gender were obscured. Political tactics like Waliuba's became less viable. Rendered unto the marketplace, prices were no longer seen to be the domain of citizen-state negotiation. Instead of appeals by disappointed *wananchi*, the value of goods would be worked out through the logics of buying and selling alone. When Tanzanians experienced shortages under socialism, they spoke of *bidhaa hewa* (ghost commodities) and they blamed the party-state; as public provisioning has waned, shortages still exist, but the inability to buy goods is now imagined as a problem of insufficient income – that is, of poverty – rather than of insufficient supply. Many farmers did want better prices for their produce, but it was neither evident at the time nor with hindsight that market-oriented regimes were capable of doing so. The results of marketization have varied by region, crop, and year, with some farmers receiving a higher proportion of international prices for their export crops but also being subjected to greater price volatility and cumbersome procedures. On the whole, "producing countries [have] less secure market outlets, a weaker bargaining position, and more difficult planning."[66]

---

[66] Stefano Ponte, *Farmers and Markets in Tanzania* (James Currey, 2002), pp. 164–166.

In practice, people did not so easily surrender their aspirations for collectively governing worth. Insurrections and protests against marketization multiplied across the continent.[67] Others showed their disappointment through foot dragging and other forms of silent subversion. These histories, of course, are not the subject of this book, but as these histories are written, it is worth attending to how the government of value was remade, not erased. Narrow enclaves within states, especially ministries of finance and central banks, were authorized to govern value in new ways, purposefully insulated from popular claims-making.[68] Marketized currency regimes that replaced fixed exchange rates did mark an end to direct authority over the price of money, as well as the bureaucratic controls that I discussed in Chapter 4; yet, the state continues to intervene in currency valuation to this day. In part, central banks do so by adjusting the rate of interest they pay on deposits and sovereign bonds (i.e., the price offered to banks in exchange for their reserves). In part, they do so through public statements that try to cajole and convince financiers to not collapse the national reserves of foreign capital on which the countries depend but over which they have less direct authority.[69] In part, they do so by encouraging their citizens to take jobs abroad and send foreign money home. States continue, in other words, to govern value, albeit in ways that would make it difficult for Noah Waliuba's descendants to articulate legitimate claims.

---

[67] See the collection "When 'Adjusted' People Rebel," in *International Review of Social History* 66(S29) (2021).

[68] Jason Hickel, "The (Anti)Politics of Central Banking: Monetary Policy, Class Conflict and the Limits of Sovereignty in South Africa," *Economy and Society* 50(1) (2021): 57–77; Jens van't Klooster, "The Ethics of Delegating Monetary Policy," *Journal of Politics* 82(2) (2020): 587–599.

[69] Douglas Holmes, *Economy of Words: Communicative Imperatives in Central Banks* (University of Chicago Press, 2013).

Archival Collections Consulted

Kenya

Central Bank of Kenya Library
Kakamega Records Centre (KRC)
Kenya National Archives, Nairobi (KNA)
Macmillan Library

Tanzania

Arusha Records Centre (ARC)
Bank of Tanzania Library
Tanzania National Archives, Dar es Salaam (TNA)
Tanzania National Library
Tanzania National Record Centre, Dodoma
University of Dar es Salaam East Africana Section

Uganda

Bank of Uganda (BoU)
Bank of Uganda Library
Bugisu Cooperative Union (BCU)
Bundibugyo District Archive (BDA)
Jinja District Archive (JDA)
Kabarole District Archive (KDA)
Lira District Archive (LDA)
Makerere Institute for Social Research (AR/MISR)
Makerere University Africana Special Collections
Mbale District Archive (MBL)
Uganda National Archives (UNA)

United Kingdom

Bank of England (BoE)
Barclays Bank (DCO)
United Kingdom National Archives (UKNA)

United States of America

International Monetary Fund (IMF)
Papers of Joseph S. Nye, Harvard University

Bibliography

Ackrill, Margaret and Leslie Hannah. *Barclays: The Business of Banking 1690–1996* (Cambridge University Press, 2001).

Adams, Bert and Mike Bristow. "The Politico-Economic Position of Ugandan Asians in the Colonial and Independent Eras." *Journal of Asian and African Studies* 13(3–4): 151–166.

Aiyar, Sana. *Indians in Kenya: The Politics of Diaspora* (Harvard University Press, 2015).

Alami, Ilias, Carolina Alve, Bruno Bonizzi, Annina Kaltenbrunner, Kai Koddenbrock, Ingrid Kvangraven, and Jeff Powell. "International Financial Subordination: A Critical Research Agenda." *Review of International Political Economy* 30(4) (2023) : 1360–1386.

Aminzade, Ronald. *Race, Nation, and Citizenship in Postcolonial Africa* (Cambridge University Press, 2013).

Amsden, Alice. "A Review of Kenya's Political Economy since Independence." *Journal of African Studies* 1(4) (1974): 417–440.

Anderson, David. "'Yours in Struggle for Majimbo': Nationalism and the Party Politics of Decolonization in Kenya, 1955–64." *Journal of Contemporary History* 40(3) (2005): 547–564.

Anderson, David and David Throup. "Africans and Agricultural Production in Colonial Kenya: The Myth of the War as a Watershed." *Journal of African History* 26(4) (1985): 327–345.

Angelo, Anais. *Power and the Presidency in Kenya: The Jomo Kenyatta Years* (Cambridge University Press, 2020).

Apter, Andrew. *The Pan-African Nation: Oil and the Spectacle of Culture in Nigeria* (University of Chicago Press, 2005).

Apter, David. *The Political Kingdom in Uganda: A Study of Bureaucratic Nationalism*, 3rd ed. (Routledge, 1997 [1961]).

Arrighi, Giovanni. "The African Crisis." *New Left Review* II(15) (2002).

Arrighi, Giovanni and John Saul. *Essays on the Political Economy of Africa* (Monthly Review Press, 1973).

Ashforth, Adam. "Witchcraft." In Gaurav Desai and Adeline Masquelier (eds.), *Critical Terms for the Study of Africa* (University of Chicago Press, 2018), pp. 365–380.

Asiimwe, Godfrey. *The Impact of Post-Colonial Policy Shifts in Coffee Marketing at the Local Level in Uganda: A Case Study of Mukono District, 1962–1998* (Institute of Social Studies, 2002).
  "From Monopoly Marketing to Coffee Magendo: Responses to Policy Recklessness and Extraction in Uganda, 1971–79." *Journal of Eastern African Studies* 7(1) (2013): 104–124.
Asiwaju, A. I. "Migrations as Revolt: The Example of the Ivory Coast and the Upper Volta before 1945." *Journal of African History* 17(4) (1976): 577–594.
Askew, Kelly. *Performing the Nation: Swahili Music and Cultural Politics in Tanzania* (University of Chicago Press, 2002).
Atieno-Odhiambo, E. S. "'Seek Ye First the Economic Kingdom': A History of the Luo Thrift and Trading Corporation 1945–1956." In B. A. Ogot (ed.), *Hadith 5* (East African Publishing House, 1975), pp. 218–256.
Balibar, Etienne. "The Nation Form: History & Ideology." *Review* 13(3) (1990): 329–361.
Bangura, Yusuf. *Britain and Commonwealth Africa* (Manchester University Press, 1983).
Banks, Elizabeth, Robyn d'Avignon, and Asif Siddiqi. "The African-Soviet Modern." *Comparative Studies of South Asia, Africa & the Middle East* 41(1) (2021): 2–10.
Bantebya-Kyomuhendo, Grace and Marjorie McIntosh. *Women, Work & Domestic Virtue in Uganda, 1900–2003* (James Currey, 2006).
Basu, S. K. *Central Banking in the Emerging Countries: A Study of African Experiments* (Asia Publishing House, 1967).
Bates, Robert. *Markets and States in Tropical Africa: The Political Basis of Agricultural Policies* (University of California Press, 1981).
  Open-Economy Politics: The Political Economy of the World Coffee Trade (Princeton University Press, 1997).
Bates, Robert, et al. *The Reorganization of the Marketing and Processing of Crops in Uganda: Report to the Ministry of Cooperatives and Marketing* (University of California Press, 1981).
Bauer, P. T. *West African Trade: A Study of Competition, Oligopoly, and Monopoly in a Changing Economy* (Cambridge University Press, 1954).
Bayart, Jean-François. "Africa in the World: A History of Extraversion." *African Affairs* 99(395) (2000): 217–267.
  The State in Africa: The Politics of the Belly, 2nd ed. (Polity Press, 2009).
Bear, Laura. "Time as Technique." *Annual Review of Anthropology* 45(1) (2016): 487–502.
Bear, Laura, Karen Ho, Anna Tsing, and Sylvia Yanagisako. "Gens: A Feminist Manifesto for the Study of Capitalism." *Cultural*

Anthropology, 2015. www.culanth.org/fieldsights/652-gens-a-feminist-manifesto-for-the-study-of-capitalism.

Becker, Felicitas. *Politics of Poverty: Policy-Making and Development in Rural Tanzania* (Cambridge University Press, 2019).

Bell, Stephanie. "The Hierarchy of Money." Levy Institute Working Paper No. 231 (1998).

Ben Gadha, Maha, et al. (eds.). *Economic and Monetary Sovereignty in 21st Century Africa* (Pluto Press, 2022).

Bender, Mathew. *Water Brings No Harm: Management Knowledge and the Struggle for the Waters of Kilimanjaro* (Ohio University Press, 2019).

Berman, Bruce. *Control & Crisis in Colonial Kenya: The Dialectic of Domination* (James Currey, 1990).

Berman, Bruce and John Lonsdale. *Unhappy Valley. Book One* (James Currey, 1992).

Bernards, Nick. "States, Money and the Persistence of Colonial Financial Hierarchies in British West Africa." *Development and Change* 54(1) (2023): 64–86.

Biersteker, Thomas. "Self-Reliance in Theory and Practice in Tanzanian Trade Relations." *International Organization* 34(2) (1980): 229–264.

Binhammer, H. H. *The Development of a Financial Infrastructure in Tanzania* (East African Literature Bureau, 1975).

Birch, Kean and Fabian Muniesa. *Assetization: Turning Things into Assets in Technoscientific Capitalism* (MIT Press, 2020).

Birla, Ritu. *Stages of Capital: Law, Culture, and Market Governance in Late Colonial India* (Duke University Press, 2009).

Bjerk, Paul. "Agency and the Arusha Declaration: Nyerere, NUTA, and Political Discourse in Tanzania, 1966–67," *Journal of African History* (forthcoming).

Building a Peaceful Nation: Julius Nyerere and the Establishment of Sovereignty in Tanzania (University of Rochester Press, 2015).

"Postcolonial Realism: Tanganyika's Foreign Policy under Nyerere, 1960–1963." *International Journal of African Historical Studies* 44(2) (2011): 215–247.

"A Preliminary History of the Bank of Tanzania," in Salvatory Nyanto (ed.), *A History of Post-Colonial Tanzania: Essays in Honor of Prof. Isaria N. Kimambo* (James Currey, forthcoming).

"Sovereignty and Socialism in Tanzania: The Historiography of an African State." *History in Africa* 37 (2010): 275–319.

Bloch, Maurice and Jonathan Parry (eds.). *Money and the Morality of Exchange* (Cambridge University Press, 1989).

Blumenthal, Erwin. *The Present Monetary System and Its Future: Report to the Government of Tanganyika* (Government Printer, 1963).

Blunt, Robert. *For Money and Elders: Ritual, Sovereignty, and the Sacred in Kenya* (University of Chicago Press, 2019).
Bockman, Johanna. "The Long Road to 1989: Neoclassical Economics, Alternative Socialisms, and the Advent of Neoliberalism." *Radical History Review* (112) (2012): 9–42.
  "The Struggle over Structural Adjustment: Socialist Revolution versus Capitalist Counterrevolution in Yugoslavia and the World." *History of Political Economy* 51 (2019): 254–276.
Boone, Catherine. *Political Topographies of the African State: Territorial Authority and Institutional Choice* (Cambridge University Press, 2003).
  "State Building in the African Countryside: Structure and Politics at the Grassroots." *Journal of Development Studies* 34(4) (1998): 1–31.
Bosa, George. *The Financing of Small-Scale Enterprises in Uganda* (Oxford University Press, 1969).
Boserup, Esther. *Woman's Role in Economic Development* (George Allen & Unwin, 1970).
Bostock, Frances. "The British Overseas Banks and Development Finance in Africa after 1945." *Business History* 33(3) (1991): 157–176.
Bowles, B. D. "Economic Anti-Colonialism and British Reaction in Uganda, 1936–1955." *Canadian Journal of African Studies* 9(1) (1975): 51–60.
Bradley, A. W. "Legal Aspects of the Nationalisations in Tanzania." *East African Law Journal* 3(3) (1967): 149–176.
Branch, Daniel. *Defeating Mau Mau, Creating Kenya: Counterinsurgency, Civil War, and Decolonization* (Cambridge University Press, 2009).
  Kenya: Between Hope and Despair, 1963–2011 (Yale University Press, 2011).
  "Public Letters and the Culture of Politics in Kenya, c.1960–75." *Journal of Eastern African Studies* 15(2) (2021): 339–357.
Brennan, James. "Blood Enemies: Exploitation and Urban Citizenship in the Nationalist Political Thought of Tanzania, 1958–75." *Journal of African History* 47(3) (2006): 389–413.
  "Julius Rex: Nyerere through the Eyes of His Critics, 1953–2013." *Journal of Eastern African Studies* 8(3) (2014): 459–477.
  "Lowering the Sultan's Flag: Sovereignty and Decolonization in Coastal Kenya." *Comparative Studies in Society and History* 50(4) (2008): 831–861.
  Taifa: Making Nation and Race in Urban Tanzania (Ohio University Press, 2012).
Brett, E. A. *Colonialism and Underdevelopment in East Africa: The Politics of Economic Change, 1919–1939* (NOK Publishers, 1973).
Brownell, Emily. *Gone to Ground: A History of Environment and Infrastructure in Dar Es Salaam* (University of Pittsburgh Press, 2020).

"Re-territorializing the Future: Writing Environmental Histories of the Oil Crisis from Tanzania." *Environmental History* 27(4) (2022): 747–771.
Bunker, Stephen. *Peasants Against the State: The Politics of Market Control in Bugisu, Uganda, 1900–1983* (University of Chicago Press, 1991).
Burke, Timothy. *Lifebuoy Men, Lux Women: Commodification, Consumption, and Cleanliness in Modern Zimbabwe* (Duke University Press, 2005).
Byres, T. J. "Of Neo-Populist Pipe-Dreams." *The Journal of Peasant Studies* 6(2) (1979): 210–244.
Cain, P. J. and A. G. Hopkins. *British Imperialism: Crisis and Deconstruction 1914–1990* (Longman, 1993).
Callaci, Emily. *Street Archives and City Life: Popular Intellectuals in Postcolonial Tanzania* (Duke University Press, 2017).
Callon, Michel, Yuval Millo, and Fabian Muniesa (eds.). *Market Devices* (Wiley-Blackwell, 2007).
Caselli, Clara. *The Banking System of Tanzania* (Milan, 1975).
Cattelino, Jessica. *High Stakes: Florida Seminole Gaming and Sovereignty* (Duke University Press, 2008).
Chalfin, Brenda. *Neoliberal Frontiers: An Ethnography of Sovereignty in West Africa* (University of Chicago Press, 2010).
Chatterjee, Partha. *The Politics of the Governed: Popular Politics in Most of the World* (Columbia University Press, 2004).
Cherkaev, Xenia. *Gleaning for Communism: The Soviet Socialist Household in Theory and Practice* (Cornell University Press, 2023).
Clark, P. G. "The Role of an East African Central Bank in Accelerating Development." Economic Development Research Paper No. 46 (Makerere Institute of Social Research, 1964).
Clark, W. Edmund. *Socialist Development and Public Investment in Tanzania, 1964–1973* (University of Toronto Press, 1978).
Comaroff, Jean, and John L. Comaroff. "Alien-Nation: Zombies, Immigrants, and Millennial Capitalism." *South Atlantic Quarterly* 101(4) (2002): 779–805.
Cooper, Frederick. *On the African Waterfront: Urban Disorder and the Transformation of Work in Colonial Mombasa* (Yale University Press, 1987).
  Africa in the World: Capitalism, Empire, Nation-State (Harvard University Press, 2014).
  Citizenship between Empire and Nation: Remaking France and French Africa, 1945–1960 (Princeton University Press, 2014).
  Citizenship, Inequality, and Difference (Princeton University Press, 2018).
  Decolonization and African Society: The Labor Question in French and British Africa (Cambridge University Press, 1996).

Coulson, Andrew. *Tanzania: A Political Economy*, 2nd ed. (Oxford University Press, 2013).
Crossley, Julian and John Blandford. *The DCO Story: A History of Banking in Many Countries 1925–71* (Barclays Bank International Limited, 1975).
Cullen, Poppy. "Adapting to Independence: The East Africa Association, Post-Colonial Business Networks and Economic Development." In Véronique Dimier and Sarah Stockwell (eds.), *The Business of Development in Post-Colonial Africa* (Palgrave Macmillan, 2020), pp. 69–97.
  Kenya and Britain after Independence: Beyond Neo-Colonialism (Palgrave Macmillan, 2017).
Daly, Samuel Fury Childs. *History of the Republic of Biafra: Law, Crime, and the Nigerian Civil War* (Cambridge University Press, 2020).
  "The Survival Con: Fraud and Forgery in the Republic of Biafra, 1967–70." *Journal of African History* 58(1) (2017): 129–144.
Das, Veena and Deborah Poole. *Anthropology in the Margins of the State* (SAR Press, 2009).
Daston, Lorraine and Peter Galison. *Objectivity* (Zone Books, 2007).
Davis, Muriam Haleh. *Markets of Civilization: Islam and Racial Capitalism in Algeria* (Duke University Press, 2022).
Day, Sophie, Euthymios Papataxiarchēs, and Michael Stewart. *Lilies of the Field: Marginal People Who Live for the Moment* (Westview Press, 1999).
De, Rohit. *A People's Constitution: The Everyday Life of Law in the Indian Republic* (Princeton University Press, 2018).
De, Rohit and Robert Travers. "Petitioning and Political Cultures in South Asia." *Modern Asian Studies* 53(1) (2019): 1–20.
De Boeck, Filip. "Domesticating Diamonds and Dollars: Identity, Expenditure and Sharing in Southwestern Zaire (1984–1997)." *Development and Change* 29(4) (1998): 777–810.
De Haas, Michiel. "Moving Beyond Colonial Control? Economic Forces and Shifting Migration from Ruanda-Urundi to Buganda, 1920–60." *Journal of African History* 60(3) (2019): 379–406.
De Haas, Michiel and Kostadis Papaioannou. "Resource Endowments and Agricultural Commercialization in Colonial Africa: Did Labour Seasonality and Food Security Drive Uganda's Cotton Revolution?" EHES Working Papers in Economic History No. 111 (2017).
Decker, Alicia. "An Accidental Liberation: Ugandan Women on the Front Lines in Idi Amin's Economic War." *Women's History Review* 22(65) (2013): 954–970.
  "Idi Amin's Dirty War: Subversion, Sabotage, and the Battle to Keep Uganda Clean, 1971–1979." *International Journal of African Historical Studies* 43(3) (2010): 489–513.

In Idi Amin's Shadow: Women, Gender, and Militarism in Uganda (Ohio University Press, 2014).

Decker, Stephanie. "Decolonising Barclays Bank DCO? Corporate Africanisation in Nigeria, 1945–69." *Journal of Imperial and Commonwealth History* 33(3) (2005): 419–440.

Desai, Gaurav. *Commerce with the Universe: Africa, India, and the Afrasian Imagination* (Columbia University Press, 2016).

Desan, Christine. *Making Money: Coin, Currency, and the Coming of Capitalism* (Oxford University Press, 2014).

Dias, Clarence. "Tanzanian Nationalisations: 1967–1970." *Cornell International Law Journal* 4(1) (1970): 59–79.

Dieng, R. S. "Adversely Incorporated Yet Moving Up the Social Ladder?" *Africa Development* 47(3) (2022): 133–166.

Dietrich, Christopher. *Oil Revolution: Anticolonial Elites, Sovereign Rights, and the Economic Culture of Decolonization* (Cambridge University Press, 2017).

Dobler, Gregor. "The Green, the Grey and the Blue: A Typology of Cross-Border Trade in Africa." *Journal of Modern African Studies* 54(1) (2016): 145–169.

Dodd, Nigel. *The Social Life of Money* (Princeton University Press, 2014).

Doganova, Liliana. "Discounting the Future: A Political Technology." In Sandra Kemp and Jenny Andersson (eds.), *Futures* (Oxford University Press, 2021), pp. 379–394.

Donovan, Kevin P. "*Uhuru Sasa!* Federal Futures and Liminal Sovereignty in Decolonizing East Africa." *Comparative Studies in Society & History* 65(2) (2023): 372–398.

Doyle, Shane. "Immigrants and Indigenes: The Lost Counties Dispute and the Evolution of Ethnic Identity in Colonial Buganda." *Journal of Eastern African Studies* 3(2) (2009): 284–302.

Eagleton, Catherine. "Designing Change." In Ruth Craggs and Claire Wintle (eds.), *Cultures of Decolonisation* (Manchester University Press, 2016), pp. 222–244.

Earle, Jonathan. *Colonial Buganda and the End of Empire: Political Thought and Historical Imagination in Africa* (Cambridge University Press, 2017).

Eckert, Andreas. "Regulating the Social: Social Security, Social Welfare and the State in Late Colonial Tanzania." *Journal of African History* 45(3) (2004): 467–489.

Eich, Stefan. *The Currency of Politics: The Political Theory of Money from Aristotle to Keynes* (Princeton University Press, 2022).

Fabian, Johannes. *Out of Our Minds: Reason and Madness in the Exploration of Central Africa* (University of California Press, 2000).

Feierman, Steven. "Reciprocity and Assistance in Precolonial Africa." In Warren Ilchman et al. (eds.), *Philanthropy in the World's Traditions* (Indiana University Press, 1998), pp. 3–24.

Ferguson, James. *Give a Man a Fish: Reflections on the New Politics of Distribution* (Duke University Press, 2015).

Ferry, Elizabeth. "'Deep in the Earth a Shining Substance': Sequestration and Display in Gold Mining and Central Banks." *Journal of Cultural Economy* 14(4) (2021): 416–434.

Feyissa, Dereje and Markus Hoehne. *Borders & Borderlands as Resources in the Horn of Africa* (James Currey, 2015).

Fitzpatrick, Sheila and Robert Gellately. "Introduction to the Practices of Denunciation in Modern European History." *Journal of Modern History* 68(4) (1996): 747–767.

Fourcade, Marion. "Cents and Sensibility: Economic Valuation and the Nature of 'Nature'." *American Journal of Sociology* 116(6) (2011): 1721–1777.

Frank, Billy. "The 'Private' Face of African Development Planning during the Second World War." In J. M. Hodge et al. (eds.), *Developing Africa* (Manchester University Press, 2014), pp. 111–132.

Fuller, Harcourt. *Building the Ghanaian Nation-State: Kwame Nkrumah's Symbolic Nationalism* (Palgrave Macmillan, 2014).

Geiger, Susan. *TANU Women: Gender and Culture in the Making of Tanganyikan Nationalism, 1955–1965* (Heinemann, 1997).

Gershenberg, Irving. "Banking in Uganda since Independence." *Economic Development and Cultural Change* 20(3) (1972): 504–523.

"The Impact of Independence on the Role of Commercial Banking in Uganda's Economic Development" (Makerere Institute of Social Research, 1969), pp. 1–15.

Geschiere, Peter. *The Perils of Belonging: Autochthony, Citizenship, and Exclusion in Africa and Europe* (University of Chicago Press, 2009).

Getachew, Adom. *Worldmaking after Empire: The Rise and Fall of Self-Determination* (Princeton University Press, 2019).

Geteria, Wamugunda. *Black Gold of Chepkube* (Spear Books: Published by Heinemann Kenya, 1988).

Gettler, Brian. *Colonialism's Currency: Money, State, and First Nations in Canada 1820–1950* (McGill-Queen's University Press, 2020).

Ghai, D. P. "Territorial Distribution of the Benefits and Costs of the East African Common Market." In C. Leys and P. Robson (eds.), *Federation in East Africa* (Oxford University Press, 1965), pp. 72–82.

Ghai, Dharam (ed.). *Economic Independence in Africa* (Kenya Literature Bureau, 1973).

Gheewala, Mahesh. "The Early Days of the Central Bank of Kenya." In P. Njoroge and V. Murinde (eds.), *50 Years of Central Banking in Kenya* (Oxford University Press, 2021), pp. 197–249.

Giblin, James. *A History of the Excluded: Making Family a Refuge from State in Twentieth-Century Tanzania* (Ohio University Press, 2005).

Gilbert, Paul Robert. "The Crown Agents and the CDC Group: Imperial Extraction and Development's 'Private Sector Turn'." In G. K. Bhambra and J. McClure (eds.), *Imperial Inequalities: The Politics of Economic Governance Across European Empires* (Manchester University Press, 2022), pp. 299–318.

Glassman, Jonathon. *War of Words, War of Stones: Racial Thought and Violence in Colonial Zanzibar* (Indiana University Press, 2011).

Goswami, Manu. *Producing India: From Colonial Economy to National Space* (University of Chicago Press, 2004).

Grace, Joshua. *African Motors: Technology, Gender, and the History of Development* (Duke University Press, 2021).

Graeber, David. "Dead Zones of the Imagination: On Violence, Bureaucracy, and Interpretive Labor." *HAU: Journal of Ethnographic Theory* 2(2) (2012): 105–128.

"It Is Value That Brings Universes into Being." *HAU: Journal of Ethnographic Theory* 3(2) (2013): 219–243.

Greaves, Ida. "The Colonial Sterling Balances." Essays in International Finance No. 20 (September 1954).

Green, Reginald. "The Economics of Disintegration: Tanzania, 1982–83" (1983). https://opendocs.ids.ac.uk/opendocs/handle/20.500.12413/4775.

"A Guide to Acquisition & Initial Operation: Reflections from Tanzanian Experience, 1967–74." In Julio Faundez and Sol Picciotto (eds.), *The Nationalisation of Multinationals in Peripheral Economies* (Macmillan, 1978), pp. 17–70.

Magendo in the Political Economy of Uganda (Institute of Development Studies, 1981).

Green, Toby. *A Fistful of Shells: West Africa from the Rise of the Slave Trade to the Age of Revolution* (Penguin Books, 2020).

Gregory, Robert. *South Asians in East Africa: An Economic and Social History 1890–1980* (Westview Press, 1993).

Grilli, Matteo and Frank Gerits. *Visions of African Unity: New Perspectives on the History of Pan-Africanism and African Unification Projects* (Springer International Publishing, 2020).

Grillo, R. D. *African Railwaymen: Solidarity and Opposition in an East African Labour Force* (Cambridge University Press, 1973).

Guha, Ranajit. *Dominance without Hegemony: History and Power in Colonial India* (Harvard University Press, 1998).

Guyer, Jane. *Legacies, Logics, Logistics: Essays in the Anthropology of the Platform Economy* (University of Chicago Press, 2016).
Marginal Gains: Monetary Transactions in Atlantic Africa (University of Chicago Press, 2004).
"Prophecy and the near Future: Thoughts on Macroeconomic, Evangelical, and Punctuated Time." *American Ethnologist* 34(3) (2007): 409–421.
"Soft Currencies, Cash Economies, New Monies." *Proceedings of the National Academy of Sciences* 109(7) (2012): 2214–2221.
"Wealth in People, Wealth in Things." *Journal of African History* 36(1) (1995): 83–90.
Guyer, Jane and Karin Pallaver. "Money and Currency in African History." In Thomas Spear (ed.), *Oxford Research Encyclopaedia of African History* (Oxford University Press, 2018), pp. 1–28.
Hancock, I. R. "The Uganda Crisis, 1966." *Australian Outlook* 20(3) (1966): 263–277.
Hansen, Holger. "Uganda in the 1970s: A Decade of Paradoxes and Ambiguities." *Journal of Eastern African Studies* 7(1) (2013): 83–103.
Hansen, Thomas Blom. "Sovereignty in a Minor Key." *Public Culture* 33(1) (2021): 41–61.
Hanson, Holly. *Landed Obligation: The Practice of Power in Buganda* (Heinemann, 2003).
To Speak and Be Heard: Seeking Good Government in Uganda, c.1500–2015 (Ohio University Press, 2022).
Harvey, David. *The Limits to Capital* (Verso, 2006 [1982]).
Hazlewood, Arthur. *Economic Integration: The East African Experience* (St. Martin's Press, 1975).
Heald, Suzette. *Controlling Anger: The Sociology of Gisu Violence* (James Currey, 1989).
Manhood and Morality: Sex, Violence, and Ritual in Gisu Society (Routledge, 1999).
Helleiner, Eric. *The Making of National Money: Territorial Currencies in Historical Perspective* (Cornell University Press, 2002).
States and the Reemergence of Global Finance: From Bretton Woods to the 1990s (Cornell University Press, 1996).
Herbst, Jeffrey. *States and Power in Africa: Comparative Lessons in Authority and Control* (Princeton University Press, 2000).
Hickel, Jason. "The (Anti)Politics of Central Banking: Monetary Policy, Class Conflict and the Limits of Sovereignty in South Africa." *Economy and Society* 50(1) (2021): 57–77.
Hirschman, Albert. *Exit, Voice, and Loyalty: Responses to Decline in Firms, Organizations and States* (Harvard University Press, 1981).

Hodgson, Dorothy. *Once Intrepid Warriors: Gender, Ethnicity, and the Cultural Politics of Maasai Development* (Indiana University Press, 2001).

Holmes, Douglas. *Economy of Words: Communicative Imperatives in Central Banks* (University of Chicago Press, 2013).

Hood, Andrew James. "Developing the East African: The East Africa Royal Commission, 1953–1955, and Its Critics." PhD dissertation, Rice University, 1997.

House-Midamba, Bessie and Felix Ekechi (eds.). *African Market Women and Economic Power: The Role of Women in African Economic Development* (Greenwood Press, 1995).

Huber, Gunther. "Private Savings in Uganda." In Peter Marlin (ed.), *Financial Aspects of Development in East Africa* (Weltforum Verlag, 1970), pp. 93–174.

Hudson, Peter James. *Bankers and Empire: How Wall Street Colonized the Caribbean* (University of Chicago Press, 2018).

Hughes, Geoffrey, Megnaa Mehtta, Chiara Bresciani, and Stuart Strange. "Ugly Emotions and the Politics of Accusation." *Cambridge Journal of Anthropology* 37(2) (2019): 1–20.

Humphrey, Caroline. *The Unmaking of Soviet Life: Everyday Economies after Socialism* (Cornell University Press, 2002).

Hundle, Anneeth Kaur. "1970s Uganda: Past, Present, Future." *Journal of Asian and African Studies* 53(3) (2018): 455–475.

  "Insecurities of Expulsion: Emergent Citizenship Formations and Political Practices in Postcolonial Uganda." *Comparative Studies of South Asia, Africa and the Middle East* 39(1) (2019): 8–23.

Hunt, Diana. *Credit for Agricultural Development: A Case Study of Uganda* (East African Publishers House, 1975).

Hunter, Emma (ed.). *Citizenship, Belonging, and Political Community in Africa: Dialogues between Past and Present* (Ohio University Press, 2016).

  "'Economic Man in East Africa': Ethnicity, Nationalism, and the Moral Economy in Tanzania." In Bruce Berman, André Laliberté, and Stephen J. Larin (eds.), *The Moral Economies of Ethnic and Nationalist Claims* (UBC Press, 2016), pp. 101–122.

  "A History of Maendeleo: The Concept of 'Development' in Tanganyika's Late Colonial Public Sphere." In Joseph M. Hodge, Gerald Hödl, and Martina Kopf (eds.), *Developing Africa: Concepts and Practices in Twentieth-Century Colonialism* (Manchester University Press, 2014), pp. 87–107.

  Political Thought and the Public Sphere in Tanzania: Freedom, Democracy and Citizenship in the Era of Decolonization (Cambridge University Press, 2015).

Hyden, Goran. *Beyond Ujamaa in Tanzania: Underdevelopment and an Uncaptured Peasantry* (University of California Press, 1980).
Idrissa, Rahmane. "Countries without Currency." *London Review of Books*, December 2, 2021.
Iliffe, John. *A Modern History of Tanganyika* (Cambridge University Press, 1979).
Ironside, Kristy. *A Full-Value Ruble: The Promise of Prosperity in the Postwar Soviet Union* (Harvard University Press, 2021).
Rowe, J. W. F. *The World's Coffee* (Her Majesty's Stationery Office, 1963).
Jamal, Vali. "Asians in Uganda, 1880–1972: Inequality and Expulsion." *The Economic History Review* 29(4): 602–616.
Jamal, Vali and John Weeks. *Africa Misunderstood* (Macmillan, 1993).
Jayal, Niraja Gopal. *Citizenship and Its Discontents: An Indian History* (Harvard University Press, 2013).
Jerven, Morton. *Economic Growth and Measurement Reconsidered* (Oxford University Press, 2014).
Jones, Gareth and Stuart Corbridge. "The Continuing Debate about Urban Bias." *Progress in Development Studies* 10(1) (2010): 1–18.
Kajubi, W. Senteza. "Coffee and Prosperity in Buganda: Some Aspects of Economic & Social Change." *Uganda Journal* 29(2) (1965): 135–147.
Karimi, Joseph and Philip Ochieng. *The Kenyatta Succession* (Transafrica, 1980).
Kasfir, Nelson. *The Shrinking Political Arena: Participation & Ethnicity in African Politics* (University of California Press, 1976).
  "State, Magendo, and Class Formation in Uganda." *Journal of Commonwealth & Comparative Politics* 21(3) (1983): 84–103.
Kasozi, A. B. K. *The Social Origins of Violence in Uganda, 1964–1985* (McGill-Queen's University Press, 1994).
Kassum, Al Noor. *Africa's Winds of Change: Memoirs of an International Tanzanian* (I.B. Tauris).
Katongole, Emmanuel. *A Future for Africa: Critical Essays in Christian Social Imagination* (Wipf & Stock Publishers, 2017).
Kennedy, Dane. *Islands of White: Settler Society and Culture in Kenya and Southern Rhodesia, 1890–1939* (Duke University Press, 1987).
Khanakwa, Pamela. "Male Circumcision among the Bagisu of Eastern Uganda: Practices and Conceptualisations." In Axel Fleisch and Rhiannon Stephens (eds.), *Doing Conceptual History in Africa* (Berghahn Books, 2016), pp. 115–137.
  "Reinventing *Imbalu* and Forcible Circumcision: Gisu Political Identity and the Fight for Mbale in Late Colonial Uganda." *The Journal of African History* 59(3) (2018): 357–379.
Killingray, David and Richard Rathbone (eds.). *Africa and the Second World War* (Palgrave Macmillan, 1986).

Kiwanuka, Semakula. *Amin and the Tragedy of Uganda* (Weltforum Verlag, 1979).
Klooster, Jens van't. "The Ethics of Delegating Monetary Policy." *Journal of Politics* 82(2) (2020): 587–599.
Koselleck, Reinhart. *Futures Past: On the Semantics of Historical Time* (Columbia University Press, 2004).
Kratz, Joachim. "The East African Currency Board." *Staff Papers (International Monetary Fund)* 13(2) (1966): 229–255.
Krozewski, Gerold. "Finance and Empire: The Dilemma Facing Great Britain in the 1950s." *International History Review* 18(1) (1996): 48–69.
Kusimba, Sibel. "Money, Mobile Money and Rituals in Western Kenya: The Contingency Fund and the Thirteenth Cow." *African Studies Review* 61 (2) (2018): 158–182.
la Fontaine, Jean. "The Power of Rights." *Man* 12(3/4) (1977): 421–437.
Lal, Deepak. *The Poverty of "Development Economics"*, 2nd ed. (Institute for Economic Affairs, 1997).
Lal, Priya. *African Socialism in Postcolonial Tanzania: Between the Village and the World* (Cambridge University Press, 2015).
   "Self-Reliance and the State: Multiple Meanings of Development in Early Post-Colonial Tanzania." *Africa* 82(2) (2012): 212–234.
Latour, Bruno. "Why Has Critique Run out of Steam? From Matters of Fact to Matters of Concern." *Critical Inquiry* 30(2): 225–248.
Lee, Christopher. *Making a World after Empire: The Bandung Moment and Its Political Afterlives* (Ohio University Press, 2010).
Leopold, Mark. *Idi Amin: The Story of Africa's Icon of Evil* (Yale University Press, 2021).
Letiche, John. "Dependent Monetary Systems and Economic Development: The Case of Sterling East Africa." In Willy Sellekaerts (ed.), *Economic Development and Planning: Essays in Honour of Jan Tinbergen* (Palgrave Macmillan, 1974), pp. 186–236.
Leys, Colin. *Underdevelopment in Kenya: The Political Economy of Neo-Colonialism, 1964–1971* (University of California Press, 1975).
Leys, Colin and Peter Robson (eds.). *Federation in East Africa: Opportunities and Problems* (Oxford University Press, 1966).
Lipton, Michael. *Why Poor People Stay Poor: A Study of Urban Bias in World Development* (Temple Smith, 1977).
Little, Peter, et al. "Avoiding Disaster: Diversification and Risk Management among East African Herders." *Development and Change* 32(3) (2001): 401–433.
Lofchie, Michael. "Agrarian Crisis and Economic Liberalisation in Tanzania." *Journal of Modern African Studies* 16(3) (1978): 454–455.

Lombard, Louisa. "Denouncing Sovereignty: Claims to Liberty in Northeastern Central African Republic." *Comparative Studies in Society and History* 60(4) (2018): 1066–1095.

Lonsdale, John. "The Moral Economy of Mau Mau." In Bruce Berman and John Lonsdale (eds.), *Unhappy Valley. Book Two* (James Currey, 1992), pp. 265–468.

Low, D. A. and John Lonsdale. "Introduction: Toward the New Order 1945–1963." In D. A. Low and Alison Smith (eds.), *The History of East Africa*, vol. 3 (Clarendon Press, 1976), pp. 1–63.

Loxley, John. "The Berg Report and the Model of Accumulation in Sub-Saharan Africa." *Review of African Political Economy* 27/28 (1983): 197–204.

"The Development of the Monetary and Financial System of the East African Currency Area, 1950 to 1964." PhD dissertation, University of Leeds, 1966.

"Financial Planning and Control in Tanzania." In J. E. Rweyemamu et al. (eds.), *Towards Socialist Planning* (Tanzania Publishing House, 1972), pp. 54–55.

"Rural Credit and Socialism." In Lionel Cliffe (ed.), *Rural Cooperation in Tanzania* (Tanzania Publishing House, 1975).

"Sterling Reserves and the Fiduciary Issue in East Africa." *Economic Affairs* 11(5) (1996): 217–226.

"Structural Change in the Monetary System of Tanzania." In Lionel Cliffe and John S. Saul (eds.), *Socialism in Tanzania Volume 2: Policies* (East African Publishing House, 1972), pp. 102–111.

Lumba, Allan E. S. *Monetary Authorities: Capitalism and Decolonization in the American Colonial Philippines* (Duke University Press, 2022).

Lynch, Gabrielle. *I Say to You: Ethnic Politics and the Kalenjin in Kenya* (University of Chicago Press, 2011).

"The Wars of Who Belongs Where: The Unstable Politics of Autochthony on Kenya's Mt Elgon." *Ethnopolitics* 10(3–4) (2011): 391–410.

MacArthur, Julie. *Cartography and the Political Imagination: Mapping Community in Colonial Kenya* (Ohio University Press, 2016).

"Decolonizing Sovereignty: States of Exception along the Kenya-Somali Frontier." *The American Historical Review* 124(1) (2019): 108–143.

Macdona, Brian. "Financing Development in Africa: The Role of the Commercial Banks and Their Overseas Investment Corporations." *African Affairs* 66(265) (1967): 324–328.

Macharia, Keguro. "Loving Moi." Popula, https://popula.com/2018/08/20/loving-moi/.

Maliyamkono, T. L. and Mboya Bagachwa. *The Second Economy in Tanzania* (Ohio University Press, 1990).

Mamdani, Mahmood. *Citizen & Subject: Contemporary Africa and the Legacy of Late Colonialism* (Princeton University Press, 1996).
Imperialism and Fascism in Uganda (Heinemann Educational Books, 1983).
Neither Settlers nor Native: The Making and Unmaking of Permanent Minorities (Harvard University Press, 2020).
Politics and Class Formation in Uganda (Monthly Review Press, 1976).
Manji, Ambreena. *The Struggle for Land & Justice in Kenya* (James Currey, 2020).
Mann, Michael. "The Autonomous Power of the State: Its Origins, Mechanisms and Results." *European Journal of Sociology* 25(2) (1984): 185–213.
Marris, Peter and Anthony Somerset. *African Businessmen* (Routledge 1971).
Marshall, T. H. *Citizenship & Social Class* (Cambridge University Press, 1950).
Masefield, G. B. "Agricultural Change in Uganda, 1945–1960." Food Research Institute Studies (1962).
Mau, Søren. *Mute Compulsion* (Verso, 2023).
Maurer, Bill. "The Anthropology of Money." *Annual Review of Anthropology* 35(1) (2006): 15–36.
Mutual Life, Limited: Islamic Banking, Alternative Currencies, Lateral Reason (Princeton University Press, 2005).
Maxon, Robert. "The Kenya Currency Crisis, 1919–21 and the Imperial Dilemma." *Journal of Imperial and Commonwealth History* 17(3) (1989): 323–348.
Mazrui, Ali A. "Casualties of an Underdeveloped Class Structure: The Expulsion of Luo Workers and Asian Bourgeoisie from Uganda." In William Shack and Elliott Skinner (eds.), *Strangers in African Societies* (University of California Press, 1979), pp. 261–279.
"Tanzania versus East Africa: A Case of Unwitting Federal Sabotage." *Journal of Commonwealth Political Studies* 3(3) (1965): 209–225.
Mbembe, Achille. "At the Edge of the World: Boundaries, Territoriality, and Sovereignty in Africa." *Public Culture* 12(1) (2000): 259–284.
"Necropolitics." *Public Culture* 15(1) (2003): 11–40.
On the Postcolony (University of California Press, 2001).
McDow, Thomas. *Buying Time: Debt and Mobility in the Western Indian Ocean* (Ohio University Press, 2018).
McGovern, Mike. *A Socialist Peace?: Explaining the Absence of War in an African Country* (University of Chicago Press, 2018).
Médard, Claire. "Elected Leaders, Militias and Prophets: Violence in Mount Elgon (2006–2008)." Les Cahiers d'Afrique de l'Est, The General Elections in Kenya, 2007 (2009), pp. 339–361.

Meiu, George Paul. *Ethno-Erotic Economies: Sexuality, Money, and Belonging in Kenya* (University of Chicago Press, 2017).

Mensah, Anthony. "The Process of Monetary Decolonization in Africa." *Utafiti* 4(1) (1979): 45–63.

Milford, Ismay, Gerald McCann, Emma Hunter, and Daniel Branch. "Another World? East Africa, Decolonisation, and the Global History of the Mid-Twentieth Century." *Journal of African History* 62(3) (2021): 394–410.

Mirowski, Philip. "Defining Neoliberalism." In Philip Mirowski and Dieter Plehwe (eds.), *The Road from Mont Pèlerin: The Making of the Neoliberal Thought Collective* (Harvard University Press, 2015), pp. 417–456.

Mitchell, Timothy. "Infrastructures Work on Time." *E-Flux* (January 2020), www.e-flux.com/architecture/new-silk-roads/312596/infrastructures-work-on-time/.

  Rule of Experts: Egypt, Techno-Politics, Modernity (University of California Press, 2002).

Mittelman, James. *Ideology and Politics in Uganda from Obote to Amin* (Cornell University Press, 1975).

  "Underdevelopment and Nationalisation: Banking in Tanzania." *Journal of Modern African Studies* 16(4) (1978): 612–613.

  Underdevelopment and the Transition to Socialism: Mozambique and Tanzania (Academic Press, 1981).

Miyazaki, Hirokazu. "Between Arbitrage and Speculation: An Economy of Belief and Doubt." *Economy and Society* 36(3) (2007): 396–415.

  Arbitraging Japan: Dreams of Capitalism at the End of Finance (University of California Press, 2013).

Mizes, James C. "Investing in Independence: Popular Shareholding on the West African Stock Exchange." *Africa* 92(4) (2022): 644–662.

Mkandawire, Thandika. "The Spread of Economic Doctrines and Policymaking in Postcolonial Africa." *African Studies Review* 57(1) (2014): 171–198.

Monnet, Eric. *Controlling Credit: Central Banking and the Planned Economy in Postwar France* (Cambridge University Press, 2019).

Monnet, Éric. "Une coopération à la française. La France, le dollar et le système de Bretton Woods, 1960–1965." *Histoire@Politique* 19(1) (2013): 83–100.

Morgan, D. J. *Official History of Colonial Development: A Reassessment of British Aid Policy, 1951–1965* (Macmillan Press, 1980).

Morris, James. "'Cultivating the African': Barclays DCO and the Decolonisation of Business Strategy in Kenya, 1950–78." *Journal of Imperial and Commonwealth History* 44(4) (2016): 649–671.

Moskowitz, Kara. *Seeing Like a Citizen: Decolonization, Development, and the Making of Kenya* (Ohio University Press, 2019).

Mosley, Paul. *The Settler Economies: Studies in the Economic History of Kenya and Southern Rhodesia, 1900–1963* (Cambridge University Press, 1983).

Moyn, Samuel. *Not Enough: Human Rights in an Unequal World* (Belknap Press, 2018).

Mtei, Edwin. *From Goatherd to Governor: The Autobiography of Edwin Mtei* (Mkuki na Nyota, 2005).

Mugabi, Edward. "The Development of Towns in Uganda, 1970–1980: Political Change, the Decline of a Nation's Capital, and the Spread of Small Towns." UCL Development Planning Unit, Working Paper No. 39 (1992).

Mujaju, Akiiki. "The Gold Allegations Motion and Political Development in Uganda." *African Affairs* 86(345) (1987): 479–504.

Mukwaya, A. B. *Land Tenure in Buganda: Present Day Tendencies* (East African Institute of Social Research, 1953).

Muniesa, Fabian. "A Flank Movement in the Understanding of Valuation." *The Sociological Review* 59 (2011): 24–38.

Murillo, Bianca. *Market Encounters: Consumer Cultures in Twentieth-Century Ghana* (Ohio University Press, 2017).

Musandu, Phoebe. *Pressing Interests: The Agenda and Influence of a Colonial East African Newspaper Sector* (McGill-Queen's University Press, 2018).

Musisi, Nakanyike. "Baganda Women's Night Market Activities," in Felix K. Ekechi and Bessie House-Midamba (eds.), *African Market Women and Economic Power: The Role of Women in African Economic Development* (Greenwood Press, 2005), pp. 132–140.

Mutibwa, Phares. *The Bank of Uganda (1966–2006): A Historical Perspective* (Bank of Uganda, 2006).

Mutongi, Kenda. *Worries of the Heart: Widows, Family, and Community in Kenya* (University of Chicago Press, 2007).

Mwangi, Wambui. "Of Coins and Conquest: The East African Currency Board, the Rupee Crisis, and the Problem of Colonialism in the East African Protectorate." *Comparative Studies in Society and History* 43 (4) (2001): 763–765.

"The Lion, the Native and the Coffee Plant: Political Imagery and the Ambiguous Art of Currency Design in Colonial Kenya." *Geopolitics* 7 (1) (2002): 31–62.

"The Order of Money: Colonialism and the East African Currency Board." PhD dissertation, University of Pennsylvania, 2003.

Mwase, Ngila. "Decision-Making in Tanzania's National Bank of Commerce: Controls and Participation Dichotomy." *Economics Research Bureau Paper* 75(9) (1975): 1–49.

Nakileza, Bob. "A True Story of Coffees Magendo through Mount Elgon (Uganda)." *Etudes rurales* 180 (2007): 131–136.

Narsey, Wadan. *British Imperialism and the Making of Colonial Currency Systems* (Palgrave Macmillan, 2016).

Ndegwa, Duncan. *The Kenya Shilling: Within and Across the Frontiers* (Nairobi, 1977).

Walking in Kenyatta Struggles (Kenya Leadership Institute, 2011).

Ndegwa, Philip. *The Common Market and Development in East Africa* (East African Publishing House, 1968).

Nembhard, Jessica Gordon. *Collective Courage: A History of African American Cooperative Economic Thought and Practice* (Penn State University Press, 2014).

Newell, Sasha. "Ethnography in a Shell Game: Turtles All the Way Down in Abidjan." *Cultural Anthropology* 34(3) (2019): 299–327.

Newlyn, Walter Tessier. *Money in an African Context* (Oxford University Press, 1967).

"Comparative Analysis of Central Bank Acts." East African Institute of Social Research, EDRP 101, 1966.

Ngau, Peter. "Tensions in Empowerment: The Experience of the 'Harambee' (Self-Help) Movement in Kenya." *Economic Development and Cultural Change* 35(3) (1987): 523–538.

Nsekela, Amon. "The Public Corporation as an Instrument of Economic Development in Africa." *Mbioni* 7(3) (1972): 5–37.

"The Role of Commercial Banking in Building a Socialist Tanzania." *African Review* 4(1) (1974): 25–42.

"The Role of Commercial Banking in Building a Socialist Tanzania." In *Socialism and Social Accountability* (Kenya Literature Bureau, 1978).

"Social Accountability of a Public Enterprise." In *Socialism and Social Accountability* (Kenya Literature Bureau, 1978).

Socialism and Social Accountability (Kenya Literature Bureau, 1978).

"Some Practical Problems of Nationalization." *Mbioni* 5(4) (1969): 21–22.

Nsibambi, Apolo. "Increased Government Control of Buganda's Financial Sinews since the Revolution of 1966." *Public Administration and Development* 10(2) (1971): 100–112.

Nubukpo, Kako. "Politique monétaire et servitude volontaire." *Politique Africaine* 105(1) (2007): 70–84.

Nugent, Paul. *Boundaries, Communities and State-Making in West Africa* (Cambridge University Press, 2019).

Smugglers, Secessionists & Loyal Citizens on the Ghana-Togo Frontier (James Currey, 2002).

"States and Social Contracts in Africa." *New Left Review* II(63) (2010): 35–68.

Nyamnjoh, Francis. "Incompleteness: Frontier Africa and the Currency of Conviviality." *Journal of Asian and African Studies* 52(3) (2017): 253–270.
Nyamunda, Tinashe. "Money, Banking and Rhodesia's Unilateral Declaration of Independence." *Journal of Imperial and Commonwealth History* 45(5) (2017): 746–776.
Nye, Joseph. *Pan-Africanism and East African Integration* (Harvard University Press, 1965).
Nyerere, Julius. "Public Ownership in Tanzania." Reprinted in the *Arusha Declaration, and TANU's Policy of Socialism and Self-reliance* (Government Printer, 1967), pp. 21–25.
Nzomo, Maria. "Democracy, Gender, Equity, and Development in Africa, with Special Reference to Kenya." In Julius E. Nyang'oro and Timothy M. Shaw (eds.), *Beyond Structural Adjustment in Africa* (Praeger Publishers, 1992), pp. 99–118.
Obbo, Christine. *African Women: Their Struggle for Economic Independence* (Zed Books, 1980).
  "The Effects of Land Tenure Change upon Women in East African Smallholder Agriculture," Land Tenure Center Paper 124 (University of Wisconsin-Madison, 1985).
  "Women's Careers in Low Income Areas as Indicators of Country and Town Dynamics" paper presented at International African Institute Seminar on Town and Country (Lusaka, 1972).
Ocobock, Paul. *An Uncertain Age: The Politics of Manhood in Kenya* (Ohio University Press, 2017).
Ogle, Vanessa. "'Funk Money': The End of Empires, The Expansion of Tax Havens, and Decolonization as an Economic and Financial Event." *Past & Present* 249(1) (2020): 213–249.
Okoth, Godfrey. "Intermittent Tensions in Uganda-Kenya Relations: Historical Perspectives." *Transafrican Journal of History* 21 (1992): 69–92.
Oloya, J. J. *Some Aspects of Economic Development with Special Reference to East Africa* (East African Literature Bureau, 1968).
Olukoshi, Adebayo and Thandika Mkandawire. *Between Liberalisation and Oppression: The Politics of Structural Adjustment in Africa* (Codesria, 1996).
Onah, Emmanuel, Chinwe Okoyeuzu, and Chibuike Uche. "The Nationalisation of British Banks in Post-Colonial Tanzania: Did the Banks' Net Capital Export Position and Home Government Support Influence Compensation Negotiation Outcomes?" *Business History* 64(6) (2022): 1088–1109.
Oonk, Gijsbert. *Settled Strangers: Asian Business Elites in East Africa, 1800–2000* (SAGE, 2013).

Osei-Opare, Nana. "If You Trouble a Hungry Snake, You Will Force It to Bite You." *Journal of African History* 62(1) (2021): 59–78.
Osokina, Elena. *Stalin's Quest for Gold: The Torgsin Hard-Currency Shops and Soviet Industrialization* (Cornell University Press, 2021).
Ossome, Lyn. "Can the Law Secure Women's Rights to Land in Africa?" *Feminist Economics* 20(1) (2014): 155–177.
Pallaver, Karin. "'The African Native Has No Pocket': Monetary Practices and Currency Transitions in Early Colonial Uganda." *International Journal of African Historical Studies* 48(3) (2015): 471–499.
  "A Currency Muddle: Resistance, Materialities and the Local Use of Money during the East African Rupee Crisis." *Journal of Eastern African Studies* 13(3) (2019): 546–564.
Park, Emma. *Infrastructures of Attachments: Austerity, Sovereignty, and Expertise in Kenya* (Duke University Press, forthcoming).
  "Intimacy and Estrangement: Safaricom, Divisibility, and the Making of the Corporate Nation-State" *Comparative Studies of South Asia, Africa, and Middle East* 41(3) (2021): 423–440.
  "The Right to Sovereign Seizure? Taxation, Valuation, and the Imperial British East Africa Company." In Gurminder K. Bhambra and Julia McClure (eds.), *Imperial Inequalities: The Politics of Economic Governance Across European Empires* (Manchester University Press, 2022), pp. 79–97.
Parkin, David. *Palms, Wine, and Witnesses* (Intertext Books, 1972).
Parreñas, Juno. *Decolonizing Extinction: The Work of Care in Orangutan Rehabilitation* (Duke University Press, 2018).
Pauw, Ernest-Josef. "Banking in East Africa." In Peter Marlin (ed.), *Financial Aspects of Development in East Africa* (Weltforum Verlag, 1970), pp. 175–258.
Peebles, Gustav. *The Euro & Its Rivals: Currency & the Construction of a Transnational City* (Indiana University Press, 2011).
  "Inverting the Panopticon: Money and the Nationalization of the Future." *Public Culture* 20(2) (2008): 233–265.
  "Rehabilitating the Hoard: The Social Dynamics of Unbanking in Africa and Beyond." *Africa* 84(4) (2014): 595–613.
Perrone, Nicolás. *Investment Treaties and the Legal Imagination: How Foreign Investors Play by Their Own Rules* (Oxford University Press, 2021).
Peterson, Derek. "Colonial Rule and African Politics (1930–1963)." In Nic Cheeseman, Karuti Kanyinga, and Gabrielle Lynch (eds.), *The Oxford Handbook of Kenyan Politics* (Oxford University Press, 2020), pp. 29–42.
  Ethnic Patriotism and the East African Revival: A History of Dissent, c.1935–1972 (Cambridge University Press, 2014).

"Government Work in Idi Amin's Uganda." *Africa* 91(4) (2021): 620–640.
"The Politics of Archives in Uganda." In *Oxford Research Encyclopedia of African History* (Oxford University Press, 2021), https://doi.org/10.1093/acrefore/9780190277734.013.982.
"Violence and Political Advocacy in the Lost Counties, Western Uganda, 1930–64." *The International Journal of African Historical Studies* 48 (1) (2015): 51–72.
Peterson, Derek and Edgar Taylor. "Rethinking the State in Idi Amin's Uganda: The Politics of Exhortation." *Journal of Eastern African Studies* 7(1) (2013): 58–82.
Pigeaud, Fanny and Ndongo Samba Sylla. *Africa's Last Colonial Currency: The CFA Franc Story* (Pluto Press, 2021).
Plehwe, Dieter. "The Origins of the Neoliberal Economic Development Discourse." In Philip Mirowski and Dieter Plehwe (eds.), *The Road from Mont Pèlerin: The Making of the Neoliberal Thought Collective* (Harvard University Press, 2015), pp. 238–279.
Ponte, Stefano. *Farmers and Markets in Tanzania* (James Currey, 2002).
Porter, Theodore M. *Trust in Numbers: The Pursuit of Objectivity in Science and Public Life* (Princeton University Press, 1995).
Pratt, Cranford. *The Critical Phase in Tanzania: Nyerere and the Emergence of Socialist Strategy* (Cambridge University Press, 1976).
Prestholdt, Jeremy. "Politics of the Soil: Separatism, Autochthony, and Decolonization at the Kenyan Coast." *Journal of African History* 55 (2) (2014): 249–270.
Proctor, J. H. "The Effort to Federate East Africa: A Post-Mortem." *Political Quarterly* 37(1) (1966): 46–69.
Prunier, Gérard. "Le Magendo: Essai sur quelques aspects marginaux des echanges commerciaux en Afrique orentale." *Politique Africaine* 9 (1983): 53–62.
Quayson, Ato. *Oxford Street, Accra: Street Life and the Itineraries of Transnationalism* (Duke University Press, 2014).
Raeymaekers, Timothy. *Violent Capitalism and Hybrid Identity in the Eastern Congo* (Cambridge University Press, 2014).
Reid, Richard. *A History of Modern Uganda* (Cambridge University Press, 2017).
Resnick, Idrian. *The Long Transition: Building Socialism in Tanzania* (Monthly Review Press, 1981).
Richards, Audrey (ed.). *Economic Development and Tribal Change: A Study of Immigrant Labour in Buganda* (East African Institute of Social Research, 1954).
Richards, Audrey, Ford Sturrock, and Jean M. Fortt. *Subsistence to Commercial Farming in Present-Day Buganda: An Economic and Anthropological Survey* (Cambridge University Press, 1973).

Roberts, George. *Revolutionary State-Making: African Liberation and the Global Cold War, 1961–1974* (Cambridge University Press, 2021).
Robertson, A. F. "Bugerere: A County Case History." In Audrey Richards, Ford Sturrock, and Jean M. Fortt (eds.), *Farming in Present-Day Buganda: An Economic and Anthropological Survey* (Cambridge University Press, 1973), p. 261.
Rockenbach, Ashley. "Contingent Homes, Contingent Nation: Rwandan Settlers in Uganda, 1911–64." PhD dissertation, University of Michigan, 2018.
Roitman, Janet. *Fiscal Disobedience* (Princeton University Press, 2005).
Rothchild, Donald. *Racial Bargaining in Independent Kenya: A Study of Minorities and Decolonization* (Institute of Race Relations, 1973).
Roy, Srirupa. *Beyond Belief: India and the Politics of Postcolonial Nationalism* (Duke University Press, 2007).
Russell, Aidan. *Politics and Violence in Burundi: The Language of Truth in an Emerging State* (Cambridge University Press, 2019).
Rweyemamu, Justinian. "Restructuring the International Monetary System." *Development Dialogue* 1980(2): 75–91.
Saeteurn, Muey. *Cultivating Their Own: Agriculture in Western Kenya during the "Development" Era* (University of Rochester Press, 2020).
Sanchez-Sibony, Oscar. "Capitalism's Fellow Traveller: The Soviet Union, Bretton Woods, and the Cold War, 1944–1958." *Comparative Studies in Society & History* 56(2) (2014): 290–319.
Schama, Simon. *The Embarrassment of Riches: An Interpretation of Dutch Culture in the Golden Age* (Vintage Books, 1988).
Schatzberg, Michael. *Political Legitimacy in Middle Africa: Father, Family, Food* (Indiana University Press, 2001).
Schenk, Catherine. "Monetary Institutions in Newly Independent Countries: The Experience of Malaya, Ghana and Nigeria in the 1950s." *Financial History Review* 4(2) (1997): 181–198.
Scherz, China. *Having People, Having Heart: Charity, Sustainable Development, and Problems of Dependence in Central Uganda* (University of Chicago Press, 2014).
Schmidt, Elizabeth. *Cold War and Decolonization in Guinea* (Ohio University Press, 2007).
Schneider, Leander. *Government of Development: Peasants and Politicians in Postcolonial Tanzania* (Indiana University Press, 2014).
  "The Maasai's new clothes: A developmentalist modernity and its exclusions." *Africa Today* 53(1) (2006): 101–131.
Scotton, Carol M. M. "Some Swahili Political Words." *Journal of Modern African Studies* 3(4) (1965): 531–533.
Seidman, Ann. *Comparative Development Strategies in East Africa* (East African Publishing House, 1972).

Selsjord, Mikael. "Recent Developments in Commercial Banking in East Africa: A Statistical Analysis." *Economic & Statistical Review* 1966 (20): VIII–XXII.

Semboja, Joseph and S. M. H. Rugumisa. "Price Control in the Management of an Economic Crisis: The National Price Commission in Tanzania." *African Studies Review* 31(1) (1988): 47–65.

Sharma, Nandita. *Home Rule: National Sovereignty and the Separation of Natives and Migrants* (Duke University Press, 2020).

Shepherd Jr., George. *They Wait in Darkness* (John Day Company, 1955).

Shipton, Parker. *Bitter Money: Cultural Economy and Some African Meanings of Forbidden Commodities* (American Anthropological Association, 1989).

Credit between Cultures: Farmers, Financiers, and Misunderstanding in Africa (Yale University Press, 2011).

Mortgaging the Ancestors: Ideologies of Attachment in Africa (Yale University Press, 2009).

The Nature of Entrustment: Intimacy, Exchange, and the Sacred in Africa (Yale University Press, 2007).

Shivji, Issa. "Capitalism Unlimited: Public Corporations in Partnership with Multinational Corporations." *African Review* 3(3) (1973): 359–381.

Class Struggles in Tanzania (Tanzania Publishing House, 1976).

Julius Nyerere: Development as Rebellion, vol. 3 (Mkuki na Nyota, 2020).

"The Rule of Law and Ujamaa in the Ideological Formation of Tanzania." *Social & Legal Studies* 4(2) (1995): 147–174.

Siegel, Benjamin. "Modernizing Peasants and 'Master Farmers': Progressive Agriculture in Early Independent India." *Comparative Studies of South Asia, Africa and the Middle East* 37(1) (2017): 64–85.

Skinner, Kate. *The Fruits of Freedom in British Togoland: Literacy, Politics and Nationalism, 1914–2014* (Cambridge University Press, 2015).

Slobodian, Quinn. *Globalists: The End of Empire and the Birth of Neoliberalism* (Harvard University Press, 2018).

Smith, Lahra. *Making Citizens in Africa: Ethnicity, Gender, and National Identity in Ethiopia* (Cambridge University Press, 2013).

Sorensen, Pernille. "Commercialization of Food Crops in Busoga, Uganda, and the Renegotiation of Gender." *Gender & Society* 10(5) (1996): 608–628.

Stein, Howard. *Beyond the World Bank Agenda: An Institutional Approach to Development* (University of Chicago Press, 2008).

Stein, Howard and Ernest Wilson. "The Political Economy of Robert Bates: A Critical Reading of Rational Choice in Africa." *World Development* 21(6) (1993): 1035–1053.

Stockwell, Sarah. *The British End of the British Empire* (Cambridge University Press, 2018).

Summers, Carol. "Grandfathers, Grandsons, Morality, and Radical Politics in Late Colonial Buganda." *International Journal of African Historical Studies* 38(3) (2005): 427–447.
  "Lending to the Empire: Savings Campaigns in Uganda during World War II." Paper presented at European Conference on African Studies 2016.
  "Local Critiques of Global Development: Patriotism in Late Colonial Buganda." *International Journal of African Historical Studies* 47(1) (2014): 21–35.
  "Radical Rudeness: Ugandan Social Critiques in the 1940s." *Journal of Social History* 39(3) (2006): 741–770.
  "Ugandan Politics and World War II." In Ahmad Alawad Sikainga et al. (eds.), *Africa and World War II* (Cambridge University Press, 2015), pp. 480–498.
Suruma, Ezra Sabiti. *Advancing the Ugandan Economy: A Personal Account* (Brookings Institution Press, 2014).
Swartz, Lana. *New Money: How Payment Became Social Media* (Yale University Press, 2020).
Taoua, Phyllis. *African Freedom: How Africa Responded to Independence* (Cambridge University Press, 2018).
Taylor, Edgar. "1959 and 1972: Boycott, Expulsion, and Memory." *Awaaz*, www.awaazmagazine.com/volume-19/issue-2-volume-19/cover-story-issue-2-volume-19/1959-and-1972-boycott-expulsion-and-memory
Taylor, Edgar Curtis. "Asians and Africans in Ugandan Urban Life, 1959–1972." PhD dissertation, University of Michigan, 2016.
  "Claiming Kabale: Racial Thought and Urban Governance in Uganda." *Journal of Eastern African Studies* 7(1) (2013): 143–163.
  "Eddembe." In Dilip Menon (ed.), *Changing Theory: Concepts from the Global South* (Routledge, 2022), pp. 111–126.
Taylor, Ian. "France à Fric: The CFA Zone in Africa and Neocolonialism." *Third World Quarterly* 40(6) (2019): 1064–1088.
Taylor, Keeanga-Yamahtta. *Race for Profit: How Banks and the Real Estate Industry Undermined Black Homeownership* (University of North Carolina Press, 2019).
Thompson, Gardner. *Governing Uganda: British Colonial Rule and Its Legacy* (Fountain Publishers, 2003).
Tignor, Robert. *Capitalism and Nationalism at the End of Empire: State and Business in Decolonizing Egypt, Nigeria, and Kenya, 1945–1963* (Princeton University Press, 1997).
Tripp, Aili. *Changing the Rules: The Politics of Liberalization and the Urban Informal Economy in Tanzania* (University of California Press, 1997).

Truitt, Allison. "Money." In Felix Stein (ed.), *Open Encyclopedia of Anthropology* (Open Knowledge Press, 2020), www.anthroencyclopedia.com/entry/money.

Turner, Terence. "Marxian Value Theory: An Anthropological Perspective." *Anthropological Theory* 8(1) (2008): 43–56.

Twaddle, Michael (ed.). *Expulsion of a Minority: Essays on Ugandan Asians* (Athlone Press, 1975).

Uche, Chibuike U. "British Government, British Businesses, and the Indigenization Exercise in Post-Independence Nigeria." *Business History Review* 86(4) (2012): 745–771.

Van de Walle, Nicolas. *African Economies and the Politics of Permanent Crisis, 1979–1999* (Cambridge University Press, 2001).

van der Laar, Aart J. M. "Foreign Business and Capital Exports from Developing Countries: The Tanzanian Experience." In Lionel Cliffe and John Saul (eds.), *Socialism in Tanzania Volume 1* : Politics (East African Publishing House, 1972), pp. 83–87.

Van Zwanenberg, R. M. A. with Anne King. *An Economic History of Kenya and Uganda, 1800–1970* (Macmillan Press, 1975).

Vaughan, Chris. "The Politics of Regionalism and Federation in East Africa, 1958–1964." *The Historical Journal* 62(2) (2019): 519–540.

Vaughan, Chris, Julie MacArthur, Emma Hunter, and Gerard McCann. "Thinking East African: Debating Federation and Regionalism, 1960–1977," in Matteo Grilli and Frank Gerits (eds.), *Visions of African Unity: New Perspectives on the History of Pan-Africanism and African Unification Projects* (Palgrave Macmillan, 2021), pp. 49–75.

Verdery, Katherine. *What Was Socialism, and What Comes Next?* (Princeton University Press, 1996).

Vokes, Richard, Derek R. Peterson, and Edgar C. Taylor. "Photography, Evidence and Concealed Histories from Idi Amin's Uganda, 1971–79." *History of Photography* 44(2–3) (2020): 151–171.

von Hayek, Friedrich. "The Pretence of Knowledge." Lecture to the Memory of Alfred Nobel, 1974.

Wagner, Gunter. *The Bantu of North Kavirondo: Volume 1* (Oxford University Press, 1949).

The Bantu of North Kavirondo: Volume 2 (Oxford University Press, 1956)

Waters, Tony. "Beyond Structural Adjustment: State and Market in a Rural. Tanzanian Village." *African Studies Review* 40(2) (1997): 59–89.

Weber, Isabella. *How China Escaped Shock Therapy: The Market Reform Debate* (Taylor & Francis Group, 2021).

Weber, Max. "Politics as a Vocation." In H. H. Gerth and C. Wright Mills (eds.), *From Max Weber: Essays in Sociology* (Oxford University Press, 1946), pp. 77–128.

Economy and Society (University of California Press, 1978).

Weiss, Brad. "'Buying Her Grave': Money, Movement and Aids in North-West Tanzania." *Africa: Journal of the International African Institute* 63(1) (1993): 19–35.

The Making and Unmaking of the Haya Lived World: Consumption, Commoditization, and Everyday Practice (Duke University Press, 2012).

Sacred Trees, Bitter Harvests: Globalizing Coffee in Northwest Tanzania (Heinemann, 2003).

Weitzberg, Keren. *We Do Not Have Borders: Greater Somalia and the Predicaments of Belonging in Kenya* (Ohio University Press, 2017).

Wekesa, Peter Wafula. "The History of Community Relations across the Kenya-Uganda Boarder." PhD Dissertation, Kenyatta University, 2011.

"Magendo and Survivalism: Babukusu-Bagisu Relations and Economic Ingenuity on the Kenya-Uganda Border 1962–1980." In Dereje Feyissa and Markus Virgil Höhne (eds.), *Borders & Borderlands as Resources in the Horn of Africa* (Boydell & Brewer, 2010), pp. 151–167.

White, Luise. *Unpopular Sovereignty: Rhodesian Independence and African Decolonization* (University of Chicago Press, 2015).

Whittaker, Hannah. "Frontier Security in Northeast Africa: Conflict and Colonial Development on the Margins." *Journal of African History* 58(3) (2017): 381–402.

Whitworth, Alan. "Price Controls Techniques in Poor Countries: The Tanzanian Case." *World Development* 10(6) (1982): 475–488.

Wilk, Richard. "Poverty and Excess in Binge Economies." *Economic Anthropology* 1(1) (2014): 66–79.

Willis, Justin. *Potent Brews: Social History of Alcohol In East Africa 1850–1999* (Ohio University Press, 2002).

"Thrift, Citizenship, and Self-Improvement: Savings and Borrowings in Uganda from c.1940 to 1970" (unpublished manuscript).

Willis, Justin and George Gona. "Pwani C Kenya? Memory, Documents and Secessionist Politics in Coastal Kenya." *African Affairs* 112(446) (2013): 48–71.

Windel, Aaron. *Cooperative Rule: Community Development in Britain's Late Empire* (University of California Press, 2022).

Wise, Norton M. *The Values of Precision* (Princeton University Press, 1997).

Wood, Ellen Meiksins. "The Separation of the Economic and the Political in Capitalism." *New Left Review* I(127) (1981): 66–95.

Wrigley, C. C. *Crops and Wealth in Uganda: A Short Agrarian History* (East African Institute of Social Research, 1959).

Yaffey, M. J. H. *Balance of Payments Problems of a Developing Country: Tanzania* (Brill, 1970).

Yeh, Rihan. "Visas, Jokes, and Contraband: Citizenship and Sovereignty at the Mexico–U.S. Border." *Comparative Studies in Society and History* 59(1) (2017): 154–182.

Young, Alden. "A Currency for Sudan." In Stephen J. Macekura and Erez Manela (eds.), *The Development Century: A Global History* (Cambridge University Press, 2018), pp. 130–149.

  Transforming Sudan: Decolonization, Economic Development, and State Formation (Cambridge University Press, 2018).

Young, Crawford, Neal Sherman, and Tim Rose. *Cooperatives & Development: Agricultural Politics in Ghana and Uganda* (University of Wisconsin Press, 1981).

Zatlin, Jonathan. *The Currency of Socialism: Money and Political Culture in East Germany* (Cambridge University Press, 2008).

Znoj, Heinzpeter. "Hot Money and War Debts: Transactional Regimes in Southwestern Sumatra." *Comparative Studies in Society and History* 40(2) (1998): 193–222.

Index

accounting standards, 29, 121, 126, 135, 154–156, 161, 179–183, 185, 195, 197–201, 223, 249, 283–284, 318
accusation, economy of, 217, 235, 243, 261
Africanization, 33, 82, 135, 158, 176, 188–189, 214, 244
Amin, Idi, 9, 12, 34, 46, 92, 98, 124, 127–130, 135–136, 141, 214–215, 224, 233, 244–245, 249–250, 259, 266, 273, 276–278, 282, 316
arbitrage, 8, 24, 40, 264–265, 267–269, 276, 281–282, 284, 286–287, 294, 296, 299, 302–303, 306, 311
Arusha Declaration, 30, 150, 152, 156, 159, 164–166, 169–170, 173, 177, 179, 183, 188, 194, 205
Arusha Initiative, 314–315
Asians (South Asians), 13, 17–21, 25–26, 30, 34, 38, 40, 46, 55, 73, 91, 97–98, 100, 102–103, 117, 124, 128, 132, 135–141, 158, 162, 164, 170, 189, 207, 209, 214, 217, 219–221, 230, 244, 259, 269–270
assets, 54, 59, 64, 81, 86–87, 90, 138–140, 155–156, 160, 170, 178–181, 199, 218, 290, 301
assimilation, *See* belonging
Association Internationale Pour La Promotion et la Protection Des Investments Prives en Territoiries Etrangers, 175–176

balance of payments, 77, 141, 219, 277, 317
Bank of England, 51, 53, 57, 62, 68, 80, 82, 89, 149, 172, 175, 188
Bank of Tanzania, 86–87, 157, 166, 171, 173, 187, 196, 202, 205, 207, 315

Bank of Uganda, 1, 11, 26, 31, 39, 41, 49, 79, 87, 93, 96–97, 113–115, 125–126, 129, 132–133, 138–140, 144–146, 176, 227, 234, 248–249, 316
Banking, *See* Uganda Commercial Bank, *See* Uganda Credit & Savings Bank, *See* Barclays Bank, *See* National Bank of Commerce, *See* savings, *See* credit
Barclays Bank, 12, 27, 29, 56, 90, 101, 129, 138, 148–150, 153–157, 160–163, 166–170, 174, 176–185, 188, 192, 195, 197, 199–204
belonging, 15, 34, 36–40, 44, 46–47, 54, 71, 97–98, 119, 132, 135–138, 140–141, 214, 217, 219, 230, 244, 265, 303, 310
binge economy, 264, 275, 287, 289, 294, 298
Blumenthal, Erwin, 68–71
Bomani, Paul, 18, 52–53, 68, 70, 73, 78, 86, 186
bonds, 22, 95–96, 98, 118, 120–124
borders, 2, 7, 12, 24–27, 34, 37–40, 79, 88, 90–91, 96–98, 133, 136–137, 139–140, 142–143, 146, 207, 213, 217, 219, 230, 244, 264, 269, 272, 280, 286, 311
Brown, Roland, 180, 202–203
Buganda, 9, 13, 18, 21, 41, 44, 71, 95, 99–100, 105–106, 110, 115, 213, 270–271
Bugisu, 18, 21, 99–100, 266, 271, 273, 276, 281
Busoga, 21, 99, 106, 111, 121, 123, 132, 137, 224, 231–232, 236, 244, 253, 258

356

Index 357

calculation, *See* accounting standards
Central Bank of Kenya, 87–88, 277, 310
central banks, 5, 7–8, 22, 24–25, 53, 60, 69, 80, 83, 85, 88–90, 269, 310, 315, 326
CFA franc, 23
Chepkube, 263, 273–277, 279, 282–285, 288–292, 297–300, 302–303
citizenship, 2, 11, 14, 35–40, 43, 45, 47, 87, 93–98, 112–113, 117, 132–133, 135, 137, 147, 186, 205, 218, 227, 231, 236, 258, 260, 262, 265–267, 282, 303, 306–307, 309
  credible citizenship, 16, 32, 35–38, 45, 87, 93, 112–113, 118, 193, 213, 223, 235–236, 256, 259, 324
  pluralistic, 37, 40, 47, 146, 219, 261–262, 265, 267, 303, 306
coffee, 4–5, 10, 17–18, 26, 42, 44, 46, 48, 95, 98, 100–101, 106, 116, 125, 130, 132–133, 141, 173, 195, 213, 215, 218, 221–223, 225–227, 229, 233, 246–247, 251, 254, 261, 263, 265–273, 275, 277–285, 289–291, 295, 297–298, 300–304, 307, 312, 322
  history of, 269
Cold War, 164–166, 204
common market, 61, 68–69, 73–75, 77, 79
compensation, 148, *See* nationalization
constellation of interests, 42–43, 46, 121, 223, 227, 234, 265, 273, 301, 303, 310, 315
controlled conversion, 5, 7, 24, 56, 135, 142, 145, 249, 267, 269, 286, 317
cooperatives, 18, 29–31, 47, 100–102, 118, 129, 150, 171, 191, 194–195, 221–225, 232, 276, 300
cotton, 4–5, 18, 21, 34, 95, 98, 101, 110–111, 116, 131–133, 173, 195, 213, 218, 221–224, 226–227, 232, 251, 253, 261, 270
counterfeit, 8, 297–299
credit, 6–7, 21, 23, 30, 32–33, 35, 42, 49–50, 53, 60, 66, 69, 72, 93, 98, 101–102, 105–109, 112, 114, 117–118, 128, 133–135, 151–153, 170–171, 188, 190–192, 195, 204, 209, 218, 221–223, 248, 310, 320, 322–323, *See also* loans
currency, 2, 24–25, 38, 41–42, 52, 73, 78, 89–91, 94, 96–97, 133, 171, 249, 269, 306, 310
currency controls, *See* exchange controls

debt, *See* credit
decolonization, 2–3, 11–12, 14–15, 28, 30, 38, 53, 58, 61, 68, 71–72, 80, 93, 169, 309, 318
development, 19, 22, 37, 45–46, 51, 53, 56, 59, 65, 77, 93, 113–114, 125, 172, 174, 231
domestic currency, 5, 7, 85, 88, 94, 234
domestic labor, 4, 221, 228–229, 289, 291–292

East Africa & Mauritius Association, 165, 175–176
East Africa Royal Commission, 35
East African Currency Board, 22, 51–54, 56–57, 59, 61–70, 74, 78, 80, 82, 84, 89, 114, 168, 171
East African Federation, 53, 61, 68, 70, 72–73, 76, 78, 102, 311
East African Royal Commission, 19, 108
East African shilling, 22, 51–52, 54–55, 64–66, 75, 79, 83, 91, 202
economic crimes, 34, 48–49, 211, 217, 219, 231, 243–245, 251, 253, 255, 257, 259
Economic Crimes Tribunal, *See* economic crimes
Economic War, 135, 214, 244, 278
essential commodities, 49, 123, 216, 218, 229, 234, 239, 241, 253, 256, 273, 277, 300, 304, *See* sugar
exchange controls, 1, 4, 7, 34, 56–57, 69, 77, 82, 90, 133–134, 137, 140–141, 143, 172, 227, 248–249, 316–317, 321
export crops, 1, 3, 5, 8, 17, 22, 27–28, 36, 49–50, 54, 93, 101, 111, 132–133, 169–170, 213, 215, 221–222, 228, 233, 270, 276–277, 287, 310, 312, 315, 324–325
expulsion, *See* belonging

foreign exchange, 1–3, 5–8, 10, 22–23, 25–27, 29, 33, 42, 46–48, 60, 69, 84–85, 88, 91–92, 94–95, 97, 114, 121, 133–134, 138–139, 141–142, 145–146, 153–154, 157, 170, 172–173, 178, 189, 208, 218, 224–227, 230, 234, 237–238, 248–249, 273, 277, 300, 310, 312, 314, 316–317, 326, See also exchange controls

foreign reserves, See foreign exchange

formula, 21, 154, 156, 179, 181–185, 197–199, 201

Gichuru, James, 70, 78, 83
gorogoro, 284–285
government of value, 2, 10, 24, 26, 34, 43, 46, 49–51, 53, 62, 75, 84, 86, 88–89, 93, 119, 134, 140, 143, 153–154, 206, 214, 229, 246, 251, 261, 264, 292–293, 302–303, 308–309, 313, 315–317, 319, 323, 325–326

Green, Reginald, 180, 184, 202–203, 312

hoarding, 7, 34, 48, 131, 194, 211, 214–215, 230, 243, 247, 250, 253, 256–258, 261, 273

independence, 2, See decolonization
inequality, 19, 37, 39, 54, 75–76, 80, 93, 106–107, 113, 132, 159
inflation, 24, 34, 46–47, 62, 88, 213, 230, 246, 313–314, 317
International Monetary Fund, 68, 70, 79, 89, 114, 125, 172, 313–315, 317, 319, 322, 328

Jamal, Amir, 83, 86, 148, 152, 154, 166–167, 186, 199, 201–203, 209, 270

Kenyatta, Jomo, 70, 73, 76–77, 81–82, 84–85, 88–89, 176, 289, 299–300, 308
kinship, 26, 97, 219, 260, 280, 282, 292, 294–295, 303
kujitegemea, 15, 45, 150, 169–170, 186, 193, See also self-reliance

loans, 2, 6, 16, 21, 28, 30, 32–33, 35, 37, 45, 59, 66, 79, 94–95, 101, 104–106, 108–109, 111–112, 116–118, 125, 132, 135, 170–171, 173, 175, 190, 194, 208, 222, 232, 234, 245, 310, 322, 324, See also credit

Loynes, John, 51–52, 62–66, 68, 70, 72, 78, 80–81, 83

mafuta mingi, 214, 223, 231, 259
magendo, 8, 48, 214, 223, 232, 241, 246, 248, 252, 257, 260–261, 263, 265, 267–269, 273–274, 277–288, 290–291, 294–297, 299–301, 303, 305, 309, See also smuggling
marketing, 5, 42, 51, 102, 133, 194, 222, 226, 247, 257, 269, 271–272, 283, 285, 291, 303, 310–311, 318, 320–322
measurement, 4, 226, 230, 268, 283–285, 287
moneychanger state, 5, 7–8, 86, 90, 133, 142, 213, 269, 316–317
monopoly on valuation, 3, 5, 8, 18, 24, 26, 38–39, 41–44, 47, 49, 95, 124, 127, 143, 145, 153, 205–206, 208, 217, 247, 259, 261, 264, 267, 273, 276, 303, 307, 318, 324
Mount Elgon, 10, 12, 263–264, 266, 268, 270–271, 277, 280–281, 287, 293, 303
Mtei, Edwin, 166–167, 173, 178, 315–316
Mubiru, Joseph, 31, 114–115, 126, 176
Musazi, Ignatius, 99, 101
mwananchi, 307–309, 325, See also citizenship

Namfua, J.D., 154, 180, 184–185, 197–203
National & Grindlays, 27, 56, 127, 150, 160, 162, 179, 183
National Bank of Commerce, 29, 33, 152, 154, 161, 180, 183, 186–192, 194, 196–197, 203–204, 206, 208–209
nationalism, 6, 24, 44, 79–80, 92, 96, 122, 131, 137, 146, 205, 238, 271
nationalization, 28–29, 85, 114, 149, 151–153, 155, 157, 160, 162–168,

Index 359

170, 174, 176–178, 182, 186–187, 189, 193, 199–200, 204, 206
neocolonialism, 14, 16
neoliberalism, 38, 315–321, 323–325
New International Economic Order, 15, 29, 169, 314
Nsekela, Amon, 28, 30, 154, 180, 186, 188, 191, 193, 195, 202–203, 208, 210
Nyerere, Julius, 15–16, 29, 52, 61, 68, 70, 72–73, 86–87, 148–149, 151–153, 158, 164–169, 176–178, 182–183, 186, 203, 205, 311, 314–316, 322

Obote, Milton, 12, 41, 70, 73–75, 88, 98, 114–115, 117, 124, 140, 250, 272
Oginga Odinga, 18, 28, 81
oil crises, 206, 219, 246, 312
overcharging, 34, 48, 211, 305

policing, 27, 35, 89, 133, 136, 143, 145, 157, 161, 211, 214, 219, 229, 232, 242, 244–245, 247–248, 253–255, 257–259, 269, 277–278, 280, 282, 298–299, 301, 305, 309
Post Office Savings Bank, 88, 125–126, 194
price, 4–5, 10, 18, 21, 29–30, 46, 48, 68–69, 100, 112, 153–156, 168, 173–174, 177, 179, 198, 200, 207–208, 211, 222, 225–226, 241, 247, 253, 255, 259, 261, 263, 265, 267, 270, 281, 283–285, 306, 313, 315–316, 319–320, 322, 324–326
price control, 208, 251
price setting, 4, 321–323
productivism, 35–36, 45, 86–87, 131, 222, 237, 265

racial capitalism, 3, 18, 55, 64, 81, 108, 135, 162, 168, 192, 244
redistribution, 37, 81, 112, 118, 220, 242, 246, 318, 325
regional turn, 11

savings, 6, 31, 55, 57, 79, 87–88, 92, 95, 97–98, 102–103, 109, 113, 116, 119, 121, 123, 125–126, 128, 131, 137, 140, 151–152, 163, 170, 186, 191, 193, 310

Seebohm, Frederic, 148–149, 154, 156, 168, 199, 201–204
self-determination, 3, 22, *See* sovereignty
self-reliance, 15, 29, 45, 86, 150, 152–154, 158, 165, 169, 190, 193–194, 205, 228, 311
shortages, economic, 34, 36, 46, 48, 130, 207, 213, 215–216, 218–219, 221, 230, 232, 236, 243, 246, 260–261, 306, 313, 317, 325
smugglers, *See* magendo
smuggling, 8, 10, 12, 26–27, 34, 40, 44, 48–49, 100, 143, 145, 211, 214–215, 218, 228, 230, 232, 243–244, 247, 253–254, 261, 266–267, 271, 273, 277–278, 298, 303–304, *See also* magendo
social citizenship, 37, 147, 324
socialism, 29, 33, 49, 154, 158, 193, 205, 209–210, 318, 323
sovereignty, 2, 4, 8, 11, 14, 16, 22–23, 26, 29, 31, 40–41, 43–44, 46, 49, 53, 63, 73, 76, 85, 90, 92–93, 97–98, 133, 152, 177, 202, 205, 213, 219, 226–227, 234, 249, 261, 309, 311, 313, 316
Standard Bank, 27, 56, 150, 160, 167
Steen Hansen, H. C., 179–180, 184, 198–199
sterling, 1–2, 5–6, 23, 55–57, 59–60, 63–65, 73, 81, 84–85, 87, 90–91, 136–137, 141, 163, 175, 183, 197, 201–202, 269
structural adjustment, *See* neoliberalism
subsistence, 9, 31, 40, 47–48, 92, 131, 186, 233–234, 242, 261, 266, 271, 312
sugar, 49, 143, 216, 218, 220–221, 235–237, 239, 241, 243, 246, 277, 282, 295, 300, *See* essential commodities
Swai, Nsilo, 67, 73, 80, 82, 167

taxation, 17, 34, 54, 121, 218, 272
tea, 4, 140, 216, 237–238, 240–241, 244
territory, 2, 6–8, 13, 15, 24–28, 39, 43, 49, 59–60, 80–81, 88, 90, 93, 98, 128, 134–135, 140, 143, 153, 192,

213, 247, 269, 276–277, 281–282, 287
Toro, 111, 118, 121–124, 132, 215, 224, 237–239, 255
transactional territories, 26, 34, 40, 49, 91, 146, 221, 281, 310

Uganda Commercial Bank, 31–32, 92, 113, 116–118, 125, 127–131, 138, 140, 221, 225, 234, 248
Uganda Credit & Savings Bank, 95, 102–103, 105–106, 108–110, 112, 114, 116–117
Uganda shillings, 1, 6, 41–42, 93, 96, 134, 142–144, 224
ujamaa, 15, 150, 152–153, 170, 186, 193–194, 209
uneven and combined development, 51, 73, 75, 79, 128, 311
urban bias, 321, 325

valuation, 4, 8–9, 24, 27, 29, 43, 92, 143, 148, 154–156, 177, 179, 182, 184–185, 198–199, 202, 207, 224, 227, 231, 254, 259, 261, 264, 268–270, 285–286, 306, 309, 312, 315–316, 318, 323, 326, *See also* monopoly on valuation
value, 2, 6, 9, 22, 96, 112, 129, 135, 149, 156, 198, 205, 210, 218, 242, 247–248, 264, 268, 287, 291, 296, 319, 325, *See also* government of value
capitalist value, 50
export value, 3, 24, 35, 47, 54, 89, 94, 101, 132, 265, 310
values, 9–10, 15–16, 44, 46, 49, 124, 155, 197, 296, 319, 324

wananchi, *See* mwananchi
World Bank, 108, 114, 117, 175, 317, 319–320, 322–323

African Studies Series

1 *City Politics: A Study of Leopoldville, 1962–63*, J. S. La Fontaine
2 *Studies in Rural Capitalism in West Africa*, Polly Hill
3 *Land Policy in Buganda*, Henry W. West
4 *The Nigerian Military: A Sociological Analysis of Authority and Revolt, 1960–67*, Robin Luckham
5 *The Ghanaian Factory Worker: Industrial Man in Africa*, Margaret Peil
6 *Labour in the South African Gold Mines*, Francis Wilson
7 *The Price of Liberty: Personality and Politics in Colonial Nigeria*, Kenneth W. J. Post and George D. Jenkins
8 *Subsistence to Commercial Farming in Present-Day Buganda: An Economic and Anthropological Survey*, Audrey I. Richards, Fort Sturrock, and Jean M. Fortt (eds)
9 *Dependence and Opportunity: Political Change in Ahafo*, John Dunn and A. F. Robertson
10 *African Railwaymen: Solidarity and Opposition in an East African Labour Force*, R. D. Grillo
11 *Islam and Tribal Art in West Africa*, René A. Bravmann
12 *Modern and Traditional Elites in the Politics of Lagos*, P. D. Cole
13 *Asante in the Nineteenth Century: The Structure and Evaluation of a Political Order*, Ivor Wilks
14 *Culture, Tradition and Society in the West African Novel*, Emmanuel Obiechina
15 *Saints and Politicians*, Donal B. Cruise O'Brien
16 *The Lions of Dagbon: Political Change in Northern Ghana*, Martin Staniland
17 *Politics of Decolonization: Kenya Europeans and the Land Issue 1960–1965*, Gary B. Wasserman
18 *Muslim Brotherhoods in the Nineteenth-Century Africa*, B. G. Martin
19 *Warfare in the Sokoto Caliphate: Historical and Sociological Perspectives*, Joseph P. Smaldone
20 *Liberia and Sierra Leone: An Essay in Comparative Politics*, Christopher Clapham
21 *Adam Kok's Griquas: A Study in the Development of Stratification in South Africa*, Robert Ross
22 *Class, Power and Ideology in Ghana: The Railwaymen of Sekondi*, Richard Jeffries
23 *West African States: Failure and Promise*, John Dunn (ed)

24 *Afrikaaners of the Kalahari: White Minority in a Black State*, Margo Russell and Martin Russell
25 *A Modern History of Tanganyika*, John Iliffe
26 *A History of African Christianity 1950–1975*, Adrian Hastings
27 *Slaves, Peasants and Capitalists in Southern Angola, 1840–1926*, W. G. Clarence-Smith
28 *The Hidden Hippopotamus: Reappraised in African History: The Early Colonial Experience in Western Zambia*, GywnPrins
29 *Families Divided: The Impact of Migrant Labour in Lesotho*, Colin Murray
30 *Slavery, Colonialism and Economic Growth in Dahomey, 1640–1960*, Patrick Manning
31 *Kings, Commoners and Concessionaries: The Evolution of Dissolution of the Nineteenth-Century Swazi State*, Philip Bonner
32 *Oral Poetry and Somali Nationalism: The Case of Sayid Mahammad 'Abdille Hasan*, Said S. Samatar
33 *The Political Economy of Pondoland 1860–1930*, William Beinart
34 *Volkskapitalisme: Class, Capitals and Ideology in the Development of Afrikaner Nationalism, 1934–1948*, Dan O'Meara
35 *The Settler Economies: Studies in the Economic History of Kenya and Rhodesia 1900–1963*, Paul Mosely
36 *Transformations in Slavery: A History of Slavery in Africa*, 1st edition, Paul Lovejoy
37 *Amilcar Cabral: Revolutionary Leadership and People's War*, Patrick Chabal
38 *Essays on the Political Economy of Rural Africa*, Robert H. Bates
39 *Ijeshas and Nigerians: The Incorporation of a Yoruba Kingdom, 1890s–1970s*, J. D. Y. Peel
40 *Black People and the South African War, 1899–1902*, Peter Warwick
41 *A History of Niger 1850–1960*, Finn Fuglestad
42 *Industrialisation and Trade Union Organization in South Africa, 1924–1955*, Stephen Ellis
43 *The Rising of the Red Shawls: A Revolt in Madagascar 1895–1899*, Stephen Ellis
44 *Slavery in Dutch South Africa*, Nigel Worden
45 *Law, Custom and Social Order: The Colonial Experience in Malawi and Zambia*, Martin Chanock
46 *Salt of the Desert Sun: A History of Salt Production and Trade in the Central Sudan*, Paul E. Lovejoy

47 *Marrying Well: Marriage, Status and Social Change among the Educated Elite in Colonial Lagos*, Kristin Mann
48 *Language and Colonial Power: The Appropriation of Swahili in the Former Belgian Congo, 1880–1938*, Johannes Fabian
49 *The Shell Money of the Slave Trade*, Jan Hogendorn and Marion Johnson
50 *Political Domination in Africa*, Patrick Chabal
51 *The Southern Marches of Imperial Ethiopia: Essays in History and Social Anthropology*, Donald Donham and Wendy James
52 *Islam and Urban Labor in Northern Nigeria: The Making of a Muslim Working Class*, Paul M. Lubeck
53 *Horn and Crescent: Cultural Change and Traditional Islam on the East African Coast, 800–1900*, Randall L. Pouwels
54 *Capital and Labour on the Kimberley Diamond Fields, 1871–1890*, Robert Vicat Turrell
55 *National and Class Conflict in the Horn of Africa*, John Markakis
56 *Democracy and Prebendal Politics in Nigeria: The Rise and Fall of the Second Republic*, Richard A. Joseph
57 *Entrepreneurs and Parasites: The Struggle for Indigenous Capitalism in Zaire*, Janet MacGaffey
58 *The African Poor: A History*, John Iliffe
59 *Palm Oil and Protest: An Economic History of the Ngwa Region, South-Eastern Nigeria, 1800–1980*, Susan M. Martin
60 *France and Islam in West Africa, 1860–1960*, Christopher Harrison
61 *Transformation and Continuity in Revolutionary Ethiopia*, Christopher Clapham
62 *Prelude to the Mahdiyya: Peasants and Traders in the Shendi Region, 1821–1885*, Anders Bjorkelo
63 *Wa and the Wala: Islam and Polity in Northwestern Ghana*, Ivor Wilks
64 *H.C. Bankole-Bright and Politics in Colonial Sierra Leone, 1919–1958*, Akintola Wyse
65 *Contemporary West African States*, Donal Cruise O'Brien, John Dunn, and Richard Rathbone (eds)
66 *The Oromo of Ethiopia: A History, 1570–1860*, Mohammed Hassen
67 *Slavery and African Life: Occidental, Oriental, and African Slave Trades*, Patrick Manning
68 *Abraham Esau's War: A Black South African War in the Cape, 1899–1902*, Bill Nasson

69 *The Politics of Harmony: Land Dispute Strategies in Swaziland*, Laurel L. Rose
70 *Zimbabwe's Guerrilla War: Peasant Voices*, Norma J. Kriger
71 *Ethiopia: Power and Protest: Peasant Revolts in the Twentieth-Century*, Gebru Tareke
72 *White Supremacy and Black Resistance in Pre-Industrial South Africa: The Making of the Colonial Order in the Eastern Cape, 1770–1865*, Clifton C. Crais
73 *The Elusive Granary: Herder, Farmer, and State in Northern Kenya*, Peter D. Little
74 *The Kanyok of Zaire: An Institutional and Ideological History to 1895*, John C. Yoder
75 *Pragmatism in the Age of Jihad: The Precolonial State of Bundu*, Michael A. Gomez
76 *Slow Death for Slavery: The Course of Abolition in Northern Nigeria, 1897–1936*, Paul E. Lovejoy and Jan S. Hogendorn
77 *West African Slavery and Atlantic Commerce: The Senegal River Valley, 1700–1860*, James F. Searing
78 *A South African Kingdom: The Pursuit of Security in the Nineteenth-Century Lesotho*, Elizabeth A. Eldredge
79 *State and Society in Pre-colonial Asante*, T. C. McCaskie
80 *Islamic Society and State Power in Senegal: Disciples and Citizens in Fatick*, Leonardo A. Villalón
81 *Ethnic Pride and Racial Prejudice in Victorian Cape Town: Group Identity and Social Practice*, Vivian Bickford-Smith
82 *The Eritrean Struggle for Independence: Domination, Resistance and Nationalism, 1941–1993*, Ruth Iyob
83 *Corruption and State Politics in Sierra Leone*, William Reno
84 *The Culture of Politics in Modern Kenya*, Angelique Haugerud
85 *Africans: The History of a Continent*, 1st edition, John Iliffe
86 *From Slave Trade to "Legitimate" Commerce: The Commercial Transition in Nineteenth-Century West Africa*, Robin Law (ed)
87 *Leisure and Society in Colonial Brazzaville*, Phyllis Martin
88 *Kingship and State: The Buganda Dynasty*, Christopher Wrigley
89 *Decolonization and African Life: The Labour Question in French and British Africa*, Frederick Cooper
90 *Misreading the African Landscape: Society and Ecology in an African Forest-Savannah Mosaic*, James Fairhead and Melissa Leach
91 *Peasant Revolution in Ethiopia: The Tigray People's Liberation Front, 1975–1991*, John Young
92 *Senegambia and the Atlantic Slave Trade*, Boubacar Barry

93 *Commerce and Economic Change in West Africa: The Oil Trade in the Nineteenth Century*, Martin Lynn
94 *Slavery and French Colonial Rule in West Africa: Senegal, Guinea and Mali*, Martin A. Klein
95 *East African Doctors: A History of the Modern Profession*, John Iliffe
96 *Middlemen of the Cameroons Rivers: The Duala and Their Hinterland, c.1600–1960*, Ralph Derrick, Ralph A. Austen, and Jonathan Derrick
97 *Masters and Servants on the Cape Eastern Frontier, 1760–1803*, Susan Newton-King
98 *Status and Respectability in the Cape Colony, 1750–1870: A Tragedy of Manners*, Robert Ross
99 *Slaves, Freedmen and Indentured Laborers in Colonial Mauritius*, Richard B. Allen
100 *Transformations in Slavery: A History of Slavery in Africa*, 2nd edition, Paul E. Lovejoy
101 *The Peasant Cotton Revolution in West Africa: Cote d'Ivoire, 1880–1995*, Thomas J. Bassett
102 *Re-imagining Rwanda: Conflict, Survival and Disinformation in the Late Twentieth Century*, Johan Pottier
103 *The Politics of Evil: Magic, State Power and the Political Imagination in South Africa*, Clifton Crais
104 *Transforming Mozambique: The Politics of Privatization, 1975–2000*, M. Anne Pitcher
105 *Guerrilla Veterans in Post-War Zimbabwe: Symbolic and Violent Politics, 1980–1987*, Norma J. Kriger
106 *An Economic History of Imperial Madagascar, 1750–1895: The Rise and Fall of an Island Empire*, Gwyn Campbell
107 *Honour in African History*, John Iliffe
108 *Africans: A History of a Continent*, 2nd edition, John Iliffe
109 *Guns, Race, and Power in Colonial South Africa*, William Kelleher Storey
110 *Islam and Social Change in French West Africa: History of an Emancipatory Community*, Sean Hanretta
111 *Defeating Mau Mau, Creating Kenya: Counterinsurgency, Civil War and Decolonization*, Daniel Branch
112 *Christianity and Genocide in Rwanda*, Timothy Longman
113 *From Africa to Brazil: Culture, Identity, and an African Slave Trade, 1600–1830*, Walter Hawthorne
114 *Africa in the Time of Cholera: A History of Pandemics from 1817 to the Present*, Myron Echenberg

115 *A History of Race in Muslim West Africa, 1600–1960*, Bruce S. Hall
116 *Witchcraft and Colonial Rule in Kenya, 1900–1955*, Katherine Luongo
117 *Transformations in Slavery: A History of Slavery in Africa*, 3rd edition, Paul E. Lovejoy
118 *The Rise of the Trans-Atlantic Slave Trade in Western Africa, 1300–1589*, Toby Green
119 *Party Politics and Economic Reform in Africa's Democracies*, M. Anne Pitcher
120 *Smugglers and Saints of the Sahara: Regional Connectivity in the Twentieth Century*, Judith Scheele
121 *Cross-Cultural Exchange in the Atlantic World: Angola and Brazil during the Era of the Slave Trade*, Roquinaldo Ferreira
122 *Ethnic Patriotism and the East African Revival*, Derek Peterson
123 *Black Morocco: A History of Slavery and Islam*, Chouki El Hamel
124 *An African Slaving Port and the Atlantic World: Benguela and Its Hinterland*, Mariana Candido
125 *Making Citizens in Africa: Ethnicity, Gender, and National Identity in Ethiopia*, Lahra Smith
126 *Slavery and Emancipation in Islamic East Africa: From Honor to Respectability*, Elisabeth McMahon
127 *A History of African Motherhood: The Case of Uganda, 700–1900*, Rhiannon Stephens
128 *The Borders of Race in Colonial South Africa: The Kat River Settlement, 1829–1856*, Robert Ross
129 *From Empires to NGOs in the West African Sahel: The Road to Nongovernmentality*, Gregory Mann
130 *Dictators and Democracy in African Development: The Political Economy of Good Governance in Nigeria*, A. Carl LeVan
131 *Water, Civilization and Power in Sudan: The Political Economy of Military-Islamist State Building*, Harry Verhoeven
132 *The Fruits of Freedom in British Togoland: Literacy, Politics and Nationalism, 1914–2014*, Kate Skinner
133 *Political Thought and the Public Sphere in Tanzania: Freedom, Democracy and Citizenship in the Era of Decolonization*, Emma Hunter
134 *Political Identity and Conflict in Central Angola, 1975–2002*, Justin Pearce
135 *From Slavery to Aid: Politics, Labour, and Ecology in the Nigerian Sahel, 1800–2000*, Benedetta Rossi

136 *National Liberation in Postcolonial Southern Africa: A Historical Ethnography of SWAPO's Exile Camps*, Christian A. Williams
137 *Africans: A History of a Continent*, 3rd edition, John Iliffe
138 *Colonial Buganda and the End of Empire: Political Thought and Historical Imagination in Africa*, Jonathon L. Earle
139 *The Struggle over State Power in Zimbabwe: Law and Politics since 1950*, George Karekwaivanane
140 *Transforming Sudan: Decolonisation, Economic Development and State Formation*, Alden Young
141 *Colonizing Consent: Rape and Governance in South Africa's Eastern Cape*, Elizabeth Thornberry
142 *The Value of Disorder: Autonomy, Prosperity and Plunder in the Chadian Sahara*, Julien Brachet and Judith Scheele
143 *The Politics of Poverty: Policy-Making and Development in Rural Tanzania*, Felicitas Becker
144 *Boundaries, Communities, and State-Making in West Africa: The Centrality of the Margins*, Paul Nugent
145 *Politics and Violence in Burundi: The Language of Truth in an Emerging State*, Aidan Russell
146 *Power and the Presidency in Kenya: The Jomo Kenyatta Years*, Anaïs Angelo
147 *East Africa after Liberation: Conflict, Security and the State since the 1980s*, Jonathan Fisher
148 *Sultan, Caliph, and the Renewer of the Faith: Ahmad Lobbo, the Tārīkh al-fattāsh and the Making of an Islamic State in West Africa*, Mauro Nobili
149 *Shaping the African Savannah: From Capitalist Frontier to Arid Eden in Namibia*, Michael Bollig
150 *France's Wars in Chad: Military Intervention and Decolonization in Africa*, Nathaniel K. Powell
151 *Islam, Ethnicity, and Conflict in Ethiopia: The Bale Insurgency, 1963–1970*, Terje Østebø
152 *The Path to Genocide in Rwanda: Security, Opportunity, and Authority in an Ethnocratic State*, Omar Shahabudin McDoom
153 *Development, (Dual) Citizenship and Its Discontents in Africa: The Political Economy of Belonging to Liberia*, Robtel Neajai Pailey
154 *Salafism and Political Order in Africa*, Sebastian Elischer
155 *Performing Power in Zimbabwe: Politics, Law and the Courts since 2000*, Susanne Verheul
156 *Revolutionary State-Making in Dar es Salaam: African Liberation and the Global Cold War, 1961–1974*, George Roberts

157 *Race and Diplomacy in Zimbabwe: The Cold War and Decolonization, 1960–1984*, Timothy Lewis Scarnecchia
158 *Conflicts of Colonialism: The Rule of Law, French Soudan, and Faama Mademba Sèye*, Richard L. Roberts
159 *Invoking the Invisible in the Sahara: Islam, Spiritual Mediation, and Social Change*, Erin Pettigrew
160 *Wealth, Land, and Property in Angola: A History of Dispossession, Slavery and Inequality*, Mariana P. Candido
161 *Trajectories of Authoritarianism in Rwanda: Elusive Control before the Genocide*, Marie-Eve Desrosiers
162 *Plunder for Profit: A Socio-environmental History of Tobacco Farming in Southern Rhodesia and Zimbabwe*, Elijah Doro
163 *Navigating Local Transitional Justice: Agency at Work in Post-Conflict Sierra Leone*, Laura S. Martin
164 *Arming Black Consciousness: The Azanian Black Nationalist Tradition and South Africa's Armed Struggle*, Toivo Tukongeni Paul Wilson Asheeke
165 *Child Slavery and Guardianship in Colonial Senegal*, Bernard Moitt
166 *African Military Politics in the Sahel: Regional Organizations and International Politics*, Katharina P. W. Döring
167 *Black Soldiers in the Rhodesian Army: Colonialism, Professionalism, and Race*, M. T. Howard
168 *Ethiopia's "Development State": Political Order and Distributive Crisis*, Tom Lavers
169 *Money, Value, and the State: Sovereignty and Citizenship in East Africa*, Kevin P. Donovan
170 *New Sudans: Wartime Intellectual Histories in Khartoum*, Nicki Kindersley

Printed in the United States
by Baker & Taylor Publisher Services